Lecture Notes in Computer Science 2816

Edited by G. Goos, J. Hartmanis, and J. van Leeuwen

Springer
Berlin
Heidelberg
New York
Hong Kong
London
Milan
Paris
Tokyo

Burkhard Stiller   Georg Carle
Martin Karsten   Peter Reichl (Eds.)

Group Communications and Charges

Technology and Business Models

5th COST 264 International Workshop
on Networked Group Communications, NGC 2003
and 3rd International Workshop
on Internet Charging and QoS Technologies, ICQT 2003
Munich, Germany, September 16-19, 2003, Proceedings

Springer

Volume Editors

Burkhard Stiller
University of Federal Armed Forces Munich, UniBwM
Information Systems Laboratory, IIS
Werner-Heisenberg-Weg 39, 85577 Neubiberg, Germany -and-
Computer Engineering and Networks Laboratory, TIK
Swiss Federal Institute of Technology Zürich, ETH Zürich
Gloriastr. 35, 8092 Zürich, Switzerland
E-mail: stiller@tik.ee.ethz.ch

Georg Carle
University of Tübingen, Wilhelm-Schickard-Institute for Computer Science
Auf der Morgenstelle 10 C, 72076 Tübingen, Germany -and-
Fraunhofer Institute FOKUS
Kaiserin-Augusta-Allee 31, 19589 Berlin, Germany
E-mail: carle@informatik.uni-tuebingen.de

Martin Karsten
University of Waterloo
School of Computer Science
200 University Ave W, Waterloo, ON, N2L 3G1, Canada
E-mail: kalli@bbc.uwaterloo.ca

Peter Reichl
Forschungszentrum Wien, FTW
Donau-City-Str. 1, 1220 Wien, Austria
E-mail: reichl@ftw.at

Cataloging-in-Publication Data applied for

A catalog record for this book is available from the Library of Congress.

Bibliographic information published by Die Deutsche Bibliothek
Die Deutsche Bibliothek lists this publication in the Deutsche Nationalbibliografie;
detailed bibliographic data is available in the Internet at <http://dnb.ddb.de>.

CR Subject Classification (1998): C.2, H.3, H.4, H.5, D.2

ISSN 0302-9743
ISBN 3-540-20051-7 Springer-Verlag Berlin Heidelberg New York

Springer-Verlag Berlin Heidelberg New York
a member of BertelsmannSpringer Science+Business Media GmbH

http://www.springer.de

© Springer-Verlag Berlin Heidelberg 2003
Printed in Germany

Typesetting: Camera-ready by author, data conversion by Olgun Computergrafik
Printed on acid-free paper   SPIN: 10950036   06/3142   5 4 3 2 1 0

Preface

This volume of the Lecture Notes in Computer Science series contains the set of papers accepted for the two co-located NGC/ICQT 2003 workshops, i.e., the 5th COST 264 International Workshop on Networked Group Communications (NGC) and the 3rd International Workshop on Internet Charging and QoS Technology (ICQT), both of which took place at the University of the Federal Armed Forces Munich (UniBwM), Germany and were hosted by the Information and Systems Laboratory, IIS.

NGC 2003 was the fifth workshop in a continuing series of highly successful technical meetings on group communications within the framework of the COST Action 264 "Networked Group Communications," following previous events in Pisa, Italy, 1999, Stamford, USA, 2000, London, UK, 2001, and Boston, USA, 2002. ICQT 2003 was the latest edition of a vivid workshop on Internet economics and charging technology; previous events took place in the framework of the Annual Meeting of the German Society for Computer Science (GI) and the Austrian Computer Society in 2001 in Vienna, Austria, and in Zürich, Switzerland in 2002, co-located with the QofIS 2002 workshop.

The combination of group communications and charging addresses is an interesting facet of research and business modelling. Communication by technical means forms the major interconnection for distributed electronic applications, ranging from business processes to entertainment. While networked group communications in particular raise technology and protocol challenges, charging for Internet services inter-relates and enriches those techniques with economic models. In addition, the rise of peer-to-peer systems has gained a lot of attention and many of their inherent mechanisms are based on group management-driven methods. Both workshops target the identification of solutions, investigations of their feasibility, and a consolidation of technical and economic mechanisms to enable a fast, guaranteed, and efficient provisioning of networked group communications in the Internet. The range of session topics exactly reflects this situation, covering Application Multicast Support, Anycast and Search in P2P, Peer-to-Peer Systems, Security and Multicasting, Multicast Mechanisms, Control Algorithms, Multicast Pricing and Traffic, Routing and Economics, and Pricing and Resource Management.

Since the specific motto of these two co-located workshops, "Group Communications and Charges – Technology and Business Technology," was chosen deliberately in order to reflect current developments in this research area, NGC and ICQT brought together researchers from the area of group communications technology and economy in both industry and academia to discuss key advancements and to support further progress in these fields. Due to the major success of the same format in the past, NGC 2003 and ICQT 2003 followed a single-track and three-day program, in order to stimulate interaction and active participation. In summary, the technical sessions of the NGC and ICQT workshops contained 17 and 8 full papers, respectively. NGC introduced for the first time 6 short papers in a dedicated session to open up a discussion of new and fascinating ideas, ones deemed of high importance to reviewers but which have not reached full maturity yet. All of these full and short papers were selected after a thorough reviewing process out of 51 and 27 submissions for NGC and ICQT, respectively. Showing a truly international scope, the final program of both workshops included 12 European, 11 North American, and 2 Asian full papers.

NGC/ICQT 2003 was based upon the continued support of a number of different organizations and persons. Firstly, following the event series established during recent years, COST Action 264 – formally closed, but research-wise still active – forms the steering lead, reflected in the NGC Steering Committee. Secondly, we are very happy to see the work being performed in cooperation with ACM SIGCOMM. Finally, both workshops' technical and research success depended on all members of the two distinct technical program committees and additional reviewers, who devoted their excellent knowledge as well as many hours of their time to provide the basis of a highly qualified technical program. Furthermore, we would like to express our thanks to Jan Gerke, Danny Heerlein, Arnd Heursch, Pascal Kurtansky, Peter Racz, and Jürgen Sauerland, who performed a brilliant job in maintaining the NGC/ICQT 2003 Web servers, managing the electronic system ConfMan for paper submission and review, dealing with cameraready papers, and maintaining local networking equipment. In addition, all of them assisted us in all phases of the workshops' preparations with technical and administrative help. Thanks go also to Annette and Pietro Schicker, who ran the NGC/ICQT 2003 registration, and to Anna Meyer, Heidi Müller, and Gaby Grobauer, who operated the on-site office and provided our participants with an excellent service. Finally, we would like to address our thanks to the Springer-Verlag for a smooth cooperation on finalizing these proceedings. Last, but not least thanks go to the UniBw München and the Information Systems Laboratory (IIS) for hosting the NGC/ICQT 2003 workshop in a convenient environment.

July 2003

Burkhard Stiller
Georg Carle
Martin Karsten
Peter Reichl

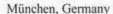

München, Germany

Organization

General Chair

Burkhard Stiller   *University of the Federal Armed Forces Munich*
                            (UniBwM), Germany and ETH Zürich, Switzerland

Steering Committee

Jon Crowcroft   *Univ. of Cambridge, UK*
Christoph Diot   *Intel Research, USA*
Serge Fdida   *Laboratoire LIP6-CNRS, France*
Luigi Rizzo   *ICSI Center for Internet Research, USA*

Program Co-chairs NGC 2003

Burkhard Stiller   *UniBwM, Germany and ETH Zürich, Switzerland*
Michael Smirnow   *FhG FOKUS, Germany*

Program Co-chairs ICQT 2003

Martin Karsten   *University of Waterloo, Canada*
Peter Reichl   *FTW Vienna, Austria*

Program Committee NGC 2003

Kevin Almeroth   *University of California, Santa Barbara, USA*
Mostafa Ammar   *Georgia Institute of Technology, USA*
Daniel Bauer   *IBM Zürich Research Lab, Switzerland*
Elizabeth Belding-Royer   *University of California, Santa Barbara, USA*
Samrat Bhattacharjee   *University of Maryland, USA*
Ernst Biersack   *Institut Eurecom, France*
Bob Briscoe   *BT Exact Technologies, UK*
John Byers   *Boston University, USA*
Georg Carle   *University of Tübingen, Fraunhofer FOKUS, Germany*
Jon Crowcroft   *University of Cambridge, UK*
Walid Dabbous   *INRIA, France*
Jordi Domingo-Pascual   *Universitat Politecnica de Catalunya, Spain*
Derek Eager   *University of Saskatchewan, Canada*
Wolfgang Effelsberg   *University of Mannheim, Germany*
Hiroshi Esaki   *University of Tokyo, Japan*
Serge Fdida   *Laboratoire LIP6-CNRS, France*

Program Committee ICQT 2003

Local Organization

Danny Heerlein, Arnd Heursch, Peter Racz,
Jürgen Sauerland, Gaby Grobauer, Anna Meyer,
Heidi Müller   *UniBwM, Germany*
Jan Gerke, Pascal Kurtansky   *ETH Zürich, Switzerland*
Annette and Pietro Schicker   *Ringwil-Hinwil, Switzerland*

Reviewers

Serious and detailed commenting on papers submitted to NGC/ICQT 2003 was performed by reviewers. Therefore, it is of great pleasure to the Program Committee Co-chairs to thank all those reviewers for their important work; they are listed below in addition to the reviewing PC members.

Complete NGC 2003 Program Committee

Complete ICQT 2003 Program Committee

Additional Reviewers:

P. Antoniadis
G. Caronni
J. Cushnie
M. Dramitinos
M. Dunmore
M. Garschhammer
I. Gojmerac
W. Haidegger
F. Hammer
A. Hanemann
T. Jensen
H. Reiser
H. Rlle
S. Schmid
D. Schmitz
M. Sifalakis
S. Simpson
P. Smith
A. Soppera
M. Waldvogel
S. Wolland

NGC/ICQT 2003 Supporters

ACM SIGCOMM

COST

University of the Federal Armed Forces Munich, Germany

Information Systems Laboratory, IIS, Germany

Swiss Federal Institute of Technology, ETH Zürich, Switzerland

Computer Engineering and Networks Laboratory TIK, ETH Zürich, Switzerland

Table of Contents

Networked Group Communications (NGC)

Application Multicast Support

Anycast and Search in P2P

Peer-to-Peer Systems

Security and Multicasting

Internet Charging and QoS Technology (ICQT)

Multicast Pricing and Traffic

Routing and Economics

Pricing and Resource Management

Author Index

User-Interest Driven Video Adaptation
for Collaborative Workspace Applications

Jeremiah Scholl, Stefan Elf, and Peter Parnes

Department of Computer Science & Electrical Engineering, Media Technology Division,
Luleå University of Technology,
971 87 Luleå, Sweden
{jeremiah.scholl,stefan.elf,peter.parnes}@cdt.luth.se
http://media.sm.luth.se/

Abstract. This paper presents a bandwidth sharing scheme for group video conferencing. The key features of the scheme are the monitoring of implicit user-hints
and message passing, which are used by each client in order to identify and report
their interest in other group members. Information about user interest is then used
by each video sender in order to adjust their frame-rate, resolution, and ultimately
bandwidth consumption in an attempt to satisfy the current interests of the receivers. A general framework and initial prototype are presented together with
experimental results.

1 Introduction

Collaborative workspace applications based on IP-multicast offer a scalable solution
for computer supported human-to-human communication. Even though Internet-wide
multicast access is not a reality, these applications are making their way into work
and educational environments due to the growing use of multicast in subnets, such as
corporate and campus networks. While workspaces come in many flavors, the main
function of these applications is to provide participating members with shared tools and
a sense of presence. Video streams from the participating members are a key component
of presence and multiple video streams can be resource intensive, making bandwidth
sharing schemes for group video conferencing a key design component in applications
of this type.

While many straight forward solutions can be applied, the human aspect and variety
of contexts in which workspaces are used make designing a robust bandwidth-sharing
scheme difficult. For example, the simplest solution is to allocate an equal portion of the
session bandwidth to all users, but this will be inefficient when some participants in the
group are of greater importance than others and could enhance the group's experience
by using a larger share of available resources. An alternative approach that is suitable in
some situations would be to allocate bandwidth based on floor control, but this is also
inflexible as it can only be applied to settings where one participant should be the focus
of the group at any given time.

At Luleå University of Technology collaborative workspaces are used daily in a
wide variety of situations. Example uses include allowing students to view classroom
lectures from home, enabling members of discussion groups to interact from distance,

B. Stiller et al. (Eds.): NGC/ICQT 2003, LNCS 2816, pp. 3–12, 2003.
© Springer-Verlag Berlin Heidelberg 2003

and providing members of projects and research divisions with increased presence of each other throughout their work day. The last mentioned case, referred to as the "e-corridor", can be viewed with particular interest in terms of bandwidth sharing due to the large variety of use-cases that it must serve. In the e-corridor members of the session can be active or passive and possible uses of the workspace range from giving or listening in on a formal presentation to passive monitoring of video. It may also include the occasional idle participant (i.e. out of the office). Thus, the number of "important" video streams in the session can vary widely over time.

This paper presents a bandwidth sharing scheme for group video conferencing aimed at a general use collaborative workspace environment, such as the e-corridor. The scheme operates by first identifying session participants that are of high importance to other group members and then allocating them a larger share of the session bandwidth. This is achieved primarily through the implicit detection of user-hints, such as the configuration of a user's desktop, and utilizes message passing so that receivers can reflect their interests back to the senders in question.

1.1   Related Work

The use of implicit user-hints in resource control has been applied to a wide range of multimedia applications, with each scheme being limited in scope to a specific domain. For example, Kulju et al. [1] investigated user hints in the context of video streaming, while Ott et al. [2] focused on its use within their own 3D landscape. In addition, recent work in collaborative workspaces has investigated how hints may be used in order to dynamically control the use of reliable multicast [3]. The work most similar to that presented in this paper is the SCUBA protocol [4], which also uses the detection of user interest in order to allocate bandwidth in video conferencing. SCUBA described the basic architectural components for schemes of this type, but little research has been done in this area since its introduction and new ideas as well as refinement on several points are still possible.

2   Design of a User-Interest Driven Video Adaptation Scheme

The bandwidth sharing scheme described in this section follows the same architecture as SCUBA, but also differs from it in several ways. The first is that a novel approach for bandwidth sharing is used that seeks to first fulfill the minimal needs of all senders before dividing the remaining bandwidth among important group members. In addition, information about user interest is used to help each sender select the correct parameters in the tradeoff between image resolution and frame rate, which is something that SCUBA does not take into consideration. Another key difference is that optimizations for message passing are presented in the context of empirical observations made about how humans interact with collaborative workspaces, whereas SCUBA presented an alternative method based on statistical sampling. Finally, greater flexibility is shown in the number and types of user-hints explored.

In order to determine the video streams that are of interest to a particular receiver one must answer the question, *"Who is this user currently viewing, and in what context?"*

Fig. 1. Video windows included in the Marratech Work Environment.

In regards to viewing context, the range of possible answers is defined by the video windows provided inside the application user interface. The Marratech Work Environment [5], which we have used for prototyping, is shown in Fig. 1 and includes video panels in several different windows. These windows are designed to compliment each other and allow each participant to view other members in a variety of ways. Similar to the well known research application vic [6], Marratech provides users with a "Participants" window, which gives a thumbnail overview of the video streams currently received from the group, and a "Focus" window that displays the video obtained from a single group member at higher resolution. In addition to these windows, Marratech also contains a small video panel in each private chat display, which allows two participants to easily obtain response clues such as posturing and facial gestures (smiling etc.) while chatting in private.

Table 1. Video windows in Marratech client.

Window	Purpose of Panel	Pixel Resolution	Min. Frame Rate
Focus	high level of presence	702 x 576, 352 x 288, 176 x 144	5 fps
Private Chat	response clues	176 x 144, 88 x 72	1 fps
Participants	overview of activity	88 x 72	.2 fps

Table 1 lists each of these windows' specific role in presence delivery along with their individual resource requirements including resolution and minimum "acceptable" frame rate, which was obtained from a variety of sources. In regards to the Focus window, the minimum acceptable rate is derived from the various work summarized by Chen

[7]. This includes work by Tang et al. [8], who noted that users consider 5 fps to be tolerable, and Watson et al. [9], who found that users do not perceive audio and video to be synchronized at frame rates lower than 5 fps. Other studies have also shown little difference in communication behavior or task outcome between 5 fps and 25 fps [10], [11], [12]. Together, this work suggests that 5 fps will provide users with an adequate experience in a variety of situations requiring a high amount of attention. The values provided for the Focus window and private chat windows were obtained through a survey conducted of expert Marratech users, and reflect the values most typically reported as "tolerable" for the each of the respective windows.

2.1   Identifying Important Video Streams

The primary method for detecting user interest is to monitor user interface parameters that will reveal the video senders currently loaded in each of the video panels described above. In our case, this leads to a host giving one of four possible classifications to each sender, one for each of the separate video window configurations and one classification for members that are currently not viewed in any available panel. For some applications it may also be desirable to create classifications that describe senders contained in multiple panels simultaneously, but with the Marratech environment this is not necessary because the frame rate and resolution required for panels delivering a high level of presence will also be sufficient for each lower level. Thus, a video stream that is delivered for the Focus window will also be sufficient for the Participants window and so on.

Cross-media clues can also be used to detect an important video stream [4] with the most useful example being the monitoring of audio. The current audio sender is usually a leading presenter or an otherwise important participant in group discussions so the Marratech application gives users the option of selecting "video follows audio", which will automatically move the current speaker into the Focus window. Monitoring the content of the Focus window will still be sufficient to detect an important stream in this case, but the audio clue can be useful to reduce the latency it takes for a sender to realize its importance and to further prioritize audio senders over other "focused" participants as described in the next subsection.

The whiteboard and chat can also provide useful clues, but of a somewhat different nature than audio and video. While drawing with the whiteboard pen or sending a chat message may be a sign that a user has become interesting to other users, this will likely only be for a short period of time while they "check out" the user's activity. Therefore, when a sender has a low frame rate (under 1 fps) an event from either of these media can be used in order to have him send an extra frame or two.

2.2   Identifying Expendable Video Streams

At times user interface monitoring and cross-media clues can be misleading and may cause a client to identify senders as important when in fact their video feeds are expendable. E-corridor participants can for example typically leave their office for an extended period of time, which may result in a client that continues to act on the behalf of its user even though no one is in the room to view the video streams received. One strategy that can be adopted in order to minimize the impact from this type of misidentification is to obtain hints regarding events external to the application before making decisions on behalf of the client. Hints of this type work to downgrade a sender that would otherwise be identified as important, and can further refine the process of detecting user importance. Several example hints in this category are listed below.

Detecting Idle Receivers. It is pointless for a receiver to continue requesting video from senders when no one is actively using the computer. One primary method for detecting an idle receiver is to monitor the user's screen saver. This can be complemented by other techniques, such as the monitoring of peripheral input devices like the keyboard and mouse, and/or the detection of a lack of movement in front of the user's camera.

Window Placement. When windows from other applications cover up a video panel, it is a solid indication that the user is not interested in the incoming video stream [1]. This should also be true if the video window in question is minimized.

Limited Resources. Even if a user can benefit from receiving additional data it does not guarantee that he has enough resources to do so. This can be especially true when using a mobile client as they are often more limited by CPU and memory resources than available bandwidth.

2.3   Video Adjustment Algorithm

The video adjustment algorithm we have designed works first to provide each sender with the minimum acceptable frame rate and proper image resolution for its most interested receiver, with unused bandwidth beyond that point distributed evenly among the highest priority senders in the group. The rationale for using this "minimum requirements first" strategy is that it allows important senders to deliver the richest experience possible while keeping them from punishing less important senders. The main drawback of this method is that it may not be appropriate for use with sessions that have very limited bandwidth, for example those which intend to support modem users, because the aggregate requirements of even the least demanding senders may be hard to meet. However, sessions of this type are today generally viewed as a special case and most likely need a scheme that is optimized specifically for use with low bandwidth sessions [7], rather then a scheme that is designed for general use like the scheme that is described in this paper.

Obviously it is not realistic to assume that the minimum acceptable requirements will be the same in every situation. In practice the administrator of the session should have the option of setting these values. However, in order to make the creation of sessions more user friendly it is important to have a workable set of default values that can be used when the administrator does not exercise this option. With this in mind we have done an analysis of expected bandwidth usage when sending at several of the appropriate frame rates and image resolutions discussed in Table 1.

Table 2 includes this information and can be used as a reference when trying to determine how well a minimum requirements approach will scale in the real world. The bandwidth measurements included were taken from a Marratech e-meeting client while sending video data at various frame rates and resolutions included in Table 1. The fourth column in Table 2 shows bandwidth measurements taken during "typical" use, with the low value representative of users that are fairly still in front of their computer, and the

Table 2. Estimated bandwidth usage for each sender.

Window	Frame Rate	Resolution	Bandwidth Usage
Focus	5 fps	352 x 288	55 kb/s - 160 kb/s
Private Chat	1 fps	88 x 72	8 kb/s - 20 kb/s
Participants	.2 fps	88 x 72	less than 1 kb/s - 4 kb/s

high value taken during moments of high activity, such as the user moving about or interacting with another person in the office. It should be mentioned that although the private chat and Focus windows have variable resolutions our measurements were taken with the default settings applied.

The numbers in Table 2 should only be treated as estimates, as variations in bandwidth consumption can be expected due to real-world factors, such as the camera type in use and the amount of motion between frames. They do however show that for a typical session (less than 50 users) it is not difficult to meet the minimum requirements for the Participants window due to the low bandwidth required by each sender. In practice this is also true for private-chat users because the concurrent number of chats is usually equal to a small fraction of the number of session participants. However, the requirements of each "more important" sender, defined as those currently sending audio or being viewed in the Focus window, may be difficult to meet if the attention of the group is too "spread out" or if the session has low to medium available bandwidth (256 Kb/s - 500 Kb/s).

Each sender operates within the scheme by classifying itself on a scale from 0 to 4 based on how it is viewed by other group members and whether or not it is currently sending audio. These classifications are: 4 - audio sender; 3 - Focus-window sender; 2 private-chat sender; 1 Participants-window sender; and 0 - no interested receivers. A host uses information about its class in order to determine its frame rate and resolution as given in Table 1, and measures the incoming bandwidth consumption of other members in order to determine the amount of bandwidth available to it. This information is then used by the sender in order to adapt its video using the priority scheme described below.

Step 1: Bandwidth is divided evenly between all the senders until each sender can send at the minimum frame rate and resolution for the Participants window.
Step 2: If there is still session bandwidth available after step 1, it is allocated between the senders of class 2 or higher until they are sending at the minimal frame rate and resolution for the private chat window.
Step 3: If there is still available bandwidth after step 2, it is divided between senders of class 3 or or higher until they can send at the necessary frame rate and resolution for the Focus window. This is done first for class 4 senders, and then for class 3 senders.
Step 4: All remaining bandwidth is divided evenly between each class 3 and 4 sender.

2.4   Receiver Feedback

In order for a sender to be aware of how it is viewed by other group members a mechanism needs to be in place that allows each receiving host to communicate their interests via messages. The simplest way to do this is to have each receiver automatically send a message each time an event occurs that causes it to reclassify a sender. This approach may of course end up in unnecessary messages being passed but it is not clear if this will consume enough bandwidth to significantly reduce the performance of the application.

Several techniques can be applied in order to reduce the number of unnecessary messages with the most obvious example occurring when someone starts to send audio, which will cause them to be moved into the Focus window by several participants simultaneously. In this situation a more efficient approach then having each receiver send a message is to instead have each receiver inform the group when they change the "video follows audio" option, which will enable the accurate use of the audio clue mentioned in sect. 2.1.

Table 3. User interactions logged during empirical study and influence on sender class.

Event	Bandwidth class	Up- or Down-grading
Un-muting audio	4	Up
Muting audio	4	Down
Viewing or maximizing main video	3	Up
Minimizing or closing main video	3	Down
Opening private media	2	Up
Closing private media	2	Down
Un-muting participant video	1	Up
Muting participant video	1	Down

An unnecessary message may also be created when a receiver views a sender in a new context while already receiving enough video. For example, if a sender has a frame rate of 5 fps due to the actions of other receivers, it is pointless to send it a message when opening up a private chat window, as this requires a refresh rate of only 1 fps. Messages of this type can be reduced by having each receiver monitor the frame rate and resolution of incoming streams and pass messages only when they are deemed to be inadequate. The drawback of this technique is that it will make it difficult for senders to know exactly whom every receiver is watching, and will thus require an additional mechanism so that each sender can find out when they should reduce their bandwidth after receivers have lost interest in them. A simple way to handle this is to include information about how each sender is viewed in RTCP receiver reports, which will solve the problem but will also introduce latency in the bandwidth reduction process. SCUBA takes a different approach towards feedback and uses statistical sampling rather than obtaining messages from the entire group. The advantage of this method is that it improves overall scalability because the number of messages grows logarithmically rather than linearly as the session size increases.

Because messages should only be created based on specific user interactions it is not clear if any of the above message reduction strategies are necessary, or if these interactions will typically be infrequent enough to make the number of messages passed in the session negligible. In order to gain further understanding of the potential amount of bandwidth that messages may consume, we conducted an empirical study of a research group consisting of nine daily Marratech users. This was done by creating a prototype version of Marratech, which generates messages based on specific user interactions as summarized in Table 3, and distributing it among these users. The messages were logged over a three day period under normal working conditions, which included a formal research discussion on the last day, as well as periods of more "common" use.

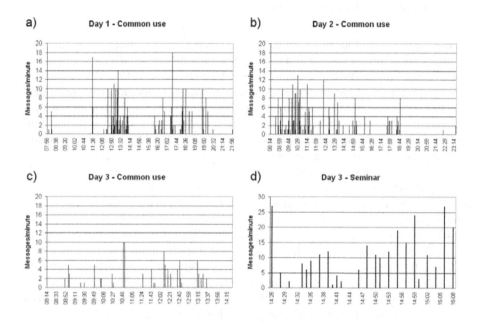

Fig. 2. Graphs showing the total number of interactions within a 9 user research group over a three day period. (Note the scale difference in (d).)

Figure 2 shows four graphs of activity during the logging period, in which a total of 1046 interactions were detected, corresponding to 119244 bytes worth of data. The average message length was 114 bytes, which included a sender id, timestamp and an indication of the interaction in question. It should be noted that these messages were not optimized in any way, so in practice it should be possible to reduce this size. Graphs **a**, **b** and **c** show activity during "common use" periods and are highlighted by a fairly low amount of activity, with some short bursts occurring that correspond to increased interaction between the users.

As expected the most intensive period of message creation by far occurred during the research discussion on the last day, which is shown in graph **d**. This included the hour of highest activity during the three days, in which 380 messages were sent. The peak minute of usage during the research discussion resulted in a total of 27 interactions, which corresponds to an average bandwidth consumption of less than .05 KB/s and a total bandwidth consumption of 3068 bytes. This shows that even if all the messages during the most active minute of the discussion were created simultaneously that the amount of bandwidth consumed would be negligible.

Thus, a conclusion can be drawn from this study that during normal use the total number of messages expected should consume a tiny portion of the session bandwidth, even if no optimizations are in place.

3   Summary and Conclusions

We have introduced a framework for bandwidth sharing in video conferencing that uses the implicit detection of user interest as a metric for resource allocation. Schemes of this type contain three architectural components, which are the detection of user interest, message passing, and bandwidth adjustment algorithms. In the area of user-interest detection we have described several methods for identifying users' interests and have introduced new ways to reduce the number of false positives in this process. In addition, we have expanded the area of bandwidth adjustment in order to help senders correctly identify their optimal frame rate and image resolution in each situation and have done so by adopting a "minimum requirements first" strategy. This strategy attempts to provide each sender with the minimum frame rate and image resolution for its most interested receiver before assigning the remaining session bandwidth to the senders deemed to be most important.

We have also discussed several different mechanisms designed to reduce the number messages created, and have conducted an empirical study in order to determine how necessary they are during real use. This study was conducted by deploying a prototype we created among a research group at our university that allowed us to monitor the messages they generated. We concluded from this study that, given the interactions from Table 3, messages will occur infrequently enough during normal use that such message reduction mechanisms are of little use in practice, even though they may be academically interesting.

3.1   Future Work

Our first priority in the future is to make a complete, user friendly prototype that can be distributed among the Marratech test users. This will require us to look into several issues including user-interface options so that users can "opt out" of the dynamic bandwidth process. In the real world this will be necessary because there are some situations when it is most beneficial to allow certain users in the session to set their bandwidth consumption manually. We also plan to study the performance of our scheme in this type of mixed environment.

In addition, robust user studies are needed in order to find further ways of refining the scheme. In particular, it is not clear at this time if it is best to divide all the extra bandwidth between only the important senders in the group as stated in sec. 2.3, or if there is a more optimal strategy. In some situations for example it may be better for a portion of the extra bandwidth to be used in order to increase the frame rate of clients in the Participants window.

Acknowledgments

This work is supported the Centre for Distance-spanning Technology, the Swedish Research Institute for Information Technology, the VITAL project and the Mäkitalo Research Centre. Stefan Elf is also with Ericsson AB, SE-931 87 Skellefteå, Sweden. Views expressed in this paper are his own and not necessarily shared by his employer.

References

1. Kulju, W., Lutfiyya, H.: Design and implementation of an application layer protocol for reducing udp traffic based on user hints and policies. In: 5th IFIP/IEEE International Conference on Management of Multimedia Networks and Services, MMNS 2002. (2002)
2. Ott, M., Michelitsch, G., Reininger, D., Welling, G.: An architecture for adaptive qos and its application to multimedia systems design. Special Issue of Computer Communications on Guiding Quality of Service into Distributed Systems (1997)
3. Scholl, J., Elf, S., Parnes, P.: Efficient workspaces through semantic reliability. In: 10th International Conference on Telecommunications, ICT 2003. (2003)
4. Amir, E., McCanne, S., Katz, R.H.: Receiver-driven bandwidth adaptation for light-weight sessions. In: ACM Multimedia. (1997) 415–426
5. Marratech: - The e-meeting company. URL[1] (2003) Visited March 30th, 2003.
6. McCanne, S., Jacobson, V.: vic : A flexible framework for packet video. In: ACM Multimedia. (1995) 511–522
7. Chen, M.: Achieving effective floor control with a low-bandwidth gesture-sensitive video-conferencing system. In: ACM Multimedia. (2002)
8. Tang, J.C., Isaacs, E.A.: Why do users like video? studies of multimedia-supported collaboration. Computer-Supported Cooperative Work: An International Journal (1993) 163–196
9. Watson, A., Sasse, M.A.: Evaluating audio and video quality in low-cost multimedia conferencing systems. Interacting with Computers **8** (1996) 255–275
10. Jackson, M., Anderson, A.H., McEwan, R., Mullin, J.: Impact of video frame rate on communicative behaviour in two and four party groups. In: ACM Computer Supported Cooperative Work. (2000) 11 – 20
11. Masoodian, M., Apperly, M.: Video support for shared work-space interaction: An empirical study. Interacting with Computers **7** (1995) 237–253
12. Ghinea, G., Thomas, J.: Qos impact on user perception and understanding of multimedia video clips. In: ACM Multimedia. (1998)

---

[1] <http://www.marratech.com>

Improving Efficiency of Application-Level Multicast with Network Support

Takeshi Sano, Taku Noguchi, and Miki Yamamoto

Department of Communications Engineering,Graduate School of Engineering,
Osaka University 2-1 Yamadaoka,Suita,Osaka,565-0871, Japan
{take4,noguchi,yamamoto}@post.comm.eng.osaka-u.ac.jp
http://www2b.comm.eng.osaka-u.ac.jp

Abstract. Large parts of the Internet are still incapable of native multi-cast, and ubiquitous deployment of multicast will take a long time. There are two approaches to provide wide-area multicast service in today's Internet. One is tunneling approach and the other is application-level multicast approach. In this paper, we focus on application-level multi-cast approach and propose a new scheme which improves the perfor-mance penalties of application-level multicast by making use of network support. Because in application-level multicast, endhosts provide multi-cast functionality instead of routers, application-level multicast delivery tree is inherently less efficient than IP multicast tree. Therefore, in our scheme, the router on the application-level multicast delivery tree alters the tree based on network-level delivery path. We evaluate our scheme with simulation experiment. Our simulation results indicate that our scheme improves the performance of application-level multicast. Further we compare our scheme to the tunneling approach from the viewpoint of transmission performances. The results reveal applicable domains of both approaches.

1 Introduction

IP multicast [1] is an efficient way for multi-point packet delivery at the network level. However, since its deployment imposes replacement of routers to multicast-capable ones, full deployment has been long in coming. Today's IP multicast is limited to "islands" of network domains under single administrative control or local area networks, and large parts of the Internet are still incapable of native multicast. There are two approaches to provide wide-area multicast service in the Internet. One is tunneling approach [3,4] and the other is application-level multicast approach. Tunneling approach offers bridging service between multi-cast islands with unicast tunneling. MBone [2] is the most popular tunneling approach. On the other hand, application-level multicast approach shifts the multicast functionality from routers to endhosts. In application-level multicast, multicast related features, such as group membership management, multicast routing and packet replication, are implemented at endhosts. Multicast delivery tree is constructed in the application layer, so all nodes in this tree are endhosts.

B. Stiller et al. (Eds.): NGC/ICQT 2003, LNCS 2816, pp. 13–22, 2003.

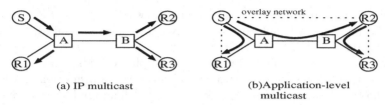

(a) IP multicast   (b)Application-level
multicast

Fig. 1. Example to illustrate IP Multicast and Application-level Multicast

Packet transmission between endhosts uses conventional IP unicast service. Since all packets are transmitted as unicast packets, the network infrastructure need not be changed. However, multicasting at endhosts incurs some performance penalties. Since endhosts do not have the topology information of network layer, they must rely on end-to-end measurements upon which the endhost multicast delivery tree is built. Therefore multicast delivery tree in the application-level multicast is inherently less efficient than the IP multicast tree. It is impossible to completely prevent multiple overlay edges from traversing the same physical link and thus some duplicate traffic on physical links is unavoidable. Further, communication path between endhosts involves other endhosts, which potentially increases endhost-perceived latency.

We propose a scheme which improves the transmission performance of application-level multicast protocols by using network support. In our scheme, a router on the application-level multicast delivery tree alters the tree to achieve more efficient application-level multicast transmission. To realize this network support, higher level function should be implemented in a router. Active network technology [5] is the most promising way for this higher level operation in a router. In this paper, we refer to the network support capable router as network-support router. We evaluate the performance of our scheme with computer simulations. Further we compare our scheme with the tunneling approach, i.e. MBone, to examine which approaches are appropriate as the solution toward wide-area multicast service.

The rest of the paper is structured as follows. In Section 2, we present an overview of application-level multicast and its performance penalty. In Section 3, we give an overview and operation of our scheme. We present our performance evaluation methodology in Section 4, and study the performance of our technique through detailed simulation in Section 5. Finally, we present our conclusions in Section 6.

2   Application-Level Multicast

Figure 1 presents the differences of the forwarding path between IP multicast and application-level multicast, where A and B are routers, and S, $R1$, $R2$, and $R3$ are endhosts. The solid lines are physical links. The case where S sends multicast data to all other endhosts is depicted in this figure.

Figure 1-(a) shows the IP multicast transmission. Here, only one packet is sent once by the sender (S), and reaches every destination with making replication of the packet at routers (A, B) inside the network. In IP multicast, routers should be implemented multicast related function, such as multicast routing and replication of packets. Exactly one copy of the packet traverses any given physical link and thus duplicate transmission on physical links is avoidable.

Figure 1-(b) shows the application-level multicast transmission. Logically, the endhosts form an overlay network (the dotted line), and application-level multicast tree is constructed on the overlay network. S sends a packet to $R1$ and $R2$ directly, and $R2$, the relay point on the overlay tree, replicates it and forwards to $R3$. Unlike the IP multicast, packet replication and forwarding are implemented at endhosts and all packets are transmitted as unicast packets. Therefore, constructed overlay network incurs two performance penalties. First, as shown in Fig. 1-(b), link S-A carries duplicate copies of the packet. Second, the data delivery path from S to $R3$ includes redundant round-trip path between B and $R2$. This causes the increase of endhost-perceived delay.

3   Overview and Operation of Our Proposed Scheme

It was pointed out in Section 2 that application-level multicast incurs performance penalties. There is a limitation for a trial to improve the transmission performance of application-level multicast by optimizing application-level multicast delivery tree with making use of only application-level information, such as end-to-end delay. However, the transmission performance may be further improved by exploiting network-level information, such as network-level delivery path information. Therefore we propose a new scheme which improves the transmission performance by exploiting network-level information. In our scheme, the router on the application-level multicast delivery tree alters the tree based on network-level delivery path information and implements multicast forwarding functionality instead of endhost. In this section, we provide detailed description of our scheme.

3.1   Overview

We illustrate the overview of our scheme in Fig. 2. In Fig. 2-(i), the sender S sends data packets to receivers $R1$, $R2$, and $R3$ by application-level multicast. Here, $R2$ and $R3$ receive the packets relayed by $R1$, therefore the path $B - R1$ is a redundant path. Due to this redundant path, their perceived delay increases compared to direct unicast transmission. To resolve this issue, we propose the scheme that reduces the redundant path. A router on the application-level multicast delivery tree monitors the delivery path. If a router detects the redundant path, it replicates packets and forwards them instead of endhosts. In the example of Fig. 2-(ii), when router B detects the redundant path between B and $R1$, it relays the arrived packet to $R2$ and $R3$, so redundant path between B and $R1$ is deleted. However, it is impossible that these intelligent processes, i.e. monitoring and multicast forwarding, are executed by a legacy router, so these processes require network-support routers, e.g. routers equipped with active network technology [5].

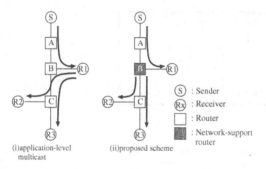

Fig. 2. Overview of our scheme

3.2   Operation

We present the details of our scheme using an example shown in Fig. 3. In Fig. 3-(a) and (b), the sender S sends packets to $R1$ and $R1$ replicates and forwards the packets to $R2$ by application-level multicast protocol. In our proposed scheme, at first multicast delivery tree of application-level multicast is constructed. After establishment of application-level multicast delivery tree, a router monitors packet forwarding and searches redundant paths. When it finds out redundant paths, it starts relaying packets. Before starting the relay, the router notifies its intention of relaying to endhosts. We would like to explain about these operation in detail.

Monitoring. In Fig. 3-(a), network-support routers A and B are monitoring the application-level multicast packets going through them. When a packet from S to $R1$ arrives at A and B (①), they caches packet header information, such as the Source IP address, Destination IP address, Sequence number, and Multicast group ID (②). Then, when the packet from $R1$ to $R2$ arrives at A and B, they cache packet header information in the same way (Fig. 3-(b), ③, ④).

Notification. In Fig. 3-(c), the router B examines headers, which have the same Sequence number and Multicast group ID, in its cache (⑤). If one header's Source IP address and another header's Destination IP address are matched, the router B finds there is a redundant path between B and the endhost indicated by that IP address. In this example, the router B detects the redundant path between B and $R1$ (⑤). Then, B notifies $R1$ that B has intention of forwarding packets to $R2$ instead of $R1$ by sending *stop_forward_message*. $R1$ stops forwarding packets to $R2$ upon reception of this *stop_forward_message* (⑥).

At the same time, in Fig. 3-(d), exactly as with B, the router A finds redundant path between A and $R1$ (⑦) and then notifies $R1$ that A forwards packets to $R2$ (⑧). Like this example, when multiple network-support router are on the redundant path, their multicast forwarding incurs duplicate packets. To avoid this issue, when the network-support routers relay

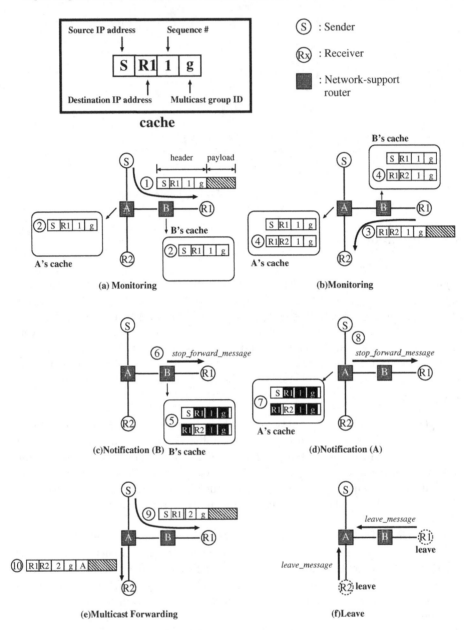

Fig. 3. Operation of our scheme

the *stop_forward_message* from another one, they stop the corresponding multicast forwarding. In this example, B stops forwarding to R2 in relying *stop_forward_message* from A to R1.

Multicast Forwarding. As shown in Fig. 3-(e), when the router A receives packets from S to $R1$ (⑨), it replicates packets and forwards to $R2$ (⑩). At that time, its IP address is added onto the packet header. This IP address is used when multicast member leaves the group.

When an endhost leaves from application-level multicast, multicast delivery tree is re-constructed in the conventional application-level multicast. In our proposed scheme, a router supports multicast transmission, so some additional operation is necessary.

Leave. When $R1$ leaves the group, it notifies A that with *leave_message* as shown by Fig. 3-(f). This *leave_message* is different from a leave message that $R1$ sends to another multicast group members when it leave from overlay network in application-level multicast protocol. The router A deletes the caches related to $R1$ upon reception of this *leave_message* from $R1$. While the router A has stopped forwarding packets to $R2$, at that time, application-level multicast delivery tree is re-constructed and another endhost forwards packets to $R2$.

When $R2$ leaves the group, it notifies A that with *leave_message* as shown in Fig. 3-(f). A stops forwarding packets to $R2$ upon reception of this *leave_message* from $R2$.

In our scheme, network-support router alters the application-level multicast delivery tree with signaling message (*stop_forward_message, leave_message*) between network-support router and endhost, and reduces the redundant path in application-level multicast. There is another implementation of our proposed cut-through method at a network-support router. In the above description, a network-support router is assumed to monitor all data flow of application-level multicast, which causes heavy loaded operation at a network-support router. When end-to-end level signaling is introduced in application-level multicast, this heavy loaded operation at a network-support router can be prevented. In this end-to-end level signaling, end hosts send a signaling packet on the same path of data packets only at initial phase (i.e. at the moment of a host would like to join application-level multicast) and at leaving phase. Network-support routers only capture this (special) signaling packet to construct or re-shape the transmission path of application-level multicast, which will reduce monitoring load of a network-support router. This approach also has another advantage that network support operation in the network can be managed by the end user, i.e. an end host can ask network support operation only when it sends a signaling packet.

4   Simulation Methodology

We have evaluated the performance of our scheme, and compared it to the tunneling approach using simulation experiments. In this section, we discuss the network model, performance metrics, placement of network-support routers, and tunneling approach, i.e. MBone.

4.1   Network Model

We used two different models to generate network topologies for our simulations.

WAXMAN [6]. The model considers a set of n vertices on a square in the
plane and places an edge between two points with a probability of $\alpha e \frac{-d}{\beta*L}$,
where L is the length of the longest possible edge, d is a random variable
between 0 and L, and α and β are parameters.

BRITE [7]. The model is assumed to have hierarchical structure of two layers,
a backbone network and access networks. Each network has power lows of
the form $f_d \propto d^\alpha$, where the frequency, f_d, of an outdegree, d, is proportional
to the outdegree to the power of a constant, α.

In our simulations, we used topology sizes consisting of 1000 routers and 3000
links, and multicast groups of 256 members. Narada [3] protocol is used to build
the application-level multicast tree for our simulation.

4.2   Placement of Network-Support Routers

Implementation of network support to all routers in the network takes a seriously
long time and the case of not all routers being network-support routers should
be general. Therefore, in order to achieve good performance with limited number of network-support routers, it is necessary to place network-support routers
strategically. We evaluate the performance over the following three placement
policies.

random Network-support routers are placed on the network randomly.
degree This is a strategic placement where a network-support router is placed
    at the vertex of large outdegree in order of outdegree size.
gateway This is another strategic placement where a network-support router is
    placed at the gateway between the backbone network and an access network
    in order of outdegree size.

The path between the branch point in network-level delivery path and the end-
host (for example, router B in Fig. 2) tends to be the redundant path. Routers
with large degree or gateway routers have higher probability of being these
branch point, so above strategic placements of the degree and gateway policies
may achieve good performance in our scheme.

4.3   Performance Metrics

We use the following performance metrics which are used in almost application-
level multicast related papers.

Relative Delay Penalty(RDP): RDP is defined as $\frac{1}{N} \sum_{i=1}^{N} \frac{d_i'}{d_i}$, where N is
    the number of group members, d_i' is the multicast transmission delay per-
    ceived by member i in our scheme, and d_i is the unicast delay between the
    sender and the member i.
Tree Cost: Tree Cost is defined as $\sum_{i=1}^{L} S_i$, where L is the number of links
    active in data transmission, and S_i is the Link Stress of link i, which is the
    number of identical copies of a packet carried by a physical link.

4.4   Tunneling Approach -MBone-

MBone connects IP multicast islands by unicast tunnels. Here, endhosts participating in the MBone session have to be connected to the IP multicast enabled
router. Therefore, in our MBone model, we assume that all the edge routers,
directly connected to endhosts, are IP multicast enabled routers. We compared
our scheme to this MBone model from the viewpoint of Tree Cost[1].

5   Simulation Results

Figures 4 and 5 show RDP vs. the ratio of network-support router over different
placement policies of network-support router. The network topology is WAX-
MAN in Fig.4, and BRITE in Fig. 5. The case of 0% network-support router
indicates the performance of pure application-level multicast without network
support. As shown in the result of both of the topology, the RDP decreases with
the increase of the ratio of network-support router. The RDP decreases more effectively in the case of strategic placement (degree and gateway) than in the case
of random placement. As previously discussed, these results have indicated that
routers of large degree and at gateway tend to be starting points of redundant
paths.

Figures 6 and 7 show Tree Cost vs. the ratio of network-support router. As
in the case of RDP performance, Tree Cost decreases with the increase of the
ratio of network-support router.

Figures 8 and 9 show Tree Cost vs. the ratio of network-support router
with comparing our scheme to MBone model. The placement policy of network-
support routers is the degree policy in these graphs. As described above, at least
all edge routers should be multicast-capable routers (network-support routers)
in MBone model. Thus, performance curve of MBone model in these graphs
starts at the point of 30% network-support routers in a network, i.e. 30% of
routers are edge routers in our topology model. With increase of ratio of multicast capable routers, these additional network-support routers are assumed to be
located randomly in a core network. As shown in these graphs, MBone model is
more effective than our scheme in the region of more than 30% network-support
routers[2].

Placement policy of network-support router in MBone model (edge router)
and in our scheme (degree and gateway) is quite different, so seamless shift of
placement policies between MBone approach and our scheme is unrealistic. But
our simulation results show that our scheme can improve delivery tree performance of application-level multicast and is applicable to the situation that not

---

[1] In the MBone session, the data being sent through the shortest path, so we compared
in terms of Tree Cost only.

[2] This result (MBone approach is better than application-level multicast) intuitively
seems to be straightforward. However, in fact, it isn't. This is because MBone approach with 30% network-support routers include a lot of unicast transmissions
between multicast islands, which may cause redundant transmission.

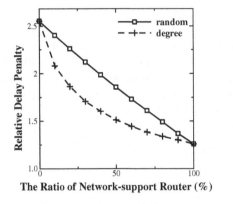

Fig. 4. RDP performance (WAXMAN)

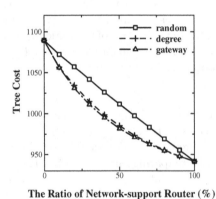

Fig. 5. RDP performance (BRITE)

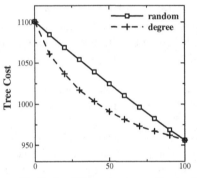

Fig. 6. Tree Cost performance (WAXMAN)

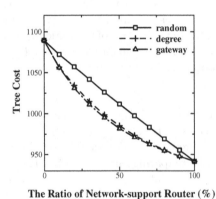

Fig. 7. Tree Cost performance (BRITE)

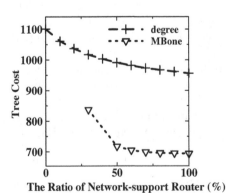

Fig. 8. Tree Cost performance: Proposal versus MBone (WAXMAN)

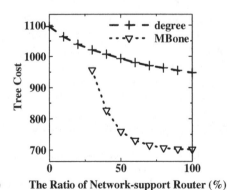

Fig. 9. Tree Cost performance: Proposal versus MBone (BRITE)

so many routers are network-support router one. In the situation that multicast capable routers are implemented all over the network, say over 30% of routers in the network, MBone approach is attractive and should be promoted.

6   Conclusions

In the paper, we have proposed and evaluated a scheme reducing the redundant path in application-level multicast by making use of network support. Our simulation results show that it is possible to improve the performance penalties of application-level multicast effectively by strategic placement of network-support routers. Then, we have compared the performance of our scheme to MBone approach. The simulation results show that our scheme and MBone approach should be implemented respectively according to the deployment of the network-support routers. We believe that the results will be a guideline for multicast deployment.

Acknowledgments

We would like to thank anonymous reviewers of NGC'03 for valuable comments.

References

1. S. Deering, D. R. Cheriton, "Host Groups: A Multicast Extension to the internet Protocol", RFC-966, December 1985.
2. H. Eriksson, "MBONE: The multicast backbone", Communications ACM, 37, 54-60, August 1994.
3. Yang-hua Chu, Sanjay G. Rao and Hui Zhang, "A case for end system multicast", IEEE JSAC, vol.20, pp.1456-1471, October 2002.
4. Suman Banerjee, Bobby Bhattacharjee and Christopher Kommareddy, "Scalable Application Layer Multicast", In Proc. of SIGCOMM 2002, Pittsburgh, Pennsylvania, August 2002.
5. K. Psounis, "Active Networks: Applications, Security, Safety and Architectures", IEEE Communi. Surveys, First Quarter 1999.
6. B. Waxman, "Routing of Multiple Connections", IEEE Jounal on Selected Areas in Communications, vol.6, no.9, pp.1617-1622, December 1988.
7. A. Medina, I. Matta, J. Byers, "On the Origin of Power Lows in Internet Topologies", ACM Computer Communication Review, vol.30, no.2, pp.18-28, April 2000.

An Adaptive Method for Dynamic Audience Size Estimation in Multicast

Maziar Nekovee, Andrea Soppera, and Trevor Burbridge

BT Exact, Adastral Park
Martlesham, Suffolk IP5 3RE, UK
{maziar.nekovee,andrea.2.soppera,trevor.burbridge}@bt.com

Abstract. We develop an end-to-end protocol for real-time estimation of the size of dynamic multicast groups. Unlike previously proposed methods our approach alleviates feedback implosion in a dynamic setting, and is scalable to large groups. The protocol is based on probabilistic polling combined with adaptive feedback control, and the use of a time-dependent Wiener filter to enhance estimation accuracy. We examine the performance of our protocol through simulations for multicast groups with up to 10,000 members, and different scenarios of group membership dynamics. Our simulation studies show that the method is capable of tracking, in a scalable manner, the size of dynamic multicast groups with high accuracy in the face of large dynamic variations.

1 Introduction

IP multicast provides an efficient and scalable solution for mass delivery of live content and data via the Internet. Tracking the size of a multicast group is important for the working of several protocols such as RTP [1,2] SRM [3], and NORM [4]. It is also crucial in deployment of multicast as the enabling technology for Internet TV (since the revenue generated from this application is mainly from advertising, for which the audience ratings are critical). Finally, tracking the number of receivers in a multicast group is of relevance to the accounting and pricing of multicast by network providers [5]. Measurements of multicast audience size (and other statistics) can be performed on the network layer by capturing memory tables from network routers [6]. However, current standards do not require multicast routers to maintain an exact count of local receivers. Furthermore, this approach requires support from (and access to) network routers, and does not scale well to applications involving multiple multicast groups.

Several papers have addressed multicast audience size estimation via an end-to-end approach based on probabilistic polling [7,8,9,10]. In this approach, the sender samples feedback from a randomly selected subgroup of members during several polling rounds, and infer the size of the group from the received replies.

The above methods, however, focus mainly on estimating the size of static multicast groups. In reality, the groups size is a time-dependent and stochastic quantity, which can vary significantly during the session. In particular, in the membership build-up (and membership termination) phase, the group size could

B. Stiller et al. (Eds.): NGC/ICQT 2003, LNCS 2816, pp. 23–33, 2003.
© Springer-Verlag Berlin Heidelberg 2003

increase (or decrease) by orders of magnitude, imposing the problems of *feedback implosion* and *poor estimation accuracy* on these protocols. Recently Alouf, Altman and Nain [11] proposed a probabilistic polling method for estimating the size of dynamic multicast groups. In this method sender obtains an instantaneous estimate of the group size by probabilistic polling, and reduces statistical errors in this estimate with the help of a linear Kalman filter. The main focus of these authors has been on optimizing the filtering operation, and they do not address the issue of feedback implosion during the polling session, a shortcoming which limits the scalability of their method.

In this paper we describe an adaptive protocol for estimating the size of dynamic multicast groups. We show through simulations that our protocol is scalable to very large groups, and is capable of tracking the group size with high accuracy in the face of large dynamic variations. In our method the volume of feedback is controlled via a time-dependent response probability $p(t)$ which dynamically adapts to variations in the upper-bound of the multicast group size. This adaptive approach ensures that feedback implosion is avoided throughout the session, and at the same time the maximum possible volume of feedbacks, below an implosion threshold, is generated. Furthermore, we describe an alternative filtering method for noise reduction which, unlike previous work, is based on time-dependent Wiener filter. The advantages of this filtering approach are that it requires only an approximate knowledge of the time-dependent power spectrum (spectrogram) of signal and noise, and that filter parameters can be adapted during the measurement to accommodate dynamic changes in the group size dynamics.

The rest of the paper is organized as follows. In section 2 we describe the steps involved in our algorithm. In section 3 we validate the algorithm through computer simulations for multicast groups with up to $10,000$ members, using a number of different models for the group membership dynamics. We also investigate the robustness of the method against losses in the network, and suggest a method for correcting the effect of losses. We conclude in section 4.

2 An Adaptive Group Size Estimation with Feedback Control

We consider multicast transmission to a group whose membership size, N, is in general time-dependent and stochastic. The aim of our protocol is to track the size of the group through probabilistic polling, under the constraint that the number of replies, r, received at each polling must remain below a predefined implosion threshold r_{max}. The protocol is composed of several sub-algorithms. In the following we describe each sub-algorithm in detail before giving an overview of the full protocol.

2.1 Group Size Estimation with Probabilistic Polling

Polling takes place during a multicast session at times $t_1, t_2, \ldots$ (these times are not necessarily equidistant). At each polling round the sender multicasts a feedback request to group members that contains a response probability p $(0 < p \leq 1)$. Upon receiving this request, each receiver returns a feedback with probability p. As a result of N independent and identically distributed Bernoulli trials, the total number r of replies sent has a binomial probability distribution $B(p, N)$ [8]. The statistical inference problem is to find an estimate $\tilde{N}$ of the group's size, based on the returned responses, and a knowledge of p. A rigorous way for obtaining such an estimate is using the maximum likelihood estimation (MLE) method [12], applied to a Binomial distribution. The likelihood function of the unknown parameter N given observation r is:

$$\mathcal{L}(N|r, p) = \binom{N}{r} p^r (1 - p)^{N-r} \approx \frac{(Np)^r}{r!} e^{-Np}, \tag{1}$$

where we have used Poisson approximation of the binomial distribution [13]. Maximizing $\mathcal{L}$ (or its logarithm) with respect to N yields the desired point estimator of the group size

$$\tilde{N}(r, p) = \frac{r}{p} \ , p \neq 0. \tag{2}$$

In a situation where losses in the network occur, and assuming spatially independent and homogeneous loss probabilities $\pi_i = \pi$ along each sender-receiver link, the probability of success of each Bernoulli trial becomes $p_i' = (1 - \pi)^2 p$, and we obtain the modified estimator:

$$\tilde{N}(p, \pi, r) = \frac{r}{p(1 - \pi)^2} = \tilde{N}(p, \pi = 0, r) \frac{1}{(1 - \pi)^2}. \tag{3}$$

2.2 Estimating an Upper Bound and Dynamic Feedback Control

In order to avoid feedback implosion, the sender chooses the response probability such that the number of feedback messages stays below some pre-defined implosion threshold r_{max} even in the worst-case scenario (i.e. when N reaches the value of an estimated upper bound N_{max}). At the start of a session this upper bound is set to some safe initial value, based on prior knowledge. However, as the session progresses, the upper bound is estimated from the returned feedbacks, such that its value adapts to actual variations in the size of the group. Given the response count r and the response probability p corresponding to a measurement instant, we obtain an estimate of the upper bound for that instant in the following way. Using Bayes' theorem [12], we have:

$$\Pr(N|r) \propto \Pr(N)\Pr(r|N) = \Pr(N)\binom{N}{r} p^r (1 - p)^{N-r} \tag{4}$$

where $\Pr(N)$ is the prior distribution of the audience size. Assuming a uniform distribution (in the interval $[0, \infty]$) for the prior $\Pr(N)$ and using Poisson approximation, we obtain:

$$\Pr(N|r; p) \propto \frac{(Np)^r}{r!} e^{-Np}. \tag{5}$$

The conditional probability that the audience size exceeds some value N_{max} is:

$$\Pr(N \geq N_{max}|r) = 1 - \frac{p}{\Gamma(r+1)} \int_0^{N_{max}} dN (Np)^r e^{-Np}, \qquad (6)$$

from which we obtain an estimate for the upper bound of the group size by requiring this probability to be at least as large as $1 - \epsilon$, where ϵ ($0 \leq \epsilon \leq 1$) is a design parameter whose value controls how tightly the upper bound follows the group size. Imposing this condition results in the following nonlinear equation for $\tilde{N}_{max}$:

$$P(r+1, p\tilde{N}_{max}) = 1 - \epsilon. \qquad (7)$$

where P denotes the incomplete Gamma function [14]. Since P is a monotonically increasing function of $p\hat{N}_{max}$, this equation has a unique solution, which is easily found by iteration. In the case that no replies are returned to sender ($r = 0$) Eq. (7) could be solved analytically, yielding

$$\tilde{N}_{max}(r = 0) = -\frac{\ln(\epsilon)}{p}; \qquad (r = 0). \qquad (8)$$

Given the above estimate for the upper bound, and a predefined implosion threshold r_{max}, the number of feedback messages in the next measurement instant is controlled by choosing the new value of p such that the risk of feedback implosion stays below a predefined threshold δ. This yields:

$$\Pr(r > r_{max}|\tilde{N}_{max}) = \delta, \qquad (9)$$

which can be written as:

$$1 - \int_0^{r_{max}} \binom{\tilde{N}_{max}}{r} p^r (1-p)^{\tilde{N}_{max}-r} = \delta, \qquad (10)$$

which can be further simplified to:

$$I_p(r_{max} + 1, \tilde{N}_{max} - r_{max}) = \delta. \qquad (11)$$

In the above equation I_p is the incomplete Beta function [14]. Since I_p is a monotonically increasing function of p, the above equation is easily solved by iteration to yield the required value of p.

2.3   A Time-Dependent Wiener Filter for Noise Reduction

The instantaneous estimate $\tilde{N}(t_k)$ contains rather large statistical errors [11], which could be viewed as a time-dependent noise $n(t_k)$ superimposed on the signal we are trying to measure, the audience size $N(t_k)$. Methods from filtering theory can then be used to reduce this noise. We use an online time-dependent Wiener filter, whose operation is defined by:

$$\hat{N}(t) = \int_{t'} dt' h(t, t') \tilde{N}(t') \Theta(t - t'). \qquad (12)$$

Here $h(t, t')$ is a linear filter kernel and Θ denotes the step function. The transform $H(t, f)$ of the filter kernel in the joint time-frequency domain, is obtained from [15]

$$H(t, f) = \frac{P_N(t, f)}{P_N(t, f) + P_n(t, f)} \tag{13}$$

where $P_N(t, f)$, $P_n(t, f)$ are the physical power spectra (spectrogram) of signal and noise, respectively. Obtaining the optimum Wiener filter from the above equation requires a knowledge of time-dependent power spectra of both signal and noise, which is generally not available. We circumvent this problem by modeling the signal and noise spectra with the following parametrized functions[1]:

$$\tilde{P}_N(t, f) = K(t) \frac{\alpha(t)}{f^2 + \alpha^2(t)}; \qquad \tilde{P}_n(t, f) = A(t), \tag{14}$$

where $\alpha(t)$, $K(t)$ and $A(t)$ are time-dependent adjustable parameters. These parameters are obtained by evaluating the spectrogram of the measured signal $\tilde{N}$ over a sliding window, and fitting the results to the sum $\tilde{P}_N(t, f) + \tilde{P}_n(t, f)$.

With the above choice of model spectra, the corresponding Wiener filter in the time-time domain takes the following form:

$$h(t, t') = \gamma(t) e^{-\beta(t)(t-t')} \theta(t - t') \tag{15}$$

with

$$\beta^2(t) = \alpha^2(t) \left(1 + \frac{K(t)}{A(t)}\right) \tag{16}$$

and $\gamma(t)$ a normalization factor. The filtered estimates $\hat{N}(t_k)$ and $\hat{N}_{max}(t_k)$ are obtained from

$$\hat{N}(t_k) = \gamma(t_k) \sum_{j \leq k} e^{-\beta(t_k - t_j)} \tilde{N}(t_j) \tag{17}$$

$$\hat{N}_{max}(t_k) = \gamma(t_k) \sum_{j \leq k} e^{-\beta(t_k - t_j)} \tilde{N}_{max}(t_j) \tag{18}$$

2.4   Protocol Overview

We conclude this section by summarizing our complete estimation algorithm. In the protocol described below we assume that polling takes place at times $t = iT$, $i = 1, 2 \ldots$, with T a user-defined (inverse) polling frequency.

initialization
Set initial guess for N_{max}, β, and calculate p from Eq. 11 (ϵ and δ are fixed design parameters.)

---

[1]   Our Lorenzian model for $P_n(t, f)$ was motivated by the fact that for $\alpha \to 0$ it corresponds to the power spectrum of a constant audience size while with $\alpha \neq 0$ we expected it to represent a rather reasonable model for the autocorrelation function of most time-varying multicast audiences.

kth measurement step

- *Sender multicast a request for feedback, containing p.*
- *Upon receiving the request, each receiver replies with probability p.*
- *Sender collects and counts feedbacks for this round and computes $\tilde{N}(t_k)$, $\hat{N}(t_k)$, $\tilde{N}_{max}(t_k)$ and $\hat{N}_{max}(t_k)$, using Eqs. (2), (17), (7) and (18), respectively.*
- *Sender uses $\hat{N}_{max}(t_k)$ to determine the response probability $p(t_{k+1})$ from Eq. 11, and sends the next feedback request containing $p(t_{k+1})$.*
- *If required, the spectrogram of $\tilde{N}$ is re-calculated and the parameters α, K, A, and β are updated by least square fitting of $P_{\tilde{N}}$.*

3   Simulation Studies

In this section we examine through a set of simulations the ability of our protocol to track with high accuracy, and in a scalable manner (i.e. avoiding feedback implosion), the size of large dynamic multicast groups. We also investigate the impact of packet loss on the protocol performance. Our simulations are performed for multicast groups with up to 10,000 members, using a number of different model scenarios for group membership dynamics. Our choice for the maximum group size was motivated by real-life webcasting applications over networks of large corporations [16], where the audience size is of such an order of magnitude. The frequency of measurements, T, was set equal to one simulation timestep throughout[2].

3.1   Models for Group Size Dynamics

As a first example we consider a scenario where the population of a multicast group follows a death-immigration (DI) stochastic model [13]. In this model members join a group at the arrival times of a Poisson process with rate $\lambda > 0$, while they leave the group at the departure rate $\mu N(t_k)$, where $N(t_k)$ is the size of the group at time t_k, and $\mu > 0$. This model is asymptotically Poisson distributed with parameter $\rho = \lambda/\mu$, and is equivalent to the non-stationary occupation process of a $M/M/\infty$ queue, which was previously considered by Alouf *et al.* [11]. These simulations were performed using $\lambda = 0.75$, $\mu = 0.000075$, and an initial group size $N(t_0) = 100$. As a second example we consider a deterministic model where the audience size shows very large harmonic fluctuations around a constant value of 5,000 (we call this the H model). This model serves as an stringent test of the adequacy of our assumptions in deriving the optimal Wiener filter, since, unlike the DI model, the power spectrum of the H model deviates significantly from a Lorenzian shape. Furthermore, a more sophisticated version of the model might be relevant to multicast applications in which the group size shows harmonic variations, e.g. corresponding to time of the day, without ever saturating to some stationary value.

---

[2] We have also applied our algorithm to systems with both larger and smaller group sizes, and have obtained results similar to those discussed below.

3.2   Simulations with No Packet Loss

All simulations were performed using three different values of feedback implosion threshold: $r_{max} = 25, 100, 200$. The filter parameter β was optimized offline in all simulations by fitting the entire signal plus noise spectrum to the forms given by Eq. (14), and was found to be $\beta = 0.05$ for the DI model and $\beta = 0.5$ for the H model. The initial guess for the upper bound of the groups was set at $N_{max} = 10,000$. Time variations of both models are shown in the upper panels of Figure 1, together with the online estimates $\hat{N}$ and $\hat{N}_{max}$, obtained for $r_{max} = 100$. The middle panels show time variations of the automatically generated response probability p, for $r_{max} = 25$ and $r_{max} = 100$, respectively. Finally, the lower panels display the corresponding number of returned feedback responses as a function of time. It can be seen that, despite a great difference in their membership dynamics, our estimates tightly track the actual group size for both models. In the case of the DI model the accuracy is less satisfactory towards the end of simulations where the number of sampled receivers is $\sim 1\%$ of the group size, but is still very high. Note also that as session proceeds, $\hat{N}_{max}$ adjusts to variations in the group size providing a 'safe' estimate of the upper-bound of this quantity. As can be seen from the middle panels of Figure 1, variations in p follow time variations in the group size, while its magnitude is controlled by the value of implosion threshold r_{max}. The lower panels of the figure display variations in the number of returned feedbacks replies as a function of time. Also shown are the corresponding feedback thresholds $r_{max} = 25$ and $r_{max} = 100$. The number of returned feedbacks fluctuates around 10 and 60, respectively but it never exceeds the corresponding implosion threshold.

Table 1. Mean value of the relative error $\delta N = |N - \hat{N}|/N$ for different choices of r_{max} is given for the death-immigration (DI) and harmonic(H) models.

r_{max}	δN (DI)	δN (H)
25	5.0%	15.5%
100	1.7%	5.6%
200	1.4%	1.1%

The relative estimation errors $\delta N = |N - \hat{N}|/N$, averaged over all timesteps are given in Table 1, for both models and three different values of r_{max}. The estimation accuracy is very high even when less that 25 feedbacks are allowed per polling round, and, as expected, increases when the allowed implosion threshold is increased. The filtered estimates are systematically better for the DI model than the H model, indicating that our filtering operation is more effective for this model of group size dynamics.

Another interesting situation is a "step response" scenario [2,17] where the size of the group changes by several orders of magnitude in the between successive measurement instants. We found that the current algorithm performs less satisfactory in such "step-join"[2] scenarios (in terms of feedback implosion

3.3   Impact of Packet Losses

In order to investigate the impact of packet loss on the performance of our protocol we considered a model where losses occur at the link adjacent to sender, with a probability Q, and independently at the receivers' link to the backbone, with a probability π. This model incorporates the main features of packet loss characteristics found in experimental [18] and simulation studies of the Mbone, which indicate that spatial correlations in packet loss is small, except for losses occurring close to multicast source.

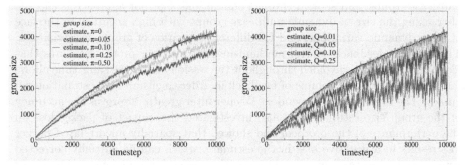

Fig. 2. The impact of packet loss is shown on group size estimate when only un-correlated losses occur at receiver links (left panel), and when they occur adjacent to the sender's link (right panel). Results are shown for a multicast group following the death-immigration process, and for several values of loss probabilities π and Q.

We performed simulations with packet loss for multicast groups whose membership size followed the above-mentioned DI and H dynamics, as well as groups with time-independent membership size. Figure 2 shows results of our simulations for the DI model (similar results were obtained for the other two models but are not shown due to space restriction). In the left panel of this figure we show results of simulations in which Q is set to zero while the probability of uncorrelated losses at receivers' links π is gradually increased from 0 (no loss) to 0.5. It can be seen that in this case the impact of packet loss is to introduce a bias ΔN in our estimation. We found that the magnitude of this bias is rather well described by $\Delta N = \tilde{N}/(1 - \pi)^2$, in agreement with our previous analysis (Eq. (4)). The above result suggests that the robustness of the estimation against uncorrelated losses could be improved by requiring receivers to measure their average loss (e.g. by detecting gaps in packet sequences) over the session, and report this to the sender when sending a reply. The sender can then estimate the average loss per receiver from this data, and incorporate this in its estimate of the group size, via Eq. (3).

In the right panel of Figure 2 we show the results for the case where π is set to 0 while Q is increased from 0 to 0.25. In this case the occurrence of a loss during a measurement round means that sender does not receive any replies at all at that round $(r = 0)$, and cannot make a valid instantaneous estimate $\tilde{N}$. This has a larger impact on our estimation than the previous case. However, as can be seen from the figure, our protocol is not extremely vulnerable to such a loss since our Wiener filter is capable of partially filtering out invalid instantaneous estimates. Thus, even with a fully correlated loss probability as high as $Q = 0.1$, the average relative error is no more than 15%.

4   Conclusions

In this paper we presented a scalable algorithm for estimating the size of dynamic multicast groups, and showed through simulations that our approach is capable of tracking the size of dynamic multicast groups with high accuracy in the face of large dynamic variations, and for different scenarios of group size dynamics. The dynamic feedback control mechanism built into our protocol ensures that feedback implosion is avoided throughout the session and at the same time allows for maximum possible volume of feedback in order to ensure high estimation accuracy. The use of a time-dependent Wiener filter greatly improves the accuracy of the group size estimate. We also investigated the impact of packet loss on the performance of the protocol and showed that spatially uncorrelated packet loss results in a negative bias in the estimate, which can be partially corrected using measurements of an (effective) average loss per group member. The use of Wiener filter improves the robustness of the estimate against highly correlated packet losses.

In the present study both the filter parameter and the measurement frequency T were held fixed throughout the session. Our methodology, however, allows for online adaptation of filter parameters in real scenarios. To achieve this the sender could evaluate the time-dependent power spectra of signal plus noise over and sliding window and adjust the filter parameter by fitting the resulting spectrum to the forms given by Eq. (14). Future work will focus on fully developing a full adaptive Wiener filter along the above lines, and a method for adjusting the measurement frequency to dynamics of multicast group size. We are also making good progress in implementing our methodology in a publish-subscribe protocol, in which estimates of time-varying listeners' interests in published topics are used for dynamic protocol configuration. This should allow us to further investigate the performance of the algorithm in a real scenario.

References

1. H. Schulzrinne, S. Casner, R. Fredrick, and V. Jacobson, "RTP: a transport protocol for real-time applications", RFC 1889, Network Working Group, January 1996.
2. J. Rosenberg and H. Schulzrinne, "Timer reconsideration for enhanced RTP scalability" in Proc. of IEEE INFOCOM98, San Francisco, USA, 1998, pp 488-496.
3. S. Floyd, V. Jacobson, S. McCanne, C. Liu, and L. Zhang, "A reliable multicast framework for light-weight session and application level framing", in Proc. of ACM SIGCOMM'95, New York, USA, 1995, pp. 342-356.

4. M. Handley, C. Bormann, B. Adamson, "NACK-oriented reliable multicast (NORM) Protocl Bulding Blocks", INTERNET-DRAFT, September 2003 www.potaroo.net/ietf/ids/draft-ietf-rmt-bb-norm-05.txt.
5. See, e.g., T. Henderson and S. N. Bhatti, "Protocol independent multicast pricing", in 10th International Workshop on Network and Operating Systems Support for Digital Audio and Video (NOSS-DV'00), The University of North Carolina, USA June 2000.
6. K. Almeroth and M. Ammar, "Collecting and modeling of join/leave behavior of multicast group members in MBone", in Proc. of HPDC'96, Syracuse, NY USA, August 1996, pp. 209-216.
7. J.-C. Bolot, T. Turletti, and I. Wakeman, "Scalable feedback control for multicast video distribution in the Internet", in Proc. of ACM SIGCOMM'94, London, UK, September 1994, pp. 58-67.
8. T. Friedman and D. Towsley, "Multicast session membership size estimation", in Proc. of IEEE INFOCOM'99, New York, NY USA, March 1999, vol. 2 pp 965-972.
9. J. Nonnenmacher, "Reliable multicast to large groups", Ph.D. thesis, EPFL, Laussane, Switzerland, July 1998; J. Nonnenmacher and E. W. Biersack, "Scalable feedback for large groups" IEEE/ACM Transactions on Networking, June 1999, pp 375-386.
10. C. Liu and J. Nonnenmacher, "Broadcast audience estimation", in Proc. of IEEE INFOCOM 2000, Tel Aviv, Israel, March 2000, vol 2, pp 952-960.
11. S. Alouf, E. Altman and P. Nain, "Optimal on-line estimation of the size of a dynamic multicast group", in Proc. of IEEE INFOCOM 2002, New York, NY, USA, March 2002, vol 2, pp 952-960.
12. P. M. Lee, "Bayesian Statistics: An Introduction", Arnold Publishing, London, UK, 1997.
13. G. R. Grimmet and D. R. Stirzaker, "Probability and Random Processes", Clarendon Press, Oxford, UK, 1992.
14. M. Abramovitz and I. Stegun. "Handbook of Mathematical Functions", Dover Publications, New York, USA, 1972.
15. See F. Hiaswatsch, G. Matz, H. Kirchauer, and W. Kozek. "Time-frequency formulation, design, and implementation of time-varying optimal filters for signal estimation", IEEE Transactions on Signal Processing, Vol. 48, pp. 1417-1432, and references therein.
16. R. J. Jacobs, M. D. Walker, and R I M Jeffry. "Intranet.tv – automated multimedia content delivery", BT Technology Journal, Vol. 20, pp. 75-83.
17. We thank the anonymous referee for drawing our attention to this scenario.
18. M. Yanjik, S. Moon, J. Kurose, and D. Towsley. "Measurement and modeling of the temporal dependence in packet loss", in Proceedings of IEEE INFOCOM'99, Los Alamitos, California, 1999.

Anycast in Locality-Aware Peer-to-Peer Overlay Networks

Rongmei Zhang and Y. Charlie Hu

Purdue University, West Lafayette IN 47907, USA
{rongmei,ychu}@purdue.edu

Abstract. This paper advocates implementing anycast in peer-to-peer (p2p) overlay networks. We argue that anycast in p2p overlays (exemplified by Pastry, Tapestry, Chord, CAN) combines the advantages of IP anycast and existing application-layer anycast services. We show that anycast can leverage the locality-awareness embedded in existing p2p overlays. The locality-awareness of the p2p routing substrates can be extended to support anycast and anycast is achieved as the result of the enhanced locality-aware routing. We have implemented anycast in Pastry, and experiments confirm that with high probability, a message addressed to an anycast group is routed to the closest node in the group according to the proximity metric. We also evaluate the performance of anycast using a realistic failure trace and the results show that our implementation of anycast is resilient to node failures.

1   Introduction

Anycast for IP was first introduced in RFC 1546 [1]. A message addressed to an anycast address is routed by the network to at least one of the servers that accept messages for that anycast address (see Fig. 1). IP anycast can provide automatic service discovery in the Internet. By assigning the same anycast address to replicated FTP servers, users can download from the closest server without manually choosing from a list of mirrors. IP anycast can also support host autoconfiguration by assigning an anycast address to the DNS service; after moving to a new network, a host can continue to contact the DNS anycast address instead of being re-configured with the new local DNS server.

Application-layer anycast has also been proposed [2,3,4]. While IP anycast relies on network routers to find the closest receiver, application-layer anycast involves anycast address resolvers to obtain application specific measurements.

The drawbacks of both IP anycast and application-layer anycast have been well known. Anycast does not comply with the hierarchy of the Internet and thus IP anycast is difficult to scale. In [5], Katabi and Wroclawski show that it is possible to provide scalable global IP anycast service. However, IP anycast needs support from network routers and its wide usage relies on wide deployment of supporting routers. Application-layer anycast requires the support of Internet distance services and scalable network measurement is still under continuous research efforts.

B. Stiller et al. (Eds.): NGC/ICQT 2003, LNCS 2816, pp. 34–46, 2003.

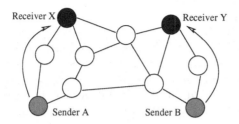

Fig. 1. Illustration of anycast. Sender A and sender B are sending to the same anycast group and their messages are routed to the closest group members receiver X and receiver Y respectively.

In the last few years peer-to-peer systems have gained popularity, from the pioneering Napster [6], Gnutella [7], and FreeNet [8] to the second-generation systems such as CAN [9], Chord [10], Pastry [11], and Tapestry [12]. These second-generation systems all build self-organizing and decentralized overlay networks. Unicast in these systems has been extensively studied. The unicast routing algorithms are highly scalable and efficient; routing is typically finished within a small number of overlay hops. Multicast on top of these p2p overlay have also been studied [13,14,15,16]. This paper advocates integrating anycast into p2p overlay networks to leverage their inherent scalability and efficiency.

Implementing anycast in p2p overlays has several advantages. First, each node in the p2p network volunteers as a router and maintains a routing table. Thus implementing anycast in p2p networks has the advantage of easy access to the "routers" while IP routers are more difficult to access and manipulate. Second, p2p overlay networks employ a flat address space by hiding the hierarchical structure and other details of the underlying Internet, which simplifies the implementations. Third, p2p overlays are highly scalable from their decentralized organization. Routing in a p2p overlay is usually completed within $logN$ hops, and by taking into account network proximity during p2p routing (called locality-aware routing), very low routing stretch and network stress are incurred. Therefore p2p overlays are deployable in large networks. Fourth, as in previous application-level anycast systems, p2p overlays can support multiple proximity metrics for anycast such as routing delay or network bandwidth.

A major issue in implementing anycast is how to route to the closest group member in an anycast group. We argue that a locality-aware p2p overlay provides an ideal environment for implementing anycast. The key observation is that locality-aware p2p overlays exploit locality in the underlying physical network in performing routing in the overlays [17,18], and this "locality-awareness" can be naturally exploited in implementing anycast, which by definition routes each message to the closest node among all candidate nodes.

The rest of the paper is organized as follows. Section 2 gives an overview of one of the locality-aware structured p2p overlays, Pastry. Section 3 describes how to integrate anycast into Pastry. Section 4 presents simulation results showing the effectiveness of anycast in finding the closest group member. Section 5 discusses related work and Section 6 concludes the paper.

2   Background

In this section, we give a slightly detailed description of Pastry [11,19], since we propose to support anycast by extending Pastry's unicast substrate. Pastry is a scalable, fault-tolerant, peer-to-peer substrate. Each Pastry node has a unique, uniformly randomly assigned *nodeId* (node identifier) in a circular 128-bit identifier space. Given a 128-bit key, Pastry routes the associated message towards the live node whose nodeId is numerically closest to the key.

Routing State. For the purpose of routing, nodeIds and keys are thought of as a sequence of digits in base 2^b. A node's routing table is organized into $128/b$ rows and 2^b columns. The 2^b entries in row n of the routing table contain the IP addresses of nodes whose nodeIds share the first n digits with the present node's nodeId; the $(n+1)$th nodeId digit of the node in column m of row n equals m. A routing table entry is left empty if no node with the appropriate nodeId prefix is known.

Each node also maintains a *leaf set*. The leaf set is the set of l nodes with nodeIds that are numerically closest to the present node's nodeId, with $l/2$ larger and $l/2$ smaller nodeIds than the current node's nodeId. The leaf set ensures reliable message delivery and is used to store replicas of application objects.

Routing. At each routing step, a node seeks to forward the message to a node whose nodeId shares with the key a prefix that is at least one digit (or b bits) longer than the current node's shared prefix. If no such node can be found in the routing table, the message is forwarded to a node whose nodeId shares a prefix with the key as long as the current node, but is numerically closer to the key than the present node's nodeId.

Node Joining. A new node with nodeId X joins the network by asking an existing, nearby Pastry node A to route a join message using X as the key. The message is routed to the existing node Z with the nodeId numerically closest to X. Node X then obtains the leaf set from Z and appropriate routing table entries from nodes encountered along the path from A to Z. After initializing its state, node X notifies other nodes that need to know of its arrival and thereby updates their routing states accordingly.

Routing Table Maintenance. To prevent the deterioration of the locality of routing table entries when the underlying network changes over time, Pastry employs a *routing table maintenance* mechanism. Periodically, each node selects a random entry from each row of its routing table, and requests from the associated node a copy of that node's corresponding routing table row. Each entry from the returned routing table row is then compared to the corresponding entry in the local routing table row. If they differ, the closer node is installed based on the proximity metric.

When a routing table entry is replaced during the maintenance, it can be stored in the routing table as a backup for the primary node. When the primary node fails, the closest live backup node is used. Storing backup nodes effectively extends the routing table to three-dimensional [19]. In this paper, the routing table entry size is set to 10.

2.1 Locality-Aware Routing

Through its locality-aware node join process and routing table maintenance mechanism, Pastry maintains a proximity-aware overlay by minimizing the distance, according to a proximity metric such as network delay, to each of the nodes that appear in a node's routing table. More precisely, Pastry ensures the following invariant for each node's routing table:

Proximity Invariant: *Each entry in a node X's routing table refers to a node that is near X, according to the proximity metric, among all the live Pastry nodes with the appropriate nodeId prefix.*

Because of the above proximity invariant and prefix-based routing, Pastry routing exhibits *low delay stretch* – the total delay experienced by Pastry routing relative to the delay between the source and destination via the underlying IP routing is usually below two [11,19].

3   Anycast in Locality-Aware p2p Overlays

In this section, we discuss how to implement anycast in structured p2p overlays. We use Pastry [11] as a concrete example in our description. In principle, anycast can be implemented in any other structured p2p substrate that supports locality-aware routing [18], such as CAN [9], Chord [10], or Tapestry [12].

3.1   Overview

Our design of anycast-enabled Pastry extends the original Pastry in two major ways: (1) An (anycast) nodeId can correspond to multiple physical nodes (anycast group members). The anycast group members are required to maintain consistent leaf sets. (2) Leaf sets are maintained based on locality and may be two-dimensional by configuration. As a result, each anycast entry in the leaf set points to nodes close to the local node in the proximity space.

The above extensions effectively leverage Pastry's locality-aware routing to support anycast. In Pastry routing, each overlay hop is either taken from the leaf set or the routing table. Since both are maintained based on the proximity metric in anycast-enabled Pastry, each hop is always close to the current node. As a result, anycast-enabled Pastry always routes a message destined to an anycast group to an anycast group member that is near the source.

3.2   Anycast NodeIds

In structured p2p overlays, nodeIds are identifiers of nodes in the overlay network and are assumed to be unique. Furthermore, the mapping between nodeIds and

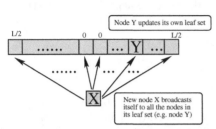
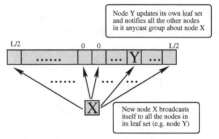

(a) Case 1: Node Y has seen the nodeId of node X before and it simply updates its own leaf set according to the proximity metric.

(b) Case 2: Node Y is seeing the nodeId of node X for the first time and updates its own leaf set. If node Y is an anycast node, it also informs all the other nodes in the same anycast group of the arrival of node X.

Fig. 2. The leaf set update process during node join.

IP addresses is assumed to be one-to-one. To incorporate anycast, the above assumption is extended to allow multiple nodes to share the same anycast nodeId. These nodes form an anycast group.

3.3   Node Joining

In anycast-enabled Pastry, the routing of a join message and the initialization of the new node's routing state is the same as in the original Pastry. However, the leaf set update process after the node joining is distinctive in two aspects, as shown in Fig. 2.

Locality-Aware Leaf Set Update. As in the original Pastry, at the end of the join process, the joining node broadcasts its arrival to the nodes in the inherited leaf set so that those nodes can update their leaf sets. In anycast-enabled Pastry, this update takes locality into account. For example, in Fig. 2(a) as the new node X notifies node Y in its inherited leaf set, if node X does not represent a new nodeId but is closer in the proximity space to node Y than the corresponding entry in node Y's current leaf set, node Y replaces that old entry with node X. The replaced node is kept as a backup in case failures should happen.

Maintaining Leaf Set Consistency. When anycast is incorporated into Pastry, there are multiple nodes in the overlay network corresponding to an anycast nodeId. By definition, the leaf sets of these nodes should contain the same set of nodeIds. Leaf set consistency is a necessary condition for the correct routing behavior of a Pastry overlay network; it guarantees that a message is always routed to the node whose nodeId is numerically closest to the message key.

   Leaf set inconsistency can potentially occur at the end of a node join process when the newly joined node X announces its existence to an anycast node Y in its inherited leaf set and node Y sees the nodeId of X for the first time, as shown in Fig. 2(b). If node Y does not notify other nodes in the same anycast group, those nodes will not be aware of the existence of the new nodeId of node X. To avoid this inconsistency, upon receiving from node X, node Y informs all the other anycast group members about node X, using a group communication mechanism.

Anycast Group Communication. We use multicast to support group communication within each anycast group. Any prefix-based p2p multicast protocol [13,14,15] can be used. The multicast address (multicast nodeId) of an anycast group is obtained by a deterministic mapping from the anycast nodeId, for example, by adding 2^{127} to the anycast nodeId (modulo 2^{128}). An update message is propagated from any node to all the other nodes by traversing the multicast tree.

3.4   Locality-Aware Routing in Anycast-Enabled Pastry

Anycast-enabled Pastry inherits locality in routing tables from the original Pastry. In addition, it also extends locality to leaf sets.

Extended Proximity Invariant: *Each entry in a node X's routing table refers to a node that is near X, according to the proximity metric, among all the live Pastry nodes with the appropriate nodeId prefix. Each entry in a node X's leaf set refers to a node that is near X, according to the proximity metric, among all the live Pastry nodes that share the same nodeId.*

When a new node X joins the network, it will be routed to a node Z with the numerically closest nodeId. If node Z belongs to an anycast group (e.g., when node X and Z are from the same anycast group), then node Z is also among the closest to node X in the proximity space among all the existing anycast group members. Assuming the triangle inequality holds in the proximity space, if the nodes in node Z's leaf set are close to node Z, they are also close to node X after node X inherits them as its own leaf set. On the other hand, if node Z has a unique nodeId, the anycast nodes in its inherited leaf set may not be close to node X. In this case, the locality of the inherited leaf sets will be improved over time by the leaf set update procedures including leaf set maintenance (see Section 3.5).

At the end of the join process, nodes from node X's inherited leaf set are notified of its arrival. These nodes are close to node X in the proximity space and may update their own leaf sets based on proximity comparison (Section 3.3). On the other hand, those nodes whose nodeIds fall inside the range of but are not included in node X's leaf set are likely to be distant in the proximity space. Therefore they are not notified of the new node X since they are unlikely to benefit from the update. The exception to this is that when node X represents a new nodeId in the p2p network, all anycast members of each anycast node in the inherited leaf set will be notified (Section 3.3).

In summary, as a result of the node join protocol and the leaf set updating procedures, the *proximity invariant* of Pastry routing is automatically extended to include the leaf set of each node when anycast is integrated into the overlay network. Since the locality in routing tables are initialized and maintained as in the original Pastry, an anycast nodeId in the routing table also points to a close node in the corresponding anycast group according to the proximity metric.

3.5   Handling Node Failures

Node Failures in Routing Tables. The anycast-enabled Pastry uses the same reactive procedure as in the original Pastry to lazily repair failed entries in the routing table. The routing algorithm chooses an alternative node to forward the message if the best choice from the routing table is found to have failed. If the down stream node has a routing table entry that matches the next digit of the message key, it automatically informs the upstream node of that entry. In addition, as in the original Pastry, the periodic routing table maintenance also repairs failed entries.

Node Failures in Leaf Sets. Anycast-enabled Pastry uses a mechanism called *leaf set maintenance* to repair failed leaf set entries: each live leaf set entry is asked to return its own leaf set and the returned leaf set is merged with the local leaf set. In addition to repairing failed entries, the local leaf set is also updated based on the proximity metric: if both the local entry and the returned entry are alive, the closer one in the proximity space is installed. Similar to routing table maintenance, those nodes that fail in the proximity comparison can be stored in the leaf set as backups to the primary node[1]. Storing backup nodes effectively extends the leaf set to two-dimensional. In this paper, the leaf set entry size is set to 10.

The backups can be used to help routing as well as leaf set maintenance. When the primary node fails, the closest live backup node can be used for routing or requesting leaf set during leaf set maintenance. The above leaf set maintenance can also be invoked periodically to prevent locality deterioration in leaf sets when the network is dynamic. Therefore, the impacts of leaf set maintenance are two fold: first, it effectively recovers leaf sets from node failures; second, it also helps to maintain the locality of leaf sets.

Node Failures in Multicast Trees. Node failures in multicast trees used for maintaining consistency among leaf sets of anycast group members are handled by the corresponding multicast protocol. For example, when the Scribe [13] multicast protocol is used, each node probes its parent periodically and re-joins the multicast tree if the current parent is found to have failed. The prefix-based routing guarantees that a valid, i.e., loop free, tree is always formed.

4   Evaluation

We have implemented anycast in FreePastry [20], following the descriptions in the previous section. This section presents the simulation results using a realistic network topology model and a node failure trace.

---

[1] Backup nodes are also produced during the leaf set update after a new node joins the p2p network (Section 3.3)

4.1   Experiment Setup

The experiments are performed on a network with 1050 routers (50 in transit domains and 1000 in stub domains). The router network is generated by GT-ITM using the transit-stub model [21]. End nodes are assigned randomly to the 1000 stub routers with uniform probability. The routing policy weights generated by the GT-ITM generator are used to calculate the shortest path between any two nodes.

The p2p network is formed by 32000 end nodes with unique nodeIds and an additional number of anycast nodes, each belonging to an anycast group. The anycast groups are modeled by the Zipf distribution: $Sub(r) = \lfloor N(r + 1)^{-1.25} + 0.5 \rfloor$, where r is the group rank and $Sub(r)$ stands for the group size. The group rank ranges from 0 to 15 in the simulations. The largest group has 256 members and the smallest has 8. For each group rank, 12 groups with distinct anycast nodeIds are created, and there are 192 anycast groups in total. Group members are randomly selected with uniform probability from the end nodes in the underlying physical network. Overall, there are a total of 7992 anycast nodes in the simulation.

To evaluate the performance of anycast in the presence of failure and recovery of anycast nodes in the p2p network, we use a trace of node arrivals and departures from a study measuring the availability of desktop computers in a corporate network [22]. The original trace contains the liveness states of 65000 nodes over a period of 840 hours. We use 7792 of the nodes during a period of 60 hours. There are an average about 6538 live anycast nodes in the entire p2p network at each hour in the simulation. We assume that nodes fail silently and the failed node is not discovered by another node until that node tries to route through it a message, either a data packet, or a control message as part of the maintenance procedures. We also assume that an anycast node always comes back with the same anycast nodeId.

At each hour in the simulations, 256 messages are sent from random sources among the 32000 non-anycast nodes to each of the 192 anycast groups. We measure the success rate of anycast routing and the routing performance of anycast, such as the relative delay penalty and the number of routing hops. The *success rate* for each message addressed to an anycast group is defined as the percentage rank, according to the proximity to the message source node, of the actual receiving member out of all the members in that anycast group. For example, the closest and second closest group members to the source node out of 5 group members have a rank of 100% and 80%, respectively. The *relative delay penalty* (RDP) is defined as the ratio between the distance traversed in the overlay network and the distance traversed if it were routed directly by the underlying IP network. If the message is forwarded to a node that has failed in the simulation, the round trip delay to the failed node is added to the total delay experienced by the message to account for the effects of node failure.

In our implementation, Scribe [13] is used to implement anycast group communication. Multicast tree maintenance are invoked at each hour to repair multicast trees for anycast groups. Failures in leaf sets are repaired on demand by

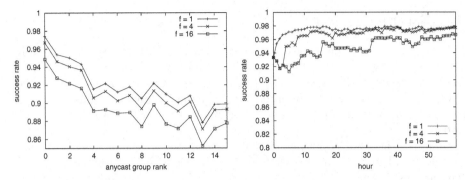

Fig. 3. Success rate of anycast for groups of varying sizes.

Fig. 4. Success rate of anycast for groups of size 256.

triggering leaf set maintenance. Routing table maintenance is invoked periodically at varying intervals (every 1, 4, and 16 hours, as represented by the symbol f in the figures shown below) to study the correlation between the success rate of anycast and the locality of the p2p network. The nodeId base of Pastry (b) is configured to 2 and the size of the leaf set (l) is set to 16.

4.2 Success Rate

Fig. 3 shows the average success rate of anycast for groups of varying sizes (group ranks). It shows the more frequent the routing table maintenance, the higher the success rate. This confirms that the locality of anycast is improved when the locality of routing table entries is improved by routing table maintenance. It also shows that the success rate decreases as the anycast group becomes smaller. This is because the smaller the anycast group, the larger the gap between adjacent ranks of anycast group members.

Fig. 4 shows the distribution of average success rate of anycast routing over the 60 hours of simulation time for groups of 256 nodes (group rank 0). For a fixed maintenance frequency, the success rate improves in the beginning of the simulation and then converges to a steady value. This suggests that the initial locality of the p2p overlay is improved by the maintenance procedures (Section 3.4).

Fig. 5 and Fig. 6 show the cumulative distribution of the success rate of anycast routing for each message and of the average success rate for messages destined to each anycast group, respectively. Under any routing table maintenance frequency, about 80% of all messages have a success rate of about 90%. The average success rates for almost all the anycast groups are above 80%.

The above simulation results suggest that the performance of anycast routing is improved as the locality of the Pastry routing is improved via periodical routing table maintenance. In principle, periodically leaf set maintenance should have similar impacts. However, due to the extremely sparse distribution (less than 1%) of anycast nodeIds within the entire Pastry nodeId space in our simu-

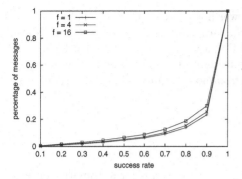

Fig. 5. Cumulative distribution of the success rate of anycast for all messages.

Fig. 6. Cumulative distribution of the average success rate of anycast for each anycast group.

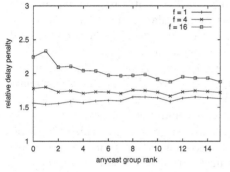

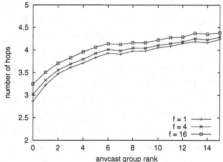

Fig. 7. Relative delay penalty of anycast for groups of varying sizes.

Fig. 8. Number of routing hops of anycast for groups of varying sizes.

lations, periodical leaf set maintenance does not affect the results as noticeably as routing table maintenance.

Note that our implementation does not always route to the closest node in the proximity space with the appropriate anycast nodeId. This can be explained by the fact that the locality-aware mechanism in Pastry is based on heuristics and thus does not produce perfect routing tables and leaf sets in anycast-enabled Pastry. Building optimal routing tables and leaf sets requires a global view of the p2p network at each node, which is very costly in practice because of the communication overhead. Nevertheless, our implementation of anycast achieves close to optimal performance without incurring excessive communication overhead.

4.3   Routing Delay and Routing Hops

Fig. 7 and Fig. 8 show the average RDP and the average number of p2p routing hops by anycast. First, both metrics are improved by routing table maintenance which improves the locality in routing table entries. Second, the higher the group rank, the fewer the routing hops. This is because the larger the anycast group, the closer the closest member, and the fewer hops it takes to reach that member. Third, RDP largely remains the same for anycast groups of different ranks for $f = 1$ and $f = 4$. This is because RDP is relative to the distance by direct IP routing between the source and the destination. The graduate decrease for $f = 16$ indicates that the initial locality from node joining is improved gradually at this maintenance frequency.

5   Related Work

Anycast was first introduced in RFC 1546 [1] as a means for automatic service discovery and host configuration. IP-anycast has also been proposed to improve IP multicast routing efficiency [23,24]. Global IP-Anycast (GIA) [5] is an architecture for scalable global IP-anycast in which inter-domain IP-anycast is implemented by edge domains maintaining efficient routes to popular anycast groups and supporting inexpensive routes to unpopular groups. Recent work related to anycast also includes global distance measurement services [25,26] and server selection techniques based on distance estimation [27].

Application-layer anycast [2] is designed to support server replication and selection without network-layer support, and is provided by anycast domain name resolvers that measure and maintain server performance metrics [3,4].

Recently, anycast has been proposed as a communication primitive in the Internet Indirection Infrastructure [28]. An anycast group is identified by a k-bit prefix and the remaining bits are used for encoding application-specific preferences. Two possible techniques of encoding location are proposed: zip code or latency based as in [26]. As pointed out in [28], zip code can not always represent network distance accurately. Latency based encoding requires the support of a measurement infrastructure, such as landmark nodes.

6   Conclusions

In this paper, we have shown that anycast can be easily integrated into locality-aware p2p overlays, using Pastry as an example. The resulting anycast-enabled p2p overlay is a more general paradigm for p2p routing since it degenerates into the original "unicast"-only overlay if nodeIds are unique. Our implementation of anycast is effective in locating the closest anycast group member in the proximity space, and retains the low routing penalty of locality-aware p2p overlays. The performance of anycast is closely related to the locality of the p2p networks, and node failures can be tolerated using simple overlay maintenance mechanisms.

Acknowledgment

We thank Peter Druschel and the anonymous reviewers for their helpful comments. This work was supported by an NSF CAREER award (ACI-0238379).

References

1. Partridge, C., Mendez, T., Milliken, W.: Host Anycast Service. RFC 1546. (1993)
2. Bhattacharjee, S., Ammar, M.H., Zegura, E.W., Shah, V., Fei, Z.: Application Layer Anycasting. In Proc. IEEE INFOCOM. (1997)
3. Fei, Z., Bhattacharjee, S., Zegura, E.W., Ammar, M.H.: A Novel Server Selection Technique for Improving the Response Time of a Replicated Service. In Proc. IEEE INFOCOM. (1998)
4. Zegura, E.W., Ammar, M.H., Fei, Z., Bhattacharjee, S.: Application-layer Anycasting: a Server Selection Architecture and Use in a Replicated Web Service. IEEE/ACM Transactions on Networking (2000)
5. Katabi, D., Wroclawski, J.: A Framework for Scalable Global IP-Anycast (GIA). In Proc. ACM SIGCOMM. (2000)
6. Napster. http://www.napster.com/.
7. The Gnutella protocol specification. http://dss.clip2.com/GnutellaProtocol04.pdf. (2000)
8. Clarke, I., Sandberg, O., Wiley, B., Hong, T.W.: Freenet: A Distributed Anonymous Information Storage and Retrieval System. In Workshop on Design Issues in Anonymity and Unobservability. (2000)
9. Ratnasamy, S., Francis, P., Handley, M., Karp, R., Schenker, S.: A Scalable Content-Addressable Network. In Proc. ACM SIGCOMM. (2001)
10. Stoica, I., Morris, R., Karger, D., Kaashoek, M.F., Balakrishnan, H.: Chord: A Scalable Peer-to-peer Lookup Service for Internet Applications. In Proc. ACM SIGCOMM. (2001)
11. Rowstron, A., Druschel, P.: Pastry: Scalable, distributed object location and routing for large-scale peer-to-peer systems. In Proc. Middleware. (2001)
12. Zhao, B.Y., Kubiatowicz, J.D., Joseph, A.D.: Tapestry: An Infrastructure for Fault-Resilient Wide-area Location and Routing. Technical Report UCB//CSD-01-1141, U. C. Berkeley (2001)
13. Rowstron, A., Kermarrec, A.M., Castro, M., Druschel, P.: Scribe: The design of a large-scale event notification infrastructure. In Proc. NGC'01. (2001)
14. Zhuang, S.Q., Zhao, B.Y., Joseph, A.D., Katz, R.H., Kubiatowicz, J.: Bayeux: An Architecture for Scalable and Fault-tolerant Wide-Area Data Dissemination. In Proc. NOSSDAV'01. (2001)
15. Zhang, R., Hu, Y.C.: Borg: A hybrid protocol for scalable application-level multicast in peer-to-peer systems. In Proc. NOSSDAV'03. (2003)
16. Ratnasamy, S., Handley, M., Karp, R., Shenker, S.: Application-level Multicast using Content-Addressable Networks. In Proc. NGC'01. (2001)
17. Ratnasamy, S., Shenker, S., Stoica, I.: Routing Algorithms for DHTs: Some Open Questions. In Proc. IPTPS'02. (2002)
18. Castro, M., Druschel, P., Hu, Y.C., Rowstron, A.: Exploiting Network Proximity in Distributed Hash Tables. In Proc. FuDiCo. (2002)
19. Castro, M., Druschel, P., Hu, Y.C., Rowstron, A.: Exploiting network proximity in peer-to-peer overlay networks. Technical report MSR-TR-2002-82 (2002)
20. FreePastry. http://www.cs.rice.edu/CS/Systems/Pastry/FreePastry/.
21. Zegura, E., Calvert, K., Bhattacharjee, S.: How to Model an Internetwork. In Proc. IEEE INFOCOM. (1996)
22. Bolosky, W.J., Douceur, J.R., Ely, D., Theimer, M.: Feasibility of a Serverless Distributed File System Deployed on an Existing Set of Desktop PCs. In Proc. SIGMETRICS. (2000)

23. Katabi, D.: The Use of IP-anycast for Building Efficient Multicast Trees. In Proc. Global Internet Symposium. (1999)
24. Kim, D., Meyer, D., Kilmer, H.: Anycast RP mechanism using PIM and MSDP. RFC 3446. (2001)
25. Francis, P., Jamin, S., Jin, C., Jin, Y., Raz, D., Shavitt, Y., Zhang, L.: IDMaps: A Global Internet Host Distance Estimation Service. IEEE/ACM Transactions on Networking. (2001)
26. Ng, T.S.E., Zhang, H.: Predicting Internet Network Distance with Coordinates-Based Approaches. In Proc. IEEE INFOCOM. (2002)
27. Ratnasamy, S., Handley, M., Karp, R., Shenker, S.: Topologically-Aware Overlay Construction and ServerSelection. In Proc. IEEE INFOCOM. (2002)
28. Stoica, I., Adkins, D., Zhaung, S., Shenker, S., Surana, S.: Internet Indirection Infrastructure. In Proc. ACM SIGCOMM. (2002)

Scalable Application-Level Anycast
for Highly Dynamic Groups

Miguel Castro[1], Peter Druschel[2],
Anne-Marie Kermarrec[1], and Antony Rowstron[1]

[1] Microsoft Research, 7 J J Thomson Avenue, Cambridge, CB3 0FB, UK
[2] Rice University, 6100 Main Street, MS-132, Houston, TX 77005, USA*

Abstract. We present an application-level implementation of anycast
for highly dynamic groups. The implementation can handle group sizes
varying from one to the whole Internet, and membership maintenance
is efficient enough to allow members to join for the purpose of receiving
a single message. Key to this efficiency is the use of a proximity-aware
peer-to-peer overlay network for decentralized, lightweight group maintenance; nodes join the overlay once and can join and leave many groups
many times to amortize the cost of maintaining the overlay. An anycast implementation with these properties provides a key building block
for distributed applications. In particular, it enables management and
location of dynamic resources in large scale peer-to-peer systems. We
present several resource management applications that are enabled by
our implementation.

1 Introduction

Anycast [12] is a service that allows a node to send a message to a nearby member
of a group, where proximity is defined using a metric like IP hops or delay. In
this paper, we are interested in the application of anycast to manage distributed
resources in decentralized peer-to-peer systems. This is a challenging application
for anycast because groups can vary in size from very small to very large and
membership can be highly dynamic.

We note that resource discovery based on anycast is a powerful building block
in many distributed systems. For example, it can be used to manage dynamic
distributed resources (e.g., processing, storage, and bandwidth) using the following pattern. First, anycast groups are created for each resource type. Nodes join
the appropriate group to advertise the availability of a resource and leave the
group when they no longer have the resource available. Nodes request nearby
resources by anycasting messages to the appropriate groups.

Unfortunately, existing anycast proposals do not support this application.
Network level anycast (e.g., [10]) does not work well with highly dynamic groups
and its deployment has been hampered by concerns over security, billing, and

---

* Supported in part by Texas ATP (003604-0079-2001) and by NSF (ANI-0225660).

B. Stiller et al. (Eds.): NGC/ICQT 2003, LNCS 2816, pp. 47–57, 2003.

scalability with the number of groups. Previous application-level anycast proposals [1,9] are easy to deploy but assume that groups are small and that membership is relatively stable. We present an application-level implementation of anycast that can be used as a powerful building block in large scale peer-to-peer applications.

Our anycast system builds a per-group proximity-aware spanning tree. It efficiently supports both small and very large groups. Moreover, it supports highly dynamic groups, because nodes join and leave a group with low overhead and all membership maintenance is decentralized. The spanning trees are used to anycast messages efficiently: messages are delivered to a nearby group member with low delay and link stress. This enables very fine-grained resource management in large scale distributed systems.

The key to the efficiency of our anycast implementation is that group trees are embedded in a structured, proximity-aware overlay network. The tree is the union of the paths from the group members to a node acting as the root of the tree. When a member joins a group, it merely routes a join request towards the root of the tree using the overlay, adding overlay links to the tree as needed. When the join request reaches a node that is already a member of the tree, the request is not propagated any further. Thus, membership maintenance is fully distributed. The same overlay network can support many different independent groups, with the advantage that the overhead of maintaining the proximity-aware overlay network can be amortized over many different group spanning trees (and other applications). This is the key to lightweight membership management and the resulting ability to support large and highly dynamic groups.

We show a number of uses of our anycast implementation to manage resources in real applications. SplitStream, for instance, is a peer-to-peer streaming content distribution system that stripes content across multiple multicast trees [4]. This striping achieves increased robustness to node failures, spreads the forwarding load across all participating nodes, and allows SplitStream to accommodate participating nodes with widely differing network bandwidth. It uses anycast to locate nodes with spare network bandwidth.

The contributions of this paper are to describe a scalable application-level implementation of anycast for highly dynamic groups, and to articulate its power as a tool for resource management in distributed systems.

The rest of this paper is organized as follows. Section 2 explains group membership management and spanning tree construction. In Section 3, we show how to implement anycast and manycast using these trees. Section 4 discusses applications of our anycast implementation. We present some performance results in Section 5. Related work is described in Section 6, and we conclude in Section 7.

2   Group Management

We use Scribe [18,6], an application-level multicast system, to manage groups and to maintain a spanning tree connecting the members of each group. Scribe can handle group sizes varying from one to millions, and it supports rapid changes in group membership efficiently. All nodes join Pastry, a structured peer-to-peer overlay [16,3]. Subsequently, nodes may join and leave potentially many groups many times to amortize the cost of building the Pastry overlay. This, combined with Pastry's already scalable algorithms to join the overlay is the key to Scribe's ability to support highly dynamic groups efficiently [6].

Per-group trees are embedded in the Pastry overlay, and are formed as the union of the overlay routes from the group members to the root of the tree. In addition to supporting anycast, group trees can be used to multicast messages to the group using reverse path forwarding [8] from the root. It has been shown that Scribe multicast achieves low delay and induces low link and node stress [6].

Scribe's approach to group management could be implemented on top of other structured peer-to-peer overlay networks like CAN [14], Chord [20], or Tapestry [23]. In fact, Scribe has been implemented on top of CAN [7].

Next, we describe Pastry and the construction of group trees using Scribe in more detail.

2.1   Peer-to-Peer Overlay

Pastry is fully described in [16,3]. Here, we provide a brief overview to understand how we implement group management and anycast.

In Pastry, numeric *keys* represent application objects and are chosen from a large identifier space. Each participating node is assigned an identifier (*nodeId*) chosen randomly with uniform probability from the same space. Pastry assigns each object key to the live node with nodeId numerically closest to the key. It provides a primitive to send a message to the node that is responsible for a given key.

The overlay network is self-organizing and self-repairing, and each node maintains only a small routing table with $O(log(n))$ entries, where n is the number of nodes in the overlay. Each entry maps a nodeId to its IP address. Messages can be routed to the node responsible for a given key in $O(log(n))$ hops. The routing table maintained in each Pastry node is created and maintained in a manner that enables Pastry to exploit network locality in the underlying network. There are two particular properties of Pastry routes that are important for efficient anycast: *low delay stretch* and *local route convergence*. Simulations with realistic network topologies show that the delay stretch, i.e., the total delay experienced by a Pastry message relative to the delay between source and destination in the underlying network, is usually below two [3]. These simulations also show that the routes for messages sent to the same key from nearby nodes in the underlying network converge at a nearby node after a small number of hops.

2.2   Group Trees

Scribe uses Pastry to name a potentially large number of groups. Each group has a key called the *groupId*, which could be the hash of the group's textual name concatenated with its creator's name. To create a group, a Scribe node asks Pastry to route a ▣▣▣▣▣▣ message using the groupId as the key. The node responsible for that key becomes the root of the group's tree.

To join a group, a node routes a ▣▣▣ message through the overlay to the group's groupId. This message is routed towards the root of the tree by Pastry. Each node along the route checks whether it is already in the group's tree. If it is, it adds the sender to its children table and stops routing the message any further. Otherwise, it creates an entry for the group, adds the source node to the group's children table, and sends a ▣▣▣ message for itself. The properties of the Pastry overlay routes ensure that this mechanism produces a tree.

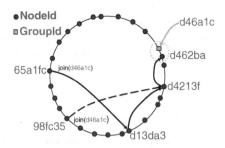

Fig. 1. Example formation of a group tree.

Figure 1 demonstrates how the trees are built using an example tree with the groupId $d46a1c$. Node $d462ba$ acts as the root for the tree, as it has the numerically closest nodeId to the groupId. Initially node $65a1fc$ routes a ▣▣▣ request using the groupId. Pastry routes the request via node $d13da3$, which takes node $65a1fc$ as a child and then forwards the request towards the groupId. Node $d4213f$ receives the request, takes $d13da3$ as a child and forwards the request. Node $d462ba$ receives the request, and takes $d4213f$ as a child. As it is the root for this group tree it does not forward the request. Subsequently, node $98fc35$ joins the group. It routes a ▣▣▣ using the groupId. Node $d213f$ receives the request and takes $98fc35$ as a child. As it is already a member of the tree the request is not forwarded to any other nodes.

If a node wishes to leave a group and it has entries in its children table for that group then it marks itself as no longer a member and does nothing else. As it has entries in its children table it is required to receive and forward messages for the group. If the departing node has no entries in its children table then it sends a ▣▣▣▣▣ message to its parent in the tree. Upon receiving a ▣▣▣▣▣ message the parent node removes the child node from its children table. If the parent node subsequently has an empty children table and it is not a member of the group, it sends a ▣▣▣▣▣ message to its parent. This process continues recursively up the tree until a node is reached that still has entries in the children table after removing the departing node, or the root is reached. Scribe's mechanisms to tolerate node failures, including root failures, and several optimizations are described in [6].

Group management scales well because Pastry ensures that the trees are well balanced and that join and leave requests are localized and do not involve any centralized node. For example, join requests stop at the first node on the route to the root that is already in the group tree. This property also holds when Scribe is implemented on top of CAN, Chord, or Tapestry.

The local route convergence property of Pastry also helps group management scalability because join and leave requests tend to traverse a small number of physical network links. Similarly, the low delay stretch property results in low latency for joins. Scribe would retain these properties only when implemented on top of other proximity-aware structured overlays, for example Tapestry.

3   Anycast and Manycast

Our anycast system allows a node to send a message to a member of a group. It relies on Scribe to create a Scribe tree for the group. If Scribe uses a proximity-aware overlay like Pastry [3] or Tapestry [23], the message will be delivered to one of the closest group members in the underlying network topology. The sender does not need to be a member of the group.

Anycast is implemented using a distributed depth-first search of the group tree, which is built as described in Section 2.2. This is efficient and scalable: anycasts complete after visiting a small number of nodes ($O(log(n))$) where n is the number of elements in the overlay), and load is balanced because anycasts from different senders start at different nodes.

Each group has an associated *groupId*. To anycast a message to a group, a sender routes a message through Pastry using the groupId as the key. The message is routed towards the node that acts as the root of the group tree. At each hop, the local node checks whether it is part of the tree for the specified groupId. If it is, then the anycast message is not forwarded; instead, a depth-first search of the group tree is initiated from that node. The search is fairly standard except that children edges are explored before parent edges and applications can define the order in which children edges are explored. For example, the order can be random or round-robin to improve load balancing, or it can use some application specific metric like an estimate of the load on each child.

We append the identifiers of the nodes that have already been visited to the message to guide the search. After all of a node's children have been visited (if any) without success, the node itself checks if it is in the group. If so, the message is delivered to the node and the search terminates. Otherwise, the anycast continues after the node adds its identifier to the list of visited nodes in the message. The identifiers of its children are then removed to keep the list small.

It is possible for the group to become empty while an anycast is in progress. This is detected when the root is visited after all its children have been visited and it is not in the group. In this case, an error message is sent back to the sender.

The search is efficient and scalable. In the absence of membership changes during the search, it completes after exploring a single path from the start node to a leaf. Our implementation uses the overlay properties to balance the load imposed by searches on the nodes that form the group tree: different senders are unlikely to explore the same path unless the group is very small. Therefore, our approach scales to a large number of concurrent senders.

In overlays with the local route convergence property (Tapestry and Pastry), the nodes in the subtree rooted at the start node are the closest in the network to the sender, among all the group members. Therefore, the message is delivered to a group member that is close to the sender in the network topology. Additionally, this leads to low link stress and delay for anycast routing.

We can also support *manycast*, i.e., the message can be sent to several group members. This is done by continuing the anycast until the message has been delivered to the desired number of members, tracking the number of recipients in the message.

Both anycast and manycast can be augmented such that the message is delivered only to group members that satisfy a given predicate. The algorithm above works efficiently when most group members satisfy the predicate. If this is not the case, the group can be split in subgroups such that most of the elements in each subgroup satisfy a given predicate. The overlay can be used to name and locate the group that should be used for a given predicate. Additionally, nodes can leave the group when they stop satisfying the predicate associated with the group.

Our anycast and manycast primitives can be secured from malicious participating nodes in the overlay, by extending earlier work on secure routing in Pastry [2]. However, the details are beyond the scope of this paper.

4   Distributed Resource Management

Existing anycast systems have been limited to small and relatively static sets of group members; accordingly, applications have been limited to tasks like server selection. Enabling anycast for highly dynamic groups whose size and membership change rapidly enables a much larger set of applications.

Applications can exploit such an anycast facility to discover and manage a much larger quantity of resources at much smaller time scales. For example, a group can be created whose members advertise some spare resource, e.g., storage capacity, bandwidth, or CPU cycles. They join the group in order to advertise availability of the resource; when they receive an anycast message from a node that seeks to consume the resource, they assign some resource units to that node. They leave the group when they no longer have any resource units available.

We next discuss some example application scenarios.

CPU cycles: Many workstations are idle for significant periods of the day, and many systems offer their spare CPU cycles for compute intensive tasks, e.g., Condor [11]. Such systems need to match spare CPU resources to jobs that need to be executed.

One approach to schedule such jobs is to create a group consisting of nodes that have pending compute jobs. Essentially, such a group acts as a job queue.

Nodes with spare CPU cycles anycast to the group, thus matching nodes with spare cycles to nodes with pending jobs. When a node has no jobs remaining it removes itself from the group. A second approach is to create a group whose members are nodes with spare CPU cycles. A node with pending jobs anycasts to the group to find a node with spare compute cycles.

The first approach works best when demand for CPU cycles is greater than supply and the second works best when the reverse is true. The two approaches can be combined by using two groups rooted at the same node.

Storage capacity: Storage systems often need to locate a node that has the spare capacity to store a replica of an object. For example, in an archival file storage system like PAST [17] a node with high storage utilization may wish to find an alternate node to store a replica on its behalf. In such a system, a group can be created consisting of nodes with spare disk capacity. A node seeking an alternate node to store a replica anycasts to the group.

Furthermore, a group can be created that consists of the nodes that store a given object. Nodes that wish to access the object anycast to the group to locate a nearby replica. The same group can also be used to multicast updates or coherence messages in order to keep the replicas consistent.

Bandwidth: Similar techniques can be used to locate nodes with spare network bandwidth. SplitStream [5,4], for instance, is a peer-to-peer content streaming system that stripes content over multiple multicast groups. This striping allows SplitStream to spread the forwarding load across the participating nodes, takes advantage of nodes with different network bandwidths, and yields improved robustness to node failures. Nodes with spare network bandwidth join a spare capacity group.

A node tries to join the groups associated with each stripe. If its default parent for a particular stripe has no spare bandwidth, the node anycasts to the spare capacity group, to find a nearby parent that can adopt it. The spare capacity group initially contains all the nodes.

In general, applications may customize the anycast primitive by controlling the DFS tree traversal order, by providing a boolean predicate on attributes of group members, and by specifying the desired number of receivers. Moreover, the low overhead of group creation and membership operations enables the use of many, potentially overlapping groups to increase the efficiency of complex queries. For instance, in addition to joining a group that indicates available storage capacity, nodes with free storage can join groups associated with more fine-grained attributes, such as a range of available storage, the expected availability of the storage node or the node's query load. Anycast queries can then be directed towards specific groups whose members are known or likely to satisfy certain attribute values, thus increasing efficiency.

5   Experimental Results

We performed an evaluation of our anycast implementation using simulations of a Pastry overlay with 100,000 nodes on a transit-stub topology [22] with 5050 routers. Each router had an attached LAN and each Pastry node was randomly assigned to one of these LANs.

We started by measuring the cost of creating 10 different anycast groups varying in size from 2,500 to 25,000 nodes. All group members joined at the same time. The average number of messages per join was 3.5 with 2,500 members and 2.3 with 25,000 members. The average cost per join decreases with the group size because the number of hops before a ▄▄▄ message reaches the group tree decreases. The cost of joining an empty group is approximately 4.1 messages. The joining load was evenly distributed, e.g., 83% of the nodes processed a single message when creating the largest group.

Then, we simulated 1,000 anycasts from random sources to each group with the predicate *true*. The average number of messages per anycast was 2.9 with 2,500 members and 2.1 with 25,000 members. The average anycast cost decreases with the group size for the same reason that the join cost decreases. The cost of anycasting to an empty group is also approximately 4.1 messages. The load to process anycasts was also evenly distributed, e.g., 99% of the nodes that processed an anycast in the group with 25,000 members only processed one or two messages and none processed more than four messages.

To evaluate whether our implementation delivers an anycast to a nearby group member, we measured the network delay between the sender and the receiver of each anycast and ranked it relative to the delays between the sender and other group members. For 90% of the anycasts to the group with 2,500 members, less than 7% of the group members were closer to the sender than the receiver. The results improve when the group size increases because the depth first search of the tree during the anycast is more likely to start at a node closer to the sender. Less than 0.15% of the group members were closer to the sender than the receiver for 90% of the anycasts to the group with 25,000 members.

6   Related Work

Related work includes IP and application-level anycast, and global resource management systems. The main contribution of our approach is the ability to perform anycast efficiently in large and highly dynamic groups.

Anycast was first proposed in RFC 1546 [12]. GIA [10] is an architecture for global IP anycast that is scalable but shares the drawbacks characteristic of network-level approaches: it requires router modifications, and it cannot exploit application-level metrics to select the destination of anycast messages.

The approach to application-level anycast proposed in [1,9] builds directory systems. Given a query, the service returns the unicast address of the closest server satisfying the query. The approach is similar to round-robin DNS. It assumes a small and static number of servers per group and does not scale to large and highly dynamic groups.

Like Scribe, Bayeux [24], and CAN-Multicast [15] are group communication systems built on top of structured peer-to-peer overlays, namely Tapestry [23] and CAN [14]. Neither Bayeux nor CAN-multicast support an anycast primitive.

While such a primitive could be added, neither protocol can support highly dynamic groups efficiently. CAN-multicast builds a separate overlay for each group, which makes joining and leaving a group relatively expensive. In our approach, the same overlay is used to host many different groups, thus amortizing the cost of maintaining the overlay.

Like Scribe, Bayeux builds per-group multicast trees on top of a peer-to-peer overlay. In Bayeux, however, a tree is the union of the overlay routes from the root to each member. This forces Bayeux to forward each join and leave request to the root, thus preventing it from handling large, dynamic groups efficiently.

The object location approach used in Tapestry and in Plaxton's work [13] can be viewed as a special case of our anycast mechanism. In these systems, the tree formed by the overlay routes from each replica holder of an object to the object's root is annotated with pointers to the nearest replica holder. Lookup messages are routed towards an object's root; when the message intercepts the tree, it uses the replica pointer to retrieve a copy of the object.

Tapestry and Plaxton use this mechanism only to locate objects. Since the trees are not fault-tolerant, objects must be periodically reinserted. Our system supports a fully general anycast primitive, supports predicate-based anycast, and maintains the group membership despite node failures. Moreover, we articulate the power of such a primitive for dynamic resource management in large-scale distributed systems.

The Internet Indirection Infrastructure (i3) [19] proposes a generic indirection mechanism supporting unicast, multicast, anycast and, mobility. i3 uses *triggers* to represent indirection points between senders and receivers. A trigger is represented by a unique id. Receivers subscribe to triggers, and senders publish to triggers. When a message arrives at a trigger, it is forwarded to one or more of the receivers registered at the trigger. In its simplest form, the i3 group membership mechanism is not scalable, because a single node maintains all members of a group. To support large groups, i3 uses a hierarchy of triggers. However, i3 has to explicitly construct and balance these trees of triggers, while in our approach, the spanning trees are formed naturally by the existing overlay routes from the group members to the group's root. Thus, our approach can handle large, highly dynamic groups with greater efficiency.

Astrolabe [21] provides a very flexible distributed resource management system. It supports generic queries on the state of the system using gossiping and it limits the rate of gossiping to achieve better scalability at the expense of increased delays. The increased delays make it unsuitable for managing dynamic resources at very small time scales.

7 Conclusions

This paper presents an efficient anycast implementation that supports large and highly dynamic groups. The properties of our anycast system enable management and discovery of resources in large-scale distributed systems at much smaller time scales than previously possible. Our systems takes a decentralized approach to group membership management, and amortizes the cost of maintaining a single overlay network over many groups and group membership changes. The system is built on top of Pastry, a scalable, proximity-aware peer-to-peer overlay and it supports multicast as well as anycast. Finally, we discuss applications that can use our anycast implementation to schedule jobs, manage storage, and manage bandwidth for content distribution. These applications demonstrate that our anycast implementation provides a powerful building block to construct large-scale peer-to-peer applications.

References

1. S. Bhattachargee, M. Ammar, E. Zegura, N. Shah, and Z. Fei. Application layer anycasting. In *Proc IEEE Infocom'97*, 1997.
2. M. Castro, P. Druschel, A. Ganesh, A. Rowstron, and D. Wallach. Secure routing for structured peer-to-peer overlay networks. In *Proc. OSDI'02*, Dec. 2002.
3. M. Castro, P. Druschel, Y. C. Hu, and A. Rowstron. Exploiting network proximity in peer-to-peer overlay networks, 2002. Technical report MSR-TR-2002-82.
4. M. Castro, P. Druschel, A.-M. Kermarrec, A. Nandi, A. Rowstron, and A. Singh. Splitstream: High-bandwidth content distribution in a cooperative environment. In *SOSP'03*, 2003.
5. M. Castro, P. Druschel, A.-M. Kermarrec, A. Nandi, A. Rowstron, and A. Singh. Splitstream: High-bandwidth content distribution in a cooperative environment. In *IPTPS'03*, February 2003.
6. M. Castro, P. Druschel, A.-M. Kermarrec, and A. Rowstron. Scribe: A large-scale and decentralized application-level multicast infrastructure. *IEEE JSAC*, 20(8), Oct. 2002.
7. M. Castro, M. Jones, A.-M. Kermarrec, A. Rowstron, M. Theimer, H. Wang, and A. Wolman. An evaluation of scalable application-level multicast built using peer-to-peer overlay networks. In *Proc. of INFOCOM'03*, 2003.
8. Y. K. Dalal and R. Metcalfe. Reverse path forwarding of broadcast packets. *Communications of the ACM*, 21(12):1040–1048, 1978.
9. Z. Fei, S. Bhattachargee, M. Ammar, and E. Zegura. A novel server technique for improving the response time of a replicated service. In *Proc IEEE Infocom'98*, 1998.
10. D. Katabi and J. Wroclawski. A Framework for Scalable Global IP-Anycast (GIA). In *Proc SIGCOMM'00*, 2000.
11. M. Mutka and M. Livny. Scheduling remote processing capacity in a workstation-processing bank computing system. In *Proc. of ICDCS'87*, 1987.
12. C. Partridge, T. Menedez, and W. Milliken. Host anycasting service. In *RFC 1546*, November 1993.
13. C. G. Plaxton, R. Rajaraman, and A. W. Richa. Accessing nearby copies of replicated objects in a distributed environment. In *Proc. 9th ACM Symp. on Parallel Algorithms and Architectures*, pages 311–320, June 1997. Newport, Rhode Island, USA.
14. S. Ratnasamy, P. Francis, M. Handley, R. Karp, and S. Shenker. A Scalable Content-Addressable Network. In *Proc. SIGCOMM'01*, Aug. 2001.
15. S. Ratnasamy, M. Handley, R. Karp, and S. Shenker. Application-level multicast using content-addressable networks. In *Proc. of NGC'01*, Nov. 2001.

16. A. Rowstron and P. Druschel. Pastry: Scalable, distributed object location and routing for large-scale peer-to-peer systems. In *Proc. Middleware'01*, 2001.

17. A. Rowstron and P. Druschel. Storage management and caching in PAST, a large-scale, persistent peer-to-peer storage utility. In *Proc. SOSP*, Oct. 2001.

18. A. Rowstron, A.-M. Kermarrec, M. Castro, and P. Druschel. Scribe: The design of a large-scale event notification infrastructure. In *Proc. NGC'01*, Nov. 2001.

19. I. Stoica, D. Adkins, S. Ratnasamy, S.Shenker, S. Surana, and S. Zhuang. Internet indirection infrastructure. In *Proc of ACM SIGCOMM*, 2002.

20. I. Stoica, R. Morris, D. Karger, M. F. Kaashoek, and H. Balakrishnan. Chord: A scalable peer-to-peer lookup service for internet applications. In *Proc. SIGCOMM'01*, 2001.

21. R. van Renesse and K. Birman. Scalable management and data mining using Astrolabe. In *IPTPS '02*, 2002.

22. E. Zegura, K. Calvert, and S. Bhattacharjee. How to model an internetwork. In *INFOCOM 96*, 1996.

23. B. Zhao, J. Kubiatowicz, and A. Joseph. Tapestry: An infrastructure for fault-resilient wide-area location and routing. Technical Report UCB//CSD-01-1141, U. C. Berkeley, Apr. 2001.

24. S. Zhuang, B. Zhao, A. Joseph, R. Katz, and J. Kubiatowicz. Bayeux: An Architecture for Scalable and Fault-tolerant Wide-Area Data Dissemination. In *Proc. NOSSDAV'01*, June 2001.

Topology-Centric Look-Up Service

L. Garcés-Erice[1], K.W. Ross[2], E.W. Biersack[1],
P.A. Felber[1], and G. Urvoy-Keller[1]

[1] Institut EURECOM
06904 Sophia Antipolis, France
{garces,erbi,felber,urvoy}@eurecom.fr
[2] Polytechnic University
Brooklyn, NY 11201, USA
ross@poly.edu

Abstract. Topological considerations are of paramount importance in the design of a P2P lookup service. We present TOPLUS, a lookup service for structured peer-to-peer networks that is based on the hierarchical grouping of peers according to network IP prefixes. TOPLUS is fully distributed and symmetric, in the sense that all nodes have the same role. Packets are routed to their destination along a path that mimics the router-level shortest-path, thereby providing a small "stretch". Experimental evaluation confirms that a lookup in TOPLUS takes time comparable to that of IP routing.

1 Introduction

Several important proposals have recently been put forth for providing a distributed peer-to-peer (P2P) lookup service, including Chord [1], CAN [2], Pastry [3] and Tapestry [4]. These lookup services are all based on *Distributed Hash Tables (DHT)*. It turns out that for many measures — like speed of lookup and potential for caching — it is highly desirable that the lookup service takes the underlying IP-level topology into account. Researchers have recently proposed modifications to the original lookup services that take topology into special consideration [5,6,7], or created Topology-aware Overlays [8].

In this paper we explore the following issues: (1) How can we design a P2P lookup service for which topological considerations take precedence? (2) What are the advantages and disadvantages of such a topology-centric design? and (3) How can the topology-centric design be modified so that the advantages of the original design are preserved but the disadvantages are abated?

To respond to the first question, we propose a new lookup service, *Topology-Centric Look-Up Service (TOPLUS)*. In TOPLUS, nodes that are topologically close are organized into groups. Furthermore, groups that are topologically close are organized into supergroups, and close supergroups into hypergroups, etc. The groups within each level of the hierarchy can be heterogeneous in size and in fan-out. The groups can be derived directly from the network prefixes contained in BGP tables or from other sources. TOPLUS has many strengths, including:

B. Stiller et al. (Eds.): NGC/ICQT 2003, LNCS 2816, pp. 58–69, 2003.

- *Stretch:* Packets are routed to their destination along a path that mimics the router-level shortest-path distance, thereby providing a small "stretch".
- *Caching:* On-demand P2P caching of data is straightforward to implement, and can dramatically reduce average file transfer delays.
- *Efficient forwarding:* As we shall see, nodes can use highly-optimized IP longest-prefix matching techniques to efficiently forward messages.
- *Symmetric:* Design lets nodes similar responsibilities.

TOPLUS is an "extremist's design" to a topology-centric lookup service. At the very least, it serves as a benchmark against which other lookup services can compare their stretch and caching performance.

This paper is organized as follows. We present related work at the end of this section. In Section 2 we describe the TOPLUS design, and we elaborate on its limitations and possible solutions in Section 3. In Section 4 we describe how we obtained the nested group structures from BGP tables and our measurement procedure for evaluating the average stretch. We then provide and discuss our experimental results. We conclude in Section 5.

Related Work. In [5], the authors show how the original CAN design can be modified to account for topological considerations. Their approach is to use online measurement techniques to group nodes into "bins". The resulting stretch remains significant in their simulation results. Paper [9] is an interesting work on Internet network distance using coordinate spaces.

In [6], the authors examine the topological properties of a modified version of Pastry. In this design, a message typically takes small topological steps initially and big steps at the end of the route. We shall see that TOPLUS does the opposite, initially taking a large step, then a series of very small steps. Although [6] reports significantly lower stretches than other lookup services, it still reports an average stretch of 2.2 when the Mercator [10] topology model is used. Coral [11] has been recently proposed to adapt Chord to the Internet topology. Coral organizes peers in clusters and uses a hierarchical lookup of keys that tries to follow a path inside one peer's cluster whenever possible. The query is passed to higher-level clusters when the lookup can't continue inside the original cluster.

Cluster-based Architecture for P2P (CAP) [12] is a P2P architecture that has been built from the ground up with topological considerations. CAP is an unstructured P2P architecture whereas TOPLUS is a structured DHT-based architecture. Unlike CAP, TOPLUS uses a multi-level hierarchy and a symmetric design. Nevertheless, although TOPLUS does not mandate a specific clustering technique to create groups, we believe those of Krishnamurthy and Wang [13,14] used in CAP are currently among the most promising.

2   Overview of TOPLUS

Given a message containing key k, the P2P lookup service routes the message to the current up node that is responsible for k. The message travels from source node n_s, through a series of intermediate peer nodes $n_1, n_2, \ldots, n_v$, and finally to the destination node, n_d.

The principal goals of TOPLUS are as follows: (1) Given a message with key k, source node n_s sends the message (through IP-level routers) to a first-hop node n_1 that is "topologically close" to n_d; (2) After arriving at n_1, the message remains topologically close to n_d as it is routed closer and closer to n_d through the subsequent intermediate nodes. Clearly, if the lookup service satisfies these two goals, the stretch should be very close to 1. We now formally describe TOPLUS in the context of IPv4.

Let I be the set of all 32-bit IP addresses[1]. Let $\mathcal{G}$ be a collection of sets such that $G \subseteq I$ for each $G \in \mathcal{G}$. Thus, each set $G \in \mathcal{G}$ is a set of IP addresses. We refer to each such set G as a *group*. Any group $G \in \mathcal{G}$ that does not contain another group in $\mathcal{G}$ is said to be an *inner group*. We say that the collection $\mathcal{G}$ is a *proper nesting* if it satisfies all the following properties:

1. $I \in \mathcal{G}$.
2. For any pair of groups in $\mathcal{G}$, the two groups are either disjoint, or one group is a proper subset of the other.
3. Each $G \in \mathcal{G}$ consists of a set of contiguous IP addresses that can be represented by an IP prefix of the form $w.x.y.z/n$ (for example, 123.13.78.0/23).

As shown in Section 4, the collection of sets $\mathcal{G}$ can be created by collecting the IP prefix networks from BGP tables and/or other sources [13,14]. In this case, many of the sets $\mathcal{G}$ would correspond to ASes, other sets would be subnets in ASes, and yet other sets would be aggregations of ASes. This approach of defining $\mathcal{G}$ from BGP tables require that a proper nesting is created. Note that the groups differ in size, and in number of subgroups (the fanout).

If $\mathcal{G}$ is a proper nesting, then the relation $G \subset G'$ defines a partial ordering over the sets in $\mathcal{G}$, generating a partial-order tree with multiple tiers. The set I is at tier-0, the highest tier. A group G belongs to tier 1 if there does not exist a G' (other than I) such that $G \subset G'$. We define the remaining tiers recursively in the same manner (see Figure 1).

Node State. Let L denote the number of tiers in the tree, let U be the set of all current up nodes and consider a node $n \in U$. Node n is contained in a collection of telescoping sets in $\mathcal{G}$; denote these sets by $H_N(n), H_{N-1}(n), \cdots, H_0(n) = I$, where $H_N(n) \subset H_{N-1}(n) \subset \cdots \subset H_0(n)$ and $N \leq L$ is the tier depth of n's inner group. Except for $H_0(n)$, each of these telescoping sets has one or more siblings in the partial-order tree (see Figure 1). Let $\mathcal{S}_i(n)$ be the set of siblings groups of $H_i(n)$ at tier i. Finally, let $\mathcal{S}(n)$ be the union of the sibling sets $\mathcal{S}_1(n), \cdots, \mathcal{S}_N(n)$.

For each group $G \in \mathcal{S}(n)$, node n should know the IP address of at least one node in G and of all the other nodes in n's inner group. We refer to the collection of these two sets of IP addresses as node n's *routing table*, which constitutes node

---

[1] For simplicity, we assume that all IP addresses are permitted. Of course, some blocks of IP addressed are private and other blocks have not been defined. TOPLUS can be refined accordingly.

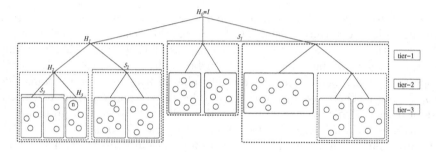

Fig. 1. A sample TOPLUS hierarchy (inner groups are represented by plain boxes)

n's state. The total number of IP addresses in the node's routing table in tier L is $|H_L(n)| + |\mathcal{S}(n)|$.

XOR Metric. Each key k' is required to be an element of I', where I' is the set of all s-bit binary strings ($s \geq 32$ is fixed). A key can be drawn uniformly randomly from I', or it can be biased as we will describe later. For a given key $k' \in I'$, denote k for the 32-bit suffix of k' (thus $k \in I$ and $k = k_{31}k_{30}\ldots k_1k_0$). Throughout the discussion below, we will refer to k rather than to the original k'.

The XOR metric defines the distance between two ids j and k as $d(j,k) = \sum_{\nu=0}^{31} |j_\nu - k_\nu| \cdot 2^\nu$. The metric $d(j,k)$ has the following properties:

- If $d(i,k) = d(j,k)$ for any k, then $i = j$.
- $\max d(j,k) \leq 2^{32} - 1$.
- Let $p(j,k)$ be the number of bits in the common prefix of j and k. If $p(j,k) = m$, $d(j,k) \leq 2^{32-m} - 1$.
- If $d(i,k) \leq d(j,k)$, then $p(i,k) \geq p(j,k)$.

$d(j,k)$ is a refinement of longest-prefix matching. If j is the unique longest-prefix match with k, then j is the closest to k in terms of the metric. Further, if two nodes share the longest matching prefix, the metric will break the tie. The Kademlia DHT [15] also uses the XOR metric. The node n^* that minimizes $d(k,n)$, $n \in U$ is "responsible" for key k.

The Lookup Algorithm. Suppose node n_s wants to look up k. Node n_s determines the node in its routing table that is closest to k in terms of the XOR metric, say n_j. Then n_s forwards the message to n_j. The process continues, until the message with key k reaches a node n_d such that the closest node to k in n_d's routing table is n_d itself. n_d is trivially the node responsible for k.

If the set of groups form a proper nesting, then it is straightforward to show that the number of hops in a look up is at most $L + 1$, where L is the depth of the partial-order tree. In the first hop the message will be sent to a node n_1 that is in the same group, say G, as n_d. The message remains in G until it arrives at n_d.

Overlay Maintenance. When a new node n joins the system, n asks an arbitrary existing node to determine (using TOPLUS) the closest node to n (using n's IP address as the key), denoted by n'. n initializes its routing table with n''s routing table. Node n's routing table should then be modified to satisfy a "diversity" property: for each node n_i in the routing table, n asks n_i for a random node in n_i's group. This way, for every two nodes in a group G, their respective sets of delegates for another group G' will be disjoint (with high probability). This assures that, in case one delegate fails, it is possible to use another node's delegate. Finally, all nodes in n's inner group must update their inner group tables.

Groups, which are virtual, do not fail; only nodes can fail. Existing groups can be partitioned or aggregated on a slow time scale, as need be. When needed, keys can be moved from one group to another lazily: when a node receives a query for a key that it is not storing, the node can perform itself a query excluding its own group. Once the key is retrieved, queries can be normally satisfied.

On-Demand P2P Caching. TOPLUS can provide a powerful caching service for an ISP. Suppose that a node n_s wants to obtain the file f associated with key k, located at some node n_d. It would be preferable if n_s could obtain a cached copy of file f from a topologically close node.

To this end, suppose that some group $G \in \mathcal{G}$, with network prefix w.x.y.z/r, at any tier, wants to provide a caching service to the nodes in G. Further suppose all pairs of nodes in G can send files to each other relatively quickly (high-speed LAN). Now suppose some node $n_s \in G$ wants to find the file f associated with key $k \in I$. Then n_s creates a new key, k_G, which is k but with the first r bits of k replaced with the first r bits of w.x.y.z/r. Node n_s then inserts a message with key k_G into TOPLUS. The lookup service will return to n_s the node n_G that is responsible for k_G. Node n_G will be in G, and all the messages traveling from n_s to n_G will be confined to G. If n_G has f (cache hit), then n_G will send f to n_s at a relatively high rate. If n_G does not have f (cache miss), n_G will use TOPLUS to obtain f from the global lookup service. After obtaining f, n_G will cache f in its local shared storage and pass a copy of f to n_s. The techniques in [16] can be used to optimally replicate files throughout G to handle intermittent nodal connectivity.

3   Drawbacks and Solutions

TOPLUS' features sacrifice other desirable properties in a P2P lookup service. Some drawbacks are:

Non-uniform population of id space: The number of keys assigned to an inner group will be approximately proportional to the number of IP addresses covered by the inner group, not to the number of up nodes in the group. Some nodes may be responsible for a disproportionate number of keys.

Lack of virtual nodes: The CAN, Chord, Pastry and Tapestry lookup services can assign virtual nodes to the more powerful peers, so that they get more keys to store. TOPLUS, as currently defined, does not facilitate the creation of virtual nodes.

Correlated node failures: As with Chord, Pastry and Tapestry, TOPLUS can replicate key/data pairs on successor nodes within the same inner group. However, if an entire inner group fails (e.g. link failure), then all copies of the data for the key become unavailable.

One first enhancement to TOPLUS is to use a non-uniform distribution when creating keys. Specifically, suppose there are J inner groups, and we estimate the average fraction of active nodes in inner group j to be q_j. Then when assigning a key, we first choose an integer (deterministically) from $\{1, 2, \ldots, J\}$ using the weights $q_1, \ldots, q_J$. Suppose integer j is selected, and group j has prefix w.x.y.z/n. We then choose a key uniformly from the set of addresses covered by w.x.y.z/n .

In order to address the lack of virtual nodes, we assign each node a permanent "virtual id" uniformly distributed over the address space of the node's inner group. More powerful nodes are assigned multiple permanent virtual ids, thereby creating virtual nodes. In the inner group table, we list the virtual ids associated with each IP address. We modify TOPLUS as follows: first the message reaches a node n such that the longest prefix match is inside the inner group of n. Then n determines in the inner group the virtual id that is the closest to the key. The responsible node is the virtual id's owner.

To solve the problem of correlated node failures, when we replicate key/data pairs, we need to distribute the replicas over multiple inner groups. Inner group failures must be detected. Due to lack space, we only sketch a partial solution here: we use K distinct hash functions to create keys, generating K different locations that are geographically dispersed with high probability.

4   Benchmarking TOPLUS

In TOPLUS, a group is defined by an IP network prefix. We have used IP prefixes obtained from two sources: the BGP routing tables of routers in the Internet, and the prefixes of well-known networks (such as corporate LANs or ISPs). As shown in [14,12], the IP prefixes obtained from BGP routing tables form clusters of hosts that are topologically close to each other. Our assumption is that this locality property is recursively preserved to some extent in coarser IP prefixes that regroup clusters (super-clusters, clusters of super-clusters, etc.).

IP network prefixes were obtained from several sources: BGP tables provided by Oregon University [17] (123,593 prefixes) and by the University of Michigan and Merit Network [18] (104,552); network IP prefixes from routing registries provided by Castify Networks [19] (143,082) and RIPE [20] (124,876). After merging all this information and eliminating reserved and non-routable prefixes, we have obtained a set of *250,562* distinct IP prefixes that we organize in a partial order tree (denoted as Prefix Tree hereafter). Studies from NLANR [21] show that about 20% of the total usable IP space was routable in 1997, and 25% in 1999. As our tree covers 35% of the IP space, we consider it a valid snapshot of the Internet in 2003.

Measuring Stretch. The stretch is defined as the ratio between the average latency of TOPLUS routing (using the Prefix Tree) and the average latency of IP routing. Ideally, we could use the `traceroute` [22] tool to measure the delay between arbitrary hosts in the Internet[2]. However, security measures deployed in almost every Internet router nowadays prevent us from using this simple and accurate measurement technique. Therefore, we have used the `King` [23] tool to obtain experimental results. King gives a good approximation of the distance between two arbitrary hosts by measuring the latency between the DNS servers responsible for these hosts.

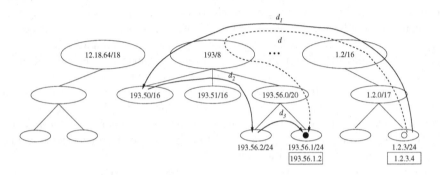

Fig. 2. Path followed by a query in the Prefix Tree

The general principle of our measurements is shown in Figure 2, where peer at address 1.2.3.4 sends a query for key k, whose responsible peer is 193.56.1.2. Following the TOPLUS routing procedure, peer 1.2.3.4 must first route the query inside the tier-1 group containing k. Peer 1.2.3.4 selects a delegate from its routing table in group 193/8, because $k/32 \subset 193/8$ (note that there cannot be another group G in tier-1 satisfying $k/32 \subset G$). Assuming the delegate is in group 193.50/16, the query is first routed along path labeled with latency d_1 in Figure 2. Then, the delegate selects the (unique) tier-2 group inside 193/8 which contains k: 193.56.0/20. Let the new delegate node be in tier-3 group 193.56.2/24. The query is forwarded to that delegate node along path d_2. Finally, the destination group 193.56.1/24 is reached with the next hop d_3 (we neglect the final forwarding of the query inside the destination group). In contrast to TOPLUS routing, the query would follow path d between 1.2.3.4 and 193.56.1.2 with IP routing. The stretch for this particular case would be $\frac{d_1+d_2+d_3}{d}$.

In general, we consider the length of the path from one peer to another as the weighted average of the length of all possible paths between them. Path weights are derived from the probability of a delegate peer to be in each of the different group at each tier. Assuming a uniform distribution of peers in the Internet, the probability of node n choosing a delegate in group G at tier i

---

[2] This can be achieved specifying one of the two host as a gateway packets must pass through.

with parent $S \in \mathcal{S}_{i+1}(n)$ can be computed as the number of IP addresses in all inner groups descendant of G divided by the number of IP addresses in all inner groups descendant of S. To simplify computations and keep them local to tier i, we approximate this probability by computing the space of IP addresses covered by the network prefix of G, divided by the space of IP addresses covered by all groups children of S (including G).

Consider a query issued by node n_s in inner group S for a key k owned by node n_d in inner group D at tier N. Let $d^T(G, G')$ be the TOPLUS latency between a node in group G and a node in group G' and $d^{IP}(G, G')$ be the corresponding direct IP latency. Let $H_0, \ldots H_N$ (as in Section 1) be the telescoping set of groups associated to node n_d (hence $H_0 = I$ and $H_N = D$). To reach n_d, n_s forwards its request to its delegate node n_g belonging to one of the inner groups G in H_1. Hence:

$$E[d^T(S, D)] = \sum_{G \subset H_1} p_G(E[d^{IP}(S, G)] + E[d^T(G, D)]) \tag{1}$$

where p_G is the probability of n_g being in G. Thus, $p_G = \frac{|G|}{|H_1|}$. Note that $E[d^{IP}(S, G)] = 0$ if ever $n_s \in H_1$, since in this case n_s is its own delegate in H_1. The process continues with n_g forwarding the query to its delegate node n'_g in one of the inner groups G' in H_2. The equation for $E[d^T(G, D)]$ is thus similar to Equation (1):

$$E[d^T(G, D)] = \sum_{G' \subset H_2} p_{G'}(E[d^{IP}(G, G')] + E[d^T(G', D)]) \tag{2}$$

where $p_{G'} = \frac{|G'|}{|H_2|}$. N recursions allow to obtain the value of $E[d^T(S, D)]$.

To obtain the average stretch of the Prefix Tree, we compute the stretch from a fixed origin peer to 1,000 randomly generated destination IP addresses using King to measure the delay of each hop. We compute the path length from the origin peer to each destination peer as the average length of all possible paths to the destination, weighted according to individual path probabilities (as described above). Finally, we compute the stretch of the Prefix Tree as the average stretch from the 1,000 previous measurements. For the experiments, we chose an origin peer at Institut Eurecom with IP address 193.55.113.1. We used 95% confidence intervals for all measurements. We detail now the different Prefix Tree configurations that we have considered in our experiments.

Original Prefix Tree is the tree resulting from the ordering of the IP prefixes using operator $\sqsubset$. The partial order tree has 47,467 different tier-1 groups (prefixes); 10,356 (21.8%) of these groups have at least one tier-2 subgroup; further, 3,206 (30%) of tier-2 groups have at least one tier-3 subgroup. The deepest nesting in the tree comprises 11 tiers. The number of non-inner group at each tier decreases rapidly with the tier depth (following roughly a power-law) and the resulting tree is strongly unbalanced.

Figure 3 (left) shows the distribution of prefix lengths in tier-1. As most prefixes of more that 16 bits do not contain nested groups, the Original Prefix Tree has a large number of tier-1 groups. Consequently, the routing tables of

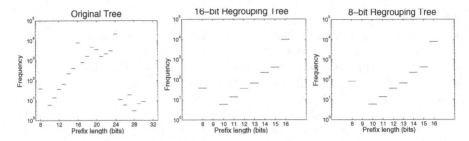

Fig. 3. Prefix length distribution for the tier-1 groups of the three Prefix Trees: Original, 16-bit regrouping and 8 bit regrouping

Table 1. Stretch obtained in each tree, depending on the tier of the destination peer

Tier	stretch TOPLUS vs. IP (± confidence interval)		
	Original	16-bit regroup.	8-bit regroup.
1	1.00 (±0.00)	1.00 (±0.00)	1.00 (±0.00)
2	1.29 (±0.15)	1.32 (±0.14)	1.56 (±0.23)
3	1.31 (±0.16)	1.30 (±0.17)	1.53 (±0.23)
4	1.57 (±0.50)	1.41 (±0.20)	1.56 (±0.50)
Mean	1.17 (±0.06)	1.19 (±0.08)	1.28 (±0.09)

each peer will be large because they have to keep track of one delegate per tier-1 group. On the other hand, since 61% of the IP addresses covered by the tree are within tier-1 inner groups, a large number of peers can be reached with just one hop.

We computed an average stretch of *1.17* for the Original Prefix Tree, that is, a query in TOPLUS takes on average 17% more time to reach its destination than using direct IP routing. In Table 1 we present the average stretch for IP addresses located in inner groups at tiers 1 to 4. As expected, we observe that the deeper we go in the tree to reach a destination, the higher the stretch becomes (because there is a higher probability of making more hops). More than half of the queries had for destination a peer in a tier-2 group.

As previously mentioned, a large number of groups are found in tier-1 and all peers in the network must know a delegate in each of those groups. In order to reduce the size of the routing tables, we modify the tree by "aggregating" small groups that have a long prefix into larger groups not present in our IP prefix sources. We consider groups to be "small" if their prefix is longer than 16 bits; this represents 38,966 tier-1 groups for our experimental data.

16-bit regrouping: A first approach consists in aggregating small groups into 16-bit aggregate prefix groups. This means that any tier-1 prefix a.b.c.d/r with $r > 16$ is moved to tier 2 and a new 16 bit prefix a.b/16 is inserted at tier-1. This process creates 2,161 new tier-1 groups, with an average of 18 subgroups in each of them. The distribution of tier-1 prefixes is shown in Figure 3 (middle).

The resulting tree contains 10,709 tier-1 groups, 50% (5,454) of which contain subgroups. We have measured an average stretch of *1.19* for that tree (see

Table 2. Mean routing table size in each tree depending on the tier of a peer. For tree entries with two columns, the left column is the full routing table size and the right column is the size without tier-1 groups

Tier	Mean routing table size						Mean routing table size		
	Original		16-bit regroup.		8-bit regroup.		Original+1	16-bit+1	3-Tier
1	47,467	0	10,709	0	8,593	0	143	143	143
2	47,565	98	10,802	93	8,713	120	436	223	105
3	47,654	187	10,862	153	8,821	228	831	288	13
4	47,796	329	11,003	294	8,950	357	1,279	428	-
5	47,890	423	11,132	423	9,016	423	696	556	-

Table 1). These results indicate that 16-bit regrouping essentially preserves the low stretch.

8-bit regrouping: We have experimented with a second approach to prefix regrouping, which consists in using coarser, 8-bit aggregate aggregate prefix groups. Any tier-1 prefix `a.b.c.d/r` with $r > 16$ is moved to tier 2 and a new 8 bit prefix `a/8` is inserted at tier-1 (if it does not already exist). This process creates 45 new tier-1 groups, with an average of 866 subgroups in each of them. The distribution of tier-1 prefixes is shown in Figure 3 (right).

The resulting tree contains 8,593 tier-1 groups (more than 5 times less than our Original Prefix Tree). 38% (3,338) of these groups contain subgroups and almost half of tier-2 groups (1,524) have again subgroups. The tree is clearly becoming more balanced and, as a direct consequence of the reduction of tier-1 groups, the size of the routing table in each peer becomes substantially smaller. We have measured an average stretch of *1.28* for the new tree (see Table 1). This remarkable result demonstrates that, even after aggressive aggregation of large sets of tier-1 groups into coarse 8-bit prefixes, the low stretch property of the original tree is preserved.

4.1   Routing Table Size

The principal motivation for prefix regrouping is to reduce the size of the routing tables. We estimate the size of the routing tables by choosing 5,000 random uniformly distributed IP addresses (peers); for each of these peers n, we examine the structure of the tree to determine the sibling sets $\mathcal{S}(n)$ and the inner group nodes $H_N(n)$, and we compute the size $|\mathcal{S}(n)| + |H_N(n)|$ of the routing table of node n.

Table 2 shows the mean routing table size depending on the tier of the peer, as well as the average. The route table size is mainly determined by the number of tier-1 groups. If we eliminate their delegates from the routing table, the size of the routing tables needed to route queries *inside* each tier-1 group remains small. Even using 8-bit regrouping, routing tables count more than 8,000 entries (see Table 2). To further reduce the routing table sizes, we transform the *Original* and the *16-bit-regrouping* trees such that all tier-1 prefixes are 8-bit long, which will limit the number of tier-1 groups to *at most* 256. We refer to the resulting

Table 3. TOPLUS vs. IP stretch in the trees where the tier-1 groups all have 8-bit prefixes

	Original+1	16-bit+1	3-Tier
stretch (TOPLUS/IP) /	1.90 /	2.01 /	2.32 /
confidence margin	(±0.20)	(±0.22)	(±0.09)

trees as *Original+1* and *16-bit+1*. For this purpose, any tier-1 prefix a.b.c.d/r with $r > 8$ is moved to tier 2 and a new 8 bit prefix a/8 is inserted at tier-1 (if it does not already exist).

We finally create another tree called *3-Tier* that has no more than 3 tiers. The top tier is formed by up to 256 groups with 8-bit long prefixes, tier 2 by up to 256 groups with 16-bit long prefixes, and the third tier by up to 256 groups each with a 24-bit long prefix. The mean routing table sizes for these three trees, presented in Table 2, on the right, shows dramatic reduction in the number of entries that must be stored by each peer. However the stretch is significantly penalized, as shown in Table 3. We clearly face a tradeoff between lookup latency and memory requirements.

5   Conclusion

TOPLUS takes an extreme approach for integrating topological consideration into a P2P service. TOPLUS is fully distributed, and is also symmetric in the sense that all nodes have the same role. TOPLUS bears some resemblance to Pastry [3,6] and Tapestry [4]. In particular, Pastry and Tapestry also use delegate nodes and prefix (or suffix) matching to route messages. However, unlike Pastry, we map the groups directly to the underlying topology, resulting in an unbalanced tree without a rigid partitioning, and in a routing scheme that initially makes big physical jumps rather than small ones. We have shown that TOPLUS offers excellent stretch properties, resulting in an extremely fast lookup service. Although TOPLUS suffers from some limitations, which we have exposed and discussed, we believe that its remarkable speed of lookup and its simplicity make it a promising candidate for large-scale deployment in the Internet.

References

1. I. Stoica, R. Morris, D. Karger, M. Kaashoek, and H. Balakrishnan, "Chord: A scalable peer-to-peer lookup service for internet applications," in *Proc. ACM SIG-COMM*, 2001.
2. S. Ratnasamy, M. Handley, R. Karp, and S. Shenker, "A scalable content-addressable network," in *Proc. ACM SIGCOMM*, 2001.
3. A. Rowstron and P. Druschel, "Pastry: Scalable, distributed object location and routing for large-scale peer-to-peer systems," in *IFIP/ACM International Conference on Distributed Systems Platforms (Middleware)*, Germany, 2001.

4. B.Y. Zhao, J. Kubiatowicz, and A.D. Joseph, "Tapestry: An infrastructure for fault-tolerant wide-area location and routing," Tech. Rep., Computer Science Division, University of California, Berkeley, 2001.

5. S. Shenker, S. Ratnasamy, M. Handley, and R. Karp, "Topologically-aware overlay construction and server selection," in *Proc. Infocom*, New York, 2002.

6. M. Castro, P. Druschel, Y.C. Hu, and A. Rowstron, "Topology-aware routing in structured peer-to-peer overlay networks," Tech. Rep., Microsoft Research, 2002.

7. A.D. Joseph, B.Y. Zhao, Y. Duan, L. Huang, and J.D. Kubiatowicz, "Brocade: Landmark routing on overlay networks," in *Proc. IPTPS'02*, (Cambridge, MA), 2002.

8. M. Waldvogel and R. Rinaldi, "Efficient topology-aware overlay network," in *Proceedings of HotNets-I*, 2002.

9. E. Ng and H. Zhang, "Predicting internet network distance with coordinates-based approaches," in *Proc. Infocom*, 2002.

10. H. Tangmunarunkit, R. Govindan, S. Shenker, and D. Estrin, "The impact of routing policy on internet paths," in *Proc. Infocom*, 2001.

11. M. Freedman and D. Mazieres, "Sloppy hashing and self-organizing clusters," in *Proc. IPTPS'03*, 2003.

12. B. Krishnamurthy, J. Wang, and Y. Xie, "Early measurements of a cluster-based architecture for P2P systems," in *ACM SIGCOMM Internet Measurement Workshop*, San Francisco, 2001.

13. B. Krisnamurthy and J. Wang, "On network-aware clustering of web sites," in *Proc. SIGCOMM*, 2000.

14. J. Wang, *Network Aware Client Clustering and Applications*. PhD thesis, Cornell University, 2001.

15. P. Maymounkov and D. Mazieres, "Kademlia: A peer-to-peer informatic system based on the XOR metric," in *Proc. IPTPS'02*, (Cambridge, MA), 2002.

16. J. Kangasharju and K. W. Ross, "Adaptive replication and replacement strategies for P2P caching," Tech. Rep., 2002.

17. "http://rv-archive.uoregon.edu/" Oregon University "Route Views" archive.

18. "http://www.merit.edu/~ipma/routing_table/" Merit Network.

19. "http://www.castify.net" Castify Networks.

20. "http://www.ripe.net/db/whois/whois.html" Whois service at RIPE.

21. "http://moat.nlanr.net/ipaddrocc/" NLANR.

22. "http://www.traceroute.org" Traceroute site.

23. K. P. Gummadi, S. Saroiu, and S. D. Gribble, "King: Estimating latency between arbitrary internet end hosts.," in *Proc. 2nd Internet Measurement Workshop*, (Marseille, France), 2002.

Service Differentiation
in Peer-to-Peer Networks Utilizing Reputations

Minaxi Gupta and Mostafa Ammar

College of Computing, Georgia Institute of Technology
Atlanta, GA, USA
{minaxi,ammar}@cc.gatech.edu

Abstract. As the population of P2P networks increases, service differentiation issues become very important in distinguishing cooperating peers from free-loaders. The basis for service differentiation could either be economic or the fact that the peers differ from each other in the type of services and resources they contribute to the system. Taking the latter approach, this paper makes three contributions: 1) it defines parameters that are suitable for service differentiation in P2P networks, 2) it proposes SDP, a protocol to accomplish service differentiation, and 3) it identifies a set of features that are necessary in a reputation system that measures the contributions of individual peers in the system.

1 Introduction

Many flavors of peer-to-peer (P2P) networks are in wide use today to access a variety of content. The popularity of these networks can be judged from the fact that Kazaa (www.kazaa.com) routinely supports of the order of two million simultaneous peers and transports more than 300 million files.

Each peer is both a client and a server in P2P networks. Perhaps this inherent notion of equality of peers is one of the reasons why service differentiation issues have not received much attention from the research community. However, as the population of these networks increases, issues like free-loading behavior[1] make it necessary to differentiate among the peers.

There are two main directions one can pursue in order to provide service differentiation in P2P networks. First, peers can be explicitly charged money depending on the class of service they belong to. However, due to the absence of the traditional client-server model of delivery in P2P networks, pricing issues in these networks are yet to be resolved. Second, the fact that the peers differ from each other in the quality of services and resources they provide (or are able to provide) can be exploited. A measure of the latter is often referred to as the *reputation* of the peer and has been explored extensively in various contexts to motivate participants to cooperate for the common good.

---

[1] Free-loaders are peers who only download content but do not serve it to the other peers.

B. Stiller et al. (Eds.): NGC/ICQT 2003, LNCS 2816, pp. 70–82, 2003.

Price and credit-based approaches have been explored in ad-hoc networks for stimulating cooperation among the nodes [1,2]. The concept of reputations has been explored toward the same goal in P2P networks [3,4,5,6,7,8]. The basic idea behind these reputation systems is to assign a reputation to each peer based on the satisfaction experienced by the other peers from the services it provides to them. While being able to find reputable peers is beneficial from the perspective of a peer wishing to retrieve content, it may serve as a disincentive for peers acting as servers to have a good reputation for the fear of being overwhelmed. An effective service differentiation scheme could serve as a motivation for peers to possess good reputations.

This paper takes the approach of using peer reputations to address service differentiation issues in P2P networks. Essentially, Kazaa uses a similar concept. Its *participation level*[2] can be viewed as a simplified form of a reputation. The participation level is used to differentiate among the peers in that peers with a higher participation level are served before others during heavy access conditions.

The goal of service differentiation is not to provide hard guarantees but to create a distinction among the peers based on their contributions to the system. The basic idea being, the more the contribution, the better the relative service. While service differentiation parameters are well understood and studied in the context of the Internet (e.g. delay, jitter, bandwidth), they are still to be defined for the P2P networks. Focusing on Gnutella like P2P networks, this paper makes three main contributions. First, it defines a set of parameters that can be used to create service differentiation in P2P networks. Second, it proposes a service differentiation protocol SDP, to accomplish service differentiation. Third, it identifies a set of features that are necessary in a reputation system to be able to use it for service differentiation.

The rest of this paper is structured as follows. Section 2 defines the parameters for service differentiation in P2P networks. Section 3 describes SDP in detail and section 4 discusses the requirements from the underlying reputation system. A discussion of security and participation issues in SDP is presented in 5. Finally, sections 6 and 7 present the evaluation and the conclusion respectively.

2   Service Differentiation in P2P Networks

In this paper, we assume that the peer reputation scores are used to map them into various LoSs. The parameters that can be used to define each LoS are discussed in section 2.1. Assuming that a service differentiation scheme consisting of three levels of service (LoS) is used, figure 1 shows an example of how the peer reputation scores (RSs) can be mapped to various LoSs using parameters a and b. In this scheme, peers for whom $RS < a$ are eligible for *basic LoS*. $a \leq RS < b$ provides *enhanced LoS* to the peers. Peers with $RS > b$ receive *premium LoS*. The parameter a and b are expected to be known to each peer in the P2P network.

Peers carry out three main functions in a P2P network: 1) bootstrapping, 2) content search, and 3) content download. The overall experience of a peer in a

---

[2] The participation level is locally updated for each peer based on the number and size of *integrity rated* files served by it.

P2P network depends on the network conditions and the services and resources provided by the other peers during each of these functions. The network conditions depend on many factors that may not be controllable within a P2P overlay topology and as a result are not considered in this paper.

Bootstrapping is required to allow peers to join the network. In Gnutella like P2P networks, to search for content, a querying peer generates a query with appropriate *keywords* and sends it to all the peers that it is directly connected to in the overlay topology. The peers who process this query reply back if they have the content in their shared directory and forward the request to the peers they are directly connected to

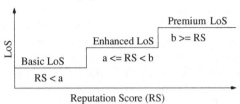

Fig. 1. An example of three levels of service in a P2P network.

depending on the *hop-count* (or the TTL) of the query. This forwarding continues until the TTL specified by the querying peer is exhausted. Upon receiving the replies, the querying peer selects a peer to download the content from. At that point, the content download typically uses a HTTP or a TCP connection with the selected peer.

2.1 Parameters for Service Differentiation

The set of parameters that can be mapped to each LoS are guided by the factors that provide service differentiation during the bootstrapping, content search, and content download functions in a P2P network; and hence the peer's perception of service quality. These factors are based on the salient features of the widely deployed unstructured P2P networks and the results of the current research on unstructured P2P networks.

Factors Affecting Bootstrapping: During the bootstrapping process, the type of peers a peer directly connects to in the overlay topology play an important role in its overall satisfaction from content search and download functions later on. For example, apart from how cooperative the connecting peers are, their actual network distance, processing power, memory, bandwidth, and storage capacity are important factors.

Factors Affecting Content Search: The following factors can be used as a basis for service differentiation because they impact the perception of service for a peer during the content search:
Number of hops: To search for content, the querying peer sets the maximum number of hops in the overlay topology its query would take, by denoting a *hop-count*. While the success of the content search phase depends on many other factors as well, the number of hops plays an important role. Hence, setting a *hop-limit* could act as a component of the service differentiation scheme.

Premium content: Peers can choose to classify some of the content they share as premium content, which they can make available only to peers eligible for certain minimum LoS. This classification can be done through some system wide guidelines.

Hard to find content: A special utility of the P2P networks for many peers comes from being able to access *hard-to-find* content. Although classifying content as hard-to-find may be based on subjective criteria, peers can potentially reserve the hard-to-find content only for peers with a certain minimum LoS.

Query caching: Sripanidkulchai [9] found that the popularity of search strings in Gnutella follows a Zipf-like distribution and that caching a small number of queries results in a significant decrease in the traffic in the Internet. In order to distinguish among the peers with various LoSs, the outcome of caching queries may be made available only to peers with a certain minimum LoS eligibility.

Cached content: Kazaa distinguishes between the functionality of *supernodes* and the rest of the peers in its P2P network. Peers with higher bandwidths can choose to become supernodes in a Kazaa P2P network. During idle periods, the supernodes actively query other peers in the network and cache the content so retrieved. This gives the supernodes access to additional content and when queries for the cached content arrive at the supernodes, they can get served faster. For faster retrieval of content in unstructured P2P networks, Cohen et. al. [10] have also proposed caching strategies. Due to its potential to improve the peer experience, caching could be used to distinguish among the service provided to peers with various LoSs.

Interest-based locality: By exploiting interest-based locality, Sripanidkulchai et. al. [11] have proposed an efficient content search solution for unstructured P2P networks. The basic idea is for peers that share similar interests to create *shortcuts* to each other. These shortcuts can then be used to locate content faster. The basic Gnutella content search paradigm remains as a backup mechanism. In creating such shortcuts, peer LoS eligibility may be used as an additional deciding factor.

Load balancing: An enhancement to maintaining a shortcut to peers that share common interests (as described above) would be to maintain the most recent load for those peers as well. Such an information can help in avoiding the already overwhelmed peers and potentially get content faster. The availability of such information however would require a periodic protocol to assess the load for the peers with similar interests. But if this information is available, it can be provided to peers eligible for certain minimum LoS during content search phase.

Factors Affecting Content Download: During the content download phase, following factors can be used as a basis for service differentiation because they impact a peer's overall experience:

Rate of transfer: During content download from the chosen peer, the rate of transfer may be dependent on the LoS the downloading peer is eligible for. The basic idea is to restrict the portion of capacity used to serve the peers with less than a certain LoS. These restriction may either be in effect all the time or may be used only during periods of heavy loads.

Scheduling policy: During periods of heavy load or even otherwise, the peers may use various scheduling policies in order to give priority in serving content to the peers with with premium LoS over the peers with enhanced LoS and to enhanced LoS over basic LoS.

3   Service Differentiation Protocol (SDP)

SDP enhances the basic functionality of Gnutella-like P2P protocols to include the service differentiation functionality. It assumes that the peers have immediate access to their own reputation scores. Assuming that the network stores reputations in a decentralized manner, one way to accomplish this is through local storage of reputations. However, security issues in such a storage need to be carefully addressed. Another alternative is to compute reputations *just-in-time* from a distributed storage. These issues are described in detail in section 4.

SDP assumes that the mapping of the reputation scores to the LoSs is known to all the peers in the P2P network. Such a mapping could be statically configured into the software or could be downloaded from the bootstrapping infrastructure[3] when a peer joins the network. SDP is flexible about the structure of peer reputations. It only requires that the structure of the reputation scores be known to all peers.

The anonymity issues in SDP are dealt with in a manner similar to those in the popular unstructured P2P protocols. The details of this and other security issues are discussed in section 5.

3.1   SDP Details

During the bootstrapping process, most popular unstructured P2P protocols provide an option to connect only to *high-capacity* (in terms of bandwidth, processing power, memory, and storage) peers. Such high-capacity peers are referred to as *supernodes* in Kazaa and *ultrapeers* in Limewire (www.limewire.com). Additionally, *binning* scheme of the type proposed in [13] can be used to allow peers to connect to peers close-by in the Internet topology. These factors impact the quality of service (QoS) perceived by the peers and can be incorporated in a service differentiation scheme. In this paper, we focus only on the service differentiation during the search and download process of the content retrieval.

For the subsequent SDP description, we build on the Gnutella specification [14]. Consequently, all enhancements proposed by SDP are on top of such a protocol and use similar terminology.

Content Search: This section describes how the content search part of unstructured P2P protocols can be modified to incorporate the service differentiation functionality using the parameters described in section 2.1.
Search phase 1: The peer who initiates the search request sends its reputation score along with the *Query* message. We refer to this enhanced query as

---

[3] The bootstrapping infrastructure used by Gnutella is called GWebCache [12].

Query_SDP. It includes the peer's reputation score in addition to the standard fields like TTL, hops, search criteria etc.

Search phase 2: Each peer who receives *Query_SDP* extracts the reputation score. This score is used to map the peer to the LoS it is eligible for and for processing the query accordingly. This mapping can be done by using parameters *a* and *b* of the type described in section 2. The LoS specific processing is referred to as the *searchProcess_SDP*. Since the processing is dependent only on the reputation score, SDP does not require any identification for the querying peer. Also, the peers who process the query do not have to cache the reputation scores for any other peer in this scheme. This is because the reputation scores may change over time.

Examples of functions that would be a part of *searchProcess_SDP* are shown in figure 2. These functions would provide appropriate LoS using the parameters described in section 2.1. Assuming three LoSs implies that there are three separate functions, one for each LoS. The functions in figure 2 assume that the number of allowable hops for basic, enhanced, and premium LoS are given by *hops_basic*, *hops_enhanced*, and *hops_premium* respectively. The basic idea behind these functions is the following. If a peer's query has already traversed more hops than it was eligible for, it is dropped immediately. However, if it has not traversed extra hops but would go farther than should (based on the TTL+Hops), then appropriate value for the TTL needs to be set. Furthermore, for enhanced and premium LoS peers, additional lookups are needed for service differentiation.

After the LoS specific processing, the query continues to be processed per Gnutella guidelines. This is denoted by *process Query* at the end of each of the functions in 2. Since *interest-based locality* and *load balancing* parameters from section 2.1 require additional protocols to be run, we eliminate them from these functions. However, if such information is available, it can be incorporated easily. As a result, the functions currently use query caching results, cached content, premium content and hard-to-find content for differentiating among the peers.

Search phase 3: Notice from the functions in figure 2 that the LoS specific query processing may amount to dropping the query. But if a query is not dropped during search phase 2, the peer forwards it on its outgoing interfaces according to Gnutella specifications. In the case a response is to be sent back to the querying peer after processing the query, *QueryHit_SDP* is sent. *QueryHit_SDP* is an enhancement to the Gnutella *QueryHit* message. It allows peers who reply to optionally put their reputation scores in the response. This is to help the querying peer make a decision about who to download the content from based on the reputation of the responders.

Content Download: This section describes how SDP enhances the content download process in unstructured P2P protocols to incorporate support for service differentiation. SDP uses the parameters described in section 2.1 for this phase.

Download phase 1: In Gnutella, after selecting a peer to download the content from, the querying peer connects to the selected peer using a TCP or HTTP

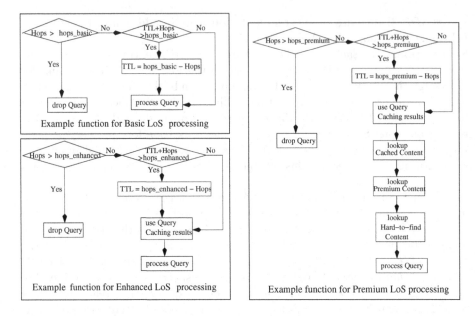

Fig. 2. Functions for service differentiation during content search.

connection. Just as in search phase 1, this phase also requires the querying peer to send its reputation score while establishing the connection for downloading.
Download phase 2: Before serving the content, the sender peer maps the reputation score to the LoS the requester peer is eligible for. Once the LoS is decided, the sender peer picks the appropriate rate of transfer and scheduling policy for the LoS.

The topic of what transfer rates to use and the particular scheduling policies employed needs more research and is beyond the current scope of this paper.

4   Reputation Scores

This section describes how the SDP requirements translate into guidelines for a reputation system. It also compares the existing reputation systems for their suitability to accomplish service differentiation using SDP. From SDP's perspective, many existing and proposed reputation systems can be evaluated along the following dimensions:

- **Centralized or decentralized:** Centralization is a reasonable choice for Ebay (www.ebay.com) and Slashdot (www.slashdot.org) style systems. However, having to retrieve reputations from a central location is not a scalable choice for SDP because even one search/download can lead to many peers attempting to retrieve the reputation of the requester peer.

- **Reputation inference:** Although reputation systems proposed in [3,4,5,6,7] store reputations in a distributed fashion, irrespective of the particular scheme chosen to store the data, they all require reputations to be computed *on-demand* which requires cooperation from the peers in performing computations. For SDP, this would introduce additional latency when the reputation scores are needed. Also, similar to the case when reputations are stored centrally, this solution will not be scalable because each search/download may require many peers to have access to the reputation scores.
- **Subjectiveness:** In order to keep the reputation computations distributed, all existing decentralized reputation systems [3,4,5,6,7] are based on a subjective assessment of reputations. Subjectiveness is part of the reason why reputation inference overheads are necessary. An *objective* reputation computation is important not only to remove the need for on-demand reputation inference, but to incorporate a detailed set of rules to judge a peer's cooperation in the P2P network.
- **Range of values:** Although several of the existing reputation systems have a limited range of values that peer reputations can assume, reputation values in most of the proposed reputation systems are *non-decreasing*. It is a relatively minor inconvenience for the mapping of reputation scores to various LoSs in SDP. This is because as the reputation values increase, this mapping may have to be changed. Thus, a desired feature would be to have a fixed range of reputation values.

A Partially Distributed Reputation System: The reputation system proposed in [8] satisfies the requirements of SDP. This partially distributed solution uses a trusted reputation computation agent (RCA) to compute scalar and objective reputations. Reliable reputation computations are ensured by having the peers collect credit for their work in the system and periodically contact the RCA to have that credit converted into a reputation equivalent. The reputation scores are encrypted by the RCA's private key to prevent tampering. However, since the RCA's key is assumed to be known to all the peers, any peer can decrypt the reputation score. Peers store their reputations locally for fast retrieval in this proposal. Also, the reputations either expire or are *used-up* by the peers. Hence, they do not always increase.

5   Discussion of Security and Participation Issues

Decentralization is one of the core strengths of the P2P networks because it makes them robust to failures. However, the same decentralization makes it hard to enforce rules in any light-weight manner. As a result, the service differentiation proposed in this paper could at most motivate peers by providing them incentives. Specifically, we focus on the discussion of security and participation issues for SDP.

Security Issues: Malicious peers can thwart SDP in two primary ways. First, they may not give better LoS to peers who are eligible for enhanced or premium

LoS. Second, they may collude with other peers and give each other a better LoS than the points justify. The latter is not a serious issue because peers often interact with a large number of other unknown peers. However, unless behavior of all peers is tracked, the occurrence of the first problem can not be eliminated. Current P2P networks do not have any provisions for isolating misbehaving peers and work on the goodwill of majority of the peers. SDP functions on the belief that if a peer trusts the reputation of the other peer, it will be willing to provide them with appropriate LoS. Moreover, the rewards from malicious behavior while providing service differentiation are limited unlike the one's that are possible by being able to assume a good reputation score without earning it.

Another important issues is that of anonymity. Gnutella like protocols do not address issues related to anonymity. Since SDP does not change the anonymity characteristics of the underlying protocol, it does not provide anonymity to the peers. However, since SDP makes the service differentiation decisions based only on the reputation scores and not on who sent it, it is independent of whether or not the underlying P2P network provides anonymity.

Participation Issues: The lack of participation in SDP may not necessarily arise out of malicious behavior. It may also be because of a peer running a version of the P2P software which is not SDP-enhanced. SDP is relatively insensitive to a small percentage of peers not providing the adequate LoS. During the search phase, the redundancy aspect is likely to offset the effect of such peers. And peers who do not send their reputation scores may be avoided for content download. The effect of participation is demonstrated by the evaluation results presented in section 6.

6   Evaluation

SDP can be evaluated along the dimensions of 1) **Effectiveness:** the actual differentiation in services provided to peers belonging to different LoSs during the content search and download phases, 2) **Sensitivity to participation:** expecting that all peers in the system run SDP for it to be effective is not possible because peers could be running different versions of the the underlying Gnutella protocol and also could be malicious. As a result, gauging the sensitivity of SDP to the extent of participation required from peers is important, 3) **Overheads:** an estimation of overheads of SDP due to the enhancements to the Gnutella *Query* and *QueryHit* messages and extra processing on the part of peers who process the content search and download requests, and 4) **Impact of parameter values:** the exact values of service differentiation parameters used while mapping them to various LoSs.

We generated connected topologies with peer populations ranging from 5000 to 25, 000. Compared to the actual populations of widely deployed P2P networks, these topologies are small. However, our main goal in the preliminary evaluation presented in this paper is to observe the general trends in the effectiveness of SDP. Each peer in the simulation topologies is connected on an average to about 4 other peers in the system.

We assume that the total number of files in each topology is the same as the peer population. The file popularities are Zipf distributed with a parameter of 1.0. At the beginning of the simulation, each peer possesses one unique file. As the peers access more files, they cache them and serve them to other peers. This leads to the file propagation. The file sizes are uniformly distributed between 0-8MBytes. Also, each peer has a *capacity-limit*, implying that it can not cache any more than a certain number of files. The requests for files in this system are uniformly distributed among all the peers with an exponential inter-arrival time of 50 requests/second. The simulation logs are 1 hour long for each topology. Furthermore, the simulations assume that three LoS (basic, enhanced, premium) are in use and that all the peers stay in the system for the entire duration of the logs and that the peer reputations do not change during that time period.

Our simulations focus on the first two parameters from the above list. To estimate the *effectiveness* of SDP in providing service differentiation, we focus on the search aspect. Furthermore, we assume that parameters like premium content, hard-to-find content, cached queries, and cached files are constant across all the LoSs. The only parameter differentiating among the peers with different LoSs is the number of hops their queries are allowed to go. These simulations assume that all the peers are running SDP and that they exhibit greedy behavior in that the number of hops specified by the peers in their searches exceed the eligibility of their reputation scores. We also estimate the *sensitivity to participation* of peers during content search. While lack of participation could also imply various kinds of malicious behavior, we only consider the lack of participation to mean that the peers are not SDP enhanced. As a result, they process the queries as they would in the case of Gnutella. The queriers exhibit greedy behavior in specifying TTL in these simulations as well.

For the above evaluations, we experimented with population sizes of 5000, 10,000, and 25,000 peers in the system. We assumed three combinations of the percentage of peers eligible for basic, enhanced, and premium LoS respectively. These combinations were $(20, 20, 60)$ $(40, 40, 20)$, and $(60, 20, 20)$. We refer to each of them as the *percentage-tuple* for simplicity. The first, second, and third entries of each percentage-tuple correspond to the percentage of peers eligible for basic, enhanced, and premium LoS respectively. For each population size and each percentage-tuple, we experimented with various cache sizes (50-1000 files) and various sets of hop-tuples. Each hop-tuple (i, j, k) corresponds to the maximum number of hops the queries for basic, enhanced, and premium LoS peers are allowed to go respectively. With all other parameters staying constant, the effect of varying population sizes was that the smaller the peer population in the topology, the more the successes during content search (and hence lesser failures). For each topology, the results across various cache sizes were identical. We now present the results for the topology with a population size of 10,000 and a cache size of 1000 files.

Figures 3(a), 3(b), and 3(c) show the effect of hop-tuple and percentage-tuple on the success of queries for the basic, enhanced, and premium LoS peers respectively. Irrespective of the particular hop-tuple, the success rates for pre-

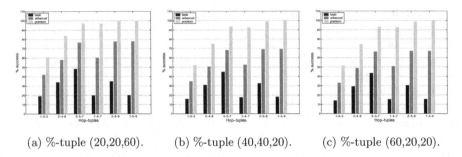

(a) %-tuple (20,20,60).   (b) %-tuple (40,40,20).   (c) %-tuple (60,20,20).

Fig. 3. Effectiveness of SDP during search.

mium LoS peers are the highest. The success rates for enhanced LoS peers are better than those of basic LoS but worse than the premium LoS peers. This shows that for the topologies tested, SDP is able to provide service differentiation for content search using just the number of hops. Comparing across graphs for peers belonging to the same LoS respectively, it becomes clear that for basic and enhanced LoS peers, as the percentage of peers eligible for the same service increases, the success rate deteriorates. This is expected because the presence of more basic and enhanced peers implies fewer premium peers and less successes during content search. The total effect is that of lesser propagation of files. Also, as expected, as the number of hops for individual LoS increase, the success rates improve as well.

Figures 4(a) and 4(b) show the effect of lack of participation on the effectiveness of SDP during content search for hop-tuples $(1, 3, 5)$ and $(2, 4, 6)$ respectively. The trends for hop-tuples $(1, 4, 7)$ and $(1, 5, 9)$ were similar to that of $(1, 3, 5)$, the only difference being the increased % successes for the former hop-tuples as expected. Similarly, the trends for hop-tuples $(2, 5, 8)$ and $(3, 5, 7)$ were similar to that of $(2, 4, 6)$. The graphs in figure 4(a) and 4(b) are for percentage-tuple $(40, 40, 20)$. The graphs for percentage-tuples $(20, 20, 60)$ and $(60, 20, 20)$ were almost identical. Since querying peers are assumed to be greedy, as fewer percentage of peers implement SDP, the overall trend in both the graphs is that of decreased service differentiation among the basic, enhanced, and premium LoS peers. This is expected because the presence of more non-SDP peers means that more querying peers will get content search replies from farther away than their LoS justifies. For figure 4(b), when the percentage of peers not participating increases beyond 30%, the difference in service diminishes quicker than for figure 4(a).

7   Conclusion

We presented SDP, a protocol for service differentiation in Gnutella like P2P networks. SDP uses parameters that affect the content search and download functions to provide different LoSs. It accomplishes this by enhancing the Gnutella

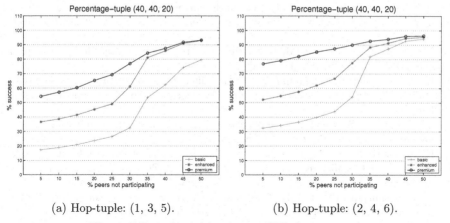

(a) Hop-tuple: $(1, 3, 5)$.   (b) Hop-tuple: $(2, 4, 6)$.

Fig. 4. Effect of participation on SDP during search.

specification. Though SDP is independent of the underlying reputation system used to decide on the LoS a peer is eligible for, a system where peers store their reputations locally is the most efficient. A preliminary evaluation of the service differentiation achieved during the search phase shows the promise of the approach.

Acknowledgment

The authors will like to thank Paul Judge for many useful insights during the initial discussions on the topic.

References

1. S. Zhong, J. Chen, and Y. R. Yang, "Sprite: A simple, cheat-proof, credit-based system for mobile ad-hoc networks," in *IEEE INFOCOM*, 2003.
2. Y. Qiu and P. Marbach, "Bandwidth allocation in ad hoc networks: A price based approach," in *IEEE INFOCOM*, 2003.
3. K. Aberer and Z. Despotovic, "Managing trust in a peer-2-peer information system," in *Ninth International Conference on Information and Knowledge Management (CIKM)*, Nov. 2001.
4. E. Damiani, S. De Capitani di Vimercati, S. Paraboschi, P. Samarati, and F. Violante, "A reputation-based approach for choosing reliable resources in peer-to-peer networks," in *9th ACM Conference on Computer and Communications Security*, Nov. 2002.
5. S. D. Kamvar, M. Schlosser, and H. Garcia-Molina, "EigenRep: Reputation management in P2P networks," Unpublished work, 2003.
6. S. Lee, R. Sherwood, and B. Bhattacharjee, "Cooperative peer groups in NICE," in *IEEE INFOCOM*, Apr. 2003.

7. L. Xiong and L. Liu, "Building trust in decentralized peer-to-peer communities," in *International Conference on Electronic Commerce Research (ICECR-5)*, Oct. 2002.

8. M. Gupta, P. Judge, and M. H. Ammar, "A reputation system for peer-to-peer networks," in *NOSSDAV*, June 2003.

9. K. Sripanidkulchai, "The popularity of gnutella queries and its implications on scalability," White Paper Featured on O'Reilly's website http://www.openp2p.com/, Feb. 2001.

10. E. Cohen and S. Shenker, "Replication strategies in unstructured peer-to-peer networks," in *ACM SIGCOMM*, Aug. 2002.

11. K. Sripanidkulchai, B. Maggs, and H. Zhang, "Efficient content location using interest-based locality in peer-to-peer systems," in *IEEE INFOCOM*, Apr. 2003.

12. "Gnutella web caching system," http://www.gnucleus.com/gwebcache/.

13. S. Ratnasamy, M. Handley, R. Karp, and S. Shenker, "Topologically-aware overlay construction and server selection," in *IEEE INFOCOM*, Apr. 2002.

14. "Gnutella spec," http://www9.limewire.com/developer/gnutella_protocol_0.4.pdf/.

Adding Structure to Unstructured Peer-to-Peer Networks: The Role of Overlay Topology

Shashidhar Merugu, Sridhar Srinivasan, and Ellen Zegura

College of Computing,
Georgia Institute of Technology,
Atlanta, GA 30032
{merugu,sridhar,ewz}@cc.gatech.edu

Abstract. Our work examines the role of overlay topology on the performance of unstructured peer-to-peer systems. We focus on two performance metrics: (a) search protocol performance, a local gain perceived directly by a user of the system and (b) utilization of the network, a global property that is of interest to network service providers. We present a class of overlay topologies based on distance between a node and its neighbors. We show, by simulation, that a particular topology instance of this class where every node has many close neighbors and few random neighbors exhibits better properties than other examined instances. In this overlay topology, the chances of locating files are high and the nodes where these files are found are, on average, close to the query source. This improvement in search protocol performance is achieved while decreasing the traffic load on the links in the underlying network. We propose a simple greedy algorithm to construct such topologies where each node operates independently and in a decentralized manner.

1 Introduction

Sharing of files is the most dominant application in use on current peer-to-peer networks [1]. Unstructured and decentralized systems (e.g., BearShare, LimeWire based on Gnutella [2], Kazaa based on FastTrack [3]) are extremely popular and attractive for their simplicity. We focus on these decentralized and unstructured peer-to-peer networks to support file searching; our goal is to examine the role of overlay topologies on the performance of such systems.

Gnutella and its family of protocols [2] use a very simple *scoped-flooding search* mechanism to locate files. A search query is propagated to all neighbors from the source node. The query is replicated and forwarded by each intermediate node to all its neighbors, up to a system-defined maximum number of overlay hops from the source. Every intermediate node compares its local contents with the requested file in the search query and responds to the query source on a match. Scoped-flooding is costly when scaled to large numbers and can only find files within the search radius. However, it is very simple and amenable to a dynamic real-world peer-to-peer network. Unlike structured peer-to-peer networks (e.g. Chord [4], CAN [5]), unstructured peer-to-peer networks do not

B. Stiller et al. (Eds.): NGC/ICQT 2003, LNCS 2816, pp. 83–94, 2003.

have any association between the content and location where it is stored, thereby eliminating the complexity of maintaining such an association in a dynamic scenario [6]. Without an association between content and location, a node does not have any information about which other nodes can best be able to resolve a query. In this case of a "blind" search, scoped-flooding reaches many search candidates as well as limits the distance traveled by a search query.

The success of a scoped-flooding search, both in terms of *quantity* of candidates searched, and the *quality* of results returned, is strongly affected by the topology of the peer-to-peer network. For example, in an overlay topology that is a k-ary tree rooted at the source of the query, a scoped-flooding search up to m hops would examine k^m candidates. On the other hand, if the source and its neighbors form a clique in the overlay topology, many nodes are revisited and hence the number of unique search candidates is lower. The quality of a result can be measured as the distance (e.g., latency, available bandwidth) in the underlying network from the hit node to the query source. A *close* result may be able to better serve the file than a far node. In an overlay topology that is constructed unaware of the underlying network, as is the case with Gnutella [7,8], the search query hits may be far from the source, even though they are within the search radius on the overlay topology. The overlay topology also determines the amount of traffic load (search queries/results) on the underlying network. For example, when most of the overlay links cross Autonomous System (AS) boundaries, there is a proportional amount of inter-AS traffic [8]. Thus the study of the characteristics of overlay topologies is very important to the performance of peer-to-peer networks, but their effect on scoped-flooding search and the traffic load on links in the underlying network has received little attention.

In this paper, we present a class of overlay topologies for decentralized and unstructured peer-to-peer networks, taking inspiration from the recent work on small-worlds [9,10]. Small-world topologies exhibit *clustering* with some random edges. It has been observed that the small-world structure is pervasive and arises "without-design" or "naturally" in many practical systems such as the World Wide Web [9,11]. Overlays, on the other hand, provide an opportunity to *design structure*. We seek the advantages of designing overlays with a small-world structure. In our model of overlay topologies, a node's links to its neighbors are divided into two categories: *short* links and *long* links. The short links connect close nodes and the long links connect nodes chosen randomly. The fraction of links that are short, called the *proximity factor* (α), is a key design parameter that controls the properties of the resultant overlay topology. When $\alpha = 0$, every link is randomly chosen, and the overlay topology is a *random graph*. On the other hand when $\alpha = 1$, every link connects to a close neighbor, and the overlay topology looks more well-ordered (e.g., grid-like). Different values of α let us span the spectrum of this class of overlay topologies. We show, using simulation, that overlay topologies with an invariant of *many close neighbors and few random neighbors* at each node exhibit the following properties: *(a)* the underlying network distance to search candidates increases with the overlay radius as we progress in the scoped flooding search; *(b)* the count of search candidates is fairly high; and *(c)* the system returns close results. We also show that the traffic load on links of the underlying network is better for these overlay topologies than random overlay topologies.

Given our results showing that these overlay topologies perform well, we turn to the practical question of constructing such topologies in a dynamic peer-to-peer environment. We propose a method of topology construction where each node operates independently and in a decentralized manner to select its own neighbors. Neighbors are selected from a pool of candidates using a simple greedy algorithm based on local information. In a practical implementation, we foresee short links connecting nodes belonging to the same AS where possible, while the long links cross AS boundaries. Given the dynamic conditions of a peer-to-peer network, nodes periodically evaluate the distance to their neighbors and replace them if necessary to maintain the invariant ratio of short and long links.

The remainder of the paper is organized as follows. We study the class of overlay topologies and desirable properties that are important for the performance of peer-to-peer networks in Section 2. In Section 3, we present our evaluation methodology and simulation results. We propose an algorithm for overlay topology construction in Section 4. Section 5 has related work followed by summary in Section 6.

2   Overlay Topologies

In this section, we present a class of overlay topologies for decentralized and unstructured peer-to-peer systems. We discuss how different instances of this class of topologies can be realized by varying a characteristic parameter. Later in this section, we present dimensions to study the effect of overlay topologies on the performance of peer-to-peer systems.

One of the key purposes of characterizing overlay topologies is to create a simple framework for an empirical analysis. Our choice for a model for the overlay topologies is inspired by the generic lattice network model for small-worlds [10]. In our class of topologies, there are two kinds of links: *short-links* and *long-links*. Every node in the system selects some *close* nodes to be its short-link neighbors and some nodes *at random* to be its long-link neighbors. An appropriate metric for distance (e.g., latency) in the underlying network defines the *closeness* of neighbors. While the short-link neighbors are carefully chosen to be close to the node, the long-link neighbors, on the other hand, being chosen randomly, are generally far from the node. We make an implicit assumption that the system has a large enough population of nodes that are spread across the underlying network ensuring the existence of close neighbors. Crawls of Gnutella peer-to-peer topologies [7,12] and live-count of active Gnutella peers [13] support this focus on a large population.

The *proximity factor* (α) of a node, defined as the ratio of the number of short links to the total number of links, is a design parameter that governs the overall structure of the topology. A node with degree d has αd short links and $(1 - \alpha)d$ long links. α takes values from 0 to 1, inclusive: $\alpha = 0$ corresponds to all long-links and $\alpha = 1$ corresponds to all short-links. Different values of α let us span the spectrum of this class of overlay topologies.

In an instance of the class of topologies with $\alpha = 0$, all the neighbors of a node are randomly chosen, and this results in a *random graph*. It is well-known that random graph topologies have a low diameter and are fairly robust in terms of connectivity [14]. The average distance between neighbors, in this all long-links case, is typically the mean node-to-node distance in the underlying network. As α increases, there is less "randomness" and more "order" in the topology. The "order" in the topology comes from the increasing number of short-links. Short-links "induce" more short-links. Intuitively, if A and B are short-link neighbors of C, then chances are that A and B are also close to each other and could be short-link neighbors themselves. This possibility of a node's neighbors being neighbors themselves introduces "clusters" in the topology. Clustering, a measure of "cliqueness" of a neighborhood, is formally defined as the fraction of allowable edges that occur among the set of neighbors of a node [9]. As α increases, the number of short-links increase and the topology is increasingly clustered. The instance of topology with $\alpha = 1$ corresponds to all short-links and we expect the topology to contain multiple clusters and to be possibly disconnected. However, an instance of the topology with many short-links but few long-links, i.e., with an α between 0.5 and 1.0, is expected to exhibit both the properties of a random graph and a clustered graph. We call such instances "small-world-like" overlay topologies. These small-world-like topologies contain multiple clusters formed by the many short-links, but their random long-links connect across clusters and keep the graph connected as well as lower its diameter.

2.1   Desirable Properties

We focus on two performance criteria of peer-to-peer systems: *(a) search protocol performance*, a local gain perceived directly by a user of the system and *(b) utilization of the network*, a global property that is of interest to network service providers. Search protocol performance is studied along the two dimensions of search space and underlying network distance to search results. Network utilization is measured by the traffic load on the links in the underlying network.

Search Space. The size of scoped-flooding search space around a query source node is measured by number of unique candidate nodes visited by the search query. Since scoped-flooding search protocol is ignorant of particular file being searched for, the chances of finding the requested file depend significantly on the size of the search space. The factors that determine the size of search space include search radius and structure of the overlay topology. It is also desirable that the overlay topology be always connected and robust from sudden departures of nodes that are quite common in a dynamic peer-to-peer network. Connectivity of the topology ensures that scoped-flooding search does not terminate early and that all nodes up to the search radius are explored.

Underlying Network Distance to Search Results. After completion of the search process when the search results are returned, the query source has a choice of selecting one of the hit nodes to serve the file. This file transfer depends on the distance between the query source and the chosen hit node in the underlying network. Though the query source and hit node are relatively close in the overlay, it is not necessary that these two nodes are close in the underlying network. If the overlay topology is *aware* of the underlying network, the scoped-flooding search mechanism can find close hit nodes. To quantify this awareness, we define *stride* at i^{th} step to be the term $(D_i - D_{i-1})$, where D_i denotes the average distance in the underlying network to all nodes that are exactly i hops away on the overlay topology.

Network Traffic. A benefit of an overlay topology being aware of the underlying network is an improvement in the utilization of links in the underlying network. One of the most common definitions of traffic load in overlay networks is the notion of *stress*. Stress [15] of a link in the underlying network is defined as the number of logical links (of the overlay topology) whose mapped paths include the underlying link.

In summary, we desire overlay topologies that satisfy a dual objective of improving the performance of scoped-flooding search protocol and minimizing the traffic load on the links of the underlying network. To realize these goals, we seek "good" structural properties on the overlay to have *(a)* a large number of unique search candidates and *(b)* an awareness of overlay topology with the underlying network. An overlay topology with structural properties similar to that of a random graph gives large number of unique search candidates, however it does not "fit" well with the underlying network. On the other hand, an overlay topology with high clustering conforms well with the underlying network, but has a lower number of unique search candidates. We aim to find a suitable balance in the structural properties of overlay topologies for these two goals of producing a higher count of search candidates and being underlying network-aware.

3   Evaluation

In this section, we analyze, by simulation, how the desirable properties described in Section 2.1 vary with the proximity factor (α) in our class of overlay topologies. We briefly explain our simulation framework followed by analysis of results from different experiments. These experiments, designed to study the role of overlay topology on the performance of peer-to-peer networks, evaluate *(1)* success of scoped flooding search queries, *(2)* underlying network distance to search results, and *(3)* stress on links in the underlying network.

3.1   Methodology

Simulation Parameters. A network topology comprising of 5152 routers was generated using the Transit-Stub graph model from the GT-ITM topology generator [16]. The link latencies are assigned values according to the type of the link, using a uniform distribution on the following ranges: [15ms, 25ms] for intra-transit domain links, [3ms, 7ms] for transit-stub links, [1ms, 3ms] for intra-stub links. In each experiment, end-hosts are attached uniformly at random to the stub routers of the underlying network topology. These end-hosts participate in the overlay network. All our experiments have 4096 end-hosts (overlay nodes) by default. All overlay nodes have at least 3 and at most 4 neighbors[1]. In order to simulate scoped-flooding search for files, 50 unique files with varying popularity are introduced into the system. Each file has multiple copies stored at different locations chosen at random. The number of copies of a file are proportional to their popularity. The count of file copies is assumed to follow Zipf distribution with 2000 copies for the most popular file and 40 copies for the least popular file. The queries that search for these files are also initiated at random hosts on the overlay topology. Again the number of queries for a file is assumed to be proportional to its popularity. Each query follows the scoped-flooding search protocol up to a maximum of 4 overlay hops from the query source[2]. Each experiment is repeated multiple times with different seeds to remove any bias in random number generation that is used in multiple stages of simulation (e.g., placement of end-hosts on the underlying network, copies and queries of files on end-hosts).

Overlay Topologies. We constructed four different instances of the class of overlay topologies described in Section 2. These four instances of topologies are compared along different dimensions of the desirable properties described in Section 2.1. The instances of topologies have proximity factors of $\{0.0, 0.33, 0.66, 1.0\}$. With a minimum degree of 3 at each node, these four values of proximity factor correspond to four combinations of numbers of short and long links: $(0, 3)$, $(1, 2)$, $(2, 1)$ and $(3, 0)$. Global information about underlying network distances to all nodes is used in deciding the short-link neighbors, whereas the long-link neighbors are randomly chosen from the node population. An overlay topology instance with $\alpha = 0.0$ ("all-long-links"), corresponds to the case where neighbors of every node are randomly chosen. Current unstructured peer-to-peer systems use a random neighbor selection scheme that results in an overlay topology which is similar to this all-long-links instance. At the other end of the spectrum, every node has close neighbors in the "all-short-links" topology with $\alpha = 1.0$. The instance of $\alpha = 0.66$ is a topology where every node has more short links than long links and has similarities to a small-world graph. We also refer to this "many-short-links" instance as "small-world-like" overlay topology.

---

[1] Several implementations of Gnutella protocol (including Limewire, GTK-Gnutella, Gnucleus) allow users to configure the number of neighbors. Typical recommended values for node degree are 4 and 5. We ran our experiments with the degree ranges of [4, 6] inclusive and the results are similar to what we present here. One key difference though is that diameter decreases with increasing degree.

[2] Though early versions of Gnutella protocol specification suggested a TTL of 7, most popular Gnutella servents including Limewire use a default TTL value of 4 to limit system resource usage.

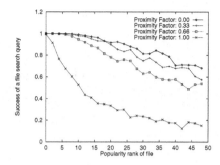

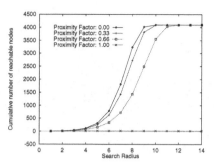

Fig. 1. Scoped-Flooding Search Query Success Rate

Fig. 2. Count of reachable nodes with increasing search radius

3.2   Simulation Results

Success of Search. A query for a file is "successful" when it finds at least one match for the requested file within the search radius. Success rate of a file is defined as the ratio of number of successful queries to the total number of queries issued for that file throughout the system. Though the number of queries we simulated per file is proportional to the popularity of that file, "success rate" is a normalized quantity across all the files. In Figure 1, we plot the success rate of queries for files with different popularity for each instance of overlay topologies. All topologies have a high success rate for more popular files because of the large number of copies for these files. However as the popularity decreases, the number of copies of files in the system decreases and the success rate for all the topologies goes down. One key observation is that the success rate for the all-short-links topology (with $\alpha = 1.0$) drops rapidly, compared to the success rate for the other three values of the proximity factor. We also note that the success rate for small-world-like topology is fairly close to that of the all-long-links topology.

The effects that we observe in Figure 1 follow directly from Figure 2. In Figure 2, we plot the cumulative number of unique nodes that are reachable as we increase the search radius of the scoped-flooding scheme. The all-long-links topology ($\alpha = 0$) reaches more nodes at each radius than all the other three topologies; but with a maximum search radius of 4 that is used in our simulation, the number of unique nodes reached by these three topologies ($\alpha = \{0, 0.33, 0.66\}$) is very similar. The small-world-like topology can access a fairly large number of nodes because each long link allows the query to reach more nodes outside its local region. The similarity in number of search candidates results in similar success rate that we observed in Figure 1 for these three topologies. Also, the low success rate of the all-short-links topology in Figure 1 is due to the small (almost constant) number of nodes that are accessed at increasing search radii. This topology causes nodes to form clusters and makes the graph disconnected. The diameters of four kinds of overlay topologies ($\alpha = \{0.0, 0.33, 0.66, 1.0\}$) are 11, 12, 14, and 6 respectively. Also the average path lengths are 7, 7, 8, and 2 respectively. Note that the diameter and the average path length of the small-world-like topology ($\alpha = 0.66$) is comparable to the more random topologies ($\alpha = \{0.0, 0.33\}$). On

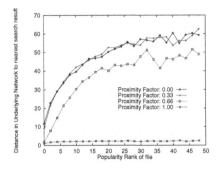
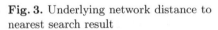
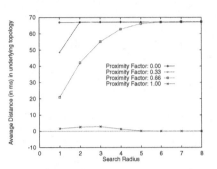

Fig. 3. Underlying network distance to nearest search result

Fig. 4. Variation of avg. underlying network distance to nodes at a given radius

the other hand, the all-short-links topology is disconnected in all our multiple trials and the values for diameter and average path length that are reported are for the connected components of the topology.

Distance to Search Results. Figure 3 plots the underlying network distance to nearest search result as a function of file popularity. Each point is an average over all the queries issued for that file. The nearest search result for small-world-like topologies ($\alpha = 0.66$) is closer than the nearest result for topologies with $\alpha = 0.0$ and $\alpha = 0.33$. Even though the all-short-links topology shows the smallest distance, most of the queries are failures. The reason for these observations follows directly from Figure 4 where we plot "stride", as defined in Section 2.1. The stride for all-long-links topology ($\alpha = 0$) is flat (zero) as all the links are randomly chosen and hence the average distance to nodes is independent of how far they are on the overlay from the source node. It can also be clearly seen that the neighborhood of nodes in small-world-like topology is closer in the underlying network (a positive stride), leading to the search results being found closer in the underlying network. On the other hand, in the all-short-links topology, all the nodes at increasing radii are very near the source and exhibit a tendency to form clusters. We also notice that, on average, after a small number of overlay hops, the all-short-links topology is disconnected.

Stress. To show the effect of traffic load by the various topologies on the underlying network, we plot the mean stress of links in the underlying network as the size of the population increases in Figure 5. The all-short-links overlay topology has extremely low mean stress because for every node, its set of neighbors is selected from nodes that are close to it and the links to those nodes are not shared by any other pair of nodes. In the case of all-long-links ($\alpha = 0.0$) topology, a node's neighbors are picked from the entire set of nodes, leading to overlay links that span the underlying network, causing underlying links to carry multiple overlay links. The many-long-links ($\alpha = 0.33$) topology is in between the two extremes. The graph shows that randomness in choosing the neighbors increases the mean stress of the underlying links. The small-world-like ($\alpha = 0.66$)

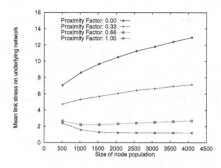

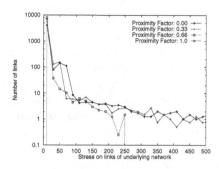

Fig. 5. Variation of mean stress on underlying network links with node population

Fig. 6. Frequency distribution of values of stress on links of the underlying network

topology, by virtue of having many short links, has a low mean stress like that of the all-short-links topology. Some of the disproportionate increase in stress of more random topologies ($\alpha = \{0.0, 0.33\}$) as the population size increases, is potentially due to the use of transit-stub graphs for our simulations. The links connecting stubs to transit nodes could possibly form bottlenecks pushing up the mean stress of a topology. To investigate this, we plot the frequency distribution of the stress on the underlying links in Figure 6. It can be clearly seen that random topologies have many more links with high stress than the all-short-links and small-world-like topologies on the same underlying network.

3.3 Summary of Results

As expected of random graphs, the all-long-links topology has a low diameter, reaches out to many candidates in a scoped-flooding search and is always connected. However, it does not utilize the links of the underlying network well and the stride is almost zero for these topologies. On the other end of the spectrum, the all-short-links topology behaves like a well-ordered graph with higher diameter, and better utilization of the links in the underlying network. However, the search space is quite small and the topology is disconnected most often. In between these two ends of the spectrum, but closer to the case of all-short-links, we observe that the topologies, with many short links and few long links, have desirable properties. They not only have low diameter, large search space and are always connected like an all-long-links topology, but are also aware of the underlying network and can utilize the links better like an all-short-links topology.

4 Overlay Topology Construction

We have shown in the previous section that overlay topologies with many close neighbors and few random neighbors at each node exhibit desirable properties.

Now we consider how to practically construct such overlay topologies in a peer-to-peer environment.

We propose an operation called Adapt that is executed by nodes in the peer-to-peer system. By executing an Adapt operation, a node selects "better" neighbors according to its local view of the system. Each node in the system has the following parameters: (1) the number d of neighbors; (2) the proximity factor α that determines the neighborhood ratio of short and long links; (3) a adapt-threshold γ of distance to determine whether another adapt operation is necessary; and (4) an adapt-epoch δ value to schedule a periodic adapt operation. The life-time of a node on the peer-to-peer system is divided into two phases: a join phase and a maintenance phase. In the join phase, a new node, say X, adapts repeatedly until its short-link neighbors are at a "satisfactory" distance. Let D_i denote the average distance in underlying network to the short-link neighbors of X after i^{th} invocation of Adapt. X adapts until: $|D_i - D_{i-1}| < \gamma$. When this condition is met, say, at time t_0, we say X has "settled" in its neighborhood. Later, in the maintenance phase, X schedules a periodic Adapt operation at every adapt-epoch δ time units, i.e., at $\{(t_0 + \delta), (t_0 + 2\delta), \ldots\}$. An Adapt operation is also triggered when one or more neighbors depart. The three input parameters to the Adapt procedure are the node-ID (u), the number of short links (s) and the number of long links (l). s and l are computed according to the node parameters d and α where $s = \alpha d$ and $l = (1 - \alpha)d$. Node u builds a candidate list of potential neighbors from its current local neighborhood. These candidates include current neighbors of u and neighbors of current neighbors, i.e., all nodes seen in a "depth-first-traversal" starting from u up to a depth of two hops. Node u measures distances to each of these candidates from itself. A new set of neighbors is formed by selecting the s "closest" candidates according to distance rank and picking l candidates at random from the rest. Thus node u acts in a greedy fashion to improve its local neighborhood.

One of the key features of the Adapt procedure is its simplicity. Adapt is similar in spirit to the simple scoped-flooding search of the unstructured peer-to-peer systems. Both schemes scout their immediate neighborhood, but for different reasons: one for closer neighbors, the other for locating files. Adapt is decentralized and does not make use of any central authority or any infrastructure. It is based only on a local view of the node and hence can be easily deployed on current peer-to-peer systems. The triggers for an Adapt operation, both based on an adapt-epoch and adapt-threshold, make this scheme amenable to dynamic arrivals and departures of nodes of a peer-to-peer system.

A preliminary evaluation of the join phase suggests that Adapt can find close neighbors. We have also examined the question of partial deployment, where only a fraction of the node population observe the invariant ratio of many close neighbors and few random neighbors. Our initial results are encouraging, but we omit them here due to lack of space and refer the reader to an extended version of our paper [17].

5   Related Work

Ripeanu et al. [7] observed a significant "mismatch" between Gnutella logical overlay and its projection on the underlying network. Another study by Saroiu et al. [12], based on a crawl of Gnutella topology, confirmed that it is highly robust to partitions indicating its similarity to a well-connected random graph. Many approaches (e.g., binning [18], beaconing [19], Tiers [20]) are proposed to construct topology aware overlay networks. All these approaches identify close nodes suitable for short-link neighbors and hence are complementary to our work. Among other considerations for constructing topologies of unstructured peer-to-peer networks, a recent proposal [21] suggests "interest-based shortcuts" to link peers that have similarity in shared content. It is possible to think of a composite metric that combines both distance in underlying topology that we use in our work with the interest based locality to select neighbors. A recent work, very similar in spirit to ours, combines the idea of small-worlds with peer-to-peer networks. In this work [22], the authors propose a new cache replacement algorithm for routing tables to improve location of data items in Freenet. We believe that the key space distance metric used in the proposed cache replacement algorithm can blend with our metric of the underlying network distance.

6   Summary

Overlay topology plays a fundamental role in the performance of an unstructured peer-to-peer network. In this paper, we have presented a class of overlay topologies and their characteristic parameter called proximity factor. Proximity factor relates to the underlying network distance between a node and its neighbors. Different instances of this class of overlay topologies are realized by varying the proximity factor. These topology instances are examined, by simulation, along two performance-related dimensions: *(a)* search protocol performance and *(b)* utilization of links in the underlying network. Our simulation results show that in a particular "small-world-like" topology instance of this class where every node has many close neighbors and few random neighbors, *(1)* the chances of locating files are high and *(2)* the nodes where these files are found are, on average, close to the query source. This improvement in search protocol performance is achieved while *(3)* decreasing the traffic load on the links in the underlying network. To demonstrate the feasibility of constructing such "small-world-like" overlay topologies in a practical peer-to-peer environment, we have proposed a simple greedy algorithm called Adapt. A node executing Adapt operates independently and in a decentralized manner to select its neighbors.

References

1. A. Oram, Ed., *Peer-to-Peer: Harnessing the Power of Disruptive Technologies*, O'Reilly, 2001.
2. "http://rfc-gnutella.sourceforge.net".

3. "http://www.fasttrack.nu".
4. I. Stoica, R. Morris, D. Karger, M. F. Kaashoek, and H. Balakrishnan, "Chord: A Scalable Peer-to-peer Lookup Service for Internet Applications," in *ACM SIGCOMM*, 2001.
5. S. Ratnaswamy, P. Francis, M. Handley, R. Karp, and S. Shenker, "A Scalable Content Addressable Network," in *ACM SIGCOMM*, 2001.
6. S. Ratnaswamy, S. Shenker, and I. Stoica, "Routing Algorithms for DHTs: Some Open Questions," in *First Intl. Workshop on Peer-to-Peer Systems*, March 2002.
7. M. Ripeanu, I. Foster, and A. Iamnitchi, "Mapping the Gnutella Network: Properties of Large Scale Peer-to-Peer Systems and Implications for System Design," *IEEE J. on Internet Computing, Special Issue on Peer-to-peer Networking*, 2002.
8. S. Sen and J. Wang, "Analyzing peer-to-peer traffic across large networks," in *Internet Measurement Workshop*, 2002.
9. D. J. Watts, *Small Worlds: The Dynamics of Networks between Order and Randomness*, Princeton University Press, 1999.
10. J. Kleinberg, "The Small-World Phenomenon:An Algorithmic Perspective," in *ACM Symposium on Theory of Computing*, 2000.
11. R. Albert, H. Jeong, and A. L. Barabási, "The Diameter of the World-Wide Web," *Nature*, 1999.
12. S. Saroiu, K. Gummadi, and S. Gribble, "A Measurement Study of Peer-to-Peer File Sharing Systems," in *Multimedia Conferencing and Networking*, Jan 2002.
13. "Gnutella network hosts: http://www.limewire.com/current_size.html".
14. B. Bollobás, *Random Graphs*, Cambridge University Press, 2001.
15. Y. Chu, S. G. Rao, S. Seshan, and H. Zhang, "A Case for End System Multicast," *IEEE Journal on Selected Areas in Communication, Special Issue on Networking Support for Multicast*, 2002.
16. E. Zegura, K. Calvert, and M. J. Donahoo, "A Quantitative Comparison of Graph-based Models for Internet Topology," *IEEE/ACM Trans. on Networking*, Dec 1997.
17. S. Merugu, S. Srinivasan, and E. Zegura, "Adding structure to unstructured peer-to-peer networks: the role of overlay topology," Tech. Rep. GIT-CC-03-31, College of Computing, Georgia Institute of Technology, 2003.
18. S. Ratnaswamy, M. Handley, R. Karp, and S. Shenker, "Topologically-Aware Overlay Construction and Server Selection," in *Infocom*, 2002.
19. N. Shankar, C. Komareddy, and S. Bhattacharjee, "Finding Close Friends over the Internet," in *International Conference on Network Protocols*, 2001.
20. S. Banerjee, C. Komareddy, and S. Bhattacharjee, "Scalable Peer Finding on the Internet," in *Global Internet Symposium, Globecom*, 2002.
21. K. Sripanidkulchai, B. Maggs, and H. Zhang, "Efficient Content Location Using Interest-Based Locality in Peer-to-Peer Systems," in *Infocom*, 2003.
22. H. Zhang, A. Goel, and R. Govindan, "Using the Small-World Model to Improve Freenet Performance," in *Infocom*, 2002.

Building Semantic Peer-to-Peer Networks upon CAN*

Jiantao Song, Yong Zhang, Chaofeng Sha, and Hong Zhu

Department of Computer Science and Engineering,
Fudan University, Shanghai, China, 200433
{011021376,012021133,cfsha,hzhu}@fudan.edu.cn

Abstract. Existing decentralized architectures for peer-to-peer (P2P) networks can be generally partitioned into two categories: unstructured (such as Gnutella) and structured (such as CAN, Chord, Pastry and Tapestry). Based on Content Addressable Networks (CAN), we propose a hybrid scheme for building Semantic Peer-to-peer Networks (SPNs) where semantically related nodes are connected to each other. The entire peer-to-peer overlay networks are overlapped by many SPNs and all these SPNs are logically organized into a hierarchy. Then we provide a searching algorithm to "focus" query propagation only in appropriate SPNs. As a result, the nodes visited for a lookup can be reduced by several orders of magnitude compared to Gnutella.

1 Introduction

Peer-to-peer (P2P) networking applications have seen explosive growth in recent years. An important feature of a P2P network is that the utility of the network is closely related to the quantity and quality of the resources available. More resources can be added by increasing the number of nodes in the network. But the number of resources available to each node may drop with the growth of the network. The ability to locate resources efficiently and effectively over a large, dynamic network is therefore crucial to the utility of the network as a whole.

Centralized indexing architectures such as Napster suffer from the single point of failure. Existing decentralized P2P architectures are generally partitioned into two categories: unstructured (such as Gnutella [6]) and structured (such as CAN [10], Chord [15], Pastry [12] and Tapestry [19]). In decentralized unstructured P2P systems, each node is responsible for maintaining the indices of only the files it stores and the P2P systems create a random overlay network. They rely on flooding for search, hence inherently supporting partial-match queries, but such expensive search does not make the systems scalable. Aiming at improving the scalability, decentralized structured P2P networks, commonly referred to as Distributed Hash Tables (DHTs), carefully distribute the file indices among participating nodes, with queries being routed directly to the node

---

* This work is supported by a grant from the Ministry of Science and Technology (grant ♯2001CCA03000), National Natural Science Fund (grant ♯60273045) and Shanghai Science and Technology Development Fund (grant ♯025115032)

B. Stiller et al. (Eds.): NGC/ICQT 2003, LNCS 2816, pp. 95–106, 2003.

responsible for the needed file index. Although DHTs provide efficient search for exact-match queries, they are not as effective for partial match queries.

Our goal is to build a scalable P2P searching system that provides efficient search even for partial-match queries. The inefficiency of decentralized unstructured P2P systems lies in that the P2P network topology is unrelated to the location of data and queries are flooded blindly in the entire network. We argue that the efficiency of decentralized unstructured P2P systems can be greatly improved by building Semantic Peer-to-peer Networks (SPNs) where semantically related nodes are connected to each other. By grouping semantically related nodes, the search space can be pruned, while on the other hand, the number of resources available to each node may increase. With this scheme, not only can millions of nodes coexist in a single system, but also partial match queries are supported and the efficiency of locating resources is boosted.

However, building SPNs is challenging in the context of self-organized and dynamic P2P networks. How are semantically related nodes organized together to form SPNs? How can a node joining the system efficiently find the right SPNs and join them? How to adapt to the changes in the contents and interests of nodes? Given a query, which SPNs are appropriate for searching? Exploiting the mature tools (e.g. [7][11][17]) of document classification, we can classify documents of each node and further classify nodes. Using Content Addressable Networks (CAN) as an infrastructure, we propose a hybrid scheme for building Semantic Peer-to-peer Networks (SPNs) where nodes with the same classes of documents are connected to each other. A node can belong to several SPNs and the entire peer-to-peer overlay networks are overlapped by many SPNs. Moreover, SPNs formed are not isolated, but are semantically related as well.

Specifically, we make the following contributions:

- Based on CAN, we propose solutions to the construction and maintenance of SPNs, and SPNs can adapt to the changes in the contents and interests of nodes. Furthermore, all SPNs formed are logically organized into a hierarchy, and such hierarchical SPNs are "embedded" into CAN. A node joining the system can efficiently find the right SPNs and join them.

- We present a search algorithm that can "focus" query propagation only in appropriate SPNs, and that can tradeoff the performance of the system and the recall level (i.e. the percentage of the matches that can be found).

- We evaluate the performance of SPNs and find that nodes visited for a lookup can be reduced by several orders of magnitude compared to Gnutella.

The rest of this paper is organized as follows. Section 2 reviews some related work. Section 3 introduces formally the conception of SPNs and describes SPNs construction and maintenance. We present a search algorithm for SPNs and provide some solutions for hot spots in section 4 and section 5 respectively. In section 6 we evaluate the performance of the search algorithm. Finally, section 7 concludes our paper.

2   Related Work

Sylvia et. al [10] proposed the Content Addressable Network (CAN) as a distributed infrastructure that provides hash table like functionality on Internet-like scales. It models the participating nodes as zones in a virtual d-dimensional Cartesian coordinate space on a d-torus. To store a pair $\langle Key, Value \rangle$, Key is mapped onto a point in the space and the $\langle Key, Value \rangle$ pair is stored at the node whose zone contains the point. Retrieving an entry corresponding to Key is reduced to the problem of routing to the node storing the $\langle Key, Value \rangle$ pair. For a d-dimensional space partitioned into N equal zones, the average routing path length is $O(dN^{\frac{1}{d}})$ hops and individual nodes maintain $O(d)$ neighbors.

To improve the effectiveness of blind search in decentralized unstructured P2P systems, much work has been done. Crespo et al. [4] introduce the concept of routing indices, which allow nodes to forward queries to their neighbors that are more likely to have answers. Three techniques for efficient search are presented in [18]: iterative deepening, Directed BFS and Local Indices. More recently, "interest-based locality" is employed in [14], where nodes directly link to nodes that satisfied previous queries. Cohen et al. [3] propose "associative search" and improve the efficiency of locating rare items. However, all these are heuristic methods that improve the performance of the system to a certain degree, so it is still hard to build a large-scale P2P system supporting partial match queries by only employing these heuristics.

More related to our work, Triantafillou et. al [16] also form clusters of nodes based on the semantic categories of the documents but they predefine the maximum number of clusters. Furthermore, there is no semantic relation between clusters formed in their paper while we organize logically all SPNs into a hierarchy. And such hierarchical systems are also advocated in [8]. Crespo et. al [5] introduce the conception of Semantic Overlay Networks (SONs), and focus on analyzing the elements necessary for the building and usage of SONs under the assumption that nodes can magically join SONs. But we explicitly present the solution for a node to join the right SPNs efficiently.

3   SPNs Construction and Maintenance

In this section, we first formally introduce the concept of SPNs, and then detail their construction and maintenance.

3.1   The Concept of SPNs

Our system consists of N nodes and M distinct documents. Let P be a set of nodes and O be a set of documents where $P = \{p_i | 1 \leq i \leq N\}$ and $O = \{o_j | 1 \leq j \leq M\}$. Each node $p_i \in P$ maintains a set of documents $O(p_i) \subseteq O$ (a particular document may be stored in more than one node). A document classifier F maps documents to classes and a document can be mapped to multiple classes. Classification is organized as a tree-like hierarchy with a single root such as the one in Fig. 1. Every document in the system naturally belongs to the class on the highest level. We assume that the classifier F may be imprecise but that it does not make mistakes. For example, A "Rock" style music document may be classified as "music" because of imprecision but it can not be classified as "Movie". Each class is given a unique name in the form of "the class name on level 0 | the class name on level 1| ... | the class name on level k". For example, in Fig. 1, we name the class "rock" as "Entertainment | Music | Rock". We denote the set of classes of p_i as $C(p_i)$ and $C(p_i) = \{F(o_j)|o_j \in O(p_i)\}$. We call the class of p_i which has the maximum number documents (ties are broken arbitrarily) the dominant class, denoted by $c^*(p_i)$.

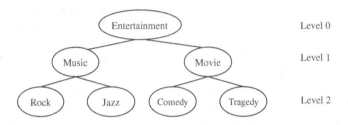

Fig. 1. A Classification Hierarchy

We formally introduce the concept of Semantic Peer-to-peer Networks (SPNs). We model a semantic peer-to-peer network as a graph SPN(c), and $SPN(c) = (P(c), E)$ where $P(c) = \{p_i \in P | c \in C(p_i)\}$ and $E = \{an\ edge\ e\ |\forall p_i \in P(c), \exists\ a\ node\ p_j \in P(c)\ such\ that\ the\ edge\ e\ links\ p_i\ with\ p_j\}$.

3.2   SPNs Construction

In this subsection, we describe our approach to construct SPNs upon CAN. The main idea of the construction of SPNs is as follows. Nodes in the system with the same dominant class c are neighbors (i.e., clustered together) in CAN and are connected to each other by green edges. We denote the set of nodes with the same dominant class c as cluster(c). If a node p_i has a non-dominant class c, then there exists a node p_j in cluster(c) connected to p_i by a blue edge. Thus all nodes in the system with the same class c are connected to each other, and a semantic peer-to-peer network SPN(c) can be formed. Furthermore, all SPNs are logically organized into a hierarchy according to the classification hierarchy, which is indispensable due to the following two facts: First, nodes having a class c and those having a class c', a subclass or a super class of c, are also semantically related. Second, the document classifier may be imprecise so that a document belonging to the class c may be classified as c' and vice versa.

The routing table of each node consists of two neighbor lists: one GreenEdge-List used for storing the coordinate neighbors with the same dominant class and one RedEdgeList storing the rest neighbors; and several BlueEdgeLists: one BlueEdgeList for each of its classes storing a "remote" node with the same class.

Pseudocode for NodeJoin algorithm

```
   //We assume that C(Pₙ) = {c¹, c², ..., cᴸ} where cⁱ = c₀ⁱ|c₁ⁱ|...|c_{kᵢ}ⁱ (1 ≤ i ≤ L).
   //We do not consider the class c₀ⁱ (1 ≤ i ≤ L).
1  for (i = 1; i ≤ L; i + +){
2    if (cⁱ is the dominant class of pₙ) {
3      KEY₁ ← c₀ⁱ|c₁ⁱ|...|c_{kᵢ}ⁱ ;
4      A1 ← hash(KEY₁); //KEY₁ is mapped onto a point A1 in the CAN space
5      Find the node p_{A1} whose zone contains  the point A1;
6      if (p_{A1} stores a pair ⟨KEY₁, IP address of a node p_{k1}⟩)
7        pₙ gets one half zone from p_{k1}  and joins the CAN routing;
8      else { //there hasn't been any node with the dominant class KEY₁
9        pₙ randomly chooses a zone  in the corner of the CAN space;
10       p_{A1} stores a pair ⟨KEY₁, IP address and the zone of pₙ ⟩;
11       for(j = 1; j ≤ kᵢ − 1; j + +){
12         KEY₂ ← c₀ⁱ|c₁ⁱ|...|c_{kᵢ−j}ⁱ ;
13         A2 ← hash(KEY₂);
14         Find the node p_{A2} whose zone contains the point A₂;
15         if(p_{A2} stores a pair ⟨KEY₂, IP address of a node⟩){
16           if(p_{A2} doesn't store a pair ⟨KEY₁, IP address of a node⟩)
17             p_{A2} stores a pair ⟨KEY₁, IP address of pₙ⟩;
18           continue;
           }
19         if((j == kᵢ − 1) && (p_{A2} doesn't store ⟨KEY₁, IP address of a node ⟩))
20           p_{A2} store a pair ⟨KEY₁, IP address of pₙ⟩;
         }
       }
     }
21   else{// cⁱ is the non-dominant class of pₙ
22     KEY₃ ← c₀ⁱ|c₁ⁱ|...|c_{kᵢ}ⁱ ;
23     if(the number of documents in class KEY₃ ≥ THRESHOLD) {
24       A3 ← hash(KEY₃);
25       Find the node p_{A3} whose zone contains the point A3;
26       if(p_{A3} stores a pair ⟨KEY₃, IP address of a node p_{k3}⟩){
27         p_{k3} stores the IP address of pₙ in the BlueEdgeList for KEY₃;
28         pₙ stores the IP address of p_{k3} in the BlueEdgeList for KEY₃;
       }
     }
   }
 }
```

Before joining the system, a node p_n first runs the document classifier F on all its documents. If there hasn't been any node whose dominant class is $c^*(p_n)$ in the system, p_n joins the routing of CAN by randomly choosing a point on the boundary of the coordinate space, inserts a pair $\langle Key, Value \rangle$ in CAN where Key is $c^*(p_n)$ and Value is its IP address and zone, and also places the $\langle Key, Value \rangle$ pair at the node storing a pair $\langle Key', Value' \rangle$ where Key' is a super class of $c^*(p_n)$. Otherwise, p_n gets its zone from one of the nodes in cluster($c^*(p_n)$), and joins the "cluster". At the same time, p_n also joins SPN(c) for each $c \in (C(p_n) - \{c^*(p_n)\})$ by simply finding a node p_d in cluster(c) and connecting to it by a blue edge. If the number of documents in a certain class c is less than the THRESHOLD ($THRESHOLD \geq 1$) prescribed by the system, we do not have it join SPN(c) since it contributes very little to the SPN as far as the maintenance overhead it brings about is concerned. If the THRESHOLD is set to 1, then all nodes with a class c join the SPN(c). Specifically, the node p_n joins the system according to the NodeJoin algorithm as above. Fig. 2 shows an example of a possible result of using this algorithm in a 2-dimensional CAN.

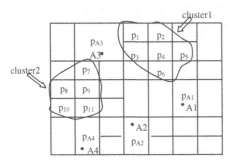

cluster1: nodes with the dominant class $c_0|c_1|c_2|c_3|c_4$
cluster2: nodes with the dominant class c $_0|c_1|c_2$
point A1=hash ($c_0|c_1$)
point A2=hash ($c_0|c_1|c_2$)
point A3=hash ($c_0|c_1|c_2|c_3$)
point A4=hash ($c_0|c_1|c_2|c_3|c_4$)
node p_{A4} stores $< c_0|c_1|c_2|c_3|c_4$, IP address of $p_1>$
node p_{A2} stores $< c_0|c_1|c_2$, IP address of $p_7>$
   and $< c_0|c_1|c_2|c_3|c_4$, IP address of $p_1 >$
node p_{A1} stores $< c_0|c_1|c_2$, IP address of $p_7>$

Fig. 2. Example a possible result of using NodeJoin algorithm in a 2-dimensional CAN

In Fig. 3a we illustrate an entire classification hierarchy for all the documents. In Fig. 3b, we show a partial classification hierarchy formed by the current classes in the system. Such a classification hierarchy is "embedded" into CAN, and is actually maintained by the nodes storing $\langle Key, Value \rangle$ pairs, each $\langle Key, Value \rangle$ pair pointing to a node in cluster(Key).

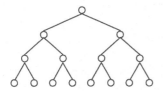   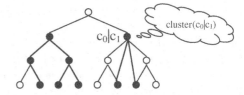

a) An entire classification hierarchy   b) A partial classification hierarchy formed by
                                                the current documents in the system

Fig. 3. Example a classification hierarchy "embedded" in the system

Let us now analyze the efficiency of a node's joining the system. Since the documents of each node can be classified offline, we do not consider the complexity of classification. If the documents of a node are classified into L classes and the maximum level of the classes is level K, then it takes $O(KLdN^{\frac{1}{d}})$ overlay hops to join the system in a d-dimensional CAN. We can make tradeoffs between the efficiency of joining the system and the precision of classification.

3.3 SPNs Maintenance

In addition to basic node departure and recovery that can be handled by CAN, some additional maintenance of SPNs should be done. Consider the following situations: when joining the system, a node may fail to find any node to connect to by a blue edge for some non-dominant class c at the 26th step of the NodeJoin algorithm even if the THRESHOLD is set to 1, because there is no node whose dominant class is c in the system currently. With the evolvement of the system, it is possible that some nodes with the dominant class c join the system and a "cluster" of nodes with the dominant class c be formed. Unfortunately, none of the nodes in cluster(c) knows the existence of the "remote" node. On the other hand, nodes may add new documents and delete old ones, so the formerly dominant classes may be changed accordingly. To adapt to these situations, each node periodically updates the BlueEdgeLists for each of its classes, and/or leaves the current "cluster" to join a new one if its dominant class is changed greatly. If a node p_i still has not found any node for a certain BlueEdgeList related to a class c' for many periods, which suggests that nodes with the class c' are not connected to each other, it temporarily takes c' as its virtual dominant class, and inserts a pair $\langle c'(virtual),\ IP\ address\ of\ p_i \rangle$ in CAN to have it connected by other nodes with non-dominant class c'. When a node p_j with the real dominant class c' joins the system, it replaces $\langle c'(virtual),\ IP\ address\ of\ p_i \rangle$ with $\langle c',\ IP\ address\ of\ p_j \rangle$.

We observe that after the first node p_k with the dominant class $c^*(p_k)$ joined the system, all the subsequent nodes with the same dominant class will split the zone occupied by p_k according to the 7th step of the NodeJoin algorithm, and all nodes with a non-dominant class $c^*(p_k)$ will connect to p_k by blue edges according to the 28th step of the algorithm. This results in two ill effects: For one thing, the zone occupied by p_k will become smaller and smaller relative to other nodes in cluster($c^*(p_k)$), leading to an extremely nonuniform partitioning of the space. For another, the connections needed to be handled by p_k will become more and more, resulting in an unbalanced load distribution. To address this problem, the node $p_{k'}$ with the largest volume of zone in cluster($c^*(p_k)$) is periodically selected. Then $p_{k'}$ inserts a pair $\langle c^*(p_k),\ IP\ address\ of\ p_{k'} \rangle$ to replace the pair $\langle c^*(p_k),\ IP\ address\ of\ p_k \rangle$.

To maintain the logically hierarchical organization of SPNs, each node storing a pair $\langle Key,\ Value \rangle$ periodically places the pair $\langle Key,\ Value \rangle$ at the node storing a pair $\langle Key',\ Value' \rangle$ where class Key' is the nearest ancestor of class Key (class Key' can be easily parsed from class Key by our naming mechanism for classes). If the node storing the pair $\langle Key',\ Value' \rangle$ finds that there are such pairs as $\langle Key,\ Value \rangle$ and $\langle Key'',\ Value'' \rangle$ stored at it where both Key and Key'' are subclasses of Key' while Key'' is also a subclass of Key, then only the pair $\langle Key,\ Value \rangle$ is reserved and the other pair $\langle Key'',\ Value'' \rangle$ is deleted.

Now we present a notion of a peer group. A Peer Group derived from a node p_i, denoted by $PG(p_i)$, is defined as a set of nodes which can be searched by recursively traversing the GreenEdgeLists from p_i, plus the nodes in the BlueEdge-List related to the class $c^*(p_i)$ of each node searched. Formally, $PG(p_i)\ =$

$cluster(c^*(p_i)) \cup \{p_j \in P \mid \exists \text{ } a \text{ } node \text{ } p_k \in cluster(c^*(p_i)), \text{ } such \text{ } that \text{ } p_j \text{ } is \text{ } stored \text{ } in$
$the \text{ } BlueEdgeList \text{ } related \text{ } to \text{ } c^*(p_i) \text{ } of \text{ } p_k\}$. It is clear that all nodes in $\mathrm{PG}(p_i)$
have a class $c^*(p_i)$. Moreover, if the THRESHOLD is set to one, each node with a
class $c^*(p_i)$ in the system belongs to $PG(p_i)$ too. That is, the peer group derived
from node p_i is the set of nodes in a semantic peer-to-peer network $SPN(c^*(p_i))$.

4   Searching SPNs

Similar to searches in WEB, users are not satisfied with a single answer but with
a small set of the whole matches. So we present our searching algorithm that
returns a certain number of results matching queries.

Given a query, the query classifier, which can be implemented by using a
proper classification algorithm (e.g. [7][11][17]), is first invoked to classify the
query. After the query is classified, it is sent to the appropriate SPNs. Since
the query may be classified imprecisely, we consider all the subclasses and super classes (excluding the class at the root) of the classification result and the
query is flooded in all the corresponding SPNs until enough results are found. To
address the message duplication issue inherent in flooding, we can employ the
method of multiple-walker random walks presented in [9] to forward the query
and set different TTLs (Time-To-Live) for different SPNs to terminate the query
propagation respectively. The searching algorithm is described as follows.

Pseudocode for SearchingSPNs algorithm

```
void SearchingSPNs(String Q, int γ ) {
   //The number of results γ is given by users or bounded by the system
   //Assuming that the query Q is classified as c (c = c₀|c₁|...|cₖ, k ≥ 1).
   for(i = 0; i ≤ k − 1; i + +){
      KEY ← c₀|c₁|...|cₖ₋ᵢ;
      A← hash(KEY) ;//KEY is mapped onto a point A in the CAN space
      Find the node pₐ whose zone contains the point A;
      if(pₐ stores a pair ⟨KEY, IP address of a node ⟩)
         break;
   }
   FloodingBySubclass(KEY);
   FloodingBySuperclass(KEY);
}
void FloodingBySubclass( String c) {
   A← hash(c);
   Find the node pₐ whose zone contains the point A;
   if( pₐ stores a pair ⟨c, IP address of a node pc ⟩){
      Flood Q in PG(pc) until γ results are found or the TTL reaches 0;
      for each ⟨c′,Value ⟩ stored at the node pₐ
         if( class c′ is a subclass of c) FloodingBySubclass(c′);
   }
}
```

```
void FloodingBySuperclass(String c){ //Assume that c = c₀|c₁|...|cₜ(1 < t ≤ k)
  for(i = 1; i ≤ t - 1; i + +){
    KEY=c₀|c₁|...|cₜ₋ᵢ;
    A← hash(KEY) ;
    Find the node pₐ whose zone contains the point A;
    if( pₐ stores a pair ⟨KEY, IP address of a node pₖ ⟩)
      Flood Q in PG(pₖ) until γ results are found or the TTL reaches 0;
  }
}
```

5 Solutions to Hot Spots

Each node storing a pair $\langle Key, Value \rangle$ is frequently visited, and is possibly overloaded. To alleviate such hot spots, we present the following three solutions.

5.1 Using Multiple Hash Functions

Multiple hash functions are used in CAN for improving data availability, and are used in [2] to achieve better load balancing for DHTs. Here, we use this simple method to alleviate hot spots. If a node p_i is the first one with the dominant class $c^*(p_i)$ joining the system, it uses h different, but universally agreed hash functions to map $c^*(p_i)$ onto h points in the coordinate space of CAN, so a single pair $\langle c^*(p_i), \text{ } IP \text{ } address \text{ } of \text{ } p_i \rangle$ can be replicated at h distinct nodes in the system. When other nodes with the class $c^*(p_i)$ join the system subsequently, they choose uniformly and randomly a hash function to map the key $c^*(p_i)$, and visit one of the nodes storing $\langle c^*(p_i), \text{ } IP \text{ } address \text{ } of \text{ } p_i \rangle$.

5.2 Exploiting Heterogeneity

It has been shown in [13] that there is significant heterogeneity in P2P systems. Exploiting heterogeneity, we can make the node with more powerful processing, storage, and bandwidth capabilities store $\langle Key, Value \rangle$ pairs. The main approach is as follows. Each node p_i storing $\langle Key, Value \rangle$ pairs periodically broadcast "election" messages in cluster($c^*(p_i)$), and the most powerful node p_j not storing any $\langle Key', Value' \rangle$ pairs is elected. Then the two nodes exchange their zones, GreenEdgeList, RedEdgeList and $\langle Key, Value \rangle$ pairs. Finally, they inform their neighbors of such changes. Note that they need not exchange their BlueEdgeLists since they are in the same cluster.

5.3 Using Replication

Replication is a commonly used technique for avoiding hot spots. Each node in cluster(c) naturally has a replication of the Key c. So if a routing path between the querying node and the node storing the desired pair $\langle c, Value \rangle$ traverses the

can be easily handled. We showed that the search performance of SPNs is significantly improved by focusing the query propagation only in appropriate SPNs, and can also be made tradeoff with the level of recall. We argue that large-scale P2P searching systems supporting efficient partial-match queries, which are vital to the success of P2P file sharing systems, can be implemented with SPNs.

References

1. Lee Breslau, Pei Cao, Li Fan, Graham Philips, Scott Shenker. Web Caching and Zipf-like Distributions: Evidence and Implications. In IEEE INFOCOM, 1999.
2. J. Byers, J. Considine, M. Mitzenmacher. Simple Load Balancing for Distributed Hash Tables. In 2nd International Workshop on Peer-to-Peer Systems (IPTPS'03).
3. E. Cohen, A. Fiat, H. Kaplan. Associative Search in Peer to Peer Networks: Harnessing Latent Semantics. In IEEE INFOCOM 2003.
4. A. Crespo and H. Garcia-Molina. Routing indices for peer-to-peer systems. In Proceedings of the 22nd IEEE International Conference on Distributed Computing Systems (ICDCS), July 2002.
5. A. Crespo and H. Garcia-Molina. Semantic Overlay Networks, Submitted for Publication. http://www-db.stanford.edu/~crespo/publications/op2p.pdf.
6. Gnutella website. http://www.gnutella.com.
7. T. Joachims. Text categorization with Support Vector Machines: Learning with many relevant features. In Machine Learning: ECML-98, Tenth European Conference on Machine Learning.
8. P. Keleher, S. Bhattacharjee, and B. Silaghi. Are virtualized overlay networks too much of a good thing? In First International Workshop on Peer-to-Peer Systems (IPTPS 02), March 2002.
9. Q. Lv, P. Cao, E. Cohen, K. Li, and S. Shenker. Search and replication in unstructured peer to peer networks. In Proceedings of the 16th annual ACM International Conference on supercomputing, 2002.
10. S. Ratnasamy, P. Francis, M. Handley, R. Karp, and S. Shenker, A scalable content addressable network. In Proc. ACM SIGCOMM, 2001.
11. B. R.-N. R. Baeza-Yates, Modern Information Retrieval, Addison-Wesley, 1999.
12. A. Rowstron and P. Druschel, Pastry: Scalable, distributed object location and routing for large-scale peer-to-peer systems. IFIP/ACM International Conference on Distributed Systems Platforms (Middleware), November 2001.
13. S. Saroiu, P. Gummadi, and S. Gribble. A Measurement Study of Peer-to-Peer File Sharing Systems. In MMCN, 2002.
14. K. Sripanidkulchai, B. Maggs, and H. Zhang. Efficient Content Location Using Interest-Based Locality in Peer-to-Peer Systems, In IEEE INFOCOM 2003.
15. I. Stoica, R. Morris, D. Karger, M. F.Kaashoek, and H. Balakrishnan, Chord: A scalable peer-to-peer lookup service for internet applications. In Proc. ACM SIGCOMM, August 2001.
16. P. Trianta.llou, C. Xiruhaki, M. Koubarakis, and N. Ntarmos. Towards high performance peer-to-peer content and resource sharing systems. In CIDR, 2003.
17. I. Witten and E. Frank. Data Mining. Morgan Kaufmann Publishers, 1999.
18. B. Yang, H. Garcia-Molina , Efficient Search in Peer-to-Peer Networks. In Proceedings of the 22nd IEEE International Conference on Distributed Computing Systems (ICDCS), July 2002.
19. Y. Zhao, J. Kubiatowicz, and A. Joseph, Tapestry: An infrastructure for fault-tolerant wide-area location and routing, Technical report, U. C. Berkeley, 2001.

Adding Reliable and Self-healing Key Distribution to the Subset Difference Group Rekeying Method for Secure Multicast

Sencun Zhu, Sanjeev Setia, and Sushil Jajodia

Center for Secure Information Systems, George Mason University, Fairfax, VA 22030
{szhu1,setia,jajodia}@gmu.edu

Abstract. We study two important issues related to the Subset Difference Rekeying (SDR) method [4]. First, we present a reliable key distribution scheme, called WFEC-BKR, that enables members to receive the current group key in a reliable and timely fashion inspite of packet losses in the network. Through simulation, we show that in most scenarios, WFEC-BKR outperforms previously proposed schemes for reliable rekey transport. Second, we present a group key recovery scheme that adds the self-healing property to SDR, i.e., our scheme enables a member that has missed up to a certain number m of previous rekey operations to recover the missing group keys without asking the key server for retransmission. The additional communication overhead imposed by our key recovery scheme is quite small (less than $3m$ additional keys).

1 Introduction

In recent years, many approaches for scalable group rekeying have been proposed, e.g. LKH [8,9,11], OFT [1], MARKS [2], Subset Difference [4] and self-healing [6]. Further, it has been proposed that groups be re-keyed periodically instead of on every membership change [5,10]. Periodic or batched rekeying can reduce both the processing and communication overhead at the key server, and improve the scalability and performance of key management protocols based on logical key trees.

In addition to the rekeying algorithm, the communication overhead of group rekeying also depends on the protocol used for reliably delivering the updated keys to the members of the group. Recently, researchers have proposed customized reliable multicast protocols for group rekeying, e.g., Proactive-FEC [10] and WKA-BKR [7], which take advantage of the special properties of the rekey payload for achieving reduced communication overhead in comparison to conventional reliable multicast protocols.

Among the rekeying protocols proposed in the literature, the Subset Difference Rekeying method (SDR) [4] is one of the few protocols that have the property of *statelessness*. In a stateless rekeying protocol, in order to decode the current group key, a member only needs to receive the keys that are transmitted by the key server during the current rekey operation. This property makes SDR

B. Stiller et al. (Eds.): NGC/ICQT 2003, LNCS 2816, pp. 107–118, 2003.

very attractive for secure multicast applications where members may go off-line frequently or experience burst packet losses. Furthermore, SDR has been shown to be very efficient in terms of communication overhead.

In this paper, we study two important issues related to the key delivery protocol used for the SDR method. First, we address the issue of reliable rekey transport for SDR. We present a key distribution scheme, called WFEC-BKR, that enables members to receive the current group key in a reliable and timely fashion despite the presence of packet losses in the network. WFEC-BKR is a hybrid protocol that combines the advantages of two previously proposed rekey transport protocols – the proactive FEC based key delivery protocol [10] and the WKA-BKR protocol [7]. Through simulation, we show that in most scenarios, WFEC-BKR outperforms the other rekey transport protocols.

Second, we examine the issue of *self-healing* group key distribution for SDR. We present a key recovery scheme that adds the self-healing property to SDR, i.e., the scheme enables a member that has missed up to a certain number m of previous rekey operations to recover the missing group keys without asking the key server for retransmission. This self-healing key recovery property results in reduced network traffic and also reduces the load on the key server, and is especially useful for group members that may experience burst packet losses. Through a detailed simulation, we found that the communication overhead imposed on the key server by our recovery scheme is quite small (less than $3m$ additional keys).

The reminder of this paper is organized as follows. In Section 2, we discuss related work and introduce the SDR method in more detail. In Section 3 we present our hybrid reliable key distribution scheme and evaluate its performance through detailed simulation. Section 4 describes our key recovery schemes and its performance. Finally, we summarize our work in Section 5.

2   Related Work

The group rekeying protocols proposed in the literature can be divided into stateful and stateless protocols. The stateful class of protocols includes several protocols based upon the use of logical key trees, e.g., LKH [8,9] and OFT [1]. In these protocols, a member must have received all the key encryption keys of interest in all the previous rekey operations; otherwise, it will be unable to decode the new (group) key being transmitted during the current rekeying operation, and will have to ask the key server to retransmit any keys it is missing. Among these protocols, neither LKH nor OFT includes any mechanisms for reliable key distribution. To address the issue of reliable key delivery for these group rekeying approaches, researchers have proposed protocols based on the use of proactive redundancy such as the proactive-FEC based key delivery protocol [10] and WKA-BKR [7]. However, these protocols only address the issue of reliable key delivery for the *current* rekeying operation.

Stateless group rekeying protocols form the second class of rekey protocols. In these protocols, a legitimate user only needs to receive the keys of interest in the current rekey operation to decode the current group key. In other words, there is no dependency between the keys used in different rekeying operations. One such protocol is the subset difference rekeying method (SDR) presented by Naor *et al* [4]. In SDR, the key server maintains a logical key tree and every member is mapped to a leaf node of the key tree. During a rekey operation the key server partitions the current members of the group into a minimal number of subsets (called a *subset cover*), and then encrypts the new group key with the common key of each subset separately. Naor *et al* show that the average number of subsets is $1.25r$ when there are totally r revoked users in the system. Thus, the communication complexity (i.e., the number of subsets) is independent of the group size, which makes this algorithm very scalable, particularly when $r \ll |N|$ (Chen and Dondeti [3] show that SDR performs better than LKH for rekeying of large batches). The number of keys stored by each user is $0.5log^2|N|$.

Another example of a stateless protocol is the self-healing key delivery protocol proposed by Staddon *et al* [6]. In addition to statelessness, this protocol has the property (referred to as self-healing) that a group member that has not received a previous group key (due to network packet loss) can recover that group key *on its own* without contacting the key server. The self-healing protocol is based on polynomial-based secret sharing techniques. We note that this protocol has two limitations that may discourage its deployment for some applications. First, in this protocol, an application's lifetime is pre-divided into a certain number of sessions, and the key server initiates a group rekeying at the beginning of each session. Thus, this protocol is not suitable for applications which have a security requirement of immediate user revocation. Second, the maximum allowed number of revoked users during these these sessions has to be pre-determined and must not be exceeded for the protocol to be secure. In Section 4, using techniques such as one-way key chains, we propose a protocol that adds the self-healing property to the SDR method with very small additional overhead. In addition, our protocol can perform immediate group rekeyings and there is no upper bound on the number of revoked users.

We note that periodic batched rekeying has been shown to improve the scalability and performance of group key management protocols [5,10]. As such, in this paper we discuss our key delivery schemes for SDR in the context of periodic batched rekeying. (Note, however, that our key delivery schemes can be used for both individual and batched rekeying.)

3   Reliable Key Delivery for SDR

In a group rekeying, the key server first executes the SDR algorithm to determine the subset cover for all the current members of the group. Then it generates a new group key, and encrypts the group key separately with the common key of each subset in the subset cover. Finally, it multicasts all the encrypted keys to the group. The question we wish to address is: how can every on-line user receive the new group key in a reliable and timely fashion in the presence of packet losses in network?

Previous work on the problem of reliable key delivery such proactive FEC based key delivery protocol [10] and WKA-BKR [7] has focussed on the LKH algorithm and not on SDR. In this section, we first discuss the application of these approaches to SDR and then present an improved hybrid approach called WFEC-BKR.

Proactive FEC-Based Key Delivery. In the proactive FEC-based approach [10], the key server packs the encrypted keys into packets of s_k keys. These packets are divided into FEC blocks of k packets. The key server then generates $\lceil (\rho - 1)k \rceil$ parity packets for each block based on Reed Solomon Erasure (RSE) correcting codes, where $\rho \geq 1$ is the pro-activity factor. A user interested in the packets from a certain block can recover all the original packets in the block as long as it receives any k out of $\lceil k\rho \rceil$ packets from the block. If a user does not receive a packet that contains the encrypted key of interest to it, but it receives $t(t < k)$ packets from the block that contains this packet, it will ask the key server for retransmission of $k - t$ new parity packets. The key server collects all the retransmission requests, and then for each block it generates and transmits the *maximum* number of new parity packets required by users. The retransmission phase continues until all the users have successfully received their keys.

WKA-BKR. The WKA-BKR scheme [7] uses a simple packet replication technique in which packets are transmitted multiple times, but it takes advantage of two properties of the rekey transport payload to minimize the overall bandwidth overhead of a rekey operation. First, the encrypted keys are assigned different replication weights, depending on the number of users interested in them and the loss rates of these users. Clearly, when a subset in the SDR method covers a larger number of users or these users have higher loss rates, the encrypted key for this subset should be given a higher degree of replication so that most of these users will receive the key reliably. Hence, in this scheme the key server first determines the weight w_i for each encrypted key K_i based upon the users interested in that key. It then packs the keys that have the same weight $\lfloor w_i \rfloor$ into the set of packets p_i. When broadcasting the packets, the key server sends packets in p_i $\lfloor w_i \rfloor$ times. This process is called weighted key assignment (WKA). Second, during the retransmission phase, since each user that has made a retransmission request only needs one encrypted key to decode the current group key, there is no need for the key server to retransmit the entire packet sent in the previous round that contained the requested key. Instead, the key server repackages the keys that need to be retransmitted into new packets before retransmitting them. This process is called batched key retransmission (BKR). The WKA-BKR scheme has been shown to have a lower bandwidth overhead than the other schemes in most scenarios.

3.1   WFEC-BKR: A Hybrid Approach

In our comparative performance evaluation of the proactive-FEC based scheme and the WKA-BKR scheme [7], we found that one reason that WKA-BKR has a lower bandwidth overhead than the proactive FEC-based approach is due to the bandwidth efficiency of its retransmission scheme, i.e., BKR. In the proactive FEC based approach, the key server retransmits the *maximum* number of required parity packets for each block. Therefore, the bandwidth overhead is dominated by retransmissions due to users experiencing high packet losses. On the other hand, we found that the proactive FEC-based approach usually has a smaller bandwidth overhead than WKA-BKR in the first round of transmission, especially when the weights of many packets in WKA are larger than 2. This is because RSE encoding used in FEC is more efficient than the simple replication used in WKA. Further, we found that proactive FEC-based protocols have a lower latency of key delivery than WKA-BKR. Based on these observations, we propose a hybrid scheme, called WFEC-BKR, which is a combination of weighted FEC and BKR.

In WFEC-BKR, the key server first packs the encrypted keys into s_p packets of s_k keys, and then divides the packets into s_b blocks of k packets. The key server then chooses an appropriate ρ and generates $\lceil (\rho - 1)k \rceil$ parity packets for each block, based on the analysis in Section 3.2. Finally, it broadcasts all the packets. In the retransmission phase, a user that has not received its key reports the missing key. The key server collects all the retransmission requests, repackages the requested keys into new packets, and then broadcasts these packets. This process is repeated until all users have received their keys successfully.

3.2   Determining the Proactivity Factor ρ

We note that, unlike the proactive FEC-based protocol discussed in [10], in our protocol the proactivity factor for different FEC blocks will typically be different depending upon the number of users interested in the keys in a particular block as well as the estimated packet loss rates of these users.

Now we consider the issue of selecting an appropriate proactivity factor ρ for each FEC block. Clearly, increasing ρ results in reduced latency at the expense of increased bandwidth overhead. We now sketch an approach that can be used to determine the ρ for each block, based on the number of users interested in the keys in each block and the loss probabilities of these users (a user can estimate its packet loss rate and piggyback this information in the NACK it sends to the key server.). Thus, we can use this approach to obtain a reasonable initial set of parameters (ρ and k) that can balance the bandwidth overhead with the key delivery latency.

Consider a user u_i with a loss probability p_i. Recall that each user is interested in exactly one key (say K) out of the keys transmitted by the key server. Let ρ_x be the proactivity factor for the FEC block B_x that contains K and let k denote the FEC block size. Let $L_x = \lceil k\rho_x \rceil$. The probability that u_i receives the packet that contains K is $1 - p_i$. In the event it does not receive the packet that contains K, it is still able to reconstruct that packet if it receives at least any k other packets out of the L_x packets in the FEC block. Therefore, the probability $p(x, i)$ that it will receive K in the first round of transmission is

$$p(x, i) = (1 - p_i) + p_i (\sum_{j=k}^{L_x - 1} \binom{L_x - 1}{j} (1 - p_i)^j (p_i^{L_x - j - 1})). \tag{1}$$

Using this approach, the key server can compute the probabilities $p(x, i)$ for all the users u_i interested in the key K. By repeating this process for all the keys in a block, adding together all the probabilities $p(x, j)$, where u_j is a user interested in one of the keys in the block B_x, and dividing the sum of the probabilities by the total number of users interested in the keys in the block, we can obtain the expected value of f_x, the fraction of users interested in the keys in block B_x that will receive their keys in the first round of the key delivery protocol.

3.3   Performance Evaluation

Metrics and Simulation Model. In this section, we evaluate the performance of WFEC-BKR scheme by comparing it to that of the proactive FEC and the WKA-BKR schemes. We use two metrics in this evaluation: (i) the *average bandwidth overhead* at the key server, defined as the ratio of the total bandwidth (including the bandwidth of the original rekey payload and the replicated and the retransmitted packets) to the bandwidth of the original rekey payload, and (ii) the *fraction of members who successfully receive the group key in the first (transmission) round* of the key delivery protocol. The second metric reflects the latency of group rekeying.

The results are obtained via simulation using a heterogeneous network packet loss model in which a fraction $\alpha = 20\%$ of the receivers have a high packet loss probability $p_h = 0.2$, whereas the remaining receivers have a low packet loss probability $p_l = 0.02$. The packet loss a user experiences is assumed to be independent. We examine the performance of the schemes using the following group characteristics. The key server constructs a binary key tree of height 13, knowing that the maximum number of users who join the group over the lifetime of the application will not exceed $2^{13} = 8092$. Initially, we assume that there are 5000 users in the group. At each rekeying event, the group membership of 100 (randomly selected) users is revoked and 100 new users join the group.

We use the method of independent replications for our simulations and all our results have 95% confidence intervals that are within 1% of the reported value. In our discussion below, we use FEC(x) to denote the proactive FEC based key delivery protocol [10] with pro-activity factor x, and WFEC(x)-BKR to denote the hybrid scheme which uses pro-activity factor x for the first round transmission and then uses BKR for retransmission.

Results

Bandwidth Overhead. Fig. 1 plots the rekeying bandwidth overhead (y-axis) of the schemes for 30 consecutive rekeying events (x-axis). We can make the following observations from this figure. First, overall, the hybrid scheme WFEC(1.2)-BKR has the smallest bandwidth overhead, whereas FEC(1.2) has the second largest bandwidth overhead (only slightly lower than FEC(1.6)). The difference between WFEC(1.2)-BKR and FEC(1.2) is significant. Since WFEC(1.2)-BKR and FEC(1.2) have the same bandwidth overhead for replication in the first round of transmission, the difference indicates that batched key retransmission is more efficient than retransmitting the maximum number of required parity packets for each block. Note that WFEC(1.6)-BKR outperforms FEC(1.6) due to the same reason.

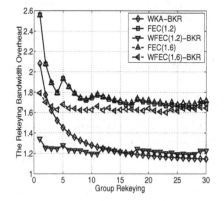 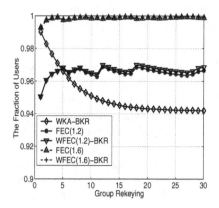

Fig. 1. Key server bandwidth overhead for different rekeying events.

Fig. 2. The fraction of members who receive their keys in the first round.

Second, the WKA-BKR scheme has a high bandwidth overhead at the beginning of the simulation, but the overhead decreases with each rekeying event. In stateful protocols such as LKH, the bandwidth overhead of WKA-BKR and FEC is mainly a function of the group size and the number of joins and leaves being processed as a batch [10,7]. Since each rekeying event in our simulation has the same number of member joins and leaves, we would not expect there to be much variation in the bandwidth overhead for different rekeying events for LKH. In contrast, for SDR the bandwidth overhead of WKA-BKR depends upon the sizes of the subsets in the subset cover. The composition of the subset cover tends to change over time. For example, the subset to which a user belongs is split when another user from the same subset is revoked and this results in two smaller subsets. As more users leave the group, most subsets become very small; as a result, their replication weights under WKA-BKR are also reduced, leading to a lower overall bandwidth overhead.

Third, the curves for FEC fluctuate at some rekeying points while the curve for WKA-BKR is very smooth. This fluctuation arises from the use of different FEC block sizes k for different rekeying events in order to minimize the overhead of packet padding.

Latency. In Fig. 2 we plot the fraction (f_r) of users who receive the group key in the first (transmission) round of the key delivery protocol for 30 consecutive rekey events. We observe that FEC(1.2) and WFEC(1.2)-BKR have the same latency as do FEC(1.6) and WFEC(1.6)-BKR. However, f_r is larger than 0.99 for FEC(1.6) and WFEC(1.6)-BKR, whereas it is around 0.97 for FEC(1.2) and WFEC(1.2)-BKR. This is not surprising since the degree of redundancy in FEC(1.6) is larger than that in FEC(1.2). For WKA-BKR, f_r decreases over time since the replication weights used by the WKA algorithm tend to be reduced as discussed above.

Overall, from Figures 1 and 2, we can conclude that WFEC-BKR has low bandwidth overhead (comparable to that of WKA-BKR), and relatively low latency (comparable to that of proactive FEC-based key delivery).

4   Self-healing Key Delivery for SDR

The reliable key delivery protocols discussed in Section 3 work well for scenarios where a user experiences random packet losses. However, a user might have to request multiple packet retransmissions until it finally receives the encrypted key of interest to it. There is no guarantee that it will receive the group key before the next group rekeying event. This is especially true for users that are experiencing intermittent burst packet losses. Another similar scenario arises when a user is off-line (while still a member of the group) at the time of group rekeying. If the user receives data that was encrypted using a group key that it has not received, it will need to obtain that group key.

A self-healing key delivery protocol allows a user to obtain missing group keys on its own without requesting a retransmission from the key server. This is accomplished by combining information from the current key update broadcast with information received in previous key update broadcasts. In this section, we will discuss two schemes that add the self-healing property to SDR. We say a scheme has *m-recoverability* if the maximum number of previous group keys a legitimate user can recover is m.

4.1   Scheme I: The Basic Scheme

Figure 3 shows a sequence of rekeying events. Let $T(i)$ be the current rekeying time, and $K(i)$ is the new group key to be distributed. A simple approach that enables a current member to recover the previous m group keys, i.e., $K(i - m), K(i - m + 1), ..., K(i - 2), K(i - 1)$, is to encrypt these m keys with the current group key $K(i)$ individually and broadcast them to the group. Hence, as long as a user receives $K(i)$ reliably (e.g., through WFEC-BKR), it will be able to recover the previous m keys. However, this approach does not enforce *backward confidentiality* [9], because a newly joined user can also recover these keys.

To solve this problem, it is important to bind the time at which user joined the group with its ability to recover a previous group key. In other words, a user should only allowed to recover the group keys that were used after it joined the group. To achieve this goal, in our scheme the key server encrypts each group

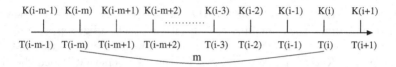

Fig. 3. Recovering the previous group keys, here $T(i)$ is the current rekey time.

key, $K(i-j), 1 \leq j \leq m$ with a key that is derived by XORing the current group key $K(i)$ with the group key $K(j-1)$. Thus, the key server broadcasts m encrypted keys as follows:

$$KeyServer \longrightarrow * : \{K(i-m)\}_{K(i-m-1) \oplus K(i)}, \{K(i-m+1)\}_{K(i-m) \oplus K(i)}, ...,$$
$$\{K(i-1)\}_{K(i-2) \oplus K(i)},$$

where $\oplus$ is the XOR operation and $\{K2\}_{K1}$ means encrypting key $K2$ with key $K1$. A user that joined the group at time $T(j)$, $i - m < j < i$, and received $K(j)$ can recover all the keys between $K(j)$ and $K(i)$ after it receives $K(i)$. A newly joined user, i.e., a user joining at $T(i)$, cannot recover the previous keys because it does not hold any previous keys. On the other hand, a user that was off-line for more than m rekeying periods cannot recover these previous keys. The communication cost is m keys for this basic scheme.

However, there are two scenarios where the security of this scheme may be compromised. The first scenario arises when a revoked user joins the group again some time in the future. For instance, a user that left the group at $T(j)$, $i - m < j < i$, and rejoins at $T(i)$ will be able to recover all the keys between $K(j)$ and $K(i)$ based on $K(j-1)$ and $K(i)$. A similar scenario arises when a user that has left the group or whose membership was revoked colludes with a newly joined user. In the above example, a user whose membership was revoked at time $T(j)$ and has the key $K(j-1)$ could collude with a newly joined user who has $K(i)$ to recover the intermediate keys that they are not authorized to have.

4.2   Scheme II: Dealing with the Rejoining/Colluding Attack

We now propose an extension to the basic scheme that addresses the rejoining/colluding attack described above. The key idea is to bind the ability of a user to recover a previous group key not only to the time at which it became a member but also to its membership duration. The scheme involves the following steps.

1. In each group rekeying, the key server generates a key chain of size $m + 1$. Let the keys in the key chain generated for the rekeying at $T(i)$ be $K^m(i), K^{m-1}(i), ..., K^1(i), K^0(i)$, where $K^0(i) = H(K^1(i)) = H^2(K^2(i)) = ... = H^m(K^m(i))$ and H is a one-way hash function such as SHA-1. Due to the one-wayness of the hash function, a user knowing $K^j(i)$ can compute all the keys $K^{j-1}(i), ..., K^0(i)$ independently, but it cannot compute any of the keys $K^{j+1}(i), ..., K^m(i)$. $K^0(i)$ is the group key that all the users should use for data encryption between $T(i)$ and $T(i+1)$.

2. The users in the group are considered to be partitioned into $m+1$ subgroups, depending upon their membership duration. Each subgroup is associated with a separate key from the one-way key chain generated in the first step. Specifically, $K^j(i)$ is the key intended for the members that joined the group at $T(i-j)$ for $0 \le j < m$, and $K^m(i)$ is the key intended for members that joined at or before $T(i-m)$. The algorithm used for key distribution is discussed in more detail later in this section.

3. The key server broadcasts m encrypted keys as shown below:

$$KeyServer \longrightarrow * : \ \{K^0(i-m)\}_{K^0(i-m-1)\oplus K^m(i)}, \cdots,$$
$$\{K^0(i-2)\}_{K^0(i-3)\oplus K^2(i)}, \{K^0(i-1)\}_{K^0(i-2)\oplus K^1(i)}.$$

From step 3, we can see clearly that the ability of a user to recover previous group keys depends on its membership duration. For a new user that only receives $K^0(i)$, it cannot contribute any keys to help any users whose membership was revoked earlier to recover the previous group keys. For a current member that has been in the group for at least m rekeying periods, it can generate all the keys in the key chain after it receives $K^m(i)$; hence it can recover all the m group keys if it has $K^0(i-m-1)$. For a current member that joined at $T(j)$, $i-m < j < i$, it will receive $K^{i-j}(i)$, which enables it to recover at most the keys between $K^0(j)$ and $K^0(i)$ even when it colludes with the early revoked nodes. But this is not an additional security leak, because the user is authorized to have these keys. Thus, this scheme is secure to the rejoining/colluding attack that appears in Scheme I.

An Example In Fig. 4 we show an example to illustrate scheme II. Let $T(10)$ be the current rekeying time and $m = 5$. Following the algorithm above, the key server first generates a random key $K^5(10)$, based on which it generates a hash key chain $K^5(10), K^4(10), ..., K^1(10), K^0(10)$. The current members of the group are considered to be divided into $m + 1 = 6$ subgroups depending upon their membership duration. The key sent to newly joined members is $K^0(10)$, while the keys sent to the remaining members are as follows: $K^1(10)$ is sent to the users that joined at $T(9)$, $K^2(10)$ is sent to the users that joined at $T(8)$, $K^3(10)$ is sent to the users that joined at $T(7)$, $K^4(10)$ joined at $T(6)$, and $K^5(10)$ to all the users that joined at or before $T(5)$. Finally it broadcasts

$$KeyServer \longrightarrow * : \ \{K^0(5)\}_{K^0(4)\oplus K^5(10)}, \{K^0(6)\}_{K^0(5)\oplus K^4(10)}, \cdots,$$
$$\{K^0(8)\}_{K^0(7)\oplus K^2(10)}, \{K^0(9)\}_{K^0(8)\oplus K^1(10)}.$$

The Key Distribution Algorithm. To evaluate the communication complexity of this scheme, we first discuss the key distribution algorithm that distributes the keys in the key chain to users of different membership durations in step 2 of the scheme. A simple approach for this is to deliver $K^m(i)$ to the current users that joined at or before $T(i-m)$ using the SDR method, while delivering all the keys $K^j(i)$, $m < j \le 0$, to the users that joined at $T(i-j)$ through unicast, encrypted individually with the leaf keys corresponding to these users.

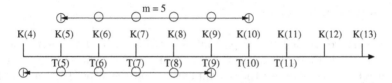

Fig. 4. An example illustrating Scheme II. Here $T(10)$ is the current rekey time.

Let $N(i)$ denote the number of users that join the group between $T(i-1)$ and $T(i)$, then the communication complexity of this scheme is $\sum_{j=i-m}^{i} N(j)$. Thus, the scalability of this approach depends on the arrival rate of the system. Below we present another algorithm that has the communication complexity of $O(m)$.

In SDR, users are mapped into the leaves of the key tree from the left to the right in the same order as their joining times. Hence, all the $N(i)$ users that join between $T(i-1)$ and $T(i)$ and are added into the key tree at $T(i)$ as a batch occupy $N(i)$ consecutive leaves of the key tree. Naturally, they form one or more subsets in the SDR algorithm. The key server uses the following process to determine the number of subsets for these $N(i)$ users:

1. Identifies the minimal full subtree $S(i)$ that covers all these $N(i)$ users. Clearly, the root of this subtree is the least common ancestor of these users.
2. Marks all the leaves in $S(i)$ which are not mapped to any of these $N(i)$ users as revoked.
3. Runs the SDR algorithm to determine the number of subsets for $S(i)$.

The key server maintains a main key tree that corresponds to all the users that joined at least m rekeying periods ago, and m subtrees that correspond to the other users that joined at different rekeying periods. From the mth rekeying on, in every rekeying the key server merges the subtree that corresponds to the users whose membership durations just exceeded m rekeying periods into the main key tree.

As in the original SDR algorithm, the number of subsets in this algorithm increases when users join and leave. The communication complexity of our approach depends upon how many *additional* subsets N_a our algorithm introduces compared to the original SDR algorithm. The value of N_a depends on the group size, the number of arrivals and the number of revoked users in each rekeying period, and the value of m. We studied this issue through extensive simulations. We found that in most cases N_a is smaller than m, whereas in other cases it lies between m and $2m$. Although we do not have an analytical proof for this conclusion, our simulations strongly indicate that the number of additional subsets is less than $2m$. Thus, taking into account the m keys broadcast in step 3 of our scheme, we conclude that we can add the self-healing property to SDR at the expense of transmitting at most $3m$ additional keys.

5 Conclusions

In this paper, we studied two important issues related to the subset difference rekeying method. First, we presented a hybrid key distribution scheme, called WFEC-BKR, that combines the advantages of the proactive FEC and WKA-BKR key delivery protocols. Through simulation, we show that WFEC-BKR has low latency as well as low bandwidth overhead. Second, we present a recovery scheme that adds the self-healing property to SDR with very small additional communication overhead.

References

1. D. Balenson, D. McGrew, and A. Sherman. Key Management for Large Dynamic Groups: One-Way Function Trees and Amortized Initialization. IETF Internet draft (work in progress), August 2000.
2. B. Briscoe. MARKS: Zero Side Effect Multicast Key Management Using Arbitrarily Revealed Key Sequences. In Proc. of First International Workshop on Networked Group Communication, NGC 1999.
3. W.Chen and L.Dondeti. Performance comparison of stateful and stateless group rekeying algorithms. In Proc. of Fourth International Workshop on Networked Group Communication, NGC 2002.
4. D. Naor, M. Naor, and J. Lotspiech. Revocation and Tracing Schemes for Stateless Receivers. In Advances in Cryptology - CRYPTO 2001. Springer-Verlag Inc. LNCS 2139, 2001, 41-62.
5. S. Setia, S. Koussih, S. Jajodia. Kronos: A Scalable Group Re-Keying Approach for Secure Multicast. In Proc. of the IEEE Symposium on Security and Privacy, Oakland CA, May 2000.
6. J. Staddon, S. Miner, M. Franklin, D. Balfanz, M. Malkin and D. Dean. Self-Healing Key Distribution with Revocation. In Proc. of the IEEE Symposium on Security and Privacy, oakland, CA, May 2002.
7. S. Setia, S. Zhu and S. Jajodia. A Comparative Performance Analysis of Reliable Group Rekey Transport Protocols for Secure Multicast. In Performance Evaluation 49(1/4): 21-41 (2002), special issue Proceedings of Performance 2002, Rome, Italy, Sept 2002.
8. C. Wong, M. Gouda, S. Lam. Secure Group Communication Using Key Graphs. In Proc. of SIGCOMM 1998, Vancouver, British Columbia, 68-79.
9. D. Wallner, E. Harder and R. Agee. Key Management for Multicast: Issues and Architecture. Internet Draft, draft-wallner-key-arch-01.txt, September 1998.
10. Y. Yang, X. Li, X. Zhang and S. Lam. Reliable group rekeying: Design and Performance Analysis. In Proc. of ACM SIGCOMM 2001, San Diego, CA, USA, August 2001, 27-38.
11. S. Zhu, S. Setia, and S. Jajodia. Performance Optimizations for Group Key Management Schemes. In Proc. of the 23rd IEEE ICDCS 2003, Providence, RI, May 2003.

Key Bundles and Parcels:
Secure Communication in Many Groups

Eunjin Jung, Xiang-Yang Alex Liu, and Mohamed G. Gouda

Department of Computer Sciences
The University of Texas at Austin
{ejung,alex,gouda}@cs.utexas.edu

Abstract. We consider a system where each user is in one or more elementary groups. In this system, arbitrary groups of users can be specified using the operations of union, intersection, and complement over the elementary groups in the system. Each elementary group in the system is provided with a security key that is known only to the users in the elementary group and to the system server. Thus, for any user u to securely multicast a data item d to every user in an arbitrary group G, u first forwards d to the system server which encrypts it using the keys of the elementary groups that comprise G before multicasting the encrypted d to every user in G. Every elementary group is also provided with a key tree to ensure that the cost of changing the key of the elementary group, when a user leaves the group, is small. We describe two methods for packing the key trees of elementary groups into key bundles and into key parcels. Packing into key bundles has the advantage of reducing the number of encryptions needed to multicast a data item to the complement of an elementary group. Packing into key parcels has the advantage of reducing the total number of keys in the system. We apply these two methods to a class of synthetic systems: each system has 10000 users and 500 elementary groups, and each user is in 2 elementary groups on average. Simulations of these systems show that our proposals to pack key trees into key bundles and key parcels live up to their promises.

1 Introduction

We consider a system that consists of n users denoted u_i, $0 \le i < n$. The system users share one security key, called the system key. Each user u_i can use the system key to encrypt any data item before sending it to any subset of the system users, and can use it to decrypt any data item after receiving it from any other system user. (Examples of such systems are secure multicast systems [1], [2], [3], [4], secure peer-to-peer systems [5], and secure wireless networks [6].)

When a user u_i leaves the system, the system key needs to be changed so that u_i can no longer decrypt the encrypted data item exchanged within the system. This requires to add a server S to the system and to provide each system user u_j with an individual key K_j that only user u_j and server S know. When a user u_i leaves the system, server S changes the system key and sends the new key to

B. Stiller et al. (Eds.): NGC/ICQT 2003, LNCS 2816, pp. 119–130, 2003.
© Springer-Verlag Berlin Heidelberg 2003

each user u_j, other than u_i, encrypted using its individual key K_j. The cost of this rekeying scheme, measured by the number of needed encryptions, is $O(n)$, where n is the number of users in the system.

Clearly, this solution does not scale when the number of users become large. More efficient rekeying schemes have been proposed in [7], [8], [9], [10], [11], and [12]. A particular efficient rekeying scheme [3] and [4] is shown to cost merely $O(\log n)$ encryptions. This scheme is extended in [13], [14], and [15], and is shown to be optimal in [16], and has already been accepted as an Internet standard [3].

This scheme is based on a distributed data structure called a key tree. A *key tree* is a directed, incoming, rooted, balanced tree where each node represents a key. The root of the tree represents the system key and each leaf node represents the individual key of a system user. The number of leaf nodes is n, which is the number of users in the system. Each user knows all the keys on the directed path from its individual key to the root of the tree, and the server knows all the keys in the key tree. Thus, in a binary key tree, each user knows $\lceil \log_2 n \rceil + 1$ keys, and the server knows $(2n - 1)$ keys.

An example of a key tree for a system of 8 users is depicted in Figure 1(a). The root of the key tree represents the system key $K_{01234567}$ that is known to all users in the system. Each user also knows all the keys on the directed path from its individual key to the root of the key tree. For example, user u_7 knows all the keys K_7, K_{67}, K_{4567}, and $K_{01234567}$.

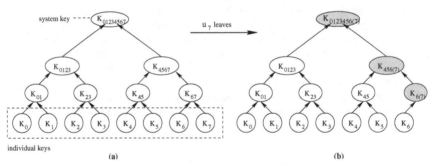

Fig. 1. A binary key tree before and after u_7 leaves

Figure 1(a) and 1(b) illustrates the protocol for updating the system key when user u_7 leaves the system. In this case, the system server S is required to change the keys $K_{01234567}$, K_{4567}, and K_{67} that user u_7 knows. To update these keys, S selects new keys $K_{0123456(7)}$, $K_{456(7)}$, and $K_{6(7)}$, encrypts them, and sends them to the users that need to know them. To ensure that u_7 cannot get a copy of the new keys, S needs to encrypt the new keys using keys that u_7 does not know. Therefore, S encrypts the new $K_{0123456(7)}$ with the old K_{0123}, encrypts the new $K_{0123456(7)}$ and the new $K_{456(7)}$ with the old K_{45}, encrypts the new $K_{0123456(7)}$, the new $K_{456(7)}$, and the new $K_{6(7)}$ with K_6. Then, S multicasts the encrypted keys to the corresponding holders of these keys. The protocol can be specified as follows.

$$S \rightarrow u_0, \cdots, u_6 : \quad \{u_0, u_1, u_2, u_3\}, \quad K_{0123} < K_{0123456(7)}|\text{chk} >$$
$$S \rightarrow u_0, \cdots, u_6 : \quad \{u_4, u_5\}, \quad K_{45} < K_{0123456(7)}|K_{456(7)}|\text{chk} >$$
$$S \rightarrow u_0, \cdots, u_6 : \quad \{u_6\}, \quad K_6 < K_{0123456(7)}|K_{456(7)}|K_{6(7)}|\text{chk} >$$

This protocol consists of three steps. In each step, server S broadcasts a message consisting of two fields to every user in the system. The first field defines the set of the intended ultimate destinations of the message. The second field is an encryption, using an old key, of the concatenation of the new key(s) and a checksum computed over the new key(s). Note that although the broadcast message is sent to every user in the system, only users in the specified destination set have the key used in encrypting the message and so only they can decrypt the message.

The above system architecture is based on the assumption that the system users constitute a single group. In this paper, we extend this architecture to the case where the system users form many groups.

2   Groups and Group Algebra

Assume that the system has m, $m \geq 1$, elementary groups: each elementary group is a distinct subset of the system users and one elementary group has all the system users. Every elementary group has a unique identifier G_j, $0 \leq j \leq m - 1$. The identifier for the elementary group that has all users is G_0. As an example, Figure 2 illustrates a system that has eight users u_0 through u_7 and five elementary groups G_0, G_1, G_2, G_3, and G_4.

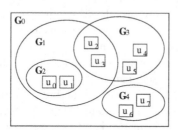

Fig. 2. A sample system

The system needs to be designed such that any user u_i can securely multicast data items to all users in any elementary group G_j. Moreover, any user u_i can securely multicast data items to all users in any group, where a group is defined recursively according to the following four rules:

i. Any of the elementary groups $G_0, \cdots, G_{m-1}$ is a group.
ii. The union of any two groups is a group.
iii. The intersection of any two groups is a group.
iv. The complement of any group is a group.(Note that the complement of any group G is the set of all users in G_0 that are not in G)

Thus, the set of groups is closed under the three operations of union, intersection, and complement.

Each group can be defined by a group formula that includes the following symbols.

- G_0 through G_{m-1}
- $\vee$ for union
- $\wedge$ for intersection
- $\neg$ for complement

Group formulae can be manipulated using the well-known laws of algebra: associativity, commutativity, distribution, De-Morgan's, and so on. For example, the group formula

$$G_1 \vee \neg(\neg G_2 \wedge G_1)$$

can be manipulated as follows:

$$
\begin{aligned}
G_1 &\vee \neg(\neg G_2 \wedge G_1) \\
&= \{\text{by De Morgan's}\}\ G_1 \vee (\neg\neg G_2 \vee \neg G_1) \\
&= \{\text{by associativity of } \vee\}\ G_1 \vee \neg\neg G_2 \vee \neg G_1 \\
&= \{\text{by definition of complement}\}\ G_1 \vee G_2 \vee \neg G_1 \\
&= \{\text{by commutativity of } \vee\}\ G_1 \vee \neg G_1 \vee G_2 \\
&= \{\text{by definition of complement}\}\ G_0 \vee G_2 \\
&= \{\text{by definition of } \vee\}\ G_0
\end{aligned}
$$

From this formula manipulation, it follows that the group defined by the formula $G_1 \vee \neg(\neg G_2 \wedge G_1)$ is the set of all system users. Thus, for a user u_i to securely multicast a data item d to every user in the group $G_1 \vee \neg(\neg G_2 \wedge G_1)$, it is sufficient for u_i to securely broadcast d to every user in the system.

In the rest of this paper, we consider solutions for the following problem. How to design the system so that any system user u_i can securely multicast data items to any group G in the system. Any reasonable solution for this problem needs to take into account that the users can leave any elementary group in the system or leave the system altogether, and these activities may require to change the security keys associated with the elementary groups from which users leave. In particular, the solution should utilize key trees, discussed in Section 1, that can reduce the cost of changing the security keys from $O(n)$ to $O(\log n)$, where n is the total number of users in the system.

The above problem has many applications. As a first example, consider a music file sharing system that has four elementary groups: Rock, Jazz, Blues, and Do-Not-Disturb. A user u_i in this system may wish to securely distribute a song of Louis Armstrong to all interested users. In this case, user u_i securely multicasts the song to all users in the group, Jazz$\wedge\neg$Do-Not-Disturb.

As a second example, consider a student registration system in some university. This system has m elementary groups G_0 through G_{m-1}, where each G_i is a list of the students registered in one course section. A professor who is teaching three sections G_5, G_6, G_7 of the same course, may wish to securely multicast any information related to the course to all the students in the group $G_5 \vee G_6 \vee G_7$.

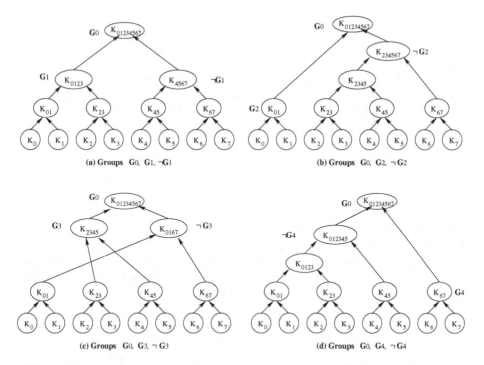

Fig. 3. The complete key trees for the elementary groups and their complements

3   Key Bundles

The above problem suggests the following simple solution (which we show below that it is ineffective). First, assign to each elementary group G_j a security key to be shared by all the users of G_j. Second, assign to the complement $\neg G_j$ of each elementary group G_j a security key to be shared by every member of this complement. Third, provide a key tree for each elementary group and another key tree for its complement. Note that the two key trees provided for an elementary group and its complement span all the users in the system. Thus, these two trees can be combined into one *complete* key tree that spans all system users in the system. Figure 3 shows the four complete key trees that are provided for the four elementary groups and their complements in the system in Figure 2.

From Figure 3(a), the key for the elementary group G_1 is K_{0123} and the key for its complement is K_{4567}. From Figure 3(b), the key for the elementary group G_2 is K_{01} and the key for its complement is K_{234567}. From Figure 3(c), the key for the elementary group G_3 is K_{2345}, and the key fro its complement is K_{0167}. From Figure 3(d), the key for the elementary group G_4 is K_{67}, and the key for its complement is K_{012345}.

Note that these complete trees have the same key for group G_0, and the same individual key for each user. Nevertheless, the total number of distinct keys in these complete trees is 19, which is relatively large for this rather simple

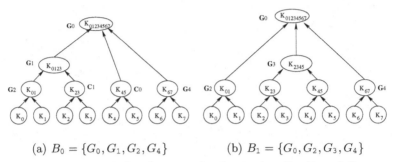

(a) $B_0 = \{G_0, G_1, G_2, G_4\}$ (b) $B_1 = \{G_0, G_2, G_3, G_4\}$

Fig. 4. The complete key trees for the two bundles B_0 and B_1

system. In general, this method requires $O(mn)$ keys, where m is the number of elementary groups and n is the number of users in the system.

To reduce the total number of needed keys, several elementary groups can be added to the same complete key tree, provided that these elementary groups are "nonconflicting". This idea suggests the following three definitions of nonconflicting elementary groups, bundles, and bundle covers.

Two elementary groups are *nonconflicting* if and only if either their intersection is empty or one of them is a subset of the other. In the system example in Figure 2, the three elementary groups G_0, G_1 and G_2 are nonconflicting since G_1 is a subset of G_0, and G_2 is a subset of G_1. On the other hand, the two elementary groups G_1 and G_3 are conflicting, because they share two users u_2 and u_3 and neither group is a subset of the other.

A *bundle* of a system is a maximal set of nonconflicting elementary groups of the system. In the system example in Figure 2, the four elementary groups G_0, G_1, G_2, G_4 constitute one bundle B_0, and the four elementary groups G_0, G_2, G_3, G_4 constitute a second bundle B_1.

A *bundle cover* of a system is a set $\{B_0, \cdots, B_{m-1}\}$ of system bundles such that the following two conditions hold:

i. *Completeness*: Each elementary group of the system appears in some bundle B_i in the bundle cover.

ii. *Compactness*: Each bundle B_i has at least one elementary group that does not appear in any other bundle B_j in the bundle cover.

Note that the set $\{B_0, B_1\}$, where $B_0 = \{G_0, G_1, G_2, G_4\}$ and $B_1 = \{G_0, G_2, G_3, G_4\}$, is a bundle cover for the system in Figure 2.

The security keys for the elementary groups in a bundle can be arranged in a complete key tree. For example, Figure 4(a) shows the complete key tree for B_0. In this tree, the key for group G_0 is $K_{01234567}$, the key for group G_1 is K_{0123}, the key for G_2 is K_{01}, and the key for G_4 is K_{67}. Note that users u_4 and u_5 in G_0 do not belong to any other elementary group in the bundle, and so they are viewed as forming a complement group C_0 whose key is K_{45}. We refer to a complete key tree that corresponds to a bundle as a *key bundle*.

Figure 4(b) shows the complete key bundle for B_1. Note that in this bundle every user in G_0 is also in another elementary group. Thus, the resulting complete key tree does not have a complement group as in the former key tree in Figure 4(a).

Comparing the two key bundles in Figures 4(a) and 4(b), one observes that each of the elementary groups G_0, G_2, and G_4 appear in both key bundles because none of them conflict with any elementary group or any group in the system. One also observes that each of these groups has the same group key in both key bundles, and that the individual key of each user is the same in both key bundles. Note that these key bundles have only 15 distinct keys compared with the 19 distinct keys in the four complete trees in Figure 3. This represents more than 20% reduction in the total number of keys in the system.

The system server S knows the two key bundles in Figure 4, and each user u_i knows only the keys that exist on the paths from its individual key K_i to the key of group G_0. Thus, each user u_i needs to collaborate with the system server S in order to securely multicast data items to any elementary group or any group that can be defined by intersection, union, and complement of elementary groups. This point is illustrated by the following four examples.

For the first example, assume that user u_0 wants to securely multicast a data item d to every user in group G_4. In this case, user u_0 can execute the following protocol.

$$u_0 \rightarrow S \qquad : K_0 < d|G_4|\text{chk} >$$
$$S \rightarrow u_0, \cdots, u_7 : G_4, \quad K_{67} < d|u_0|\text{chk} >$$

This protocol consists of two steps. In the first step, user u_0 sends a message $K_0 < d|G_4|\text{chk} >$ to server S. This message consists of three concatenated fields, namely the data item d, its intended destination G_4, and the checksum chk; the message is encrypted by the individual key K_0 of user u_0. In the second step, server S multicasts the message G_4, $K_{67} < d|u_0|\text{chk} >$ where the second field consists of the data item d, the message source u_0, and the checksum chk and is encrypted with the group key of G_4.

For the second example, assume user u_1 wants to securely multicast a data item d to the users in either group G_1 or G_3, namely the users in the union of G_1 and G_3. In this case, user u_1 can execute the following protocol.

$$u_1 \rightarrow S \qquad : K_1 < d|G_1 \vee G_3|\text{chk} >$$
$$S \rightarrow u_0, \cdots, u_7 : G_1 \vee G_3, \quad K_{0123} < d|u_1|\text{chk} >, \quad K_{2345} < d|u_1|\text{chk} >$$

In the second step of this protocol, server S multicasts the message $G_1 \vee G_3$, $K_{0123} < d|u_1|\text{chk} >$, $K_{2345} < d|u_1|\text{chk} >$ to the two groups G_1 and G_3. The users in group G_1 can get d by using the group key K_{0123} to decrypt $K_{0123} < d|u_1|\text{chk} >$ and the users in group G_3 can get d by using the group key K_{2345} to decrypt $K_{2345} < d|u_1|\text{chk} >$. Note that if it is u_2 who wants to send d to $G_1 \vee G_3$, then since u_2 belongs to both G_1 and G_3, u_2 already knows both K_{0123} and K_{2345}. Therefore, u_2 can send the encrypted d directly to the users in G_1 and G_3 as follows:

$$u_2 \to u_0, \cdots, u_7: \ G_1 \vee G_3, \quad K_{0123} < d|u_2|\text{chk} >, \quad K_{2345} < d|u_2|\text{chk} >$$

For the third example, assume that user u_4 wants to send a data item d to all the users in the intersection of G_1 and G_3. In this case, user u_4 can execute the following protocol.

$$u_4 \to S \qquad : K_4 < d|G_1 \wedge G_3|\text{chk} >$$
$$S \to u_0, \cdots, u_7: \ G_1 \wedge G_3, \quad K_{0123} < K_{2345} < d|u_4|\text{chk} >>$$

In the second step of this protocol, server S multicasts a message $G_1 \wedge G_3$, $K_{0123} < K_{2345} < d|u_4|\text{chk} >>$ to the group $G_1 \wedge G_3$. Here the concatenation of d, u_4 and chk is encrypted by both the group key of G_1, which is K_{0123}, and the group key of G_3, which is K_{2345}. The encrypted message can only be decrypted by the users that are in both G_1 and G_3 because only these users know the two group keys K_{0123} and K_{2345}.

For the fourth example, assume that user u_5 wants to send a data item d to all the users in the complement of group G_1. In this case, user u_5 executes the following protocol.

$$u_5 \to S \qquad : K_5 < d|\neg G_1|\text{chk} >$$
$$S \to u_0, \cdots, u_7: \ C_0 \vee G_4, \quad K_{45} < d|u_5|\text{chk} >, \quad K_{67} < d|u_5|\text{chk} >$$

After server S receives this message, it translates $\neg G_1$ to $C_0 \vee G_4$ then multicasts the message $G_c \vee G_4, K_{45} < d|u_5|\text{chk} >, K_{67} < d|u_5|\text{chk} >$. The users in group G_c can get d using the group key K_{45}, and the users in group G_4 can get d using the group key K_{67}.

The algorithm for the construction of a bundle cover is described in detail in the full version of this paper[17].

4   Key Parcels

A bundle is defined as a maximal set of nonconflicting elementary groups in the system. From this definition the elementary group G_0 is in every bundle since it does not conflict with any other elementary group in the system. Thus, every key bundle is a complete key tree.

This feature of bundle maximality has one advantage and one disadvantage. The advantage is that the complement of any elementary group in a bundle B_j can be expressed as the union of some other elementary groups in B_j. Thus, securely multicasting a data item to the complement of any elementary group can be carried out efficiently. The disadvantage is that the number of keys needed in each key bundle is relatively large, and so the total number of keys in the system is relatively large.

Clearly, the disadvantage of bundle maximality outweighs its advantage in systems where users never need to securely multicast data items to the complements of elementary groups. Therefore, in these systems, we use "parcels",

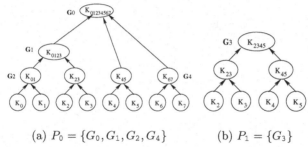

(a) $P_0 = \{G_0, G_1, G_2, G_4\}$ (b) $P_1 = \{G_3\}$

Fig. 5. The complete key trees for the parcel cover

which are not maximal, instead of bundles, which are maximal. The definitions of parcels and parcel covers are given next.

A *parcel* of a system is a set of nonconflicting elementary groups of the system.

A *parcel cover* of a system is a sequence of parcels $(P_0, \cdots, P_{s-1})$ such that the following two conditions hold:

i. *Completeness*: Each elementary group of the system appears in some parcel P_i in the parcel cover.
ii. *Compactness*: Each elementary group in each parcel P_i conflicts with at least one elementary group in each of the preceding parcels $P_0, \cdots, P_{i-1}$ in the parcel cover.

As an example, a parcel cover for the system in Figure 2 is (P_0, P_1), where $P_0 = \{G_0, G_1, G_2, G_4\}$ and $P_1 = \{G_3\}$. Figure 6 is a parcel cover (P_0, P_1) for the system in Figure 2.

The security keys for the elementary groups in a parcel can be arranged in a key tree that is not necessarily a complete tree. Figure 6(a) shows the key tree for parcel P_0 consisting of the elementary groups G_0, G_1, G_2, and G_4. Figure 6(b) shows the key tree for parcel P_1 consisting of the elementary group G_3. Note that the key tree for parcel P_1 is not a complete tree. We refer to a key tree that corresponds to a parcel as a *key parcel*.

The algorithm to construct a parcel cover is described in detail in the full version of this paper[17].

5 Simulation Results

In this section, we present the results of simulations that we carried out to demonstrate the feasibility of key bundles and key parcels. In our simulation, we used a class of synthetic systems with the following properties:

i. The number of users in each system varies from 1000 to 10000.
ii. Each system has 500 elementary groups.
iii. In each system, a user joins 2 elementary groups on average.

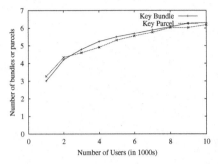

Fig. 6. Number of bundles or parcels

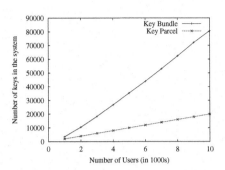

Fig. 7. Number of keys in the system

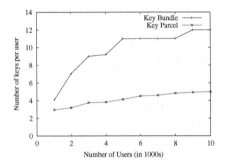

Fig. 8. Number of keys per user

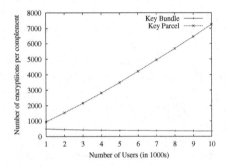

Fig. 9. Number of encryptions per complement

Each system is simulated 100 times and the averages of the following four items are computed over the 100 simulation runs for each system: the number of bundles or parcels in the system cover, the total number of keys in the system, the number of keys per user, and the number of encryptions needed to multicast a data item to the users in the complement of an elementary group. The results of these simulations are shown in Figures 6 through 9.

As shown in Figure 6, the number of bundles in a bundle cover more or less equals the number of parcels in a parcel cover. Note that this number increases logarithmically as the number of users in the simulated system grows.

Figure 7 shows that the number of keys in systems that use key bundles and the number of keys in systems that use key parcels grow linearly as the number of users in the system increases. However, the number of keys in the case of key bundles grows much faster in the case of key parcels. This is because each key bundle is a complete key tree while each key parcel is not necessarily complete.

As shown in Figure 8, the number of keys that each user needs to store increases as a logarithm function with the number of users in the system.

Figure 9 shows that when Key Bundle approach is used, the average number of encryptions performed for a complement of an elementary group decreases as the number of users increases (the actual number is from around 500 to 400). As the number of users increases, the probability of two groups' conflicting increases. Therefore, the average number of groups can be put in a bundle decreases. Since we use the keys of other groups in the same bundle of a complement of an elementary group, the number of encryptions decreases as the number of users increases.

The number of encryptions for a complement performed in Key Parcel approach is constantly larger than that in Key Bundle approach, and the difference becomes greater as the number of users grows. It is because that the number of encryptions for a complement $\neg G$ for a random elementary group G in key parcels is $O(n)$, since the server needs to use the individual keys for the users that are not in the parcel which G belongs to.

6 Conclusion

We consider a system where each user is in one or more elementary groups. In this system, arbitrary groups of users can be specified using the operations of union, intersection, and complement over the elementary groups in the system. Every elementary group is provided with a key tree to reduce the cost of changing the key of the elementary group. We propose two methods for packing the key trees of elementary groups into key bundles and into key parcels.

Packing into key bundles has the advantage of reducing number of encryptions needed to multicast a data item to the complement of an elementary group. Packing into key parcels has the advantage of reducing the total number of keys in the system. We apply these two methods to a class of synthetic systems: each system has from 1000 to 10000 users and 500 elementary groups, and a user in each system is in 2 elementary groups on average. Simulations of these systems show that our proposal to pack key trees into key bundles and key parcels provides a reasonable performance to be used. The number of keys stored per user in the case of key bundles is 12 for 10000 user system, while that in the case of key parcels is 5. Instead, the number of encryptions needed for a complement in the case of key bundles is far less than that in the case of key parcels by the magnitude of $O(\frac{n}{k})$.

As a future work, we would like to find a hybrid between these two methods, which needs less number of keys in the system than in the case of key bundles and at the same time supports complement of an elementary group with less number of encryptions than in the case of key parcels.

We are also interested in conducting a case study of these methods in a real world application. The case study includes to define appropriate scopes of elementary groups and to maintain key bundles or key parcels accordingly. As a typical application of secure group communication, a knowledge sharing system can take advantage of these methods.

As described in Section 3, if the sender of message m does not know the keys required to encrypt m appropriately, the system server has to encrypt m and multicast. This requirement for the server's help may cause performance bottleneck at the server. To reduce the workload of the system server, future work will investigate how multiple servers may be placed and coordinated to work in a distributed or a hierarchical manner.

References

1. Gong, L.: Enclaves: Enabling secure collaboration over the internet. IEEE Journal of Selected Areas in Communications **15** (1997) 567–575
2. Mittra, S.: Iolus: a framework for scalable secure multicasting. In: the Proceedings of the ACM SIGCOMM '97, ACM Press (1997) 277–288
3. Wallner, D.M., Harder, E.J., Agee, R.C.: Key management for multicast: Issues and architectures. RFC 2627 (1999)
4. Wong, C.K., Gouda, M., Lam, S.S.: Secure group communications using key graphs. IEEE/ACM Transactions on Networking (TON) **8** (2000) 16–30
5. Steiner, M., Tsudik, G., Waidner, M.: Key agreement in dynamic peer groups. IEEE Transactions on Parallel and Distributed Systems **11** (2000) 769–780
6. Gong, L., Shacham, N.: Multicast security and its extension to a mobile environment. Wireless Networks **1** (1995) 281–295
7. Ballardie, A.: Scalable multicast key distribution. RFC 1949 (1996)
8. Chang, I., Engel, R., Kandlur, D.D., Pendarakis, D.E., Saha, D.: Key management for secure internet multicast using boolean function minimization techniques. In: the Proceedings of IEEE Infocom 1999. Volume 2. (1999) 689–698
9. Naor, D., Naor, M., Lotspiech, J.: Revocation and tracing schemes for stateless receivers. In: Advances in Cryptology - CRYPTO 2001. LNCS 2139, Springer-Verlag (2001) 41–62
10. Rodeh, O., Birman, K., Dolev, D.: The architecture and performance of security protocols in the ensemble group communication system: Using diamonds to guard the castle. ACM Transactions on Information and System Security (TISSEC) **4** (2001) 289–319
11. Setia, S., Koussih, S., Jajodia, S., Harder, E.: Kronos: A scalable group re-keying approach for secure multicast. In: the Proceedings of IEEE Symposium on Security and Privacy. (2000)
12. Waldvogel, M., Caronni, G., Sun, D., Weiler, N., Plattner, B.: The versakey framework: Versatile group key management. IEEE Journal on Selected Areas in Communications **17** (1999) 1614–1631
13. Gouda, M.G., Huang, C.T., Elnozahy, E.: Key trees and the security of the interval multicast. In: the Proceedings of the 22 nd International Conference on Distributed Computing Systems. (2002) 467–468
14. Li, X.S., Yang, Y.R., Gouda, M.G., Lam, S.S.: Batch rekeying for secure group communications. In: the Proceedings of the 10th international World Wide Web conference on World Wide Web, ACM Press (2001) 525–534
15. Yang, Y.R., Li, X.S., Zhang, X.B., Lam, S.S.: Reliable group rekeying: a performance analysis. In: the Proceedings of the 2001 conference on applications, technologies, architectures, and protocols for computer communications, ACM Press (2001) 27–38
16. Snoeyink, J., Suri, S., Varghese, G.: A lower bound for multicast key distribution. In: the Proceedings of IEEE Infocom 2001. (2001) 667–675
17. Jung, E., Liu, X.Y.A., Gouda, M.G.: Key bundles and parcels: Secure communication in many groups. Technical Report TR-03-21, Dept. of Computer Sciences, the University of Texas at Austin (2003)

EBM: A New Approach
for Scalable DiffServ Multicasting

A. Striegel[1], A. Bouabdallah[2], H. Bettahar[2], and G. Manimaran[3]

[1] Dept. of Comp. Sci & Engr., Univ. of Notre Dame,
Notre Dame, IN
`striegel@cse.nd.edu`
[2] Lab Heudiasyc, Université de Technologie - Compiègne
60200 Compiègne France
`{bouabdal,hatem.bettahar}@utc.fr`
[3] Dependable Computing & Networking
Dept. of Electrical and Computer Engineering
Iowa State University, Ames, IA 50010 USA
`gmani@iastate.edu`

Abstract. The phenomenal growths of group communications and QoS-aware applications over the Internet have respectively accelerated the development of two key technologies, namely, multicasting and Differentiated Services (DiffServ). Although both are complementary technologies, their integration is a non-trivial task due to architectural conflicts between them. In this paper, we propose a new approach, Edge-Based Multicasting (EBM), for providing multicast transport across a DiffServ domain. EBM leverages the intelligence of edge routers in DiffServ and a new entity called a Multicast Broker (MB) to provide such services. Unlike traditional IP multicast, our approach keeps core routers stateless and multicast-unaware. Our approach has significant implications for multicasting regarding scalability, deployment, security, heterogeneous users, and resource management. In our paper, we outline the EBM model and propose a novel tree construction algorithm, Edge Cluster Trees (ECT), which captures the unique aspects of DiffServ and EBM. Finally, we present detailed simulation studies of our approach and contrast our approach versus previous work.

1 Introduction

Although the available bandwidth of the Internet is continually increasing, new applications are continually being developed which erode gains in network capacity. For many of these new applications (ex. video/audio on demand, peer to peer sharing, teleconferencing, distributed gaming), the traditional unicast model is highly inefficient for supporting such applications. To address such inefficiency, the concept of multicasting was proposed to eliminate such unnecessary data transmissions by reducing the connections to a multicast tree with minimal bandwidth cost.

B. Stiller et al. (Eds.): NGC/ICQT 2003, LNCS 2816, pp. 131–142, 2003.

From the perspective of both the end user and the network service provider, multicasting could offer tremendous benefit to both network efficiency and QoS. However, the issue of how to support multicasting in one of the more promising QoS models, Differentiated Services [1], has received relatively little research attention. Although the two concepts of bandwidth conservation (multicast) and scalable QoS management (DiffServ) are complementary, the emphasis on scalability by DiffServ creates architectural conflicts with multicasting that make the integration of the two technologies a non-trivial task [2].

1.1   Differentiated Services & Multicasting

The Differentiated Services (DiffServ) architecture [1] was proposed by the IETF for providing scalable QoS across the Internet. In the DiffServ architecture, intelligence is migrated to the edge of the domain in order to keep the core of the network simple and scalable. Routers in a DiffServ domain are divided into two categories, *core routers* (simple and high speed) and *edge routers* (stateful and intelligent). Core routers do not have per-flow state and differentiate packets according to the marking (DSCP - DiffServ Code Point) of the packet. In contrast, edge routers are stateful entities that are responsible for policing and/or marking all packets according to an SLA (Service Level Agreement) between the source (other ISP, user, company) and the domain, or between two domains.

Whereas DiffServ relies on only edge routers possessing intelligence and state information, multicasting relies on per-group state throughout the entire network. Thus, when trying to integrate the two technologies, one is faced with two conflicting principles, core statelessness for scalability versus per-group state information for efficiency. The natural question is, which principle is more important, state information (storage and router complexity) or maximal network efficiency (bandwidth)? It is our belief that state information is vastly more costly than bandwidth. Whereas one could argue that if one can increase bandwidth capacity, one can also increase the state storage capacity, it is the maintenance of such state information (router complexity) that is the problem. Thus, we pose a simple question: Why not follow the DiffServ approach and minimize the number of routers that must maintain such state information? If bandwidth can be thought of as significantly cheaper than maintaining state information at all routers, can one leverage the DiffServ model to provide a better and more scalable multicast?

These questions provide the motivation for our paper. In our paper, we propose a novel approach for DiffServ multicasting, Edge-Based Multicasting (EBM), which leverages the unique aspects of the DiffServ architecture to exploit the intelligence of edge routers and maintain core statelessness. Rather than employing a multicast everywhere approach, EBM reduces the problem to edge-to-edge transport across a single DiffServ domain. In addition, we introduce the concept of a Multicast Broker (MB) for group management and a novel algorithm for tree construction, (Edge Cluster Tree (ECT)), that addresses the unique characteristics of the DiffServ environment. Our approach introduces several other benefits as well:

- *Core simplicity* - In EBM, core routers do not have to support any multicast operations (routing, replication, resource management).
- *Multicast deployment* - Rather than requiring the same multicast protocol from end-to-end, the black box nature of EBM allows for seamless translation between multicast protocols.
- *Security* - The EBM architecture lends itself both to security (protection against spoofing, malicious attacks) as well as traffic management (protection against DoS attacks).
- *Resource management* - Rather than requiring core routers to negotiate resources [3], EBM simplifies the process to a single interaction between the MB and Bandwidth Broker (BB).

The rest of our paper is organized as follows. In Section 2, we describe the key components of the EBM architecture. Next, in Section 3 we describe the ECT algorithm for tree construction. In Section 4 we conduct extensive simulation studies and in Section 5, we examine related work. Finally, in Section 6 we make several concluding remarks.

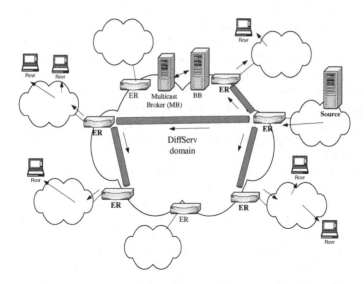

Fig. 1. EBM Network Architecture

2   EBM: Edge-Based Multicasting

The primary goal of the Edge-Based Multicasting (EBM) architecture is to provide scalable multicast transport across a single DiffServ (DS) domain. The first step is to apply the scalability principles of DiffServ to multicasting, i.e. push the state to the edge of the domain. This concept fits perfectly with the notion of a multicast transport service that allows the core routers to remain as simple, stateless routers. Figure 1 shows the fundamental principles of the EBM architecture and is summarized below:

- *Stateless core:* Core routers are multicast unaware and therefore do not maintain any multicast state information.
- *Tunneled packets:* Packets are tunneled from edge to edge, thus reducing the multicast packet to a true unicast packet in the core.
- *Edge replication:* Packets may only be replicated at edge routers. The replication information may be included in the packet (encapsulated tree) or maintained as state information at the edge router.
- *Multicast Broker:* The Multicast Broker (MB) manages all egress join/leave requests and multicast trees for the entire DS domain. In addition, the multicast broker manages all QoS interactions for multicasting (security, resource reservation, etc.).

2.1 EBM Multicast Transport

In order to provide a multicast transport service, the edge router must provide two new functions, namely packet replication/tunneling and join/leave forwarding. Both functions are fairly straightforward and require only minimal changes to the edge router.

For packet replication and tunneling functionality, an edge router must be able to recognize a multicast packet and appropriately replicate/tunnel the packet onto the domain. When a multicast packet arrives at an edge router from outside the domain, the edge router will examine its state information (provided by interactions with the MB) and replicate/tunnel the packet via a modified Minimal Encapsulation header [4] to downstream egress points in the multicast domain. If the packet should be replicated to outside of the DS domain, the encapsulation header is stripped off and the original information replaced in the multicast packet.

The second function (join/leave forwarding) involves acting as an attendant for inter-domain routing requests that require the intervention of the MB. For any join/leave request, the edge router must tunnel the request to the MB along with information about the QoS requested (PHB) and the egress point requesting the multicast service. The MB processes the join/leave request and the appropriate edge routers are updated with the new tree information. Thus, the edge router need not be concerned with the specifics of multicast routing, only the appropriate mechanisms for packet tunneling, replication, and forwarding to the MB.

2.2 EBM Multicast Broker (MB)

In order to simplify group management, the EBM architecture incorporates the use of an entity known as the Multicast Broker (MB). The responsibilities of the MB include tree construction, tree rearrangement, and security management. The MB may be either a centralized or distributed entity. In this paper, we address the MB from the perspective of a centralized entity near (but separate) from the Bandwidth Broker (BB). In order to meet the high levels of group dynamics, we propose that the MB services would be provided using a tiered scheme employing load balancing.

The centralization of all multicast information offers several significant benefits. First, QoS negotiations for a tree are greatly simplified. Due to the distributed nature of routing in traditional IP multicasting, each router may need to negotiate resources individually [5]. In contrast, the MB can negotiate with the BB for the entire multicast tree in one exchange. Second, the centralized approach lends itself towards a more robust security scheme as well. In contrast to traditional IP multicasting, the centralized approach makes it easier to force security features (authentication/encryption) on all group dynamics (topology changes, etc.) and can also serve as a starting point for managing secure groups. Finally, the centralized architecture is ideal for tree construction and tree rearrangement [6].

2.3   Member Join

In EBM, a member is defined as an egress point (edge router) that wishes to receive packets for the multicast group. An egress point may have many other downstream domains or receivers. The maximum size of an EBM multicast group is bounded by the number of edge routers (potential egress points) and is independent of the number of receivers, hence reducing the practical size of the scalability problem.

Initial Join Request: The join process begins when an inter-domain join request reaches the edge of the DS domain. The request may be sent by any of the existing multicast protocols (SSM, IGMP, PIM) and would be intercepted by an edge router. Upon receiving a join request at an edge router, the request is forwarded to the MB for the domain (known via configuration or discovery). The request is forwarded to the MB using either a signaling PHB or other appropriate low loss/reduced delay PHB. The join message includes the ID of the new egress point, the requested PHB (if possible), and the information from the inter-domain join request.

MB Processing: Upon receiving an join message, the MB must first determine the status of the group in the DS domain. If the group already exists in the domain (has ingress or egress points), the MB does not need to search for the group. However, if the multicast group does not exist in the DS domain, the MB must locate the multicast group. For cases where the join request is using SSM or CBT (Core-Based Trees) where a source address is included, the problem is vastly simplified as the location of the multicast group is easily identified. In other cases, the MB must search for the multicast group using a multicast inter-domain routing protocol such as MBGP or MSDP as the multicast group address does not necessarily imply location and thus must be discovered.

The actual edge routers to which the new egress point can be grafted to is discussed in more detail in Section 3. A simple (but not optimal) solution is to graft the new egress point to the closest on-tree edge node that satisfies the edge-to-edge PHB of the new egress point. Such topology information would be readily available from the underlying link state routing protocol.

Graft: After the MB has determined the appropriate grafting point; the MB will inform both the new egress point and the upstream edge router of the change in the multicast tree. If the tree is not being rearranged, only the two edge routers involved, the MB, and the BB (optional) need to know about the change in the multicast tree. The MB sends an update message to the two edge routers containing the ID of the new edge router (leaf), the ID of the parent edge router, the ID of the multicast group, and the DSCP for the new branch. Both of the edge routers will update their replication information and future data transmissions to the group will now flow to the new egress point. In the event that non-ingress edge routers do not keep replication state information (i.e. tree encapsulation), the MB will send the update message to the ingress router rather than the grafting point. The advantage of employing tree encapsulation is that tree rearrangement can be conveyed via a single packet to the ingress router(s) rather than all effected nodes. For single sourced multicast trees (such as SSM), such an approach may be advantageous for faster tree optimization. For multi-sourced trees (shared and many to many), multiple nodes may need to be updated.

2.4 EBM Member Leave

When an edge router wishes to leave the multicast group, it sends an leave message to the MB. It is assumed that such a message will only be sent when the edge router has no additional downstream receivers (i.e. the last of its downstream receivers sends a prune or times out). The member leave operation is less critical from the user perspective as the user no longer desires service from the multicast group. However, from the perspective of a service provider, the quick execution of a member leave operation minimizes wasted resources. Similar to the join operation, the prune operation can be conducted using the MB with the addition of domain-wide tree rearrangement for optimal packet distribution.

3   Edge-Clustered Trees (ECT)

The construction of multicast trees in an environment such as DiffServ is governed by several constraints that must/should be obeyed. These constraints include:

- *PHB priority:* An egress point with a higher priority PHB must not sit downstream from an egress point with a lower PHB. For example, a packet cannot be tunneled to a BE (Best Effort) egress point with the BE PHB and then tunneled to an EF (Expedited Forwarding [7]) egress point using the EF PHB.
- *PHB promotion:* Conversely, an egress point with a lower priority PHB should not receive a higher priority PHB for its packets than requested. For example, a packet should not be tunneled to an AF (Assured Forwarding [8]) egress point with the EF PHB and then tunneled to an EF egress point with the EF PHB.

– *Minimal hop count:* Packets should be delivered with the minimal hop count possible since no per-flow state exists to balance the cost of additional hops (i.e. shorter path is better than a longer path).

Because of these constraints, traditional multicast tree construction algorithms such as KMB [9] and others cannot be applied to the problem directly. Since existing algorithms are not sufficient for addressing such constraints, we developed a novel approach called the Edge Clustered Tree (ECT) for constructing trees in such an environment.

3.1   ECT Algorithm

The premise of the ECT algorithm is fairly simple, cluster similarly QoS-classed egress points together in an effort to balance the cost of the tree versus the additional hops required for edge-based branching. The ingress node tunnels the packets to clusters that then tunnel the packets to the egress points in their clusters and other downstream clusters. The ECT algorithm itself can be broken into two key phases, cluster construction and cluster linkage.

3.2   Cluster Construction

In the first phase, a cluster is constructed centered on each egress point of the multicast group. A cluster consists of all other egress points within H hops of an edge router (E_X) whose PHBs can be satisfied by the PHB used for packets sent to E_X [1]. The cost of the cluster consists of the costs of tunneling to the nodes in the cluster (from E_X to the cluster nodes) and the cost of the tunnel from the ingress router to E_X. The metric $M(E_X)$ for evaluating a cluster centered at node E_X is defined as:

$$M(E_X) = \frac{D(I_G, E_X) + \sum_{i=0}^{|C_X|} D(E_X, C_{X,i})}{|C_X|}$$

where $D(X, Y)$ is the number of hops between X and Y, I_G is the ingress router for the group (single source), $|C_X|$ is the number of nodes within H hops that are satisfied by E_X's PHB, and $C_{X,i}$ is the ith node in the cluster centered around E_X. A lower value of $M(E_X)$ denotes that the average cost of servicing the nodes in a cluster is lower as well. The ingress node is a special cluster whose PHB satisfies any egress point.

3.3   Cluster Linkage

In the next phase, the clusters are linked together via tunnels to connect the multicast distribution tree for the domain[2]. The algorithm proceeds by connecting the best cluster according to the metric. In the first iteration, only the ingress

---

[1] The precedence of various PHBs is a topic beyond the scope of this paper. We assume that rules to govern such precedence exist in the MB.

[2] The complete ECT algorithm is available in [10].

cluster may be tunneled from (although its cluster may not be selected). Once a cluster is selected, the cluster becomes available as a candidate for future clusters to be tunneled from provided that the PHB priority is still satisfied. Ties are resolved by connecting the highest PHB first in order to maximize the chances that other clusters may be tunneled from that cluster.

When a cluster is selected, all of the nodes inside of the cluster are removed from consideration as members of other clusters. The metric of the remaining clusters is recomputed based on the new cluster membership and the potential new grafting points of previously selected clusters (cluster centers only). An additional constraint may be imposed, cluster depth D, such that a cluster may not be more than D tunnels away from the ingress point, thus capping the maximum tunnels to an egress point at $D+1$ tunnels (tunnels to cluster+tunnel from cluster).

3.4   ECT Example

Figure 2 shows an example of the ECT algorithm with $H = 2$. In the figure, only paths between edge nodes that are egress points (members) of the group are shown. Each link label denotes the hop count between the nodes.

- *Step 1:* The clusters around each node are constructed considering all egress points within $H = 2$ hops. For the cluster centered on $N1$, it finds two nodes within 2 hops whose PHB is still satisfied by its PHB. Conversely for $N0$, although it can find $N1$ within 2 hops, it cannot offer service ($BE < AF10$). The figure shows a total of 6 clusters.
- *Step 2a:* The best cluster is linked to the tree. In this case, the ingress point (I) is the best cluster.
- *Step 2b:* The next best cluster is centered on $N1$. The cluster is linked to the tree via the ingress point and the nodes within $N1$'s cluster ($N0$ and $N2$) are removed from all other clusters. The remaining clusters ($N3, N4$) check to see if $N1$ is closer than the ingress point.
- *Step 2c:* The next best cluster is centered on $N4$. The cluster is linked to the tree via the ingress point and node $N3$ is removed from the remaining cluster.

After Step 2c, the tree is constructed covering all the egress points for the multicast group and satisfying the PHB priority rules.

4   Simulation Studies

In order to evaluate the performance of the EBM architecture, we used the ns-2 simulator for the following models:

- *Ingress-only* - Packets are tunneled out from the ingress node to all egress points in the DS domain. Replication is done only at the ingress node.

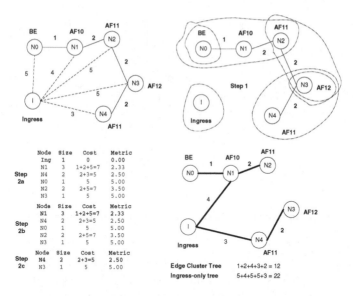

Fig. 2. Example of Edge Cluster Tree construction

- *EBM* - The EBM model is studied using two variations, the simple algorithm (outlined in EBM architecture) and ECT.
- *DSMCast* - The adaptive DSMCast model [11] is studied that selects either DSMCast or ingress-only branching depending upon which is the least cost approach.
- *Traditional IP* - Although we believe traditional IP multicasting is not scalable, it provides an excellent baseline for evaluating the relative overhead of the algorithms versus the best possible case for performance.

The simulations were conducted for a single domain scenario of varying random network topologies and varying QoS distributions (uniform and non-uniform). The models were evaluated on three performance metrics, the average bandwidth consumed per link, the average number of hops, and the average number of tunnels to an egress point. The average bandwidth consumed per link gives an indication of the relative impact of multicast traffic on each link provided that no multicast packets are dropped. The average hops and average tunnels metrics demonstrate the additional impact of tunneling that occurs since packets may take a longer router to reach edge nodes versus ingress-only tunneling. The parameters for the simulations are available in [10].

Effect of Group Density. In Figure 3(a), we examine the impact of the group size (egress points) on the performance of the various models. As would be expected, traditional IP multicast performs the best in terms of the bandwidth cost of multicasting. In order to better study the additional overhead of core statelessness, the figure shows the simulation results normalized as a ratio to the cost of traditional IP multicasting. DSMCast follows traditional IP multicast-

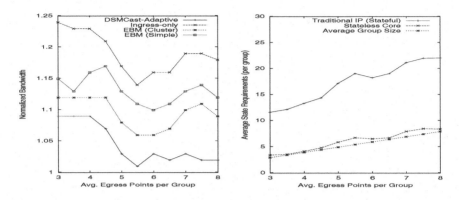

Fig. 3. Effect of group size (Uniform distribution) - (a) normalized (b) state information

ing the closest as it uses an actual multicast tree embedded inside the packet, thus achieving much of the benefit of the multicast tree. Next, the two EBM approaches follow with ECT offering a marginal improvement over the simple approach. The ingress-only approach comes in last as it sees no savings for multicasting across a given domain. Although such an approach would save on an end-to-end basis, it performs essentially the same as unicasting each packet across the domain. However, as we see in Figure 3(b), the performance of traditional IP multicast comes at a cost. Whereas the state cost of stateless core multicasting follows the predicted average group size quite closely, the state cost increases much more rapidly in traditional IP multicasting. Due to space requirements, the similar results with a non-uniform PHB distribution are not included but are available in [10].

Effect of ECT Parameters: Figure 4(a) examines the impact of the H (hops) setting on the performance of the ECT algorithm with the performance of DSM-Cast, the simple EBM algorithm, and ingress-only branching included as a baseline. With a low H, the algorithm performs similar to the simple EBM algorithm since only selected clusters can allow intermediate tunneling. With an increase in H, the cluster algorithm is able to find more nodes within reach and hence reduce the overall cost of the distribution tree. However, beyond a certain point, ECT performs worse as nodes are absorbed that would be better optimized by being in separate clusters. Figure 4(b) shows the tunneling impact on groups of AF (Assured Forwarding) classes by the hops setting. At the point where the average number of tunnels for all classes is maximized ($H = 3$), the best performance (see Figure 4) is also achieved as well. Once the threshold of $H = 3$ is passed, the clusters contain too many nodes as is evidenced by the lower average tunneling value. In fact, even the lower classed AF PHBs dramatically lower their average tunneling value and begin to converge together. In actuality, it is when the opposite effect (increased average tunneling between nodes) is seen, a more efficient multicast distribution tree is achieved.

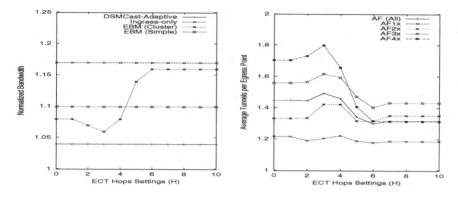

Fig. 4. Effect of cluster hops setting - uniform distribution - (a) normalized (b) average tunnels (class-wise)

5   Related Work

Most of the works that we are aware of fail to address the issue of scalability (core statelessness). In [3], the authors examine support for multicasting in a DiffServ environment using traditional IP multicasting. The work identifies the NRS (Neglected Reservation Subtree) problem regarding resource reservation issues with grafting new branches onto the multicast tree.

MBone & SGM: The closest work to EBM is the original MBone architecture. Our work differs from MBone in several key respects. First, our solution is specifically geared towards the DiffServ architecture and towards providing a transport functionality only. Whereas MBone is interested in end-to-end service, EBM focuses solely on the unique aspects of the DS domain. Second, due to the close coupling of EBM with DiffServ, EBM allows for unique functionality that cannot be offered with MBone. For example, rather than relying on other ISPs as would occur with MBone, a single ISP using EBM can force authentication for all multicast routing updates in the domain and manage the QoS impacts via the MB. Although EBM at its lowest level can essentially be thought of a specialized topology of MBone, it is the coupling of the MB, the uniqueness of the DiffServ topology, and the ECT algorithm that offer EBM its true distinction versus MBone.

Beyond MBone, the other two similar works are Small Group Multicasting (SGM) [12] and DSMCast (DiffServ MultiCast) [11]. EBM differs significantly from SGM in that the trees need not be encapsulated in the header. DSMCast represents our previous work that encapsulated the edge-to-edge multicast tree in the header and relied on stateless but multicast-aware hardware in the core.

6   Conclusions

In this paper, we proposed a new approach for DiffServ multicasting, Edge Based Multicasting (EBM) that relies on edge-based replication, tunneling, and a Multicast Broker (MB) entity to deliver a scalable multicast transport service across a single DiffServ domain. In addition, we proposed a novel algorithm, the Edge Cluster Tree (ECT), that captures the unique aspects of heterogeneous QoS management in a DiffServ domain. We believe that the EBM architecture has tremendous potential for expediting the wide scale deployment of multicasting as DiffServ is deployed. Our approach minimizes the impact of multicasting support by requiring only modifications to the edge routers and the inclusion of a Multicast Broker. Thus, we believe the EBM architecture represents a viable approach for joining the two technologies of DiffServ and multicasting.

References

1. K. Nichols, S. Blake, F. Baker, and D. Black, "Definition of the Differentiated Services field (DS Field) in the IPv4 and IPv6 headers," *IETF RFC 2474*, Dec. 1998.
2. A. Striegel and G. Manimaran, "A survey of QoS multicasting issues," *IEEE Communications*, pp. 82–87, June 2002.
3. R. Bless and K. Wehrle, "Group Communication in Differentiated Services Networks," in *Internet QoS for the Global Computing 2001 (IQ 2001), Workshop at CCGRID 2001*, Brisbane, Australia, May 2001, pp. 618–625.
4. C. Perkins, "Minimal Encapsulation within IP," *IETF RFC 2004*, Oct. 1996.
5. A. Striegel and G. Manimaran, "Dynamic DSCPs for heterogeneous QoS in DiffServ multicasting," in *Proc. of GLOBECOM*, Taipei, Taiwan, Nov. 2002.
6. R. Sriram, G. Manimaran, and C. S. R. Murthy, "A rearrangeable algorithm for the construction of delay-constrained dynamic multicast trees," *IEEE/ACM Trans. Networking*, pp. 514–529, Aug. 1999.
7. B. D. et. al, "An expedited forwarding PHB (per-hop behavior)," *IETF RFC 3246*, Mar. 2002.
8. J. Heinanen, F. Baker, W. Weiss, and J. Wroclawski, "Assured forwarding PHB group," *IETF RFC 2597*, June 1999.
9. L. Kou, G. Markowsky, and L. Berman, "A fast algorithm for Steiner trees," *Acta Informatica*, vol. 15, no. 2, pp. 141–145, 1981.
10. A. Striegel, A. Bouabdallah, H. Bettahar, and G. Manimaran, "EBM: Edge-based multicasting in DiffServ networks," in *Notre Dame CSE Technical Report*, Apr. 2003.
11. A. Striegel and G. Manimaran, "A scalable approach to DiffServ multicasting," in *Proc. of ICC'2001*, Helsinki, Finland, June 2001.
12. R. Boivie, "A new multicast scheme for small groups," *IBM Research Report RC21512*, June 1999.

Team Oriented Multicast: A Scalable Routing Protocol for Large Mobile Networks*

Yunjung Yi, Mario Gerla, Joon-Sang Park, and Dario Maggiorini

University of California at Los Angeles
California, USA
{yjyi,gerla,jspark,dario}@cs.ucla.edu

Abstract. This paper proposes a multicast protocol, called *Team Oriented Multicast* (TOM). TOM builds up a "motion aware" hierarchy to support efficient, scalable team multicast protocol. TOM identifies clusters of nodes with same affinity as teams and manages the multicast membership information using the unit of team rather than dealing with individual node members. TOM uses a two-tier data dissemination approach where the source propagates a data packet to each subscribed teams leader and each leader forwards the data to the entire team. TOM constructs a multicast mesh structure among leaders of subscribed teams, where each leader is connected to m other parent leaders, receiving duplicate packet streams from each parent. Each team leader proactively maintains the list of nodes in the same multicast mesh.

Simulation results show the effectiveness, scalability and reliability of TOM in various representative scenarios.

1 Introduction

With the advances in wireless ad hoc communications, robotics and microflyer technology, the deployment of large-scale networks with hundreds and even thousands of distributed autonomous nodes will be possible in the near future. In such large scale networks, with no fixed infrastructure, providing an efficient, scalable routing and multicast scheme is extremely challenging. In [13], the authors have shown that a hierarchical routing is essential to achieve adequate performance in very large networks. A hierarchical approach, where multicast group receivers are grouped into a few clusters, can be exploited if a stable cluster platform can be maintained. By grouping receivers, QoS protocols consider only a small number of representative nodes instead of thousands of individual members. However, the assumption of a stable cluster platform often fails in MANET scenarios where nodes move quickly and thus the membership of a cluster is extremely fragile. With an unstable cluster structure, hierarchical multicasting may not be a good solution due to excessive cluster maintenance cost.

---

* This work is supported in part by ONR "MINUTEMAN" project under contract N00014 - 01 - C - 0016

B. Stiller et al. (Eds.): NGC/ICQT 2003, LNCS 2816, pp. 143–154, 2003.

That observation leads us to conclude that developing a hierarchical multicasting protocol working for all possible scenarios is probably not feasible. Fortunately, in many large scale MANET scenarios (e.g., warfront activities, search and rescue, disaster relief operations, etc.), the mobile nodes are organized in teams with different tasks and, correspondingly, different functional and operational characteristics. In particular, nodes in the same team will have the coordinated motion. We call this model the "affinity team model". For example, various units in a division can be organized into companies and then further partitioned into task forces based on their assignments in the battlefield. In a highway, platoons of cars can be treated as a team because of their motion affinity. Other examples are search and rescue operations, disaster monitoring, and mobile sensor platforms. Our basic observation of those applications is that nodes can be grouped based on their physical location, mobility, or interests. With the affinity team model, it suffices for mobility management to keep track of only one of the nodes in each team (a representative node). Other nodes in the team can be reached through the representative node. As our affinity team model guarantees the stability of clustering (teams) in some degree, the design of an efficient scalable hierarchical multicast structure is now realistic.

Our proposed idea, *Team-Oriented Multicast* (TOM), exploits the affinity team model. It defines teams and manages the membership information using the unit of team rather than that of a set of individual nodes. A team is defined as a set of nodes that have the motion affinity and interests differentiated by subscribed multicast groups. To fully utilize that logical hierarchy of teams, TOM provides a two-tier multicasting approach where the source propagates a data packet to each subscribed team's leader and each leader forwards the data to the entire team. As one can easily expect, the performance of such a two-tier approach considerably depends on the design of first-tier communication platform among leaders. From now on, we will call the leader the "team representative node" (TRN). If the reliability and latency of data transmission to each TRN can be bounded, this two-tier approach can provide a reasonable throughput. Otherwise, this approach may perform worse than a flat multicast protocol such as ODMRP [14], because of the extra overhead to manage the logical cluster architecture. In Internet multicast, shared tree structures are often used to improve the efficiency of multicasting. Internet multicasting protocols emphasize efficiency rather than reliability because the underlying wired medium guarantees the data delivery in some degree. In MANET scenarios, this is not true anymore. Due to collisions, congestion, link errors, jamming, asynchronous links and interferences, the delivery ratio on a wireless connection varies over time and it may becomes unacceptable(e.g., less than 60%) [7]. The delivery ratio of a packet sharply drops as the traveled hops increase [7]. This unique characteristic makes the hierarchical MANET multicasting protocol distinctive from hierarchical multicasting protocols proposed in wired network. Thus, the main focus of TOM is to provide an efficient and robust platform among selected team leaders.

The rest of paper is organized as follows. Section 2 briefly overviews the related works. In Section 3, we will discuss the design issue and protocol description of TOM. Following Section 4 will show the evaluation of TOM through simulation study. Finally, we conclude our paper in Section 5.

2   Related Works

As the node mobility is one of main challenges to design MANET routing protocol, many researches have been conducted to develop a mobility model [3] [6]. The observation of group affinity is not new. In [3] [10] [16], the author already proposed a group mobility model where a set of nodes move together. There are many researches on clustering algorithms and routing algorithms considering node mobility [4] [2] [9] [8]. However, not many researches have been accomplished on hierarchical MANET multicasting protocols working with group mobility.

A few MANET multicasting protocols choose hierarchical approaches [12] [17] [5] [21]. Those ideas have been mostly focused on the efficiency and reliability in a rather small scale network. Unicast tunneling used in AMRoute and unicast transmission in MCEDAR are not scalable, since the cost of unicast grows as the number of participants or *cores* increase.

In [21], the authors proposed a hierarchical multicasting based on the scalable unicast routing LANMAR [8], called M-LANMAR. The approach and design goals of M-LANMAR are similar to TOM. M-LANMAR, however, totally depends on the underlying unicast protocol to propagate the packet to landmarks, and thus it shows the limited scalability.

TOM, divergent from previous approaches, addresses the low packet reception rate in a large network and provides a robust forwarding structure. This is important especially in a large-scale network where the cost (e.g., latency and packet overhead) of packet recovery is considerably high.

3   Algorithm Description

As a first step to a hierarchical multicasting, TOM constructs a virtual hierarchy by organizing nodes to a few teams based on affinity team model and selecting a leader for each team. With such a hierarchy, TOM provides a two-tier multicasting paradigm where the source delivers the packet to each member in two steps: (1) inter-team data forwarding: data forwarding to each team leader called a team representative node (TRN) and (2) intra-team forwarding: data dissemination within a team initiated by the TRN node. Detailed algorithm description is found in our full version paper [20].

The network that TOM considers consists of several teams $\{T\}$ and individual nodes that do not belong to any team due to the lack of affinity. A team T is a connected un-directed graph with the maximum distance D from a node i to j (i and $j \in T$). A link (i, j) implies a direct connection between i and j. A team T is defined as a set of nodes having the same mobility pattern and common interests i.e., motion affinity group. Each node discovers a team and selects a leader in a distributed manner based on the idea proposed in [9]. In the paper, for the sake of simplicity, we assume: (1) a node does not join a multicast group if it does not belong to a team; and (2) all nodes in the same team subscribe the same multicast groups. With those assumptions, inter-team membership maintenance and data forwarding become simple. Thus, this paper focuses on inter-team membership management and data forwarding.

3.1   Inter-team Group Membership Management

TOM builds up a m-ary connected multicast mesh structure among subscribed teams' leaders. In m-ary connected multicast mesh structure, each leader has at most m undirected connections with other leaders. By allowing m redundant packet receptions from connected leaders, note that each node forwards a data packet to all connected leaders except toward incoming direction, our mesh structure provides a reliable transmission platform over a tree structure. To effectively manage the mesh structure with dynamic membership changes, TOM develops a mesh maintenance algorithm, where the goals of algorithm are (1) requiring less dynamic mesh re-construction; (2) working in a distributed fashion; and (3) demanding low overhead.

To maintain a path between two leaders connected in the multicast mesh structure, TOM uses a distance vector routing protocol (DSDV). With random mobility of each team, all nodes should proactively manage the paths to leaders. Thus, each node in the network maintains the table of all the leaders who subscribed to any group and periodically exchanges and updates that table with neighbor nodes. We call the table of leaders as TRN table hereafter.

Our mesh structure is an undirected connected graph $G = (V, E)$. Each vertex $v \in V$ can have at most m edges. The redundancy factor m can be adjusted considering the overall reliability. However, to satisfy the connectivity of our graph model, m should be greater than 2 (two) [20]. As default, we use $m = 3$. Each vertex v in the graph has a unique sequence number seq_v, which is assigned at Membership Join phase. A root vertex $r \in V$, which has the lowest sequence number among V, maintains the vertices list V and the current sequence number $C(seq)_G$ to assign a new member. The sequence number is important to maintain a connected graph with dynamic membership changes i.e., new join, leave or link changes.

A Group Membership Join: TOM, because of TRN table update mechanism, can propagate the partial membership information with low overhead to the entire network. Only root vertices of multicast groups advertise the group address and the size of the multicast mesh graph to the entire network by piggybacking the information on TRN table exchange messages so that a new team can finds a point to send a Join Query by looking up its TRN table.

The Join of a new team T_i to a group m_j is a procedure to add a vertex trn_i (the leader of T_i) and edges with the minimal cost to the multicast mesh graph $G(m_j)$ while keeping $G(m_j)$ connected. When a new team T_i wants to join

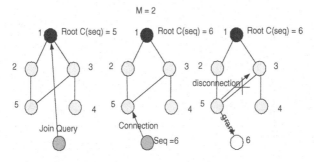

Fig. 1. Join Procedure

a multicast group m_j, the leader trn_i of T_i first looks up its local TRN table to retrieve the root vertex of $G(m_j)$ and sends a query if available. Otherwise, (i.e., this node is a new incoming node or no team has subscribed to m_j), trn_i claims itself as a root vertex in a graph $G = (\{trn_i\}, \emptyset)$ and starts advertising the membership information with TRN table exchange. Once a root vertex discovers another graph for the same group, it tries to merge two graphs (**Graph Merge Procedure**)(see [20]).

When a root vertex r receives the query packet, it increments the current sequence number $C(seq)_G$ and assign to trn_i (i.e., $seq_{trn_i} = C(seq)_G$). r returns the member list V and new sequence number seq_{trn_i} to trn_i. Each node has two connection list: the parents list CL_p and children list CL_c. For each link (v, w) where $seq_v < seq_w$, v is a parent of w and w is a child of v. To guarantee a connected graph, a vertex v should have at least one link $e_p = (v, w)$ where $seq_w < seq_v$ (i.e., $CL_p \neq \emptyset$) (The proof is given in [20]). trn_i sorts the member list V in ascending order according to the distance from trn_i based on its TRN table. Until, trn_i finds a parent node to connect, it sends a Connection Request to a node v_j i.e., j-th element in V. Upon receiving a Connection Request packet, v_j performs **Connection Establish Procedure** (see [20]). Without a link and node failure, trn_i will find at least one parent node if $m \geq 2$ (see [20]). Note that we assume that network is not partitioned.

Once trn_i is connected to G, then trn_i informs the root vertex r. The root vertex adds trn_i to V and propagates to G with the current sequence number $C(seq)_G$. To provide resilient membership maintenance in spite of a failure of the root, we duplicate the membership information to each vertex in the graph. Fig. 1 illustrates an example of Join Procedure. Once a node joins a group, it may add connections up to m links adaptively.

Membership Leave. When a team leaves a group, the leader sends an explicit Membership Leave Request. If the leader is not a root vertex, it disconnects all connections and informs the root vertex. If a root vertex wants to leave, it chooses the vertex v with the smallest sequence number and hands over the root role. A new root advertises the entire nodes in the graph the change of root address. A root without edge simply stops advertising so that each node in the network removes the entry from TRN table after a timeout.

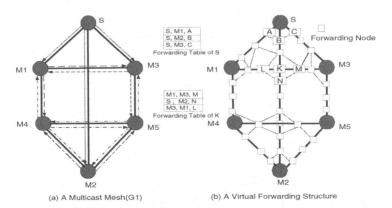

Fig. 2. Multicast Mesh and Virtual Forwarding Structure

3.2   Inter-team Data Forwarding

Inter-team data forwarding mechanism is the key to the success of TOM's two-tier data transmission approach. To design an efficient and reliable inter-team forwarding mechanism, however, is very challenging, since the average distance of data transmission is very large and the path reliability is extremely low. The path redundancy by the mesh structure does not significantly improve the reliability without a bounded packet reception rate between two connected leaders. Thus, our main goal of inter-team data forwarding scheme is to improve the path reliability in an efficient way.

TOM proposes the multi-path neighbor aggregation (MPNA) technique. MPNA builds a virtual forwarding structure including intermediate nodes and leaders in the multicast mesh. Fig. 2 illustrates an example of a multicast mesh structure and following a virtual forwarding structure. Ideally, a node in the virtual forwarding structure should relay a packet only once for efficiency. In MPNA scheme, however, a node may relay the packet more than once to propagate aggregation information, if necessary. We should note that this forwarding node concept is not new. It was already proposed in ODMRP. However, MPNA develops a different mechanism to find forwarding nodes. In ODMRP, each intermediate node sets the forwarding flag, if it receives a Join Reply packet from a neighbor, thus explicit control messages are necessary. In MPNA, a sender calculates next forwarding nodes (next hops) using TRN table and adds the aggregation header piggybacking the information to the packet. A node sets the forwarding flag, if it discovers that, by examining the aggregation header of incoming packet, a previous hop selects it as a next hop. Conceptually, it is more similar to soft-state Differential Destination Multicast (DDM) [11] than to ODMRP. In DDM, targeting a small group, each source aggregates the packet in a similar way to MPNA. DDM, however, attempts to reduce the aggregation information by deploying the synchronization between a node and the next hop. If a route is pretty stable, DDM can significantly reduce the aggregation overhead. TOM, however, is designed for a network with high mobility, and thus, the stability of a path is pretty low. More importantly, the underlying routing protocol used to update paths between leaders, DSDV, tends to change routes frequently. With DSDV, a node updates a path whenever it discovers a fresher route even though the current path is still valid [7]. Thus, the optimization of DDM is not directly applicable to TOM. Furthermore, TOM provides multi-path transmission. Thus, it differs from previous schemes [14,11].

3.3   Intra-team Membership Maintenance and Data Forwarding

We use a simple approach to handle intra-team membership. This is warranted by the fact that within the team, relative mobility is minimal and only short range because of team affinity. To maintain the team, e.g., the leader re-selection, team forming and team split/merge, each node is required to periodically exchange some information. In our implementation, each node exchanges local routing table including entries in $\frac{D}{2}$ hops from a node and a leader is selected based on the routing table information. Without deploying explicit membership join/leave messages, nodes can advertise the membership by piggybacking on the routing table update packets. The data is propagated within a team using a "scoped flooding".

4   Simulation Study

In this section, we evaluate the performance of TOM through extensive simulation experiments. As a reference for performance comparison we use ODMRP (On-Demand Multicast Routing Protocol) [14]. This benchmark choice is justified by the fact that ODMRP was shown to outperform most of the existing ad hoc multicast schemes such as CAMP [12], AMRoute [5] and ARMIS [19] in mobile scenarios [15].

Our performance metrics are as follows: (1)delivery ratio: The ratio of the number of delivered packets to each member versus the number of supposedly received packets by each member; (2) forwarding overhead: the total number of forwarded data packets versus the total number of delivered packets to members; and (3) packet latency: the average end-to-end delay of a multicast packet to each member.

We use QualNet [1] simulator, a successor of GloMoSim [18]. It provides a detailed and accurate model of the MAC, Channel and routing protocols. We use default parameters provided by QualNet. In our simulation, each source generates data in a CBR (Constant Bit Rate) fashion with UDP (User Datagram Protocol). Each source generates 4 pkts/second with 512 bytes packet size. We use IEEE 802.11 DCF MAC and two-ray ground path-loss model for the Channel. The transmission range of each node is 376m and bandwidth of the device is 2Mbits/sec.

In the network, 1000 nodes are uniformly placed within 6000 x 6000 m^2 terrain. We divide the network into 36 groups where each group has the same group mobility following "Reference Point Group Mobility (RPGM)" model [3]. Except for the mobility study, for all simulations, each team moves with 10 m/s speed with 10 seconds pause time. We assume that the whole group joins a multicast group if a node in the group joins i.e., a group defines a team if it subscribes a multicast group. Thus, maximally 36 teams can exist in the network. The average number of neighbors for each node is 10 and the scope of a team is four. For maintaining the routing structures, ODMRP uses 2 seconds interval for each Join Query and TOM uses 1 second interval for TRN table update. To maintain a team i.e., for a cluster management, each node periodically broadcast its local routing table at every 5 seconds. In our simulation study, we omit the team discovery procedure. We assume that a team is pre-fixed for the simplicity of the evaluation.

TOM, as default, uses a multicast mesh structure with $m = 3$ and MPNA scheme with the path redundancy factor $r = 2$ and a new path update interval $I_{update} = 0.25$ seconds.

4.1   Study on Scalability

One of our main contributions of TOM is the scalability as the group size and number, and network size increases. To show the advantage of TOM compared to traditional *flat* multicast protocols, we examine the throughput changes of TOM over different group number and size compared to those of ODMRP, a representative *flat* MANET multicast protocol. By deploying a large number of nodes (we use 1000 nodes through our simulation), we implicitly show the scalability of TOM with the large number of nodes. To test the scalability with the group number, we increase the number of multicast group(s) from 1 to 10 where each group has five subscribed teams with a single source. For a group size test, we fix the group number and the source number to 1 and increase the number of subscribed teams from 1 to 10.

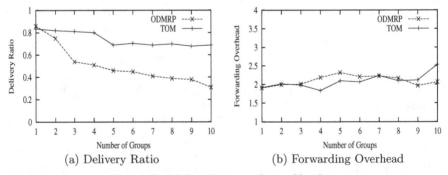

(a) Delivery Ratio   (b) Forwarding Overhead

Fig. 3. Scalability Test v.s. Group Number

Fig. 3(a) and 3(b) show the delivery ratio and forwarding overhead of TOM compared to those of ODMRP with variable group sizes. The forwarding overhead of both TOM and ODMRP slightly grows as the group number increases;

because the network becomes more congested and thus, the delivery ratio degrades. Notably, the delivery ratio of TOM is fairly stable in spite of the increase of offered load. Since TOM does not introduce major control overhead as the group size or number increases, it keeps the network status pretty stable. On the other hand, the performance of ODMRP significantly degrades as the group number increases. As ODMRP applies separate Join Query flooding for each group, the control overhead of ODMRP proportionally increases to the number of group. Thus, ODMRP suffers from heavier load due to the increase of data packets as well as Join Query flood packets as the group number increases. Those results clearly demonstrate the scalability of TOM as the group number increases.

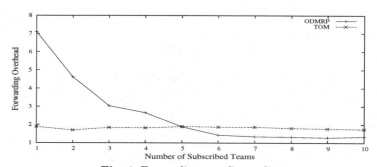

Fig. 4. Forwarding v.s. Group Size

Fig. 4 illustrates the forwarding overhead of both schemes versus the group size. Remarkably, in spite of intra-team flooding overhead, the overhead of TOM is comparable to that of ODMRP. More importantly, the overhead of TOM keeps stable. Note that, if we apply an efficient flooding scheme or ODMRP for the intra-team data forwarding as mentioned earlier, the overhead of TOM can be further reduced. On the other hand, the forwarding overhead of ODMRP is closely related to the group size and actually grows as the group size becomes smaller. Since ODMRP periodically floods a data packet with Join Query message i.e., ODMRP piggybacks the Join Query information on the data packet periodically to update the membership information, the total number of forwarded data packets is dominated by the flooding packets. Thus, the forwarding overhead decreases as the number of members delivering the packet increases. Note that we omit the comparison in terms of delivery ratio with the group size since the next simulation study implicitly shows the result.

4.2 Impact of Mesh Degree on Performance

Intuitively, the packet delivery ratio of a mesh structure will be enhanced as m increases unless the network is congested. In this simulation, we want to investigate the impact of redundancy degree m on the delivery ratio and forwarding overhead. As a reference, we build a 1-level multicast tree with $m = 0$.

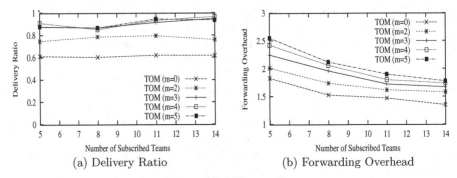

(a) Delivery Ratio   (b) Forwarding Overhead

Fig. 5. Mesh Degree Test

For the simulation, we use a multicast group with a single source. We increase the number of subscribed teams from 5 to 14.

In the results, Fig. 5(a) and 5(b), we can observe two major performance improvements between $m = 0$ and $m = 2$ and between $m = 2$ and $m = 3$. The results clearly demonstrate the benefit from the path redundancy created by using the mesh structure. However, a mesh structure with a large redundancy factor more than three does not significantly improve the throughput. Notably, with a mesh with $m = 5$ suffers and performs actually worse than $m = 4$ case due to too heavy forwarding overhead. Empirically, we recommend $m = 3$ to maximize the throughput of the proposed mesh structure.

Note that [20] includes more simulation study results.

4.3   Investigation on Forwarding Mechanisms

In this simulation, we investigate the performance of inter-team forwarding mechanisms: (1) separate unicast tunneling; and (2) multi-path neighbor aggregation technique with $r = 1$ i.e., a single path, $r = 2$ and $r = 3$. As we study the throughput of first-tier nodes, we omit the intra-team forwarding in this experiment. Thus, only team leaders become member nodes of a multicast group. And we use fixed team leaders randomly chosen at the initialization of each simulation run. We examine the performance of ODMRP over subscribed leaders, as a reference.

We use a multicast group forming the multicast mesh ($m = 3$) with a single source and variable number of members from 5 to 14.

In Fig. 6(a) and 6(b), we can observe four important facts. First, the delivery ratio of the single-path broadcast schemes used by ODMRP and MPNA with $r = 1$ are remarkably low compared to that of unicast tunneling. Still, the redundant packet transmission in the multicast mesh significantly improves the reliability i.e., TOM+MPNA ($r=1$) performs far better than ODMRP. Secondly, the multi-path mechanism considerably enhances the throughput. By adding one more path i.e., $r = 2$, the performance of TOM is improved more than 20%. As the throughput difference between $r=2$ and $r=3$ is not significant, we recommend to use $r = 2$ for MPNA technique. Thirdly, the forwarding overhead of unicast

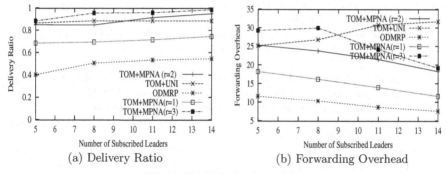

Fig. 6. Path Redundancy Test

increases as the number of connections increases. On the other hand, broadcast mechanisms reduce the overhead and efficiently forward a packet by eliminating unnecessary re-braodcasts of the same packet. Thus, broadcast mechanisms are much more scalable than unicast tunneling with group size. Lastly, our virtual forwarding structure becomes more robust and efficient with the group size. The forwarding overhead of MPNA scheme degrades but the reliability of it increases as the group size grows.

Note that, to collect the forwarding overhead of ODMRP in this simulation study, we omit the number of periodic data flooding packets (i.e., Join Query flooding packets). Thus, we consider the overhead of ODMRP as the lower bound to propagate a data within a multicast mesh structure. Considering that each team has many members, TOM does not significantly increase the forwarding overhead even though it applies multiple paths and redundant transmissions.

5   Conclusion

In the paper, we proposed a two-tier hierarchical multicasting protocol exploiting the affinity team model. Our proposed idea, TOM, contributed as follows: (1) by reducing the number of visible members from outside, TOM considerably reduces the complexity and overhead of a multicasting protocol; (2) TOM identified and corrected the low packet delivery ratio in the large-scale network, which should be addressed to develop a scalable MANET protocol; (3) TOM developed a multicast mesh structure and multi-path neighbor aggregation technique to improve the reliability; (4) through extensive study, TOM showed the scalability, reliability, flexibility and efficiency.

References

1. Scalable networks, http://www.scalble-solutions.com.
2. B. An and S. Papavassillou. A mobility-based clustering approach to support mobility management and multicast routing in mobile ad-hoc wireless networks. *International Journal of Network Management*, 2001.

3. G. Bianchi, X. Hong, M. Gerla, G. Pei, and C.-C. Chiang. A group mobility model for ad hoc wireless networks. *Proceedings of ACM/IEEE MSWiM'99*, 1999.
4. B.McDonald and F.Znati. A mobility-based framework for adaptive clustering in wireless ad hoc networks. *IEEE Journal on Selected Areas in Communications*, vol. 17, Aug. 1999.
5. E. Bommaiah, M. Liu, A. McAuley, and R. Talpade. AMRoute: Ad-hoc Multicast Routing protocol. *Internet-draft, draft-talpade-manet-amroute-00.txt*, 1998.
6. T. Camp, J. Boleng, and V. Davies. A survey of mobility models for ad hoc network research. *Wireless Communications and Mobile Computing (WCMC): Special issue on Mobile Ad Hoc Networking*, 2002.
7. D. S. J. De Couto, D. Aguayo, B. A. Chambers, and R. Morris. Effects of loss rate on ad hoc wireless routing. *technical report MIT-LCS-TR-836*, March 2002.
8. M. Gerla, X. Hong, and G. Pei. LANMAR: Landmark routing for large scale wireless ad hoc networks with group mobility. *Proceedings of IEEE/ACM MobiHOC*, 2000.
9. X. Hong and M. Gerla. Dynamic group discovery and routing in ad hoc networks. *Proceedings of the First Annual Mediterranean Ad Hoc Networking Workshop*, 2002.
10. R. Hutchins and E. Zegura. Measurement from a campus wireless network. *ICC*, 2002.
11. L. Ji and M. S. Corson. Differential destination multicast-a manet multicast routing protocol for small groups. *INFOCOM*, 2001.
12. J.J.Garcia-Luna-Aceves and E. L. Madruga. A multicast routing protocol for ad-hoc networks. *IEEE INFOCOM*, 1999.
13. F. Kamoun and L. Kleinrock. Hierarchical routing for large networks: performance evaluation and optimization. *Computer Networks*, 1977.
14. S.-J. Lee, M. Gerla, and C.-C. Chiang. On-demand multicast routing protocol. *Proceedings of IEEE WCNC*, 1999.
15. S.-J. Lee, W. Su, J. Hsu, M. Gerla, and R. Bagrodia. A performance comparison study of ad hoc wireless multicast protocols. *IEEE INFOCOM*, 2000.
16. M. Sanchez and P. Manzoni. A java based simulator for ad-hoc networks. *http://www.disca.upv.es/misan/mobmodel.htm*, 2001.
17. P. Sinha, R. Sivakumar, and V. Bharghavan. MCEDAR: Multicast core-extraction distributed ad hoc routing. *IEEE WCNC*, 1999.
18. UCLA. Glomosim: A scalable simulation environment for wireless and wired network systems.
19. C.-W. Wu and Y. Tay. A multicast protocol for ad-hoc wireless networks. *MILCOM*, 1999.
20. Y. Yi, M. Gerla, and J.-S. Park. Team oriented multicast: a scalable routing protocol for large mobile networks. *UCLA Technical Report 030034*, 2003.
21. Y. Yi, X. Hong, and M. Gerla. Scalable team multicast in wireless ad hoc networks exploiting coordinated motion. *NGC*, 2002.

Generalized Multicast Congestion Control
An Efficient Multi-rate Scheme Using Single-rate Control*

J. Li and S. Kalyanaraman

Rensselaer Polytechnic Institute, 110 Eighth Street, Troy, NY 12180
{lij6@cs,shivkuma@ecse}.rpi.edu

Abstract. In this paper, we propose a multicast congestion control called GMCC. It provides multi-rate features at low complexity by encompassing a set of *independent* single-rate sub-sessions (a.k.a layers). Various receivers can subscribe to different subsets of these layers to achieve different throughput. The sending rate in each layer is adjusted without boundary by a single-rate multicast congest control algorithm. The set of layers offered to receivers is also dynamically adapted to need. In summary, GMCC is *fully adaptive*.

Keywords: Multicast, congestion control, multi-rate,single-rate

1 Introduction

In multicast [5], the congestion control issue is complicated because we need to consider the congestion on a tree instead of that along a path. Intensive research has been conducted in this area, and researchers have proposed two categories of multicast congestion control protocols: single-rate and multi-rate.

In single-rate protocols such as ORMCC [12], PGMCC [19] and TFMCC [21], the source sends data to all receivers at a dynamically adjusted rate. The rate has to be adapted to the slowest receiver to avoid consistent congestion at any part of the multicast tree. Therefore, faster receivers suffer. Still, single-rate protocols have advantages because they are simple.

In a multi-rate multicast session, there are a set of sub-sessions, also called layers. Each layer has multicast traffic and uses a separate multicast group address. Examples are RLM [10] PLM [11], RLC [20], FLID-DL [1], FLGM [3], STAIR [2] and WEBRC [15]. Recipients have to increase or decrease their receiving rates by joining or leaving some layers[1]. Since the sending rates of these layers are not adapted to network status, the receivers have to perform join/leave operations very frequently to adapt their throughput to real time congestion. However, according to IGMP [8], join and leave operations (especially leave) need time to take effect, leading to coarse control. Moreover, a large volume of control traffic is introduced into the network, and the routers are heavily loaded

---

* This work was supported in part by a grant from Intel Corporation.

[1] Joining a layer is also called subscription, leaving a layer is also called unsubscription. In this paper we will use both sets of terms exchangeably.

B. Stiller et al. (Eds.): NGC/ICQT 2003, LNCS 2816, pp. 155–167, 2003.

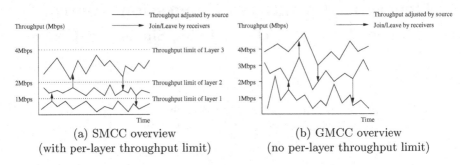

(a) SMCC overview
(with per-layer throughput limit)

(b) GMCC overview
(no per-layer throughput limit)

Fig. 1. Qualitative Comparison of SMCC and GMCC

because all the rate control burden has been shifted to them. These schemes are also called *receiver-driven* schemes.

A recently proposed scheme SMCC [9] is a hybrid of single-rate and multi-rate multicast congestion control. It combines a single-rate scheme TFMCC[21] with the receiver-driven idea. In each layer, the source adjusts sending rate *within a certain limit* based on TFMCC, and receivers join or leave layers cumulatively according to their estimated maximum receiving rates using TCP throughput formula [18]. Since the flows in each layer are adaptive to network status, the number of join and leave operations are greatly reduced. The congestion control is more effective. However, since SMCC requires static configuration of the maximum sending rates for each layer, it may require more layers than necessary for a receiver to achieve desire throughput, or fail to differentiate receivers desiring for different throughput.

Our proposed scheme GMCC solves these problems while having the merits of SMCC. Figure 1 shows the difference between SMCC and GMCC visually. In general, GMCC has the following advantages:

(1) It is *fully* adaptive. The sending rate in each layer can be adjusted without rigid limits. Together with the automatically adjusted number of layers, it always allows heterogeneous receivers to receive at different rates.
(2) The number of layers used is just enough to accommodate the differences among the throughput desired by receivers. No redundant layers are used.
(3) The source can control the overall throughput of a multicast session by limiting the number of layers to be used. In particular, if only one layer is allowed, GMCC works as a single-rate multicast congestion control scheme, which is the reason it is so named.
(4) It is not coupled with equation-based rate control mechanism such as TFMCC. The rate control mechanism at source can be replaced by others based on representative (the most congested receiver).

GMCC also addresses the issue of starting and stopping traffic within layers depending on whether there are receivers in the layers.

In the rest of this paper, we will describe the details of GMCC, and show some simulation results to demonstrate the performance of GMCC.

2   Generalized Multicast Congestion Control

The two key issues of GMCC are (1) How the source controls the throughput in each layer, (2) How and when a receiver join or leave layers to adjust its total throughput. The basic ideas of solutions are the following:

- In each layer, the source chooses a most congested receiver as *congestion representative* (CR) and adjusts the sending rate of this layer according to the CR's feedback (Section 2.2).
- The source starts traffic in a layer when the first receiver joins and stops traffic in a layer when the last receiver leaves (Section 2.3).
- Each receiver joins layers cumulatively, and is allowed to be the CR of at most one layer.
- When a receiver detects that it is much less congested than the most congested receiver (i.e. the CR) in the highest layer it has joined, meaning it can potentially receive at a higher rate, it joins an additional layer *successively* (Section 2.4).
- When a receiver detects that it is the most congested receiver in more than one layer, which means it confines or can potentially confine the sending rates of more than one layer, it leaves the highest joined layer (Section 2.5).
- Receivers make decisions of join and leave based on statistics. Statistics can be used only if (1) At least a certain number of samples have been collected, and (2) Every layer has a CR.

As shown in the above ideas, it is important for a receiver to detect whether it is more congested than another. We propose to use *Throughput Attenuation Factor* (TAF) for this purpose described in next section. After that, we describe various aspects of the GMCC scheme.

2.1   Throughput Attenuation Factor

Throughput Attenuation Factor (TAF)[2] is a metric *measured at the receiver side* to indicate how congested the receiver is. It comprises two parts, *Individual Throughput Attenuation Factor* (ITAF) and *Congestion Occurrence Rate* (COR), each describing a different aspect of congestion.

Individual throughput Attenuation Factor. ITAF is defined as

$$1 - \frac{\mu}{\lambda}$$

measured only in congestion epochs (A congestion epoch is an event when one or more consecutive packets are lost[3].) μ is the instantaneous output rate and λ is the rate of input generating this portion of output. It shows how much proportion

---

[2] This section is a self-contained overview of our technical report [13] which covers more details.

[3] We assume that packet loss is due to congestion only.

of input is lost during an instance of congestion, and therefore indicates *how serious* this instance of congestion is.

ITAF may be measured in the following way in implementation: Each data packet carries the instantaneous sending rate information, assumed to be λ_n for the packet of sequence number n. When a packet of sequence number n arrives, the receiver divides this packet size by the latest packet arriving interval and gets the instantaneous receiving rate μ_n. If the receipt of sequence number n indicates a packet loss, a ITAF is obtained as $1 - \frac{\mu_m}{\lambda_m}$ where m is the received sequence number immediate prior to n.

Congestion Occurrence Rate. COR is defined as the reciprocal of the interval between two consecutive congestion epochs. For instance, if the loss of packet n and $n + i$ $(i > 1)$ is detected at time t_1 and t_2 respectively (with the packets from $n + 1$ to $n + i - 1$ received), then a sample of COR would be $\frac{1}{t_2 - t_1}$. COR shows how frequently congestion happens.

With ITAF and COR defined, TAF is the product of these two factors, i.e.

$$TAF = ITAF \times COR$$

The larger TAF, the more congested is a receiver. To avoid unnecessary oscillation, the average values over a certain number (30 in our simulations) of ITAF and COR samples are used for TAF calculation. In GMCC, each receiver measures its own TAF *for each joined layer* and maintains the mean Θ and standard deviation Θ^σ of the latest N TAF samples for the purpose of TAF comparison.

2.2   Sending Rate Control within a Layer

Given a layer with active receivers, the source chooses a most congested receiver in this layer as congestion representative (CR) and uses its feedback for rate adaptation[4]. When the CR detects packet loss, it sends feedback packets called *congestion indications* (CIs) back to the source that decreases the sending rate by half. To avoid reducing rate too much, the source decreases the sending rate at most once per SRTT (smoothed RTT). The samples of RTT are collected by the source at the receipt of CIs. The value of a sample is the time difference between the CI arrival and the departure of the data packet triggering the CI. SRTT is calculated by exponential weighted moving average formula: SRTT = $(1 - \varepsilon)$ SRTT + ε RTT $(0 < \varepsilon < 1$, we use 0.125). At the absence of CIs, the sending rate is increased by $s/SRTT$ each SRTT, where s is the packet size.

To update CR, the source checks the following condition based on statistical inference [16], and switch CR from receiver j from i if the condition is true.

$$\Theta_i > \alpha_1 \Theta_j + \alpha_2 \sqrt{\frac{\Theta_i^{\sigma 2} + (\alpha_1 \Theta_j^\sigma)^2}{N}} \tag{1}$$

---

[4] The concept of CR here is similar to the representative receiver in DeLucia & Obraczka's work [6] and TFMCC [21].

Table 1. Some Key Symbols In Section 2

Symbol	Meaning
Θ_i	Average TAF of receiver i
Θ_i^σ	Standard deviation of receiver i's TAF
θ	Average ITAF of a receiver's highest joined layer measured during periods without bandwidth shifting
θ'	Average ITAF of a receiver's highest joined layer measured during bandwidth shifting periods
N	Number of TAF/ITAF samples kept for calculation
J	Number of positive TAF/ITAF comparison results required to join an additional layer

The symbol meanings are shown in Table 1, and α_1, α_2 are configurable parameters. We set α_1 as 1.25 since we want to bias toward the current choice of CR to avoid unnecessary oscillation, α_2 as 1.64 for a 90% confidence level.

On the receiver side, CIs are suppressed if receivers find out that condition (1) is true. The information of CR is broadcast to all receivers for the calculation.

Notice that unlike SMCC, the sending rate in each layer can be adjusted to any level required for adaptation. Besides, other rate control mechanisms such as those in PGMCC [19] and TFMCC [21] can be used in place of the current one, as long as the transmission rate is controlled by the source based on the feedback packets from the most congested receiver.

2.3 On-and-Off Control of Layers (by Source)

In any GMCC session, there is always a basic layer in which the source keeps sending packets subject to rate control. All other layers must be turned on (i.e. start traffic) or turned off (i.e. stop traffic) at right time to avoid bandwidth waste. When a receiver joins a layer which did not have any receiver yet, the source needs to start sending packets in this layer, i.e. *turn on* this layer. In an active layer, the CR keeps sending heartbeat packets to the source. If the source has not received heartbeat packets from the CR for a certain period, and no new CR is chosen, the source stops sending data in this layer, i.e. *turn off* this layer. For more details, please refer to our technical report [14].

2.4 Joining an Additional Layer (by Receiver)

Whenever a receiver enters a GMCC session, it subscribes to the basic layer of GMCC and stays there till it quits the session. Beyond this basic layer, the receiver must perform join operations to increase its total throughput rate at right time. A receiver joins an additional layer *successively* when it detects that its throughput rate can be potentially increased. There are three types of join:

Type 1: Join Operations Triggered by Normal TAF. This is the common type of join. Assume we observer receiver i, and the CR is receiver j. Receiver i

measures TAF for the *the highest layer* it is in as we defined before. Once there are at least N TAF samples of this layer, it check the following condition:

$$\Theta_j > \beta_1 \Theta_i + \beta_2 \sqrt{\frac{(\beta_1 \Theta_i^\sigma)^2 + \Theta_j^{\sigma 2}}{N}} \tag{2}$$

β_1 and β_2 are parameters. We are conservative about join, and heuristically choose $\beta_1 = 2$, $\beta_2 = 2.58$ for a 99% confidence level. If the condition in (2) is true for $J (= 30)$ consecutive times, the receiver will join an additional layer. The reason to use relatively small N for samples and J for TAF comparison results, instead of to use a single large N for samples, is that calculating the mean and deviation of a large set of samples is expensive. Meanwhile, this method can catch the dynamics of networks.

Although the TAF comparison in other layers can also stimulate the receiver to join more layers, restricting it in the highest joined layer has equivalent effect and simplifies the design.

Type 2: Join Operations Triggered by Hypothetical TAF. Sometimes the link between the source and a receiver is underutilized and the receiver does not have any TAF samples. In this case, we use *hypothetical* TAF. When a non-CR receiver notices that the CR of its highest joined layer has updated TAF statistics, this receiver gets a *hypothetical* COR sample by assuming congestion at this moment. Using this COR sample together with *unchanged* ITAF (1 for no loss), it calculates a *hypothetical* TAF and check the condition in (2). Once there are J *consecutive* positive results, a join operation is triggered.

Note that the test version of COR and TAF are not accepted as permanent samples since they are not true samples. Once used, they are discarded. Consequently, the join operations of type 1 are not interfered.

Type 3: Join Operations Triggered by Probabilistic Inter-layer Bandwidth Shifting. Under some special cases, there can be no type 1 and 2 join but join operations are still plausible. Consider a topology in Figure 2 containing two bottlenecks. Assume $R1$ is in one layer, and $R2$ is in two layers. When $R3$ enters the session, since the bandwidth in Bottleneck 1 has already be fully utilized, it will stay in only one layer. The reason is that the congestion generated by *intra-session flows* of other layers is not distinguished from that by *inter-session flows*, whereas the congestion of the former kind can actually be ignored in the context of deciding whether to join. This problem also occurs in SMCC, but the paper [9] did not consider it.

A solution can be that, for the above example, sometimes we try to send a little more in the first layer, while sending less in the second layer. If R3 does not see any increased congestion, it will know that a portion of the congestion is incurred by intra-session flows, therefore can join the second layer.

Certainly the above method should be carefully managed because sending more in a layer might cause more severe congestion on some paths. We developed the following technique called *probabilistic inter-layer bandwidth shifting* (PIBS).

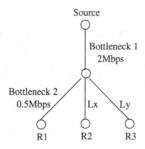

Fig. 2. A Topology Example Where Probabilistic Inter-layer Bandwidth Shifting Is Needed

Assume multiple layers (layer 1 to n, $n > 1$) are used in a multicast session. Let the period between two consecutive rate reductions (in the same layer) be a *rate control period* (RCP). At the beginning of each RCP at layer i ($1 \le i < n$), with probably ρ, the source decides that it will send data at the $(1 + \delta)$ level (otherwise send normally). That is, at any moment during this whole RCP, if the calculated sending rate is λ_i, the source will actually send packets at the rate of $\lambda_i + \min(\delta\lambda_i, \lambda_{i+1})$. At the same time, at layer $i + 1$, the actual sending rate is adjusted to $\max(0, \lambda_{i+1} - \delta\lambda_i)$. Briefly, the source "shifts" some bandwidth from layer $i + 1$ to layer i. To avoid significant unfairness to non-GMCC flows, ρ and δ must be small (both are 0.1 in our simulations). Also, at any moment, no two layers are allowed to perform bandwidth shifting simultaneously.

Given a receiver R and a multicast session the receiver is in, assume ℓ layers go through the bottleneck on the path between the source and R. If $\ell > 1$, for any layer $i < \ell$, according to the definition of ITAF (Section 2.1), the average ITAF measured by R at layer i during bandwidth shifting periods (θ') should be approximately the same as that measured during periods without bandwidth shifting (θ). On the contrary, if θ' is larger than θ, it means shifting bandwidth to layer i cause more congestion, indicating that no layer above i goes through the same bottleneck.

Assume R's highest joined layer is k, and the highest layer with traffic for the whole multicast session is L. If $k < L$, R will check the following condition at layer k once it has at least N samples for both θ and θ'.

$$\theta - \gamma\sqrt{\frac{\sigma^2 + \sigma'^2}{N}} \le \theta' \le \theta + \gamma\sqrt{\frac{\sigma^2 + \sigma'^2}{N}} \tag{3}$$

σ and σ' are the standard deviations corresponding to θ and θ' respectively. If condition (3) is true, the receiver R will join layer $k+1$. It should be noticed that although ITAF samples are distinguished under this situation, they are treated as the same for TAF calculation under situation 1 and 2.

Two Exceptional Cases. To prevent spurious join, there are two exceptional cases to be checked before the join operation really occurs.

(1) If any layer does not have a CR yet, meaning the session has not reached its sending rate limit, the join attempt should be canceled.

(2) If a receiver is already a CR for some layer, or detects that it may become a CR in any of its joined layers, meaning it will unnecessary confine the sending rates of other layers if joined, it also refrains itself from join. The detection is done by checking the following condition, assuming this receiver is i and the CR is j,

$$\Theta_i > \Theta_j + \omega\sqrt{\frac{\Theta_i^{\sigma\,2} + \Theta_j^{\sigma\,2}}{N}} \tag{4}$$

ω decides confidence level, and we used 3.5 for 99.99% level.

It is worth mentioning that we do not have "join attempt" as SMCC does. We believe that in GMCC, since both the sending rates in each layer and the number of layers can be dynamically adjusted, as a multicast session goes on, the combination of sending rate settings and the choice of layer number will evolve to the extent that will accommodate the heterogeneity among the receivers, so that a join won't cause abrupt severe congestion. Moreover, omitting join attempts significantly simplifies the design.

2.5   Leaving a Layer

A receiver always unsubscribes from the highest joined layer. After a receiver joins a layer, it needs to wait for some time to allow the network stabilize. This is achieved by collecting N more samples for TAF statistics in *all* joined layers before it checks whether to leave. Then, if the receiver is the CR or satisfies the condition in (4) in more than one layer, it leaves the highest layer it is in. The reason is the same as explained in the second exceptional case of join at the end of Section 2.4.

3   Simulations

We have run several *ns*-2 [17] simulations to test different aspects of GMCC. In these simulations, drop-tail routers are used, router buffer size is set to 20K bytes, and Reno TCP is used for background traffic.

3.1   Effectiveness of the Adaptive Layering

GMCC does not require redundant layers to satisfy heterogeneous receivers, as shown in this simulation. In Figure 3, four TCP flows go from node S to TR1∼4 respectively, and a GMCC session originates at S and ends at GR1, GR2. The bandwidth of the link between R1 and R3 is set to 5Mbps in the first simulation, and 10Mbps in the second. Ideally, two layers as the minimum are expected for both simulations, with GR1 in one layer and GR2 in two.

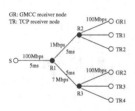

Fig. 3. Topology for layering effectiveness test

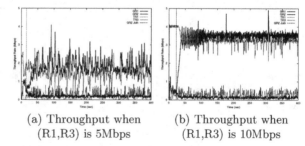

(a) Throughput when (R1,R3) is 5Mbps

(b) Throughput when (R1,R3) is 10Mbps

Fig. 4. Effective Layering Test Result

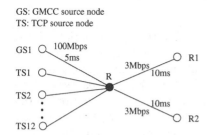

Fig. 5. Star topology for testing responsiveness to traffic dynamics

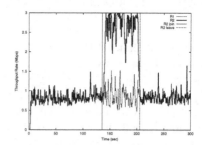

Fig. 6. Test Results of Responding to Traffic Dynamics

The throughput of the flows in these two simulations are shown in Figure 4. GR2 joined an additional layer at 15.8-th second and at 22.4-th second in the first and second simulations respectively, and stayed in two layers till the end of simulations. In contrast, GR1 only subscribed to the basic layer. This conforms to the expectation above and shows that the GMCC does not use more layers than necessary.

3.2 Responsiveness to Traffic Dynamics

There are two types of response to traffic dynamics. The first type of response is by the source that adjusts sending rates within layers. GMCC's rate adaption by source is almost the same as that in our single-rate work ORMCC [12]. Therefore, we omit the examination of source response to traffic dynamics here, and refer readers to [12]. The second type of response is by receivers by means of joining and leaving layers. It can be considered as a complementary measure of the first type response limited by CRs.

We used the star topology in Figure 5 to test the receivers' responsiveness to the dynamics of crossing traffic on the bottleneck. A GMCC session has GS1 as the source node and R1, R2 as the receiver nodes. On each of the links of (R,R1) and (R,R2), there are six TCP competing flows at the beginning of the simulation. During the period between 100-th and 200-th second, five TCP flows on the link (R,R2) pause, leaving one TCP flow as the only competing flow.

As shown in Figure 6, receiver R2 joined an additional layer at 135.412-th second. After those five TCP flows pause, the link (R,R2) became much

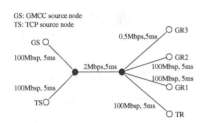

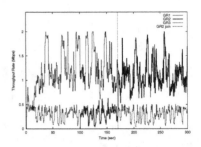

Fig. 7. Topology for testing prob. inter-layer bandwidth shifting

Fig. 8. Test Results of PIBS: Throughput of All GMCC Receivers

less congested than (R,R1). Therefore, this join operation is appropriate. There is 35-second gap between the pause and the join operation, though. That is relatively long because GMCC is conservative about join and therefore requires enough number of samples and positive TAF comparison results (see Section 2.4). However, GMCC is quicker when making decisions about unsubscription. In this simulation, R2 left the layer at 205.178-th second. On the other hand, since there is no traffic dynamics on the link (R,R1), receiver R1 remains in one single layer.

3.3   Effectiveness of Probabilistic Inter-layer Bandwidth Shifting

To verify that PIBS (Section 2.4) is a valid technique, we ran a simulation on the topology in Figure 7. A TCP flow originates at TS and ends at TR as background traffic. The GMCC flows in a multicast session go from GS to GR1,2,3. The 2Mbps bottleneck is shared by all three GMCC receivers, and the 0.5Mbps bottleneck only affects GR3. At the beginning of the simulation, only GR1 and GR3 are in the session. At 100th second, GR2 enters the session. Figure 8 shows that in one simulation instance, GR2 subscribed to an additional layer at 170.146-th second based on bandwidth shifting. Again, there is long delay because GMCC receivers need to collect enough samples before making decisions.

We noticed that in some other instances of this simulation, a join operation for another reason (in particular, under situation 2 in Section 2.4) happened before the results of bandwidth shifting took effect, and the joini operations triggered by bandwidth shifting were suppressed. This is not unexpected because the flows are dynamic and the comparisons in GMCC are all probabilistic. It is possible that during some random periods the condition in situation 2 becomes true and triggers a join operation.

3.4   Throughput Improvement

The topology in Figure 9 contains six bottlenecks and is used to test how GMCC improves the throughput of heterogeneous receivers with relatively slight difference of expected throughput. All the links are of 5ms delay. The bandwidths of

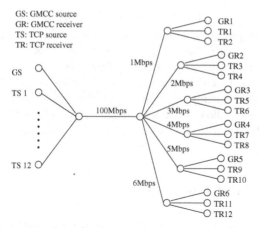

Fig. 9. Topology for testing throughput improvement

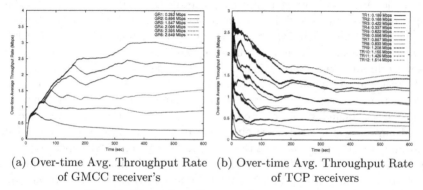

(a) Over-time Avg. Throughput Rate (b) Over-time Avg. Throughput Rate
of GMCC receiver's   of TCP receivers

Fig. 10. Throughput Improvement Test Result

the bottlenecks are from 1Mbps to 6Mbps. On each of them, there are two TCP flows as competing traffic. A GMCC session is held between the source GS and six receivers (GR1 to GR6). Simulation time is 600 seconds.

Figure 10 shows the over time average throughput rate of all receivers. Over time average throughput rate at time t is defined as the total throughput through time t divided by the total run time. We can see that the six GMCC receivers do achieve different throughput rates, with GR6 being the highest and GR1 being the lowest. Six layers are used in this simulation.

We need to mention that in this simulation, GMCC receivers achieve higher throughput than TCP correspondents. The reason is that each flow in a GMCC layer is a single-rate congestion control flow independent of other flows. It competes for bandwidth like any other flow does. For example, when GR2 subscribes to two layers, there are then two TCP flows and two GMCC flows on the 2Mbps bottleneck. The throughput of GR2 is the sum of both GMCC flows, and therefore can be approximately twice as much as each of the TCP flows. However, due to the limit by CRs in lower layers, assuming there are n TCP flows and m

GMCC flows on a bottleneck, a receiver may not get the share of $m/(m + n)$. GR6 here is an example. Although what we observed for GMCC in this simulation is different from traditional TCP-friendliness concept, we don't consider it as a serious problem, because each GMCC flow within a layer still competes in a TCP-friendly manner. This is more or less the same as people open multiple TCP connections to transmit a single object over the Internet. Moreover, using independent GMCC flows of this kind greatly simplifies the task to achieve multi-rate for multicast. Still, we will explore this issue more carefully in the future.

4   Conclusion and Future Work

We have presented a multi-rate multicast congestion scheme called GMCC. By combining single-rate congestion control and traditional multi-rate techniques (mostly joining and leaving layers by receivers) in a novel way, it provides a simple design for a perplexing problem of which most previous solutions are complicated. While having the merits of a similar previous scheme SMCC [9], it is *fully* adaptive and surmounts the limits posed by SMCC's static configurations. A new technique called *probabilistic inter-layer bandwidth shifting* is proposed as the solution to a problem not addressed by SMCC. Besides, the rate control mechanism at source can be replaced by other representative-based mechanisms.

This paper includes the first step study of GMCC. In the paper, we have seen several parameters needed at receiver side in GMCC. To study how receivers' uniformly or differently changing these parameters affects GMCC performance is important. We would also like to conduct simulations in more complex topologies and with different types of buffer management (e.g. RED) on routers as well as with different flavors of TCP. We are now in the process of developing large scale simulations (with several thousand receivers) for GMCC on the simulator of ROSS [4].

References

1. J. Byers, et al, "FLID-DL Congestion Control for Layered Multicast," *NGC 2000*.
2. J. Byers, G. Kwon, "STAIR: Practical AIMD Multirate Multicast Congestion Control", *NGC 2001*.
3. J. Byers, et al, "Fine-Grained Layered Multicast", *Infocom 2001*
4. Christopher D. Carothers, David Bauer, Shawn Pearc, "ROSS: A High-Performance, Low Memory, Modular Time Warp System", *14th Workshop on Parallel and Distributed Simulation (PADS 2000)*, May 2000
5. S. Deering, "Host Extensions for IP Multicasting", *RFC 1112*, August 1989
6. Dante DeLucia, Katia Obraczka, "A Multicast Congestion Control Mechanism Using Representatives", *Proceedings of the IEEE ISCC 1998*
7. Kevin Fall, Sally Floyd, "Simulation-based Comparisons of Tahoe, Reno, and SACK TCP", *Computer Comm. Review*, Vol. 26, No. 3, Jul. 1996, pp. 5-21
8. W. Fenner, "RFC 2236: Internet Group Management Protocol, Version 2", *IETF*

9. Gu-In Kwon, John Byers, "Smooth Multirate Multicast Congestion Control", *IEEE INFOCOM '03*, April 2003
10. S. McCanne, et al, "Receiver-driven Layered Multicast," *SIGCOMM '96*, Aug '96
11. A. Legout, E. Biersack, "PLM: Fast Convergence for Cumulative Layered Multicast Transmission Schemes", *Proc. of ACM SIGMETRICS*, 2000
12. Jiang Li, Shivkumar Kalyanaraman, "ORMCC : A Simple And Effective Single-Rate Multicast Congestion Control Scheme", *submitted work*, 2002
13. J. Li, et al, "Using Average Attenuation Factor to Locate the Most Congested Path for Multicast Congestion Control", *Technical Report, CS, RPI*, 2003, available at http://www.cs.rpi.edu/~lij6/Research/my_papers/ormcc-tr.ps.gz
14. J. Li, et al, "Generalized Multicast Congestion Control: An Efficient Multi-rate Scheme Using Single-rate Control", *Technical Report, CS, RPI*, 2003, available at http://www.cs.rpi.edu/~lij6/Research/my_papers/gmcc-tr.ps
15. Michael Luby, Vivek K. Goyal, Simon Skaria, Gavin B. Horn, "Wave and Equation Based Rate Control Using Multicast Round Trip Time," *SIGCOMM*, 2002.
16. William Mendenhall, "Introduction to Probability and Statistics: Third Edition", *Duxbury Press*, 1997
17. The Network Simulator - ns-2, available at http://www.isi.edu/nsnam/ns
18. Jitendra Padhye, et al, "Modeling TCP Throughput: A Simple Model and its Empirical Validation," *SIGCOMM 1998*, Aug. 1998.
19. L. Rizzo, "PGMCC: A TCP-friendly Single-Rate Multicast Congestion Control Scheme", *SIGCOMM '00*, Aug '00.
20. L. Vicisano, L. Rizzo and J. Crowcroft, "TCP-like congestion control for layered multicast data transfer," *INFOCOM*, Apr '98.
21. Jorg Widmer, Mark Handley, "Extending Equation-based Congestion Control to Multicast Applications", *SIGCOMM 2001*, Aug. 2001.

IP Multicast over Cable TV Networks

A. Selcuk Uluagac and Jon M. Peha

Carnegie Mellon University[1]
Dept. of Electrical and Computer Engineering
Pittsburgh, PA 15213, USA
selcuk@alumni.cmu.edu, peha@cmu.edu, www.ece.cmu.edu/~peha

Abstract. When a cable TV network that provides Internet access is connected to multiple ISPs, there are instances where multicast does not work or works inefficiently. This paper identifies causes of these problems, and proposes solutions, demonstrating that it is possible to provide efficient multicast with any of the architectures under consideration. In addition, the de facto industry standard for data transmission over cable networks, DOCSIS^{TM}, guarantees that a cable company will have the ability to block certain multicast traffic (such as traffic generated by Internet television broadcasters which compete with the cable company's core business.) This paper describes how an ISP can circumvent this. Under the assumption that there is a significant amount of multicast traffic, we show that cable companies and ISPs would be motivated to provide multicast services in all cases, but there are cases where they are not motivated to choose an efficient approach. Finally, we consider the impact of possible regulation that prohibits cable companies from blocking. In cases where this regulation has any impact, it can increase or decrease the cost of multicast services.

1 Introduction

Many companies multicast television and radio programming over the Internet [1]-[4], even though dial-up access cannot support real-time video and is marginal for quality audio. As more subscribers get broadband Internet access [5], these and other multicast applications may become common, making multicast efficiency important.

Efficient multicast mechanisms have been developed for a cable network connected to one Internet Service Provider (ISP), as was typical when Internet over cable began. However, this is changing. The US Government required Time Warner to connect its cable networks to multiple ISPs as a condition of the merger with America On Line [6]. There have also been trials with multiple ISPs in the U.S. [7]-[11]. Moreover, multiple ISPs can connect to cable data networks in Canada [12].

In this paper, we address multicast over cable platforms that support multiple ISPs. With current methods of enabling connections between cable networks and multiple ISPs, there are realistic cases in which multicast does not work or works inefficiently. We describe the causes of these problems and possible solutions. Additionally, the dominant standard for IP over cable [13] allows a cable company to block any multi-

---

[1] The authors would like to thank Professor Marvin Sirbu of Carnegie Mellon University and the reviewers for their valuable comments.

B. Stiller et al. (Eds.): NGC/ICQT 2003, LNCS 2816, pp. 168–180, 2003.

cast stream it wishes. For example, a cable company might use this capability to block services such as Internet TV that would compete with the cable company's core business [14]. We will describe the mechanism to block competing multicast traffic, and how ISPs can provide multicast services even when cable companies try to block.

Under the assumption that multicast becomes common, we will examine the conditions in which cable companies and ISPs are motivated to provide efficient multicast services, and the conditions in which a cable company would have incentive to use its blocking capability. There has been controversy regarding whether cable companies should be regulated so they cannot limit competition, or interfere with the free flow of information [15]-[17]. Under the same assumption that multicast is common, we also examine the possible consequences of regulating multicast mechanisms.

In section 2, we review architectures that permit multiple ISPs to operate over a cable network. Section 3 presents associated multicast problems on these architectures and proposes solutions. Section 4 explains how cable companies can block multicast traffic, and what an ISP can do to prevent this. Section 5 evaluates which technical design decisions would best support an effective business strategy from the perspective of a cable company and the perspective of an ISP. This section also considers the effect of a regulatory prohibition on blocking. Section 6 concludes this paper.

2   Forwarding Mechanisms that Support Multiple ISPs

Figure 1 shows a typical cable architecture [18]-[19]. Subscribers access the network through a *cable modem (CM)*. Traffic from CMs flows to a *Cable Modem Termination System* (CMTS) [20] at the cable *Head-End*. The CMTS manages traffic from or to the CMs, and allocates cable resources (i.e. bandwidth) both upstream and downstream. The CMTS is generally connected to an upstream interconnection device located at the *Regional Head-End* [20]. ISPs connect to the network at this *Regional Head-End*. The protocol suite that defines the interface and operation requirements for these devices is Data Over Cable Service Interface Specification (DOCSIS) [13].

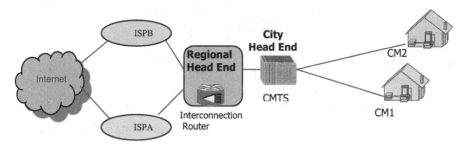

Fig. 1. Sample Cable Network Architecture with Multiple ISPs

When there are multiple ISPs connected to a cable network that uses typical routing techniques based on destination IP address at the regional head end, a subscriber's packets are not always sent upstream to their preferred ISP. Many techniques have been proposed to address this problem [21]-[26]. Among those, *Source-address based routing* (SABR) and *encapsulation* have attracted the most attention.

With source-address based routing, each cable modem's source address is assigned from the IP number pool associated with the customer's ISP [22], [23]. The router at the cable head end forwards upstream packets to the appropriate ISP based on source IP address instead of destination address. In effect, the router at the regional head end acts as though it were N *virtual routers*, one for each ISP. Each virtual router handles the packets that have source addresses in their range.

With encapsulation, a cable user's data packets are put into another packet. Generally, the outer packet is addressed to the preferred ISP and the inner packet is addressed to the final destination. The router at the cable head-end sees only the outer packets and forwards accordingly. The ISP delivers the inner packet to its final destination over the Internet. Encapsulation enables tunneling, where outer packets support tunnels between a cable user and a tunnel-terminating device (e.g. Access Concentrator). Inner packets travel inside those tunnels; each cable user has a separate tunnel running transparently through the cable network to the ISP [22], with a unique session or tunnel IDs to identify it. The encapsulation mechanism can be managed by either the cable company or the ISP [23]. In the former case, the tunnel ends on the cable network; the cable network strips off the outer packet and forwards the inner packet to the correct ISP. In the latter case, the tunnel ends at the ISP; the ISP strips off the outer packet, and the cable company knows nothing about the inner packets.

PPP over Ethernet (PPPoE) [27] and Layer Two Tunneling Protocol (L2TP) [28] are the encapsulation protocols most discussed for cable networks. Both encapsulate Point-to-Point Protocol (PPP) frames [29]. Figure 2 depicts a sample PPPoE architecture, where CM#1 and CM#2 users subscribe to ISPA and ISPB respectively.

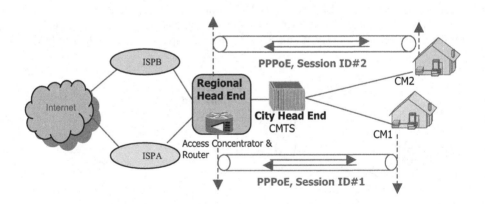

Fig. 2. Sample Cable Network Architecture with PPPoE

3   Multicast Problems and Solutions

3.1   Multicast Problems & Solutions with Source Address Based Routing

When source-address based routing (SABR) is used as the underlying technology in the cable network, the multicast transmissions pose different problems depending on the IGMP [30] *mode* of the DOCSIS devices (i.e. CM and CMTS), and whether an ISP can interpret multicast routing messages received from the cable network.

DOCSIS specifies two operational modes for the CMTS and CM devices: *active* and *passive* [31]. Active mode devices are able to terminate and initiate IGMP messages (e.g. send and receive a membership query message) like a multicast-enabled router [31]; passive mode devices cannot. Passive mode devices can only forward IGMP messages. If a DOCSIS-compliant device (i.e. CMTS or CM) acts as a router, it has to be in active mode; if it acts as bridge, it can be either active or passive.

If the CMTS is in *active mode*, multicast is not possible without protocol changes. The CMTS in active mode collects membership information from the cable modems via IGMP membership reports such as IGMP Join or Leave messages, and then summarizes these multicast activities by sending a message upstream to the regional head-end. Depending on the protocol deployed, this upstream message could be a Protocol Independent Multicast-Sparse Mode (PIM-SM) Join/Prune, a Distance Vector Multicast Routing Protocol (DVMRP) Prune/Graft, or a Multicast Open Shortest Path First (MOSPF) Link State Advertisement [32], [33]. The source address of a message sent upstream to the regional head-end is the address of the CMTS, so a source-addressed-based router at the regional head-end router cannot determine where to forward the packet. If it simply drops that packet, all multicast packets are lost.

There are two ways to make multicast possible. In one, which we call *Selective Forwarding*, the router at the regional head-end forwards upstream unicast packets based on source, and multicast packets sent by the CMTS (e.g. PIM-SM Join or DVMRP Prune) based on destination address. Whenever a new multicast connection is established, the router randomly selects an ISP, and forwards upstream multicast messages to that ISP for the duration of the multicast. Alternatively, this problem could be solved at the CMTS rather than at the regional head-end. Instead of using its own IP address as the source of membership reports sent upstream to the regional head-end (e.g. PIM-SM Join), the router at the CMTS could use the IP address of the first cable modem to subscribe to the multicast. The router at the regional head-end can then route this packet based on source address to an appropriate ISP.

Both schemes work if and only if the ISP understands these upstream multicast messages. If the cable network and the ISPs do not adopt the same protocols, this can be achieved by using an interdomain multicast protocol such as Border Gateway Multicast Protocol (BGMP) [34]. Alternatively, the router at the regional head-end could send an IGMP join message upstream to an arbitrarily selected ISP router instead of sending the multicast summary message.

With both of these approaches, it is preferable to send all packets through the ISP associated with the first cable modem to subscribe, even if that cable modem has since gone off line. Otherwise, the regional head-end may send upstream reports first to one ISP, and then to another, which would cause both ISPs to simultaneously forward the stream for extended periods.

All traffic from a given multicast stream would go through this same ISP. To be fair to all ISPs, the probability of selecting a given ISP should be proportional to the amount of multicast traffic received by that ISP's customers. If (and only if) the amount of traffic carried by an ISP is *consistently* out of proportion, then there is a fairness problem. This may occur when ISPs are selected randomly by the regional head-end, but the correct probability distribution is not known. Fairness should not be a problem if the matter is handled at the CMTS. The problem can also be prevented outside the cable network through a new ISP Signaling Protocol, where ISPs dynamically negotiate with each other to decide which ISP delivers multicast data to the customers of all of the ISPs. ISPs would exchange information about the ongoing multicast groups/applications and their members. However, the signaling protocol adds significant processing and communications overhead.

If the CMTS is operating in *passive mode*, multicast efficiency depends on the IGMP mode of the CMs. Consider the case where the two cable users in Figure 1 are associated with different ISPs and are interested in receiving the same multicast stream. If both users successfully send membership reports (MR) (i.e. IGMP Join) to their associated ISPs, then both ISPs will forward the multicast stream, causing each CM to receive two copies of each packet. If the CMs are in active mode, duplicate membership can be suppressed as follows. Every 10 seconds, customer devices send MRs upstream to the CM, where they can be forwarded upstream to the CMTS. When the CMTS receives an MR traveling upstream, the CMTS also forwards the MR on all downstream links, so all CMs see the MR. An active mode CM will suppress upstream transmission of an MR that merely duplicates an MR it has seen. Thus, multicast is efficient when CMs are active mode. In contrast, a passive mode CM will suppress an unnecessary MR only if it is holding the unnecessary MR in its buffer at the instant when it observes an equivalent MR from another CM. To solve the resulting redundancy problem that occurs when CMTS and CMs are passive mode, the Selective Forwarding Mechanism explained above could be deployed.

In summary, without protocol changes, multicast is efficient when CMs are active mode and the CMTS is passive mode, but multicast is inefficient when CMs and the CMTS are passive, and multicast fails entirely when the CMTS is active.

3.2   Multicast Problems & Solutions with Encapsulation Mechanisms

If the cable network uses a standard encapsulation scheme such as L2TP or PPPoE as described in Section 2, users will not be able to receive multicast packets without protocol modifications. With these protocols, the cable network cannot observe the multicast-related messages, such as membership reports. Consequently, when a router at the regional cable head-end receives a downstream multicast packet, the router will not recognize the multicast address, and will discard the packet.

There are two ways to make multicast work. The first is *multiple unicast*. With this technique, a router converts each downstream multicast packet that arrives from the Internet backbone to multiple unicast packets, and a packet is sent separately over the cable network to each of the interested users. If the tunnel-terminating device is within the ISP, then this conversion takes place at the ISP's gateway. If the tunnel-terminating device is within the cable network at the regional head-end, then this conversion can take place either at the head-end or the ISP's gateway. This technique requires some changes in the networking algorithms of either the ISP network or the cable network. The disadvantage of this solution is the excess resources consumed by redundant transmission of duplicate packets.

The second solution is *discriminatory encapsulation,* where multicast traffic is no longer encapsulated in the upstream and the downstream directions, but unicast traffic is encapsulated. Whenever a user wants to join a multicast application, encapsulation software residing in the user's PC does not encapsulate multicast membership report packets (i.e. IGMP Join.) This allows the cable network to be aware of the interested multicast receivers. In the same way, the tunnel-terminating device does not encapsulate multicast packets in the downstream. Thus, the implementation of this scheme requires new encapsulation software that discriminates between multicast and unicast traffic. This technique is more efficient than multiple unicast. However, as was discussed in Section 3.1, the ISP must be able to accept upstream reports from the regional head-end, either because there is an inter-domain multicast protocol such as BGMP [34], both networks use the same multicast routing protocol, or the regional head-end sends IGMP messages upstream.

4   Blocking Multicast Traffic

The DOCSIS protocol suite guarantees that a cable company can choose to block certain multicast traffic as a matter of its network policy [31]. For instance, a cable company may use this ability to block video streaming, which potentially competes with the cable company's core business. A DOCSIS-compliant CMTS can encrypt downstream multicast traffic, so that a cable modem must request the decryption key from the CMTS. The CMTS blocks the stream by denying the request [35]. In such a case, some interested customers will not be able to receive multicast streams.

However, an ISP can provide its customers with a multicast service that the cable company cannot block by using the multiple unicast technique described in Section 3.2; an ISP unicasts each packet downstream to every cable customer that wishes to receive the multicast service. The redundant transmissions obviously create higher loads than would be seen with an efficient multicast mechanism.

For multiple unicast to work, CMs must send membership reports upstream such that they reach the ISP, without being terminated en route at the CMTS or the regional head-end. Thus, upstream membership reports should be encapsulated. In systems where all upstream traffic is encapsulated, multiple unicast is always an option for ISPs. The method cannot be used in cases where software at the customer premises only encapsulates non-multicast upstream traffic as described in Section 3.2, or where source-address based routing is used and no upstream traffic is encapsulated. Thus, an ISP can use the multiple unicast technique where all upstream traffic is encapsulated, or where the ISP (and not just the cable company) provides the customer with the relevant piece of software to encapsulate the upstream membership report.

5   Multicast Strategies that Advance Business Objectives

This section examines which multicast mechanisms are likely to be adopted, assuming that multicast traffic is abundant, so there is incentive for protocol enhancements that improve multicast efficiency. Nevertheless, cable companies and ISPs do not always maximize profit by cooperating in attempts to improve efficiency.

Section 5.1 describes the extent to which cable companies and ISPs would be motivated to deploy mechanisms that would influence the efficiency of multicast under the assumption that cable companies are not restricted by regulation, or influenced by fear of regulation. Sections 5.2 and 5.3 discuss the technical options available to cable companies and ISPs, and identify which options these companies would select based on these motivations, with SABR and encapsulation respectively. In Section 5.4, we show how results would differ if regulators prohibited cable companies from using the blocking mechanism described in Section 4. Results both with and without this prohibition on blocking are summarized in Table 1 at the end of this section.

5.1   Motivation for Technical Efficiency

The pricing of Internet services influences who pays the price for inefficiency. The prices charged by cable companies can be categorized as *usage-based* or *non-usage-based* [36]. With the former, price depends on the amount of data sent and received. With the latter, price is fixed, independent of the amount of data sent and received.

With usage-based pricing, ISPs have incentive to facilitate efficient multicast where possible, so multicast becomes less expensive. Cable companies share this motivation for efficiency, except for multicast applications that directly compete with a cable company's core revenue sources such as broadcast television and pay-per-view movies. A cable company may increase its profit by causing competing services (e.g. Internet video broadcasting) to be more expensive. Nevertheless, cable companies benefit from an efficient multicast capability, because DOCSIS guarantees them the ability to block, thereby preventing competing services from using this capability.

ISPs can still provide multicast for competing services through multiple unicast, but the resulting redundancy makes multicast more expensive. Alternatively, it is conceivable that some networks may someday have the ability to offer discriminatory prices for different multicast streams, perhaps based on source address; in this case, the cable company could charge competing services more instead of blocking.

With non-usage-based pricing, cable companies always have incentive to make multicast efficient because efficiency reduces resource consumption without affecting the cable company's revenue. In contrast, ISPs have much less incentive to make multicast efficient, because they do not pay for the inefficiency. One implication is that cable companies should choose not to block multicast streams, because ISPs have the ability to circumvent this feature using the multiple unicast technique, and the resulting inefficiency increases the cost to cable companies and not to ISPs.

5.2   Source Address Based Routing

As discussed in Section 3.1, multicast traffic poses different problems in different architectural configurations. In each case, the cable company can address the problems without aid from an ISP. When the CMTS is in active mode, regardless of the IGMP mode of the CM devices, upstream multicast reports sent by the CMTS are dropped at the regional head-end so that the subscribers cannot receive multicast data. The cable company can solve this problem at the cable head-end by inserting the IP address of a subscribing cable modem as the source of membership reports sent upstream instead of using its own IP address. Alternatively, it can solve the problem at the regional head-end by using selective forwarding. If there is no interdomain multicast routing protocol, the cable company can configure the router at the regional head-end to send IGMP messages upstream. When both the CMTS and the CM are in passive mode, redundant transmissions can occur. The cable company can address this inefficiency problem via Selective Forwarding at the regional head-end. In networks where the CMTS is passive and CMs are active, multicast is always efficient.

As discussed in Section 5.1, a cable company has incentive to provide an efficient multicast service with both usage-based and non-usage-based pricing. Thus, regardless of whether the CMTS and the cable modems are in active or passive mode, all multicast is likely to be efficient unless the cable company blocks. However, as described in Section 5.1, cable companies have incentive to block competing services when there is usage-based pricing, thereby forcing ISPs to carry these competing services using the multiple unicast technique. With non-usage-based pricing, cable companies will not block, and all multicast will be efficient.

5.3   Encapsulation

As described in Section 3.2, users cannot receive multicast unless either multiple unicast or discriminatory encapsulation are adopted; both require protocols modifications. Whoever provides encapsulation software to the consumer decides whether to use discriminatory encapsulation. This could be either the cable company or the ISP. Moreover, discriminatory encapsulation requires either an interdomain multicast routing information exchange, or a change in the way the cable company's router at the regional head-end handles multicast packets, or for cable network and ISPs to use the same multicast routing protocol.

In the case where the cable company provides the encapsulation software, the cable company can choose discriminatory encapsulation, which is more efficient than multiple unicast, without aid of the ISP. As discussed in Section 5.1, a cable company has incentive to offer an efficient multicast service with either usage-based or non-usage-based pricing. Thus, cable companies would choose discriminatory encapsulation.

With non-usage-based pricing, where cable companies would not block, it is likely that all multicast traffic will use this efficient approach. In contrast, with usage-based pricing, cable companies have reason to block multicast from competing services, so an ISP has reason to use multiple unicast for this traffic. An ISP can do this without aid from the cable network. Consequently, multicast traffic from competing services will be carried inefficiently, and other multicast traffic will be carried efficiently.

In the case where the ISP provides the encapsulation software, cable companies acting alone cannot make discriminatory encapsulation work. Neither can ISPs, except in the case where the cable network and ISPs happen to use the same routing protocols. With non-usage-based pricing, cable companies prefer efficient solutions, but an ISP may or may not be willing to help. ISPs would accept the inefficiency of multiple unicast because inefficiency does not affect their cost, and ISPs would accept the vulnerability of discriminatory encapsulation to blocking, because a smart cable operator would not block in this case. The result may therefore depend on outside factors. For example, if a network has already been deployed without good support for multicast, it is easier to upgrade using inefficient multiple unicast, because this requires no change to software at the customer premises.

With usage-based pricing, a cable company would have incentive to block competing multicast services, so ISPs have incentive to deploy multiple unicast. To avoid the higher cost of multiple unicast due to redundant packet transmissions, the ISP may even choose to adopt two solutions: multiple unicast for streams that are blocked by the cable company, and the more efficient discriminatory encapsulation for other multicast traffic. The cable network does have a little incentive to support discriminatory encapsulation, perhaps with an interdomain exchange of multicast routing information. As above, whether this is enough incentive may depend on outside factors.

5.4   When Blocking Is prohibited

It is possible that regulators will prohibit cable companies from blocking competing services (e.g. Internet television), or they will use the threat of possible regulation to deter cable companies from blocking. This section evaluates the impact of such a restriction, assuming that it is the only regulatory restriction. As in Sections 5.1 to 5.3, we assume that the amount of multicast traffic is significant.

As discussed in Section 5.1, cable companies have no incentive to block when there is non-usage-based pricing, because ISPs can always resort to multiple unicast. Thus, with non-usage-based pricing, the results shown in Section 5.2 and 5.3 should be as appropriate with a prohibition on blocking as they were without the prohibition.

With usage-based pricing, there is a difference. Cable companies would prefer that multicast be inefficient and therefore expensive for competing services, but efficient for all other applications. When blocking is prohibited, they can no longer discriminate. If most multicast traffic comes from competing services, a cable company may prefer that all multicast be inefficient. If competing services are not a serious problem, and people are more likely to become cable modem customers if they can get a low price for noncompeting services that use multicast, then a smart cable company would make multicast efficient. A cable company would also be more inclined to provide efficient multicast when blocking is prohibited if the cable company is affiliated with an ISP that would benefit from the efficiency. While cable companies may or may not choose the most efficient option, recall from Section 5.1 that ISPs always prefer efficient multicast when there is usage-based pricing.

With SABR, multicast is always efficient when the CMTS is passive mode and the CMs are active mode. When the CMTS is in active mode, regardless of the mode of the CM devices, multicast is not possible unless the cable company adopts non-standard solutions, as proposed in Section 3.1. A cable company could choose to do nothing to solve the problem. This would force ISPs to offer a less efficient multicast using multiple unicast. The cable company benefits from choosing an efficient solution With usage-based pricing, a profit-maximizing cable company might choose either option, depending on demand for competing services. With non-usage-based pricing, the cable company benefits from choosing an efficient solution. The cable company has a similar choice to make if the CMTS and cable modems are both in passive mode. The cable company might choose to support efficient multicast through Selective Forwarding, as described in Section 3.1. The cable company might also choose not to do this, so when customers of different ISPs want to receive the same multicast stream, each ISP may forward the stream. This is inefficient, but not as inefficient as multiple unicast, where the stream is forwarded once for every recipient cable modem. Thus, in this case, a prohibition on blocking improves efficiency for competing services while degrading efficiency for noncompeting services.

With encapsulation, multicast is efficient or it is inefficiently transmitted via multiple unicast. With usage-based pricing, ISPs will always prefer an efficient approach. However, as demonstrated in Sections 3.2 and 5.3, the ISP cannot do this without help from the cable company except in the case where the cable network and ISPs happen to have adopted the same multicast protocols. Once again, the cable company may or may not prefer the efficient solution, depending on the impact of competing services on its core business. Thus, either outcome is possible.

Table 1. Summary of Probable Deployments from Sections 5.1 to 5.4

Forwarding Mechanism	USAGE-BASED PRICING		NON-USAGE-BASED
	No Prohibition	Blocking Prohibited	
Encapsulation (provided by ISPs)	B or D*	A or B*	A or B*
Encapsulation (provided by cable co.)	D	A or B*	A
SABR (Passive CMTS, Passive CMs)	D	A or C*	A
SABR (Passive CMTS, Active CMs)	D	A	A
SABR (Active CMTS)	D	A or B*	A
A. Multicast traffic is transmitted efficiently.			
B. Multicast traffic is inefficiently transmitted via multiple unicast. The number of copies equals the number of customers who want the stream.			
C. Multicast traffic is inefficiently transmitted. The number of copies equals the number of ISPs that have at least one customer who wants the stream.			
D. Competing multicast services are carried inefficiently via multiple unicast and other multicast traffic is carried via efficient mechanisms.			
* Depends on factors other than technical design.			

6   Summary

When multiple ISPs are providing services over cable networks, a forwarding mechanism is needed to deliver the packets traveling upstream to the correct ISP. The principal forwarding mechanisms that are currently under consideration are source address based routing (SABR) and encapsulation [20]-[23]. With these protocols, there are cases where either multicast does not work or works inefficiently.

If one of the widely discussed encapsulation protocols for cable networks (i.e. L2TP, PPPoE) is adopted, subscribers are not able to receive multicast streams, because a cable network cannot observe the presence of multicast membership reports. This problem can be solved in two ways: 1) multiple unicast, where a router, converts multicast packets to multiple unicast packets and then transmits them downstream; 2) discriminatory encapsulation, where unicast packets are encapsulated but multicast packets are not in the upstream and the downstream directions. The latter is less efficient. Both require that the ISP be able to understand the cable company's multicast packets, perhaps through an inter-domain-multicast routing protocol such as BGMP, or by translating upstream multicast routing packets into IGMP messages at the regional head-end.

If source-address based routing is the forwarding mechanism and the IGMP modes of the CMTS devices are active mode, multicast fails because the regional head end drops a received upstream multicast report (e.g. PIM-SM Join or MOSPF Link State Advertisement) that is sent by a CMTS. This problem can be solved either at the regional head-end or at the CMTS. At the regional head end, the router could filter the upstream multicast messages and forward the packet to a randomly selected ISP whenever a new multicast connection is established, which is *Selective Forwarding*. When the problem is solved at the CMTS, the CMTS would use the IP address of a subscribing cable modem as the source of membership reports sent upstream to the regional head-end instead of using its own IP address. Neither approach guarantees fairness to the ISPs; one ISP may consistently carry most of the multicast traffic. We have described mechanisms a cable company could adopt to solve this fairness problem. On the other hand, if both the CMTS and the CM are passive mode, then multicast works but users can receive more than one copy of every downstream multicast packet. This redundancy can be prevented at the cable network by adopting the above Selective Forwarding mechanism for IGMP-Joins. In only one case, where the CMTS is in passive mode and CMs are in active mode, standard multicast works efficiently.

Additionally, we have shown that DOCSIS gives a cable company the ability to block any multicast stream it wishes, including video multicast that competes the company's core business. However, an ISP can provide its customers a multicast service that the cable company cannot block through multiple unicast.

Assuming that multicast becomes quite common, cable companies and ISPs would be motivated to provide multicast services. Nevertheless, cable companies and ISPs are not always motivated to offer an efficient mechanism. We first consider the case where cable companies are free to block. Motivation depends on whether pricing is usage-based or non-usage-based. When pricing is *usage-based*, cable companies would be motivated to block multicast traffic associated with competing services, causing this traffic to be carried inefficiently via multiple unicast. All other multicast traffic would be carried with an efficient multicast service, except possibly in the case where encapsulation is used and ISPs provide the encapsulation software. In this case, it is possible that all traffic will be via multiple unicast. When pricing is *non-usage-based*, cable companies have no incentive to block because ISPs can adopt multiple unicast, which hurts cable companies. Traffic would be carried over an efficient multicast service, with the possible exception of the same case where the ISP provides encapsulation software. In this case, the ISP and cable company must work together to provide efficient multicast, which may or may not happen.

A cable company may be precluded from blocking by regulation or fear of regulation. Such a prohibition would be unnecessary with non-usage-based pricing, because cable companies would not block anyway. With usage-based pricing, there are architectures where companies provide efficient multicast. However, there are also architectures where the cable company may or may not be motivated to do so; it depends on whether cable companies profit more from making competing services expensive or from making other services inexpensive. If a cable companies chooses not to support efficient approach, then inefficient and expensive multicast will not be limited to competing services, as was the case without the prohibition. Thus, this regulation could actually increase the cost of multicast applications to consumers.

References

1. H. Jinzenji and K. Hagishima, "Real-time audio and video broadcasting of IEEE GLOBECOM '96 over the Internet using new software," *IEEE Communications Magazine*, Vol.: 35, Issue: 4, April 1997 pp. 34 –38.
2. "MediaChannel: Your Daily Guide to Internet Television & Video," *MediaChannel,* www.mediachannel.com
3. D. Gunzerath, "Radio and the Internet," *The National Association of Broadcasters*, May 5,2000, www.nab.org/Research/Reports/ RadioandInternet/sld015.htm
4. J. Careless, " Digital Television -JumpTV Fights For Retransmission," *Digital Television.com* Jun 1, 2001, www.digitaltelevision.com/2001/webcast/0801_1.shtml
5. "Broadband Subscriber Count Nears 20 Million - December 2002," *Kinetic Strategies Inc. Cable Datacom News* Dec. 1, 2002, www.cabledatacomnews.com/dec02/dec02-1.html
6. "FCC Approves AOL-Time Warner Merger," *The Federal Communications Commission Media Bureau* Oct. 25, 2001, www.fcc.gov/transaction/aol-tw-decision.html
7. Federal Communications Commission, "Annual Assessment of the Status of Competition in the Market for the Delivery of Video Programming," Ninth Annual Report, FCC Docket MB 02-145, Dec. 31, 2002.
8. R. Mark, "Cox Begins Its First Open Access Broadband Trials," *Internetnews.com* Nov. 6, 2001, www.internetnews.com/isp-news/article.php/8_917471
9. C. Grice, "AT&T to test open access to ISPs," *CNET News.com* June 7, 2000, news.com.com/2100-1033-241559.html?legacy=cnet
10. E. Joyce, "AT&T, Comcast Commit to ISP Access," *Internetnews.com* April 1, 2002, www.internetnews.com/isp-news/article.php/8_1001211
11. M. Ingebretsen and M. Siegel, "Cable slouches toward open access," *IEEE Spectrum*, Vol. 38, No. 4, April 2001, pp. 74 –79.
12. D. Menard and T. Denton, "Third Party Access to Cable Modems in Canada," Written for the FCC Open Access NOI, Docket No. 00-185. Version 2.0 Dec. 1, 2000
13. "CableLabs ≤ Certified™ Cable Modems Technical Specifications," *The CableLabs® Certified™ Cable Modem project,* DOCSIS, May 2002, www.cablemodem.com/specifications

14. S. Olsen, "Battle brews over Web streaming," *CNET News.com* May 31, 2001, news.com.com/2100-1023-267638.html
15. M. A Lemley and L. Lessig, "Written Ex Parte of Professor Mark. A. Lemley and Professor Lawrence Lessig In the Matter of Application of consent to the transfer of control of licenses MediaOne Group, Inc. to AT&T Corp," FCC CS Docket No. 99-251, Nov. 10, 1999
16. J. B. Speta, "The Vertical Dimension of Cable Open Access," *University of Colorado Law Review,* Vol. 71, No. 4, 2000, pp. 975-1010
17. T. W. Hazlett and G. Bittlingmayer, ""Open access:" the ideal and the real," *Telecommunications Policy,* Vol. 26, No. 5-6, 7 June 2002, pp 219-359
18. D. Fellows and D. Jones, "DOCSIS ™ cable modem technology," *IEEE Communications Magazine,* Vol. 39, No. 3, March 2001, pp. 202-209.
19. V. C. Majeti (Ed.), "Cable modems: current technologies and applications," *Intl. Engineering Consortium and Institute of Electrical and Electronic Engineers,* IEEE Press, 1999.
20. D. Farber, S. D. Dukes, and M. E. Laubach, "Delivering Internet Connections over Cable, Breaking the Access Barrier," *Wiley Computer Publishing, John Wiley & Sons Inc.* 2001
21. S. O'Donnell, "Broadband Architectures, ISP Business Plans, and Open Access," *Telecommunications Policy Research Conference (TPRC)* Alexandria, VA. Sept. 23-25, 2000.
22. M. E. Laubach, "Comments on the Technical Ability to Implement Open Access Provisioning via High-Speed Data over Hybrid Fiber-Coaxial Cable Television Systems in the United States," Prepared for the White House National Economic Council, May 30, 1999, www.matmos.com/whitepapers/openaccess990530.pdf
23. E. Tseng, "A Capital Cost Model For Open Access Cable Networks," *MIT Program on Internet & Telecoms Convergence Consortium (ITC),* MIT June 7, 2000, itc.mit.edu/itel
24. E. Tseng, and Sharon Gillett, "Open Access to Cable Data Networks," *MIT Program on Internet & Telecoms Convergence (ITC),* 2000, itel.mit.edu/itel/publications.html
25. "AOL OK With Policy-Based Routing - FEB. 2001," *Kinetic Strategies Inc. Cable Datacom News* Feb. 1, 2001, www.cabledatacomnews.com/feb01/feb 01-5.html
26. J. Fijolek, "Access Methods for Support of Multiple Internet Service Providers Over DOCSIS," CommWorks Corporation, a 3com Company, White Paper, June 4, 2000.
27. L. Mamakos *et al.,* "A Method for Transmitting PPP Over Ethernet (PPPoE)," Internet Engineering Task Force Request for Comments 2516, Feb. 1999, www.ietf.org/rfc/rfc2516.txt
28. W. Townsley *et al.,* "Layer 2 Tunneling Protocol (L2TP)," Internet Engineering Task Force Request for Comments 2661, August 1999, www.ietf.org/rfc/ rfc2661.txt
29. U. D. Black, "PPP and L2TP: remote access communications," *Prentice Hall,* 2000.
30. S. Deering *et al.,* "Internet Group Management Protocol," IGMP, version 3, Internet Engineering Task Force Request for Comments 3376, Oct. 2002, Proposed Standard
31. "DOCSIS Radio Frequency Interface (RFI) Specification," *The CableLabs Certified Cable Modem project* Dec. 31, 2001, www.cablemodem.com/Specs/SP-RFIv2.0-I01-011231.pdf
32. B. Mukherjee and L. H. Sahasrabuddhe, "Multicast Routing Algorithms and Protocols: A Tutorial" *IEEE Network,* vol. 14, no. 1, pp. 90-102, Jan.-Feb. 2000.
33. M. Ramalho, "Intra- and Inter-Domain Multicast Routing Protocols: A Survey and Taxonomy," *IEEE Communications Surveys & Tutorials,* First Quarter 2000, Vol. 3, www.comsoc.org/livepubs/surveys/public/1q00issue/ramalho.html
34. D. Thaler, D. Estrin, and D. Meyer, "Border Gateway Multicast Protocol (BGMP): Protocol Specification," IETF Draft, Nov. 22, 2000, work in progress, netweb.usc.edu/bgmp/draft-ietf-bgmp-spec-02.txt, www.ietf.org/internet-drafts/draft-ietf-bgmp-spec-03.txt
35. "DOCSIS Baseline Privacy Plus Interface (BPI+) Specification," *CableLabs Certified Cable Modem project,* Mar. 1, 2002, www.cablemodem.com/Specs /SP-BPI+-I08-020301.pdf
36. Q. Wang, J. M. Peha, M. Sirbu, "Optimal Pricing for Integrated-Services Networks," in *Internet Economics,* MIT Press, 1997, pp. 353-376, www.ece.cmu.edu/~peha/papers.html

Extremum Feedback with Partial Knowledge

Thomas Fuhrmann[1] and Jörg Widmer[2]

[1] Institut für Telematik, Universität Karlsruhe (TH), Germany
[2] Praktische Informatik IV, Universität Mannheim, Germany

Abstract. A scalable feedback mechanism to solicit feedback from a potentially very large group of networked nodes is an important building block for many network protocols. Multicast transport protocols use it for negative acknowledgements and for delay and packet loss determination. Grid computing and peer-to-peer applications can use similar approaches to find nodes that are, at a given moment in time, best suited to serve a request. In sensor networks, such mechanisms allow to report extreme values in a resource efficient way.

In this paper we analyze several extensions to the exponential feedback algorithm [5,6] that provide an optimal way to collect extreme values from a potentially very large group of networked nodes. In contrast to prior work, we focus on how knowledge about the value distribution in the group can be used to optimize the feedback process. We describe the trade-offs that have to be decided upon when using these extensions and provide additional insight into their performance by means of simulation. Furthermore, we briefly illustrate how sample applications can benefit from the proposed mechanisms.

1 Introduction

Feedback is crucial to many networked group applications. The classical example are multicast transport protocols where receivers send negative acknowledgments to initiate retransmissions or report parameters for congestion control [1,7]. Mobile or embedded devices with limited memory need similar mechanisms for flow-control. Feedback is also important for network health monitoring and a variety of distributed computing applications. For example, grid computing applications that employ a huge number of nodes with largely differing capabilities will want to assign each task to the node that is, at a given moment in time, best suited to process the request [2]. A peer-to-peer file-sharing application will want to find the servant that provides the best download capacity and an e-commerce application will seek for the best matching offer at the lowest price.

Although, in principle, feedback could be aggregated by multicast routers, commercial networks do not offer the required functionality. For other networks (e.g., satellite networks) aggregation is not possible at all, since there simply are no intermediate systems. In yet other networks, as for example sensor-networks, responding to feedback requests is very resource consuming, so that it is desirable that only a few nodes need to become active and transmit their responses.

B. Stiller et al. (Eds.): NGC/ICQT 2003, LNCS 2816, pp. 181–192, 2003.

(Note, that in this example we assume also asymmetric costs for reception and transmission of messages. See [4] for a potential usage scenario.)

If aggregation is not possible or inefficient, end-to-end feedback algorithms need to be employed. Such algorithms rely on spreading the feedback across a time interval that allows the group to suppress unfavorable and thus unnecessary feedback responses. The broader this spread (as compared to the network latency) the better the suppression that can be achieved.

In previous work [5,3], it has been shown that exponentially distributed timers are optimal for many feedback scenarios. The algorithms presented there guarantee feedback within a predefined time interval T and avoid feedback implosion, if T is sufficiently large as compared to the network latency τ and an upper bound N to the number of nodes is known. In [6] this exponential feedback algorithm is extended so that extreme values from a group of nodes can be determined.

This paper presents a further extension of the exponential feedback mechanism, namely a mechanism exploiting the knowledge nodes have about the distribution of the values that are to be reported. Such knowledge can typically be expected for most of the practical usage scenarios. In particular, we study cases where the values are *independent and identically distributed* to *one of several possible distributions*. Not knowing which distribution applies in a given case makes this problem hard. Again, this can be considered a rather typical case. Network measurements indicate that loss characteristics and round-trip-times follow known distributions, but the parameters of the distribution can quickly change when the network becomes congested. Sensors reporting physical values (e.g., temperature or humidity of the environment, etc.) often reflect a common distribution whose parameters change simultaneously for all sensors. Requests in file-sharing peer-to-peer networks show largely differing popularity, where a few requests can be served by a large number of nodes and a large number of requests can only be served by a few nodes. This, again, leads to uncertainty for individual request while good statistical knowledge exists about the distribution of requests in general.

In the remainder of the paper, we will discuss the different feedback mechanisms in Section 2, present further simulation results in Section 3, and conclude with Section 4.

2   Feedback Suppression Mechanisms

In this section, we propose feedback schemes for a potentially very large group of networked nodes to report extreme values to a central instance. We assume that the reported values are received by all other nodes of the group, too. This can be achieved either by using multi-source multicast, with a broadcast medium, or by having the central instance repeat reported values in a suitable manner. We *do not* assume any aggregation capabilities inside the network.

Let $v_i \in [0; 1]$ be the set of values from which we want to know $v_{\min} = \min\{v_i : i = 1, \ldots, N\}$. Generalization to other intervals (open and closed) or maximum-search instead of minimum-search is relatively straightforward by appropriately mapping the respective value interval to $[0; 1]$. From prior work [5,3] it is known that the following algorithm is optimal for the binary case $v_i \in \{0; 1\}$ (e.g., to report packet loss ($v_i = 0$) in a reliable multicast transport protocol).

Algorithm 1 (Binary feedback) *Each node with $v_i = 0$ draws a uniformly distributed random variable $x_i \in [0; 1]$ and sends a report at $t_i = T \cdot \max\{0; 1 + \log_N x_i\}$ unless it knows that another node has answered prior to that time.*

If no feedback is received from the receivers within the time interval T then $v_{\min} = 1$. Here, T is the maximum feedback delay and N is an upper bound on the number of responders.

Extending this algorithm, [6] describes an mechanism to produce $v_{\min}$ for general distributions of $v_i \in [0; 1]$. To this end, it makes use of that fact that a random variable can often be described by a probability density function $p(v)$. If the v_i are independent and identically distributed (iid), the following algorithm is optimal:

Algorithm 2 (Deterministic feedback) *Each node i calculates $x_i = P(v_i)$ and sends a report at $t_i = T \cdot \max\{0; 1 + \log_N x_i\}$ unless it knows that another node has already reported its value.*

Here, $P(v) = \int_0^v p(v') \, dv'$ is the cumulated probability distribution function. In other words, the random variable x employed in Algorithm 1 is substituted by the random variable v. This is achieved by using a mapping that turns the distribution of the values into a uniform distribution, namely the mapping $P : [0; 1] \to [0; 1]$. As a consequence, minimal values are reported early, thereby increasing the probability for suppressing unnecessary reports of non-minimal values.

Algorithm 2 is optimal for the case of an iid random variable with known probability density function $p(v)$. In practice, however, the values that are to be reported are rarely iid to *one* known probability density function. Therefore, in the following sections more complicated but also more realistic scenarios are analyzed and respective solutions are derived.

In order to judge the effectiveness of an algorithm, it is important to know the expected number of responses. Ideally, the fraction of nodes that respond at (or before) a given moment should rise exponentially over time. As described in [3] this accounts best for an unknown group size. Conversely, considering ever shorter time-intervals the fraction of nodes responding in any of these intervals should remain constant. Hence, plotting the fraction of responding nodes as area below a *response density* function on a (reversely) logarithmic axis, the ideal curve becomes constant. Note that, according to the fact that there is a finite probability for a node to not delay its answer, the origin of the time axis *does not* lie at the leftmost end of the time range. Furthermore, because of the $t = \log_N x$ relationship the response time depends also on the group size estimate N. Therefore, the following graphs are only illustrative and not

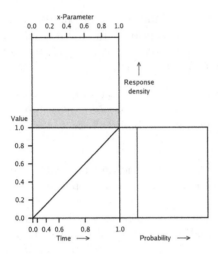

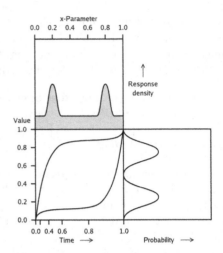

Fig. 1. Uniform distribution of values treated with Algorithm 2

Fig. 2. Response time distribution and expected number of responses for the a priori selection algorithm

exact. Since both, the probability density function and the expected number of responses as a function of time, can be plotted into a square, the resulting overall graph consists of three adjacent squares.

Figure 1 gives an illustration of Algorithm 2. Its single line shows that each value maps to one defined response time. For algorithms containing random elements, the line widens, assigning a whole range of response times to each value. Furthermore, generally, the actual shape of a response time graph does not only depend on the algorithm but also on the probability density functions.

2.1 Semi-deterministic Timers with a Priori Decision

In many cases where the values v_i are not iid to one probability distribution $p(v)$, one can find a set of probability distributions $p_j(v)$ so that with probability π_j the values are iid to $p_j(v)$. In other words, we do not know which probability distribution applies at any given moment in time, but we know that all the values are from the same probability distribution. This is what can typically be expected if the nodes are identically subject to the same causal effects of a random process. In such a scenario we have two different notions of probability:

- π_j is the probability that a distribution p_j applies.

- $P_j(v)$ is the probability of a node i to draw a value $v_i < v$ under the condition that this distribution applies.

There are two obvious algorithms for a priori determination of the response time curves:

Algorithm 3 (A priori mean) *Each node responds at time*

$$t_i = T \cdot \max\{0; 1 + \log_N \sum_j \pi_j P_j(v_i)\}$$

unless it knows that another node has already reported a smaller value.

and

Algorithm 4 (A priori selection) *Each node performs a random experiment such that it responds with probability π_j at time*

$$t_i = T \cdot \max\{0; 1 + \log_N P_j(v_i)\}$$

unless it knows that another node has already reported a smaller value.

Both algorithms are *semi-deterministic* because once the values v_i are known the response times t_i are completely determined. They are *a priori* in a sense that the decision which response time curve applies does not depend on the value v_i.

The problems that can arise from these algorithms are best illustrated by peaked distributions. Consider for example two peaked distributions each of which applies with a probability of 0.5. Using Algorithm 4 results in two significantly differing curves (Figure 2) that are equally populated with responding nodes. The two plateaus in the time domain correspond to the two mean values of the distributions (i.e., each time distribution curve tries to maximally spread out values around the corresponding mean value). Since each curve bears only 50% of the nodes and either of two curves tremendously fails to spread the values in the respective opposite case, 50% of the values are not spread out anymore. The graph shows two peaks in the response density, containing 25% of the nodes each. Only half of the nodes are uniformly distributed over the x-axis.

The mean value algorithm is performing better since it attributes two spreads corresponding to the two peak values (Figure 3). For each case, there is a constant expected number of responses with the expected response time depending on the minimal value within the group. The low value peak corresponds to early responses, the large value peak to late responses. However, compared to spreading the values in both cases over the whole interval, this scenario with a 50% chance each for the low and the high value distribution doubles the respective density of the expected number of responses. Note that the mean value algorithm corresponds to using the combined distribution together with Algorithm 2.

Hence, if the two distributions have greatly differing probabilities (e.g., 90% versus 10%) the distribution with the low a priori probability does not sufficiently contribute to the spread to avoid its values falling into a small time window. This effect thus causes a feedback implosion (see right graph in Figure 3). With a low a priori probability a large amount of responders will start responding almost at the same time. In the example shown above, this will happen at about $0.9T$.

This aptness of feedback implosion is a general and unavoidable feature of all algorithms that are based on a priori selection of a single response time

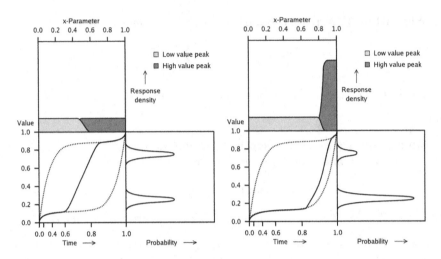

Fig. 3. Response time distribution and expected number of responses for the mean value algorithm. (Left: two peaks with 50% weight each. Right: two peaks with 90% and 10% weight)

curve. Hence, this type of feedback algorithm should not be used in case of asymmetric probabilities for two different probability distributions and in case of many largely differing probability distributions. In fact, it is hard to think of a scenario where the deterministic feedback of Algorithm 2 fails and Algorithms 4 or 3 work well.

2.2   Semi-deterministic Timers with Value-Based Decision

One way around this problem is the use of the values v_i not only to calculate the response time t_i but also to decide on the distribution curve that is used for the calculation. As in the previous case, there are two different alternatives: the use of a single mean-value curve and a value-based selection of one response curve among many.

Algorithm 5 (Value-based mean) *Each node i reports its value at time*

$$t_i = T \cdot \max\{0; 1 + \log_N \frac{\sum_j p_j(v_i) P_j(v_i)}{\sum_k p_k(v_i)}\}$$

unless it knows that another node has already reported a smaller value.

The value-based mean value algorithm can produce close to ideal behavior for certain probability distributions while it fails for others. Figure 4 shows three cases each with three peaked distributions of differing width. The response density is exemplarily shown for the case that the real distribution has a large mean value.

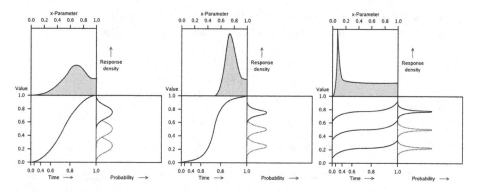

Fig. 4. Response time distribution and expected number of responses for the value-based mean value algorithm with three peaked potential distributions

1. For broad distributions the expected number of responses rises gently to a modest maximum and then falls again to the value that corresponds to an optimal spread. The function mapping values to response times is almost linear.
2. For moderately peaked distributions the rise is much sharper with a large but narrow maximum. Again, towards the limiting value the optimal response density is reached.
3. For narrowly peaked distributions the rise in the response density is very early and very sharp. Almost the whole response interval is covered by an optimal response density. Indeed, the sharp response peak is so small that the probability of a node having a value that falls into this response time tends to zero (i.e., even though the values are closely peaked, they are almost surely optimally spread over the whole response time interval).

At first sight, it might be surprising that the function mapping values to response times is not one-to-one. But a moment's thought shows that this function does not need to rise monotonically: Consider for example three almost completely separated peaks (Figure 4). Then, for each value one can tell with near certainty which of the three peaked distributions applies. Hence, each of the three peaks can be spread over the whole feedback interval, forcing the function to oscillate between early and late response. If, on the other hand, the peaks overlap, many values could either be very small values from a distribution with large mean, or reversely, large values from a distribution with small mean. Both cases would lead to exactly opposite response times. Thus, as a result, the value-based mean value algorithm averages the x-parameter. In case of medium peaks that are too broad to be entirely separated but too narrow to spread the values across a large enough interval, this can lead to a feedback implosion (see Section 3 for an example).

Algorithm 6 (Value-based selection) *Each node i performs a random experiment such that it reports its value with probability*

$$\tilde{\pi}_{ij} = \frac{p_j(v_i)}{\sum_k p_k(v_i)}$$

at time

$$t_i = T \cdot \max\{0; 1 + \log_N P_j(v_i)\}$$

unless it knows that another node has already reported a smaller value.

Algorithm 6 shows the same effect as Algorithm 5 but in a slightly different way. Instead of overshooting at the point where the large value peak becomes more likely than the middle peak, there is a continuing increase in the expected number of responses. As shown in Figure 5, we can observe a considerable risk of feedback implosion towards the end of the feedback interval where suppression is no longer effective.

Thus, although the value-based algorithms are quite capable of spreading responses over the whole feedback interval, there are certain distributions that cause feedback implosion due to peaking or delaying responses: Low value nodes delay their response to allow suppression. If a distribution with a large mean-value applies, both algorithms have to cope with the resulting delay. The mean value version does it as soon as possible and thereby in some cases too fast, causing feedback implosion. The random selection on the other hand adapts more gently but happens to be too slow in some cases.

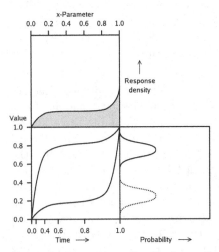

Fig. 5. Response time distribution and expected number of responses for the value-based selection algorithm

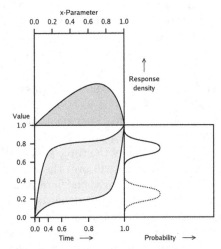

Fig. 6. Response time distribution and expected number of responses for the random spread mechanism

2.3   Randomly Spread Timers

Let $P_L(v)$ and $P_R(v)$ be the upper-left and bottom-right envelope to the cumulated distribution functions $P_j(v)$ in the sense that at least $nP_L(v)$ nodes have a value $v' < v$ and only up to $nP_R(v)$ nodes have a value $v' < v$ where n is a reasonable fraction of the maximum node number N [1].

Algorithm 7 (Random spread) *Each node i draws a uniformly distributed random number*

$$x_i \in [P_L(v_i), P_R(v_i)]$$

and reports its value at time

$$t_i = T \cdot \max\{0; 1 + \log_N x_i\}$$

unless it knows that another node has already reported a smaller value.

Like Algorithms 5 and 6, this algorithm is able to spread peaked distributions almost equally over the whole response interval (see Figure 6). Additionally, due to the randomness it is rather insensitive to exceptional value distributions. Even if all receivers report exactly the same value, this algorithm avoids a feedback implosion. Secondly, this algorithm does not require extensive calculations. However, for scenarios in which very little is known about the probability distributions, Algorithm 7 approximates the biased feedback algorithms presented in [6].

3   Simulations

To further illustrate the characteristics of the different mechanisms, we simulate the feedback process with two truncated normal distributions with peaks at 0.2 and 0.8 respectively for the distribution of values at the receivers. Both of the distributions apply with a probability of 0.5. The simulations were carried out with T set to eight times the network latency and for sizes of the receiver set n from 1 to 100,000 receivers. The upper bound on the size of the receiver set N was fixed at 100,000.

As shown in Figure 7, plain exponential feedback suppression achieves the lowest expected number of responses for a given maximum feedback delay T. However, the response times are independent of the response values, leading to an average deviation of the first reported value from the optimum of almost 0.4, when the total number of nodes is close to the estimate N (Figure 8). With deterministic feedback (not shown), the best value is always reported first while maintaining the same average number of responses. As expected, a priori selection and a priori mean frequently lead to a feedback implosion, resulting in an

---

[1] Note that for $n = N$ we would force the envelope to comprise *all* nodes. Choosing $n < N$ prevents outliers from disturbing the overall efficiency.

average number of responses only one order of magnitude lower than the number of nodes. Consequently, these algorithms cannot be recommended for general usage. By using information about the value at the receivers, one would expect to be able to improve the performance of the algorithms. Yet, only the methods of value-based random selection and random spread achieve a reasonable suppression of feedback messages. With a priori selection, feedback implosions may occur at the beginning of the feedback interval, whereas a priori mean and value-based mean lead to a feedback implosions towards the end of the feedback interval.

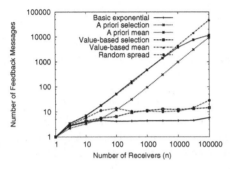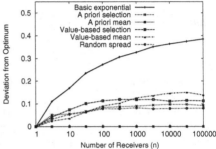

Fig. 7. Number of responses   **Fig. 8.** Quality of the first response

With all proposed mechanisms, the quality of the feedback (i.e., the deviation of the obtained response values from the real optimum of the group) improves significantly. Figure 8 shows the absolute deviation of the value of the first response from the optimal value. As before, we assume the values to be distributed between 0 and 1. A priori mean causes the optimal value or a close to optimal to be reported first almost all of the time. The performance of the other mechanisms is comparable with a deviation of roughly 0.1. Similar results are obtained when analyzing the best of the responses given, instead of the first one. However, such an analysis favors mechanisms which eventually cause a feedback implosions, since the optimal value is likely contained in the large number of responses given.

As mentioned in the previous section, particularly the value-based mean method depends to a large degree on the underlying distributions. When normal distributions with peaks further apart or closer together are used for the simulations, the method performs much better, as shown in Figure 9 for peaks at 0.1 and 0.9. While still prone to feedback implosion, the average number of feedback messages is reduced by a factor of 50. With value-based selection, which already performed very well in the previous simulation, the number of feedback messages is further reduced to around six messages. As is to be expected, the easier it is to distinguish the two distributions, the better the performance of the mechanisms.

Likewise, the number of responses is significantly better if the two normal distributions have different probabilities. In Figure 10, we depict the average number of responses when the probability that the distribution with a peak at 0.3 applies is 0.9 and the probability for the distribution with peak at 0.7 is 0.1. The number of responses for the methods where feedback implosion occurs is reduced by a factor of 10 compared to the previous simulations.

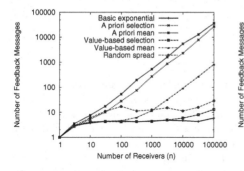 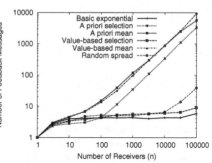

Fig. 9. Responses with peaks at 0.1 and 0.9

Fig. 10. Responses with distribution probabilities 0.9 and 0.1

Similar simulations with different distributions of response values and different probabilities for these distributions were carried out but have to be omitted for reasons of brevity.

4   Outlook and Conclusion

In this paper, we have analyzed several modifications to the basic exponential feedback mechanism. These modifications incorporate knowledge about the distribution of values that are to be reported into the feedback process. In the simple case of iid values, the distribution function can be used to obtain an optimal feedback algorithm. In more complicated cases, where one out of several potential distributions applies, a trade-off needs to be resolved: If the value distribution is either very broad or very narrow, the *value-based mean value algorithm* leads to a good spread of the responses (see Figure 4). However, for medium peaked distributions this algorithm can cause a severe feedback implosion. The *value-based random selection* and the *random spread* algorithms provide better protection against implosion while falling behind the efficiency of non-random algorithms. Both effects have also been demonstrated by means of simulations.

The proposed mechanisms greatly improve upon the quality of the feedback in case some assumptions about the underlying distribution of the response values can be made. This is often the case when measurement values are to be reported.

In future work, we intend to investigate a number of further issues. So far, the feedback process is independent of possible previous feedback rounds. Since the value distribution often changes on a much larger timescale than the duration of a feedback round, values from previous rounds can be used in addition to the current value to more reliably infer both, the underlying distribution and the group size. The latter can then be used to improve the efficiency beyond the plain exponential feedback approach. The former extends the applicability of the proposed algorithms to cases where we have no a priori assumptions about underlying distributions, thus leading to a "generic" extremum feedback algorithm.

References

1. Sally Floyd, Van Jacobson, Ching-Gung Liu, Steven McCanne, and Lixia Zhang. A reliable multicast framework for light-weight sessions and application level framing. *IEEE/ACM Transactions on Networking*, 5(6):784 – 803, December 1997.
2. Thomas Fuhrmann, Marcus Schöller, and Martina Zitterbart. Service relocation in programmable networks, 2003. Submitted for publication.
3. Thomas Fuhrmann and Jörg Widmer. On the scaling of feedback algorithms for very large multicast groups. *Special Issue of Computer Communications on Integrating Multicast into the Internet*, 24((5-6)):539–547, March 2001.
4. Alan Mainwaring, David Culler, Joseph Polastre, Robert Szewczyk, and John Anderson. Wireless sensor networks for habitat monitoring. In *Proceedings of the first ACM international workshop on Wireless sensor networks and applications*, September 2002.
5. Jörg Nonnenmacher and Ernst W. Biersack. Scalable feedback for large groups. *IEEE/ACM Transactions on Networking*, 7(3):375–386, June 1999.
6. Jörg Widmer and Thomas Fuhrmann. Extremum feedback for very large multicast groups. In *Proceedings of Third International Workshop on Networked Group Communication (NGC), London*, November 2001.
7. Jörg Widmer and Mark Handley. Extending equation-based congestion control to multicast applications. In *Proc. ACM SIGCOMM*, pages 275 – 286, San Diego, CA, August 2001.

Design and Evaluation
of a Low Density Generator Matrix (LDGM)
Large Block FEC Codec

Vincent Roca, Zainab Khallouf, and Julien Laboure

INRIA Rhône-Alpes, Planète project, France
{firstname.name}@inrialpes.fr

Abstract. Traditional small block Forward Error Correction (FEC) codes, like the Reed-Solomon erasure (RSE) code, are known to raise efficiency problems, in particular when they are applied to the Asynchronous Layered Coding (ALC) reliable multicast protocol. In this paper we describe the design of a simple large block *Low Density Generator Matrix* (LDGM) codec, a particular case of LDPC code, which is capable of operating on source blocks that are several tens of megabytes long. We also explain how the iterative decoding feature of LDGM/LDPC can be used to protect a large number of small independent objects during time-limited partially-reliable sessions. We illustrate this feature with an example derived from a video streaming scheme over ALC. We then evaluate our LDGM codec and compare its performances with a well known RSE codec. Tests focus on the global efficiency and on encoding/decoding performances. This paper deliberately skips theoretical aspects to focus on practical results. It shows that LDGM/LDPC open many opportunities in the area of bulk data multicasting.

Keywords: FEC, large block FEC codes, LDGM, LDPC, reliable multicast, ALC

1   Introduction to the Use of FEC in Reliable Multicast

Providing reliable multicast in a best-effort network where packet losses are frequent, such as the Internet, requires a reliable multicast protocol whose specific function is to compensate for these losses. Two approaches are used to provide reliability to multicast transport protocols: *Automatic Repeat Request (ARQ)*, where lost packets are retransmitted, and *Forward Error Correction (FEC)*, which transmits redundant data along with the original data. Thanks to this redundancy, up to a certain number of missing packets can be recovered at the receiver. More precisely k *source packets* (A.K.A. original or data packets) are encoded into n packets. If the FEC encoder keeps the k source packets in the set of n packets, this code is called *systematic*. The additional $n - k$ packets are then called *parity packets* (A.K.A. FEC or redundant packets). A receiver can then recover the k source packets provided it receives any k (or a bit more with LDGM/LDPC codes) packets out of the n possible. The great advantage of using FEC with multicast transmissions is that the same parity packet can recover

B. Stiller et al. (Eds.): NGC/ICQT 2003, LNCS 2816, pp. 193–204, 2003.
© Springer-Verlag Berlin Heidelberg 2003

different lost packets at different receivers. Therefore, the feedback from the receivers can be implemented at a coarser granularity. Using FEC also limits the risk of feedback implosion at the source. An extreme case is the *Asynchronous Layered Coding* (ALC) massively scalable reliable multicast protocol [6,7] which achieves reliability thanks to an intensive use of FEC. There is absolutely no feedback information from the receivers in that case.

The principal motivation for this work is our *Multicast Library (MCLv3)* [17] which implements the ALC protocol family and provides an integrated solution for the reliable and highly scalable multicast delivery of bulk data. Previous work [1,9] and the experienced gained with MCLv3 [19,18] have highlighted the importance of the two parameters (k, n) in the global efficiency achievable at application level:

- *a large n/k ratio is beneficial because it reduces the probability of packet duplication at a receiver.* Indeed, since the same set of packets (data or parity) is transmitted in a different random order in each ALC layers [19], the probability that a receiver receives the same packet on two different layers decreases if the number of packets increases.
- *a large k is beneficial because it increases the correction capacity of the FEC code.* Indeed, a parity packet can only recover an erasure in the block it belongs to. Therefore the erasure capabilities of a parity packet are inversely proportional to the number of blocks a file must be segmented into because of limitations on the k parameter. This is known as the "coupon collector problem" (section 2.5). Ideally a file may be encoded in a single block, in which case each parity packet is useful.

A Reed-Solomon erasure code (RSE) based on Vandermonde matrices [16] is intrinsically limited by the Galois Field it uses. A typical example is $GF(2^8)$ where n is at most equal to 256. With one kilobyte packets, a FEC codec producing as many parity packets as data packets (i.e. $n = 2k$) operates on blocks of size 128 kilobytes at most, and all files exceeding this threshold must be segmented into several blocks. Another drawback of RSE is a huge encoding/decoding time with large (k, n) values, which is the reason why $GF(2^8)$ is preferred in spite of its limitations on the block size. Yet RSE is optimal because a receiver can recover erasures as soon as it has received *exactly* k packets out of n. A FEC code with this property is called *MDS, or Minimum Distance Separation*. Other small block codes exist (e.g. Reed-Muller code) that all share the same fundamental limitation on the (k, n) parameters.

In this paper we describe the implementation details and performances of a large block code: Low Density Generator Matrix (LDGM), which is a particular case of Low Density Parity Check (LDPC) codes [2]. LDGM/LDPC have two main advantages: (1) they enable high speed encoding/decoding, and (2) they operate on large blocks $(k \gg 1)$.

The paper is structured as follows: Section 2 gives a brief introduction to the LDGM/LDPC codes and to iterative decoding systems. Section 3 explains how these codes can be used for the time-limited partially-reliable transmission of a large number of small objects. Section 4 describes experimental results obtained with our LDGM codec. Finally section 5 introduces related works and section 6 concludes the work.

2 Introduction to the LDPC and LDGM codes

This section gives an overview of the LDPC and LDGM codes. Interested readers can refer to [10,20] for further details.

2.1 Binary versus Packet, Symmetric versus Erasure Channels

LDPC codes were first introduced by Gallager in 1960 [2,3] and have been almost completely forgotten until Mackay and Neal rediscovered them in 1995 [11]. LDPC can operate both over Binary Symmetric Channels (BSC) and Binary Erasure Channels (BEC). With a BSC channel a bit arrives at the destination either perfectly or erroneously. It typically happens over noisy channels. On the opposite, in a BEC channel a bit either arrives perfectly or is lost in the channel. A typical example of erasure channel, which does not operate on bit streams but on packet streams, is the Internet. In that case, the main cause of packet losses is router congestion, and the CRC available in most physical layers guaranties that a packet arriving at its destination and given to IP is error-free.

If LDPC, like many codes, can operate on both types, it is much simpler with a *Packet* (resp. Bit) *Erasure Channels (PEC)* (resp. BEC). This is normal since a PEC carries more information than a BSC (i.e. the packets received are error free). In the remaining of this paper we only consider the PEC case.

2.2 Parity Check Matrix and Bipartite Graph: LDPC versus LDGM

LDPC is a linear block code with a very sparse Parity Check Matrix H (i.e. a matrix containing a large number of 0s), hence its name, "Low Density". The H matrix creates constraints between source and parity packets. Said differently, it creates a system of $n - k$ linear equations of n variables, the source and parity packets.

The H matrix can also be represented as a bipartite graph (figure 1) between left nodes, called *message nodes*, and right nodes, called *check nodes* (A.K.A. constraint nodes). The k source packets form the first k message nodes, while the parity packets form the remaining $n - k$ message nodes. There is an edge in this graph between a source node and a check node only if there is a 1 in the corresponding (column, row) entry of H. The edges represent the constraints between the various message nodes. The associated equations are given in figure 1 along each check node.

In the original LDPC approach, the H matrix, of size $n - k \times n$, and the associated bipartite graph encompass all n left nodes (source and parity nodes).

On the opposite, in the LDGM approach, the H matrix, of size $n - k \times k$ only encompasses the first k source nodes, and is associated to an I_{n-k} identity

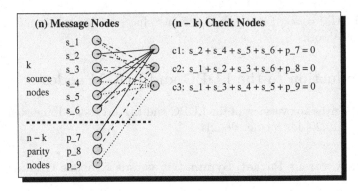

Fig. 1. Example of regular bipartite graph for LDGM, left degree 2, right degree 4.

matrix of size $n - k \times n - k$. Therefore each parity node is linked to exactly one check node. With an LDGM code a dual representation exists, where left nodes are composed only of source packets and right nodes of parity packets [20]. Nevertheless our codec and this paper use the representation of figure 1. The LDPC versus LDGM distinction is important and it impacts:

- *the encoding speed:* encoding is faster with LDGM than with LDPC.
- *the error correction capabilities:* LDPC has a major advantage over LDGM from this point of view, because parity packets are better protected. An LDPC parity packet can be recovered (because it shares edges with several check nodes) which is not possible with LDGM.

In the present paper we will essentially consider the simple case of LDGM codes. Some of the methods presented hereafter will however apply to both codes.

An LDGM code where all source nodes have the same degree, and all check nodes have the same degree, is called *regular*. In that case, the left and right degrees in the bipartite graph are linked to the (k, n) parameters by the equation:

$$k * left\_deg = (n - k) * right\_deg$$

Note that in this equation, the "check node" to "parity node" edges are not considered in the left/right degrees.

The H matrix is essentially constructed randomly, given the left and right degree constraints. An optimization is then applied to remove from the bipartite graph the cycles of length four (i.e. when two source nodes are linked to the same two check nodes) which are known to lead to suboptimal decoding.

2.3   Encoding Process

Encoding is straightforward with an LDGM code: the codec calculates each parity packet as the XOR (eXclusive OR) sum of all source nodes associated to the check node. For instance in figure 1 the parity packet p_7 is the XOR of source packets s_2, s_4, s_5, and s_6.

The encoding is more complex in case of an LDPC code since it requires solving a system of linear equations whose variables are the parity nodes. The generator matrix, G, is this solution (with LDGM H is used as a generator matrix). Encoding just consists in multiplying each source packet by G.

In both cases, since we are working on packets rather than bit streams, the XOR is calculated over all 32 bit words of the packets. Doing it on words rather than bytes is more efficient but requires that the packet length be multiple of 4 (which is not a serious constraint).

2.4   Decoding Process

Decoding Algorithms. Because decoding is exactly the same with LDPC and LDGM, we use both terms indifferently in this section. The decoding over a PEC is straightforward compared to the BSC case, and exploits the following property: *provided the value of all but one message nodes associated to a check node, the missing message node (which can be either a source or a parity packet) is equal to the XOR of all other message nodes.* The decoding process consists in solving a system of linear equations using a trivial algorithm:

- if an equation has only one remaining variable, then this variable is equal to the constant term;
- replace this variable by its value in all the other linear equations and reiterate, until blocked or until all variables have been found.

In practice, the set of linear equations are the equations associated to the check nodes, and an incoming packet contains the value of the associated variable. So, each time a fresh packet arrives, we apply the above algorithm and see if decoding can progress by one or more steps. Decoding is successful when all source packets have been received or recovered.

An equivalent algorithm exists and is often presented in the literature [20]: each time a packet arrives at a receiver (or is recovered), its value is XOR'ed to all its neighbor check nodes in the bipartite graph, and the associated edges are removed. Decoding therefore consists in searching a check node of degree one, and if one is found, recovering the missing message node and removing the now useless check node and edges from the bipartite graph. This sequence is one step of the decoding process. Of course, the newly recovered packet can itself trigger other recoveries, so the sequence is repeated recursively.

Practical Aspects. We see that the LDPC decoding process largely differs from an RSE decoding. With RSE, decoding is done all at once, as soon as exactly k packets have been received (MDS property of RSE). With LDPC we only know that decoding is not possible if less than k packets have been received, but there is no way to know in advance how many packets must be received before decoding is successful (LDPC is not an MDS code). Decoding is therefore performed *step by step*, after each packet arrival. A by-product of this feature is that the CPU load is spread over the whole reception period (even if there are more successful decoding steps at the end), rather than being concentrated at the end with RSE.

Another remark is that encoding and decoding must use the same parity matrix, H. In our codec this matrix is entirely defined once the (k, n, $left\_deg$, $seed$, H $creation$ $algorithm$) parameters are provided, where $seed$ is used by the pseudo-random number generator. The source must have a way to communicate explicitly or implicitly these values to the receivers: there can be an exchange of control parameters before transmissions take place, or it can be transmitted in-band using the FEC Object Transmission Information (FTI) header extension of ALC. Another solution is to transmit a compressed version of H to receivers.

2.5 Decoding Inefficiency and Other Practical Sources of Inefficiency

Three sources of inefficiency exist: (1) the FEC decoding inefficiency, (2) the packet duplication inefficiency, and (3) the "coupon collector problem".

LDPC is not an MDS code and introduces a decoding inefficiency: $inef\_ratio*$ k packets ($inef\_ratio \geq 1$) must be received for decoding to be successful. The $inef\_ratio$, experimentally evaluated, is therefore a key performance metric:

$$inef\_ratio = \frac{number\ of\ packets\ required\ for\ decoding}{k}$$

The use of several layers in ALC adds some more inefficiency, because the same set of packets is used for transmissions, in a random order, on the various layers. A receiver may get the same packet from several different layers, thereby creating duplicates. In this paper we will not consider this aspect (for simplicity we assume a single layer is used).

If an object is too large to be encoded in a single LDPC block, it is segmented into several blocks. Because transmissions take place in a random order [19] the "coupon collector problem" occurs [1]: packets are received for blocks already decoded while the receiver waits for the last missing packet of a non-decoded block. This problem is the *main limitation of a small block code like RSE*. Depending on the practical limitations of the LDPC codec (e.g. algorithmic or memory constraints), it can also take place with LDPC, but in a less acute way (the number of blocks is several orders of magnitude lower).

3 Exploiting the Iterative Decoding Process for the Time-Limited Partially Reliable Transmission of a Large Number of Small Objects

We now explain how the iterative decoding process of LDPC can help the partially reliable transmission of a large number of small objects. In this scenario, transmissions take place in a limited span of time, and each receiver wants to receive and decode as many objects as possible. Even if FEC is used, transmissions are globally pseudo-reliable. Our Scalable Video Streaming over ALC (SVSoA) streaming approach for hierarchically encoded videos [14,15] typically raises this problem: during each period the source needs to transmit around 1500 objects, each of them being 4.3 KB long, for a total of approximately 6.45 MB.

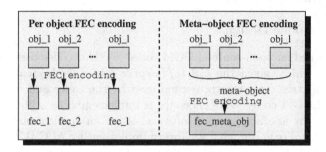

Fig. 2. Per object versus per meta-object FEC encoding.

Inadequacy of RSE. Using RSE requires to encode each object separately, so a FEC packet has only a 1/1500 probability of correcting losses in a given block. We found experimentally that a receiver experiences an average of 85% useless packets to decode all blocks, which is prohibitive! Creating meta-objects and doing cross-object encoding is therefore required to reduce the total number of blocks (figure 2).

But using RSE at meta-object level is not efficient because it creates interdependencies: let's imagine that objects 1 and 2, composed of respectively k_1 and k_2 packets, are gathered in a single meta-object which is globally FEC encoded. Therefore $k_1 + k_2$ distinct packets must be received to decode both objects at once (i.e. the meta-object). A receiver having received only $nb\_rx < k_1 + k_2$ packets cannot decode either of them, even if he received more than k_1 packets for object 1 (with a per-object encoding, decoding of object 1 would be possible then!).

The conclusion is that *RSE is not appropriate, no matter whether it operates on a small object basis or on a meta-object basis.*

The Case of LDPC/LDGM. With an LDPC encoding over the meta-object, a receiver who misses a single source packet of object 1 may take advantage of packets of object 2 because there may be common check nodes in the bipartite graph. The reception of a single packet of object 2 can then trigger the decoding of the missing packet of object 1, even if globally $nb\_rx < k_1 + k_2$. Additionally, the large block feature of LDPC improves the global efficiency since the 6.45 MB meta-object is encoded as a single block.

We found experimentally that the global inefficiency can be reduced to 11.6% additional packets with an LDPC encoding, to compare with the 85% of RSE.

LDPC/LDGM largely outperform RSE for the partially reliable transmissions of large collections of small objects.

4   Experimental Results

4.1   LDPC Codec Design

We have designed an open-source LDGM codec [5]. This codec uses the R. Neal software [13], which, given the $k, n, left\_degree$ and a seed, creates a regular parity check matrix. This matrix is then used by the coder and decoder parts of our C++ LDGM codec [5]. This codec is implemented as a library that has to be included by another piece of software, either an application or a reliable multicast protocol (e.g. our MCLv3 library implementing ALC [17]). So far our codec assumes that all source and parity packets are stored in physical memory (RAM), which creates limitations for huge blocks Future work will address this aspect and will use the dedicated virtual memory framework included in MCLv3.

4.2   Experimental Setup

The following tests use both our LDGM codec and a popular RSE codec [16]. To k source packets of a block, the codec produces $n - k = k/2$ parity packets (1.5 expansion factor). With RSE we use blocks of at most $k = 64$ source packets. Both source and parity packets are one kilobyte long (the LDGM and RSE codecs both require that all packets be the same size, which means that the application may have to pad the last packet of a block). Once encoding has been performed, the source and parity packets of all blocks are transmitted in a fully random order [4,19]. Then the receiver waits until it has received enough packets to decode all blocks of the object and then stops reception. There is no explicit loss simulation model, because random transmissions are not affected by the loss model (e.g. random or bursty losses).

During these experiments we measure the encoding/decoding times as well as the minimum number of packets required for decoding. Experiments are repeated 100 times and the minimum/average/maximum values are reported. Note that our transmission scheme leads to a *maximum decoding inefficiency equal to* $n/k = 1.5$ since $n = 1.5 * k$ packets are produced and transmitted.

4.3   Impacts of the Left/Right Degree on Decoding Inefficiency

LDPC performances are known to be highly dependent on the bipartite graph, its regular versus irregular nature, and its left and right degree distribution [12,8]. In this test we experiment with various degree values. Since we only use regular bipartite graphs, the left degree is the same for all source nodes. The right degree is implicitly defined by the $(k, n, left\_degree)$ T-uple.

Figure 3 illustrates the results obtained. We see that optimal performances are obtained with a left degree equal to 7 when $k \in [8000; 20000]$. More precisely

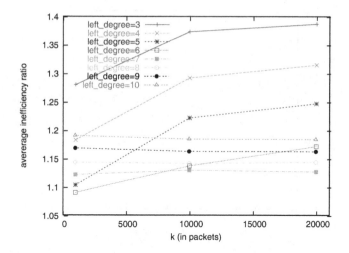

Fig. 3. LDGM left degree comparisons.

with $k = 10000$ packets and a left degree of 7, the average inefficiency ratio is 1.1284 (said differently there are 12.84% additional packets), the median is 1.1120, the 90% confidence interval around the mean is $+/-0.0484$, and the inefficiency range is $[1.101; 1.270]$. Note that these results largely differ from that of regular LDPC codes where a left degree equal to 3 is the optimum.

Our results are of course worse than those obtained with highly optimized but proprietary codes [1]. Yet they are encouraging. In the remaining of this paper we only focus on LDGM(7, 14) codes.

4.4   Comparison between LDGM(7,14) and RSE

We now compare the LDGM(7, 14) and RSE codecs. Results are given in figure 4. We see that LDGM(7,14) largely outperforms RSE for all file sizes. With a 10 MB file, the file is totally decoded with only 12.84% additional packets with LDGM whereas 18.85% additional packets are required with RSE (because of the coupon collector problem, section 2.5). It represents a 31.88% relative improvement.

The average encoding times (PIII-1GHz/Linux) with LDGM(7,14), over a single 10 MB block amounts to 0.171 seconds[1]. This is 14.5 times faster than with RSE (2.486 seconds), where 153 blocks of $k = 64$ source packets each are used[2].

Because of technical problems we didn't manage to evaluate the RSE decoding time, yet [16] indicates it is of the same order as the encoding time. The

---

[1]   This time does not include the H creation process, which amounts to 0.096 seconds. It is reasonable as this matrix can be reused over several blocks, as long as they all are of the same size.

[2]   Note that using a single block of 10000 packets with RSE would lead to prohibitive encoding/decoding times ([1] mentions times of several hours).

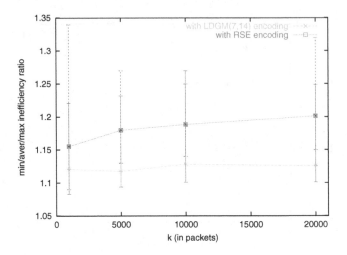

Fig. 4. LDGM(7,14) versus RSE global inefficiency ratio.

average LDGM decoding time amounts to 0.782 seconds. It is 4.6 times higher than the LDGM encoding time, but still 3.2 times faster than RSE's encoding time (and decoding time with the above assumption).

5 Related Works

In [16] the theoretical aspects and the design principles of an RSE codec are discussed. The associated open-source implementation turned out to be the most popular FEC codec in the reliable multicast community. This codec can be used either in a $GF(2^8)$, which provides good performances but is limited to $n \leq 255$, or in a $GF(2^16)$ which relieves the (k, n) constraint at the expense of major encoding/decoding times.

[1,8] introduced the basis of new FEC codes and how they can be used to create a reliable multicast protocol (which lead to the design of the ALC [6] protocol family). This code, Tornado-Z, has performances that are several orders of magnitude higher than that of Reed-Solomon FEC codes, but this is a proprietary code (see [9] for the list of patents). In fact Tornado belongs to the same category as LDPC: codes on graphs, that have been introduced in the 1960's by Gallager [2].

[9] introduces expandable codes, that can produce an infinite number of parity packets ($n \gg 1$) while operating on large blocks. Yet very little is known on the theory behind them, and just like Tornado, the LT code that falls in this category is largely protected by patents.

A lot of theoretical work has been done with LDPC (e.g. [20,12]). But to the best of our knowledge we are not aware of any public LDPC implementation for the PEC (R. Neal's LDPC software [13] is a simulator, not a codec for the PEC). The present work tries to fulfill this gap.

6   Conclusions

In this paper we describe the design of a simple large block LDGM codec, a particular case of LDPC codes, which is capable of operating on source blocks that are several tens of megabytes long. This is a major asset over the wide-spread Reed-Solomon codec which is limited to source blocks that are several orders of magnitude smaller, thereby creating important efficiency problems.

We also explain how the iterative decoding feature of LDGM can be used to protect a large number of small independent objects during time-limited partially-reliable transmissions. LDPC/LDGM enable huge performance improvements compared to RSE which is definitely not appropriate.

This paper provides several experimental results that assess LDGM's benefits. Being capable of operating on large blocks largely compensates the intrinsic decoding inefficiency of LDGM which is not an MDS code (unlike RSE). We show that LDGM yields a 31.88% relative improvement compared to RSE with 10 MByte files in terms of global inefficiency. We experimentally found that using a regular matrix with a $(7, 14)$ left/right degree distribution is the optimum in our case. We experienced an average decoding inefficiency of 12.84% (in a $[10.1\%; 27.0\%]$ range) over a 10 MB block. This is of course higher than previously published performances with highly optimized (but proprietary!) large block FEC codes. We are rather confident that our results can be improved, and at least two directions exist: (1) use LDPC rather than LDGM, and (2) use irregular graphs.

Finally encoding and decoding are considerably faster than with RSE. Producing 5000 parity packets from a 10 MB block takes 0.171 seconds on a PIII-1GHz/Linux, which represents a $\frac{5\,MB}{0.171} = 239.5$ Mbps encoding rate. Decoding is highly efficient too (0.782 seconds), even if it is slower than encoding.

Last but not least our LDGM codec [5] is distributed under an open-source license at URL: http://www.inrialpes.fr/planete/people/roca/mcl/

Acknowledgments

The authors would like to thanks Jérome Lacan, Jérome Fimes, Radford Neal, and Ousmane Diouf for fruitful discussions.

References

1. J. Byers, M. Luby, M. Mitzenmacher, and A. Rege. A digital fountain approach to reliable distribution of bulk data. In *ACM SIGCOMM'98*, Aug. 1998.
2. R. G. Gallager. Low density parity check codes. In *PhD thesis, Massachussets Institute of Technology*, 1960.
3. R. G. Gallager. Low density parity check codes. *IEEE Transactions on Information Theory*, 8(1), Jan. 1962.

4. J. Gemmell, E. Schooler, and J. Gray. Fcast multicast file distribution. *IEEE Network*, 14(1), Jan. 2000.

5. J. Labouré, V. Roca, and Z. Khallouf. *An Open-Source Implementation of a Low Density Parity Check (LDPC) Large Block FEC Code.* URL: http://www.inrialpes.fr/planete/people/roca/mcl/.

6. M. Luby, J. Gemmell, L. Vicisano, L. Rizzo, and J. Crowcroft. *Asynchronous Layered Coding (ALC) protocol instantiation*, Dec. 2002. IETF Request for Comments, RFC3450.

7. M. Luby, J. Gemmell, L. Vicisano, L. Rizzo, M. Handley, and J. Crowcroft. *Layered Coding Transport (LCT) building block*, Dec. 2002. IETF Request for Comments, RFC3451.

8. M. Luby, M. Mitzenmacher, A. Shokrollahi, and D. Spielman. Improved low-density codes using irregular graphs. *IEEE Transactions on Information Theory*, 47(2), Feb. 2001.

9. M. Luby, L. Vicisano, J. Gemmell, L. Rizzo, M. Handley, and J. Crowcroft. *The use of Forward Error Correction (FEC) in reliable multicast*, Dec. 2002. IETF Request for Comments, RFC3453.

10. D. MacKay. *Information Theory, Inference and Learning Algorithms.* Cambridge University Press, ISBN: 0521642981, 2003.

11. D. MacKay and R. Neal. Good codes based on very sparse matrices. In *5th IAM Conference: Cryptography and Coding, LNCS No. 1025*, 1995.

12. D. MacKay, S. Wilson, and M. Davey. Comparison of constructions of irregular gallager codes. *IEEE Transactions on Communications*, 47(10), Oct. 1998.

13. R. Neal. *Software for Low Density Parity Check (LDPC) codes.* http://www.cs.toronto.edu/~radford/ldpc.software.html.

14. C. Neumann and V. Roca. Multicast streaming of hierarchical mpeg-4 presentations. In *ACM Multimedia 2002*, Dec. 2002.

15. C. Neumann and V. Roca. Scalable video streaming over alc (svsoa): a solution for the large scale multicast distribution of videos. Research Report 4769, INRIA, Mar. 2003.

16. L. Rizzo. Effective erasure codes for reliable computer communication protocols. *ACM Computer Communication Review*, 27(2), Apr. 1997.

17. V. Roca and al. *MCLv3: an Open Source GNU/GPL Implementation of the ALC and NORM Reliable Multicast Protocols.* URL: http://www.inrialpes.fr/planete/people/roca/mcl/.

18. V. Roca and B. Mordelet. Design of a multicast file transfer tool on top of alc. In *7th IEEE Symposium on Computers and Communications (ISCC'02), Toarmina, Italy*, July 2002.

19. V. Roca and B. Mordelet. Improving the efficiency of a multicast file transfer tool based on alc. Research Report 4411, INRIA, Mar. 2002.

20. A. Shokrollahi. Codes and graphs. In *STACS 2000 (invited talk), LNCS No. 1770*, pages 1–12, 2000.

Overcoming Last-Hop/First-Hop Problems in IP Multicast*

Gísli Hjálmtýsson, Björn Brynjúlfsson, and Ólafur Ragnar Helgason

Reykjavik University, Department of Computer Science,
Ofanleiti 2, 103 Reykjavik, Iceland
{gisli,bjorninn,olafurr}@ru.is
http://netlab.ru.is

Abstract. Whereas much of the recent thrust in IP multicast standardization has focused on multicast routing and other supplementary infrastructure for multicast, the reach to/from end-systems from/to the multicast infrastructure constitutes a significant barrier in deploying any network layer multicast protocol. A basic problem arises from the fact that current IP multicast protocols have been designed assuming universal deployment thereby preventing end-systems that are more than one router hop away to participate in multicast. This problem is further aggravated by increasing protocol awareness of layer-2 devices effectively locking particular protocols and versions into hardware, and in part by the declining transparency of the maturing Internet due to firewalls and NATs. In this paper we describe new multicast mechanisms to address these issues. While designed as part of our research on Selfconfiguring Lightweight Internet Multicast (SLIM), the techniques and mechanisms are applicable to other multicast protocols. We discuss our implementation and experimentation over the open Internet, and show how these new protocol mechanisms have enabled us to introduce our new IP multicast to end-systems in an incremental manner without the collaboration of network administrators.

1 Introduction

As the Internet matures as the ubiquitous networking infrastructure, there is a growing interest in the realization of multicast. Although research on IP multicast dates back to the early days of the Internet, it has yet to produce a multicast service that is ubiquitously and economically available. Recently there has been a renewed effort to realize multicast. This is evident in the academic community where there is renewed interest in multicast research particularly as part of Active and Programmable networking research and related work on overlay networks. This is in addition to the reinvigorated efforts to standardize multicast supporting protocols.

Whereas much of the recent thrust in IP multicast standardization has focused on multicast routing and other supplementary infrastructure for multicast, a significant barrier occurs at the first and last hop, between the end-systems and the nearest

---

* This work (all authors) was supported in part by The Icelandic Centre for Research under grant number 020500002.

B. Stiller et al. (Eds.): NGC/ICQT 2003, LNCS 2816, pp. 205–213, 2003.

multicast capable router.   While multicast routing and other protocol related inadequacies are hindering providers from offering multicast services, the last-hop/first-hop barrier is preventing the organic growth in multicast applications and end-user community. There are three main last-hop/first-hop problems in employing multicast: Lack of ubiquity in the initial multicast infrastructure, smart layer-2 devices, and firewalls and address translators.

A major obstacle for deployment of multicast is the necessity to bridge from/to the closest multicast router to/from the end-systems. Existing IP multicast proposals [1,2] embed an assumption of universal deployment, as all routers are assumed to be multicast capable. In particular to participate in multicast an end-system must be directly connected to a multicast capable router. In part this has been addressed by building a virtual overlay network (the MBONE) such that all routers in that virtual topology are multicast capable. Still users whose first hop routers are not configured as part of this virtual topology are unable to participate in multicast. This has prevented the organic growth of multicast use as individual users require prior consent (and support) from their local administrator. Arguably, this has been a most significant barrier in the success of multicast.

Another substantial obstacle is caused by layer-2 devices – hubs and switches – that are increasingly "smart" in snooping higher level protocol packets and self-configure accordingly. While most layer-2 Ethernet devices support MAC-layer multicast in principle, these devices typically ship with the understanding of the latest version of one protocol at the time of manufacturing, rendering these capabilities obsolete upon first version change of supported protocol and incompatible with other (and new) multicast protocols. As the self-configuring properties of smart layer-2 devices drives their deployment in larger and larger local area segments, it becomes ever more critical to exploit their multicast capabilities, even for localized multicast.

The last significant part of the last-hop/first-hop problem is caused by decreasing transparency of the Internet caused by network address translators (NATs), firewalls and other gateways that invalidate the assumption of end to end visibility.   The topology management is conducted using a protocol, different and independent from the one used for the multicast distribution. Moreover, transport layer port numbers are not considered part of the identification of a multicast group. In contrast point-to-point flows embed signaling into the data transport stream and include the port numbers as part of the flow identification.   Firewalls and NATs exploit these properties to open a channel for the data stream automatically when seeing the first packets of a flow. With multicast signaled as a separate protocol and without transport level port numbers, the Firewall/NAT must understand the messages of the management protocol in order to achieve same level of automation and transparency.

Whereas the first problem is a direct consequence of assumptions and design decisions embedded in the existing IP multicast protocols, the last two problems reflect a departure from the Internet service model and as such are not rooted in any particular multicast protocol.

We have designed, implemented and experimented with a new *Self-Configuring Lightweight Internet Multicast,* SLIM [3]. While similar to [1] in that our multicast is single source, it avoids assumptions of universal deployments and avoids the use of specific multicast addresses. The novelty of our new protocol is that it does *not* require any multicast specific infrastructure beyond our new Topology Management

Protocol (TMP) that is run in the control plane of multicast capable (participating) routers. In particular TMP avoids multicast routing.

In this paper we focus on specific techniques and mechanisms to overcome the last-hop/first-hop problem that we have designed and implemented. While designed as part of our research on our new protocol, the technologies can be used for other multicast protocols. A key element in avoiding the complexities of existing multicast is that TMP employs dynamic tunneling as needed to construct a virtual topology for the multicast distribution tree through non-cooperating routers on a per tree basis. These mechanisms are also a key to solving the last-hop/first-hop problem. We discuss our implementation and experimentation over the open Internet, and show how these new protocol mechanisms have enabled us to introduce new IP multicast to end-systems incrementally without the collaboration of network administrators.

The rest of the paper is organized as follows. We begin by discussing related work in Section 2. In Section 3 we briefly describe SLIM our new lightweight self-configuring multicast. Section 4 describes how we deliver multicast to end-systems multiple hops away from multicast capable routers. In Section 5 we discuss how to overcome the layer-2 related issues, and in Section 6 we extend these mechanisms to multicast through firewalls and NATs. In Section 7 we give a brief description of our implementation using the Pronto router and the packet processor based architecture. In Section 8 we conclude.

2 Related Work

While significant amount of research has been conducted on multicast protocols and models[1,2,3,4,5] the last-hop/first-hop problem has not received significant attention from the multicast research community. In [6] UDP encapsulation is used to reach a user-level process at an end-host. Similarly, in [7] pseudo drivers (or user mode daemons) bridge across non-multicast routers. We have found tunneling to end-systems to be cumbersome and requiring too significant end-system changes to be practical. None of these methods addresses LAN issues or firewall/NAT issues addressed in this paper. Similar to PIM SM where senders tunnel to the rendezvous point, [8] uses UMTP to allow users to participate in an SSM multicast session even if their first-hop router does not support multicast. Neither address the firewall/NAT issues.

The approach most similar to our last-hop solution is [9], the last multicast hop effectively delivering a point-to-point connection to the end-system. Each hop, in particular the one to an end-system, can span multiple non-multicast routers. This part is similar to our elementary solution. However, [9] does not address the firewalls/NAT's or the LAN issues address herein.

Motivated by the desire to spark organic growth of multicast use, and frustrated by the lack of widely available network layer multicast, several researchers have concluded that multicast should first be realized as application layer overlays [10,11,12]. While we empathize with the frustration we believe that multicast will ultimately be supported at the network layer.

3 SLIM – Protocol Summary

We have designed and implemented a Self-configuring Lightweight Internet Multicast Protocol (SLIM) that avoids all multicast specific infrastructure other than topology management. SLIM is a single source multicast where a multicast channel is uniquely identified by the pair $\langle S,C \rangle$ where S is the IP address of the sender and C is the source specific channel identifier. Receivers interested in the multicast group must know both S and C, and send control messages addressed to S using normal unicast thus avoiding the need for multicast routing.

Control messages, *join* and *leave*, are sent towards S and processed by the Topology Management Protocol (TMP) running on multicast capable routers. The TMP maintains no non-local information beyond what is conveyed by the join and leave control messages. Like other sparse-mode multicast protocols TMP only forwards control messages if needed. In particular joins are suppressed at the first router already receiving the requested group. All TMP state is soft. The TMP can exploit general purpose classifiers to trigger stateful flow based forwarding, thus allowing the channel identifier C to be any legal IP address, and avoiding the need for multicast specific datapath in routers.

TMP incorporates support for incremental deployment and constructs IP tunnels through non-cooperating routers on demand, as needed, avoiding the need for and the management overhead of multicast specific virtual network.

The Join Protocol Message
JOIN messages are sent as IP packets with the router alert option and having a unique protocol id. The protocol header for a JOIN message, the only required message for the correctness of the protocol, is shown in Fig.1. It contains the following fields:
- Control: JOIN
- *Source Address (S):* IP address of the sender.
- *Channel Address (C):* IP address chosen so that the pair $\langle S,C \rangle$ is globally unique.
- *Last-Branch-Point:* IP address of the next downstream multicast enabled router in the distribution tree, or the receiver.
- *TTL@Last-Branch-Point:* TTL value of the IP header on the last branch point. Multicast enabled routers copy the TTL value in the IP header before JOIN messages are forwarded. Comparison with the corresponding value in the IP header indicates whether the last branch point is an immediate neighbor or not. If it is not a neighbor the multicast stream is sent through an IP tunnel.
- *Options:* Option identifier. If present the protocol message header is followed by an option value. An option of particular interest in this paper is the "receive as" option whose value contains the source and destination port numbers. As discussed below options facilitate our solutions to the last hop/first-hop problems.

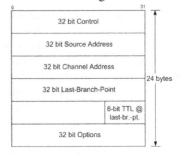

Fig. 1. The JOIN protocol header.

In addition the protocol defines a LEAVE message, designed as an optimization to accelerate resource reclaim on routers under normal conditions. All control messages are sent best effort.

The dynamic tunneling capability affords TMP the option of tunneling through non-branching multicast routers to economize on forwarding state.

Changes to End-Systems
To exploit the new multicast a receiver must acquire an application program compatible with the new multicast. This is clearly one more obstacle in mass adoption of a new multicast protocol. To mitigate this problem we have built a small launcher program that implements the TMP for end-systems, but is transparent to the datastream reception of the applications. We have tested this wrapper on a variety of applications including MS Media Player, Apple Quicktime, Netmeeting and various other commodity and freeware applications on the Windows and the Linux platforms.

4   Multicast to/from End-Users Not Directly Connected to a Multicast Router

To reach end-systems that are not directly connected to a multicast router we exploit tunneling from the last hop router. The TMP supports two options: a dynamic IP-in-IP tunnel as done between routers, and a conversion from multicast to a point-to-point (UDP) flow from the last-hop router to the end-system.

Dynamic IP-in-IP tunnel: If the end-system can dynamically construct and terminate a simple IP-in-IP tunnel, the end-system is treated as a router not directly connected to an upstream multicast capable router. The end-system sends a regular join message with the option field cleared. The multicast router receiving a join message processes the message as if it had come from a multicast router, determines that the originator of the message is not an immediate neighbor and constructs an IP-in-IP tunnel to the end-host. Upon receiving a leave message, or on soft-state expiration, the tunnel is destroyed. Besides exploiting already existing mechanisms of the TMP, this solution has the significant advantage of insulating the tunneling mechanisms from the end-host application thus requiring no changes to end-systems.

Last router point-to-point conversion: While it is attractive to use IP-in-IP tunnels, many end-systems do not have support to terminate such tunnels. To reach those end-systems the TMP supports address (or full header) swap converting the multicast packets into a regular (UDP) point-to-point connection. The requesting end-system sets the option field to "receive as" to indicate that the multicast stream must be converted to a point-to-point UDP flow. The progress is as follows:
1. The requesting host sends a TMP join message with the "receive as" option set.
2. The last-multicast-router receiving the message first checks to see if the host is an immediate neighbor. If so it sends the stream as IP multicast to the host.
3. If the host is not an immediate neighbor of the last-multicast-router the router joins the host to the corresponding multicast flow and sets up an address mapping,

swapping the channel identifier C (stored in the destination address) with the receiver host address H.

4. The host receives the multicast flow as a point-to-point unicast.

One additional advantage of the multicast to point-to-point conversion is that the receiving host may receive multicast streams to unicast applications. In fact more "active" routers (e.g., [13]) might recognize streams requested by end-hosts via unicast and join a multicast stream offering the same content, converting the multicast stream as above transparently to the receiving host. While the capabilities to perform this type of address swap is not a commodity facility on all routers, on routers that have this capability the performance hit due to conversion is minimal.

An issue raised by this type of point-to-point conversion is the potentially unlimited fan-out of any particular router. This is a real concern as long as the number of multicast routers remains small. A practical safeguard is to configure a maximum fan-out for each router, e.g., equal to the number of router ports or a multiple thereof. Once the maximum is reached the router simply forwards a join request upstream.

Multicast Senders Not Directly Connected to Multicast Routers

To facilitate the transmission of arbitrary sender that is not directly connected to a multicast router and not part of a teleconference, we have implemented a multicast relay service. An interested sender obtains a unique channel identifier from a multicast relay service. Subsequently, the sender sends a point-to-point unicast UDP stream to the relay service which relays the stream onto the multicast channel.

5 Exploiting Layer 2 Multicast Capabilities

Over the last few years LANs are increasingly built up with Ethernet switches (and hubs). Smart switches extract MAC address from observed traffic to self-configure a (minimum cost) spanning tree reaching every (active) host on the LAN. This level of self-configuration has resulted in switch based LANs (i.e. each broadcast segment) becoming larger and increasingly popular.

While observation based auto-discovery is sufficient to transparently build the MAC layer reachability graph for point-to-point connections, it is insufficient to exploit the Ethernet multicast address space. Some Ethernet switches now support the Cisco proprietary Cisco Group Management Protocol (CGMP). More commonly, however, layer-2 devices either broadcast all multicast packets or resort to snooping for layer-3 IGMP protocol messages [14]. We have found that a given device will typically only snoop one version of IGMP. Moreover, that end-system applications will similarly be limited to supporting a single version of multicast. The likelihood of finding all applications and all Ethernet switches on a given LAN supporting the same (or compatible) protocol version is small and declining as the equipment ages. With switched broadcast segments increasing in size, exploiting Ethernet level multicast capabilities is important, even for local area multicast. We believe that a new MAC address allocation protocol for multicast is warranted, perhaps a PIM-DM derivative.

To circumvent the shortcomings of IGMP snooping an interested multicast receiver host triggers the (IGMP) snooping mechanisms, simply by sending an IGMP compliant trigger packets immediately after issuing a (protocol specific) join request.

6 Multicast through Firewalls and NATs that Do Not Support Multicast

With increasing number of new and exciting services being offered over UDP transport, such as IP telephony, IP radio, some games and more, stateful symmetric UDP Firewalls are becoming widely used. Such firewalls (and similarly symmetric NATs) allow bidirectional UDP flows to pass through if they originate from the trusted segment (the inside). In essence this means that a UDP request from the inside passes through, and so does the corresponding response flow.

To deliver multicast through a symmetric firewall that does not support multicast we combine a conversion from multicast to unicast with a firewall triggering UDP request. The conversion from multicast to unicast at the last hop multicast router is described in Section 4. To get the firewall to allow the resulting unicast flow through the host sends the join message with the "receive as" option set, with the value set to source and destination ports of the anticipated UDP point-to-point flow. The join message is sent in a UDP packet from the receiver toward the source with router alert option set and picked up by the last hop multicast router. The header of the UDP packet is the inverse header of the anticipated UDP point-to-point flow and thus the converted point-to-point flow is seen by the symmetric firewall as the response to the request and the flow is allowed through.

Multicast and NAT
To extend the above to the case when a firewall is (also) a NAT is straight forward, and really only increases the amount of work required by the last hop router to convert from multicast to point-to-point unicast. We consider two cases: a static NAT where all packets sent from an internal host corresponds to an externally visible address; and the increasingly common symmetric dynamic NAT with port translation where all packets coming from multiple internal hosts are mapped to a limited pool of addresses (often one) external addresses, using port mapping to ensure uniqueness between internal and external flows.

As for a plain firewall, to get through a NAT we combine a multicast to point-to-point conversion plus a UDP trigger. The only difference occurs when the last hop multicast router compares the values of the "receive as" option to those in the header of the UDP packet carrying the join message. The difference in values indicates that the packet has been sent through a NAT. As a consequence, rather than merely swapping the destination address the router performs an address and port swap as part of the conversion of the datastream from multicast to point-to-point unicast.

Multicast Senders behind Firewalls and NATs

Multicast senders behind a firewall or a NAT can employ the above techniques using the "send as" option in place of the "receive as." A problem of equal practical significance for hosts behind a NAT is how the sender can advertise the group, as normally the end-host is oblivious to the NAT mapping, i.e., the address and port values seen by outside receivers. To combat this, the first multicast router replies to a "send as" join with a join message with a "send as reply" option containing the packet header seen at the router as the option value. This way the sender learns the values to advertise in a session description.

7 Implementation and Experimentation

We have implemented and experimented with all of the above mechanisms in our laboratories, on production LANs and over the open Internet.

Our implementation consists of a TMP daemon run on the Pronto router using packet processors [13,15]. For the purposes of this paper the Pronto router is a highly modular router supporting the composition of paths through the router from elementary packet processors. In particular, a path can have multiple branches, each branch composed of one or more packet processors. Thus branches may differ in functionality. The TMP is run as a user level process on the Pronto router.

The TMP implementation is also highly modular, with the core topology management module allowing *adaptors* to be plugged in to provide last-hop/first-hop specific functionality. This way a core router may implement only the core TMP, whereas routers closer to the edge would implement the techniques described above and possibly more. This type of modularity has been key to allowing us to experiment with various techniques without cluttering the core TMP module.

In our experimentation we have sent and received multicast in a variety of setups; in particular, where a sender or receiver or both are behind (different) firewalls and/or NATs that were not under our control. We now offer multicast streaming services to students at Reykjavik University whether on campus or accessing our services from home through their respective local ISP's firewalls and NATs. On the campus LAN we encounter the issues and employ the solutions described above. As discussed before we have implemented a small wrapper application that implements the host TMP, but is otherwise transparent to client applications, allowing users to use common applications. Our techniques incur minimal performance overhead on the last hop routers. Our experimentation validates our techniques, and has shown them robust in a wide range of environments.

8 Conclusion

In this paper we describe new mechanisms and techniques to overcome the obstacle of reaching to/from the multicast infrastructure from/to user's end-systems which still remains a significant barrier in deploying network layer multicast. We have identified three main problems: i) nearest multicast capable router is not an immediate neighbor of the end-system, ii) smart layer-2 switches do not recognize new multicast protocols, and iii) lack of transparency due to firewalls and NATs. More importantly, we have shown how each of these can be overcome or circumvented in all but the most hostile environments without help or support from network administrators. As a result we have been able to offer multicast services using our new IP multicast protocol to end-systems in an incremental manner and without the administrator support. While designed as part of our research on Lightweight Self-configuring Multicast, the problems, techniques and mechanisms are applicable to other multicast protocols. Our experimentation validates the effectiveness of our techniques.

References

[1] H. Holbrook og D. Cheriton, "IP Multicast Channels: EXPRESS Support for Large-scale Single-Source Applications," In Proceedings of SIGCOMM, 1999.

[2] B. Fenner, M. Handley, H. Holbrook and I. Kouvelas, "Protocol Independent Multicast - Sparse Mode (PIM-SM): Protocol Specification (Revised)", IETF Internet Draft, work in progress, March 2003, draft-ietf-pim-sm-v2-new-07.txt

[3] Gísli Hjálmtýsson, Björn Brynjúlfsson and Ólafur Ragnar Helgason, "Self-Configuring Lightweight Internet Multicast," in preparation.

[4] Gísli Hjálmtýsson og K. K. Ramakrishnan, "UNITE - An Architecture for Lightweight Signaling in ATM Networks," DIMACS, Networks in Distributed Computing, October 1997.

[5] Suman Banerjee, Christopher Kommareddy, Koushik Kar, Samrat Bhattacharjee and Samir Khuller, "Construction of an Efficient Overlay Multicast Infrastructure for Real-time Applications," in Proceedings of Infocom, April 2003.

[6] R. Finlayson, "The UDP Multicast Tunneling Protocol," IETF Internet draft, work in progress, September 2002, draft-finlayson-umtp-07.txt

[7] D. Thaler, M. Talwar, L. Vicisano, and D. Ooms. IPv4 Automatic Multicast Without Explicit Tunnels, Feb. 2001. Work in progress: draft-ietf-mboned-auto-multicast-00.txt.

[8] R. Finlayson, R. Perlman and Doron Rajwan, "Accelerating the Deployment of Multicast Using Automatic Tunneling," IETF Internet draft, work in progress, February 2001, draft-finlayson-mboned-autotunneling-00.txt

[9] Ion Stoica, T. S. Eugene Ng, Hui Zhang, "REUNITE: A Recursive Unicast Approach to Multicast", INFOCOM 2000, Tel-Aviv, Israel, March 2000.

[10] S. Banerjee, B. Bhattacharjee & C. Kommareddy "Scalable Application Layer Multicast," in Proceedings of ACM Sigcomm 2002, Pittsburgh, Pennsylvania, August 2002.

[11] J. Jannotti, D. K. Gifford, K. L. Johnson, F. Kaashoek, and J. W. O'Toole, "Overcast: Reliable Multicasting with an Overlay Network," in Proc. of OSDI, October 2000.

[12] M. Castro, P. Druschel, A.-M. Kermarrec, and A. Rowstron, "Scribe: A large-scale and decentralized application-level multicast infrastructure," IEEE JSAC, vol. 20, no. 8, October 2002.

[13] Gísli Hjálmtýsson, "The Pronto Platform - A Flexible Toolkit for Programming Networks using a Commodity Operating System," in the proceedings of OpenArch 2000, Tel Aviv, Israel, March 2000.

[14] B. Cain, S. Deering, I. Kouvelas, B. Fenner and A. Thyagarajan, "Internet Group Management Protocol, Version 3", RFC 3376, October 2002.

[15] Gísli Hjálmtýsson, Heimir Sverrisson, Björn Brynjúlfsson and Ólafur R. Helgason, "Dynamic packet processors - A new abstraction for router extensibility," in the proceedings of OpenArch 2003, San Francisco, April 2003.

The Performance of Software Multicast-Reflector Implementations for Multi-player Online Games

Daniel Bauer and Sean Rooney

IBM Research, Zurich Laboratory
Säumerstrasse 4
8803 Rüschlikon, Switzerland
{dnb,sro}@zurich.ibm.com

Abstract. Massive multi-player online games are large distributed applications where thousands of participants exchange data. Existing solutions based on central servers face scalability problems. We study a hybrid solution between the peer-to-peer and central server models that divides a large game into several federated small games. The central component of this architecture is a multicast reflector. We present two efficient software implementations that have been developed as Linux kernel extensions and compare them with our user-space implementation. The comparison is based on performance measurements done on actual implementations.

1 Introduction

The term Massive Multi-Player Online Game (MMPOG) has come to denote games that have a large number of participants and are played over the Internet. Current MMPOGs use a central server approach. The number of simultaneous participants a game can host is dependent on the amount of resources available on the server. Abdelkhalek et al. [1] report that processor cycles are the main bottleneck and that network bandwidth is less of a concern. Furthermore, the study of Abdelkhalek et al. revealed that compute time is equally divided between game logic and network protocol stack processing.

A better solution is one in which the total available computation to the game increases with the number of participants. Peer-to-peer games have this property; however, they only work for a small number of participants — as the number of packets sent grows as a square of the number of participants — or require communication over a broadcast medium, e.g. a LAN. It is also difficult to envisage how a pure peer-to-peer system can be made reliable and secure.

Our approach is to use a hybrid of the peer-to-peer and central-server models to obtain scalable but reliable MMPOGs. We achieve this by

- dividing a large game into several federated small games, each of a size that can be handled using a peer-to-peer model;
- using fast dedicated multicast reflectors that handle the communication for one or several of the small games;

B. Stiller et al. (Eds.): NGC/ICQT 2003, LNCS 2816, pp. 214–225, 2003.
© Springer-Verlag Berlin Heidelberg 2003

– separating the control and data planes, such that the multicast reflectors are responsible for fast data forwarding, while servers and clients continue to perform the control and management functions.

This paper reports on the performance of software multicast reflector implementations. The performance of two kernel-space implementations is evaluated against a user-space implementation.

2   Related Work

The work described in the overview paper of military simulation [6] is similar in nature to the architecture described here. For example, in the Navel Postgraduate School Net (NPSNET), the space is divided into cells in which information is multicast. One member of the cell is responsible for adding and removing others as well as giving a new member the current state of the cell. Exact details of the architecture, for example how multicast is supported are not in the public domain.

In the commercial games space OpenSkies supports large games using a federation of multicast entities [7]. In contrast to the multicast reflector described here, they use a purely user-space implementation for group communication. A network stress test [8] on computers with a 500 Mhz CPU revealed that this implementation saturates when forwarding at a rate of less than 20 Mb/s.

The Mercury system is an example of a research game architecture based on a publish-subscribe mechanism   [3]. While the approach creates an evenly balanced system, the simulation results also show that the delay scales linearly with the number of nodes and therefore limits scalability.

3   Overview of the Federated Game Architecture

We present an overview of the federated game architecture, more details can be found in [2]. Our approach divides a large game into multiple federations of smaller games. The participants of each of the smaller games belong to the same multicast group and constantly exchange data. Clients use their game-state to decide which multicast group they register in. This decision function is, in general, game specific. A simple decision function is to map the virtual location of the game characters to a multicast group. At the start of a game session, a client obtains the mapping between game's virtual locations and multicast groups from the control server. The client then adds itself to one or more of the multicast groups corresponding to these virtual locations by sending a join message to the corresponding multicast reflector.

As the players move between distinct virtual locations in the game, the client removes itself from the old multicast group and adds itself to the new one. The multicast reflector periodically checkpoints the current game state by requesting it from a client. As in principle all clients have the same game state, it does not matter which one. Clients entering a new location obtain the current state of

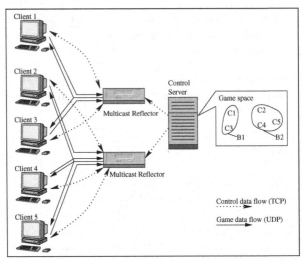

Fig. 1. Hybrid Game Architecture

the game at that location. In order to ensure a quick transition between virtual locations the application software writer may choose to be a member of not only the virtual location at which the client is resident but also of all those around it. The architecture is shown in Figure 1.

A multicast reflector maintains the list of clients resident at a given virtual location. The client sends data packets to the multicast reflector, which then forwards them to all co-located clients. The client does not know the addresses of the other clients, nor does it communicate with them directly. Multicast reflectors may all be located at the providers server farm, or scattered throughout the network. Whereas the first scenario is easier to install and manage, distributing multicast reflectors throughout the network allow better scalability — because not all data traffic is channeled through the same network access point — and is more resilient.

The multicast reflector implements the multicast function without requiring the network to support IP multicast. The clients send unicast UDP packets to the addressable multicast reflector, which in turn generates many unicast UDP packets to send to the members of the peer group. The multicast reflector in effect acts as a broadcast domain for the virtual location. A single multicast reflector supports multiple groups simultaneously, the groups are addressed using UDP port numbers.

4   Multicast Reflector Implementation

A key feature of the multicast reflector is the ability to send UDP datagrams to a set of receivers very efficiently. Efficiency is measured by both a high throughput and a low CPU load. In this section, three different multicast reflector implementations on Linux are described. As an introduction to these implementations, we

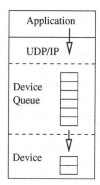

Fig. 2. Linux Network Stack Schematic Overview

provide a brief, schematic overview of the Linux network stack for UDP. We assume that packets are sent on an Ethernet device.

Figure 2 shows the different layers of the Linux network stack. UDP and IP are shown as a single layer as they are rather closely integrated. If a UDP datagram is sent, the following steps are carried out:

1. The application writes the datagram on the socket.
2. The UDP layer checks the validity of the parameters. It then creates both the UDP header and a pseudo UDP header [10]. A routing table lookup is also done to obtain the IP source address needed for the pseudo UDP header.
3. On the IP layer, a socket buffer is created and the IP header is filled in. The payload is then copied from the user space into the socket buffer[1]. The checksum is computed while copying, and therefore does not consume many additional CPU cycles. Before forwarding the packet to the device level, the MAC header is filled in.
4. On the device level, the packet is queued for transmission. Linux maintains a transmit queue for each physical device. Queuing discipline and scheduling are configurable; the default is a FIFO queue with tail dropping. If the queue is full, an error message is returned to the IP layer. Otherwise, the packet is enqueued, and the packet scheduler is started. The scheduler checks whether the device is accepting packets for transmission. If not, the scheduler stops and will be restarted as soon as the device is ready again. This is signaled through an interrupt. Scheduled packets are handed over to the device driver's transmission routine.
5. The device driver copies the contents of the packet to the buffer on the device. This is typically done using DMA transfer. If the device supports scatter/gather, then the packet does not have to be available in a single linear buffer but can be scattered across multiple buffers.

---

[1] This copy function is part of the UDP layer but accessed by a function upcall from the IP layer.

4.1   User-Space Implementation

The user-space implementation uses the BSD socket API for sending UDP datagrams. The multicast group members are maintained in a list of IP address/port tuples. Multicasting a datagram is done by traversing the list and sending the datagram to each group member. This approach is not very efficient, for each destination address, the payload data is copied from the user space to the kernel space even though the payload itself does not change. The more severe problem, is the fact that the device queue (see Figure 2) is very easily overflowed even on Gigabit Ethernet devices, as modern systems have memory transfer rates higher than 30 Gb/s [4]. The bottleneck is either the device or the PCI bus. Consequently packets are dropped, and the kernel returns the error ENOBUFS to the application[2]. The application has no other possibility than to resend the dropped packet. As the ENOBUFS error also indicates that the device queue is full, the application could sleep for some period of time before resending the packet, allowing the queue to empty itself. Unfortunately, the time granularity of Linux on Intel processors is 10 ms, which is too coarse for this purpose. For example, a 100 Mb/s fast Ethernet device sends 125 KB data in 10 ms. If we assume small packets of a few 100 B, as is typical for games, then several hundred packets can be send in 10 ms. The queue length (txqueuelen) is typically 100 packets; sleeping for 10 ms therefore dramatically reduces the throughput as the device will be idle for most of the time. The only viable choice for the application is to resend packets as fast as possible, even though this introduces a busy-waiting loop that consumes unnecessary CPU cycles.

4.2   Kernel-Space Implementation Using Scatter-Gather

A more efficient implementation can be achieved by extending the UDP layer in the Linux kernel. The principle is to maintain a list of address/port tuples per socket in the kernel. A datagram sent on the socket is then sent to each entry in the list.

   In order to achieve a performance benefit, the payload is copied and checksummed only once per multicast operation instead of once per destination. The Linux buffer-handling routines provide mechanisms to implement such a scheme. The main data structure used for handling memory in the network layer is the sk_buff [5]. The sk_buff is a control structure that contains buffer space for holding packet data. Normally, a packet including all headers is stored in a single linear sk_buff. In order to handle IP fragments efficiently, the sk_buff contains a set of pointers to memory pages where additional packet data can be stored. These pointers are maintained in the frag_list array of the sk_buff. This structure allows the following implementation of a solution:

---

[2] Per default, UDP datagrams are silently dropped and no error message is returned. Setting the IP_RECVERR option on the socket enables extended error messages, including ICMP error messages.

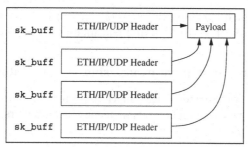

Fig. 3. Several sk_buffs sharing the same payload

1. Data sent on the socket is not, as usual, copied into a sk_buff structure but into one or more memory pages. The memory pages contain the payload without any protocol headers. During the copy operation, the checksum is computed.
2. For each entry in the address list, a sk_buff structure is allocated with sufficient buffer for holding the ethernet, IP and UDP headers. Entries in the frag_list of the sk_buff are generated that reference the memory pages containing the payload. The UDP checksum can be computed efficiently based on the previously computed checksum of the payload, the source/destination IP addresses and the UDP header.
3. After the protocol headers are filled in, the sk_buff is enqueued in the device queue for transmission. At a given point in time, multiple sk_buffs that reference the same payload exist in the queue. This is shown in Figure 3. If the enqueue operation fails, then the sk_buff is freed by the device layer. In this case, a new sk_buff structure is allocated and initialized.
4. After the last sk_buff has been enqueued, the control of the memory pages that hold the payload are returned to the kernel's memory manager. These pages will be freed after the last sk_buff has been deallocated.

The separation of headers and payload into separate buffers is efficient for network devices that support scatter-gather I/O, i.e. devices that can copy frames from non contiguous kernel memory blocks. Most of the modern network cards support this feature.

The problem of device queue overflows can be handled more elegantly in the kernel than in user space. If a packet was dropped owing to queue overflow, then the process is suspended (put to sleep) until the queue is almost empty. If the queue is drained below a low-water mark, then all processes that have been put to sleep are woken up and continue queuing packets. This is implemented using the kernel's wait queues. We have extended each device-control structure with a wait queue. If a network device can no longer accept packets, it tells the network layer to stop any transmission. The packet scheduler then stops, and the device queue eventually fills up until it overflows. If a packet is dropped, then the sending process is put to sleep on the device's wait queue. As soon as the network device is ready for transmission again, it raises an interrupt, and the packet scheduler is restarted. As soon as the queue is drained below the low-water mark, which is currently set to one eighth of the queue size, then all the sleeping processes are woken up and continue to queue packets.

4.3   Kernel-Space Implementation Using Linear Buffers

Not all devices support scatter-gather or they do not support it efficiently. For these cases, an alternate implementation using linear buffers is required. This solution works as follows:

1. Data sent on a socket is copied into a sk_buff structure such that there is enough headroom for all required headers. While the data is being copied, the checksum is computed.
2. For each entry in the address list, the original sk_buff is copied to a newly allocated sk_buff. The UDP header is computed using the previously computed payload checksum.
3. After the protocol headers have been filled in, the sk_buff is enqueued in the device queue for transmission. If the enqueue operation fails, the sk_buff is freed by the device layer and has to be copied again.
4. After all the sk_buffs have been enqueued, the original sk_buff is freed again[3].

4.4   Maintaining the Address List in Kernel Space

The kernel maintains an address list per UDP socket. The list-head and other control information are stored in the socket's transport-protocol-specific fields (union tp_pinfo). The socket's memory footprint is not increased, as tp_pinfo is typically used to hold TCP-related control information that is not needed for UDP sockets. When a UDP socket is created, the address list is empty, and the semantics of write, send and sendto operations are not changed. Applications administer the address list using two new socket options at the UDP level: UDP_MCAST_ADD is used to add a new IP address and port number to the list, whereas UDP_MCAST_DEL is used to remove a previously added entry. The semantics of the send operation changes as soon as at least one entry exists in the address list. In this case, the datagram will be sent to all addresses in the list. If the socket is closed, then the address list is freed again.

5   Results

In order to evaluate the different implementations, several measurements on various computers have been carried out. Two parameters have been measured: the throughput that was achieved and the CPU load that was generated. The

---

[3] At first glance, this seems inefficient, as the last entry in the address list could use the original sk_buff rather than a copy of it. However, if the enqueue operation fails, then the sk_buff is freed and there is no chance to send a datagram to the last receiver.

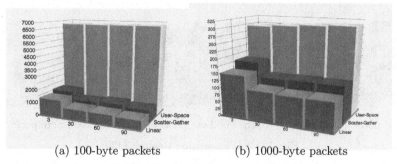

(a) 100-byte packets   (b) 1000-byte packets

Fig. 4. CPU load using Intel E100

measurements were carried out for packets of size 50, 100, 500, and 1000 bytes and for 3, 30, 60, and 90 receivers on different systems. For each parameter set, several hundred thousand packets have been sent.

Throughput has been measured at the application level by timing the **send** system calls. This also means that no protocol headers have been considered, i.e. all throughput figures report the data rate for the payload. All three implementations guarantee that no packets are lost at the sender due to buffer overflow, which was verified using a network sniffer.

CPU load was measured using the performance-monitor counters of the processor, by means of the Linux kernel extension written by Pettersson [9]. This extension provides performance counters on a per-process basis. The CPU load that a process generated was measured using a time-stamp counter, which measures the CPU cycles a process uses. As the result is inherently CPU dependent, it can only be used to compare different approaches executed on the same machine.

5.1 Measurement Series A

The first measurement series was carried out on a machine equipped with a 1.7 GHz Intel⊚ Pentium⊚ 4 processor, RAMBUS⊚ PC800 memory subsystem and an Intel⊚ EtherExpress PRO/100 VM fast Ethernet device. A modified Linux kernel version 2.4.20 with the original Intel⊚ E100 device driver version 2.2.21 and the default txqueuelen of 100 was used. The throughput measurements show that all three implementations achieve the same figures, independently of the number of receivers. The differences between implementations are very small and always below 1%. For 50-byte packets, all three implementations achieved 35 Mb/s net throughput. For 100-, 500- and 1000-byte packets, the results are 60, 88 and 94 Mb/s, respectively. The situation with respect to CPU load is different. Figure 4 shows the results for different numbers of receivers and packet sizes of 100 bytes and 1000 bytes. The ordinate gives the CPU load in millions of clock ticks.

The following observations can be made:

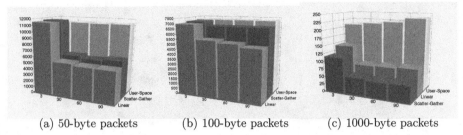

(a) 50-byte packets   (b) 100-byte packets   (c) 1000-byte packets

Fig. 5. CPU load using Realtek 8139

- The kernel-space implementations operate several times more efficiently than the user-space implementation. When using the E100 device, this effect is more pronounced for smaller packets.
- The efficiency of the kernel-space implementations improves with the number of receivers. This is because in the case of very few receivers, more CPU-intensive copy operations from user space to kernel space occur. Hence, referencing the payload buffer as done by "scatter-gather" or even copying within the kernel as done by "linear" is more efficient.
- A somewhat unexpected result is that the "linear" solution performs slightly better than the "scatter-gather" solution does. In the case of "linear", the payload is copied each time into a linear buffer, which is transferred in a single DMA operation from the kernel space to the card's memory. In the case of "scatter-gather", the payload is merely referenced. Two DMA transfers are required to transfer the packet to the card. The first transfer copies the Ethernet, IP and UDP header, and the second transfer copies the payload. For the EtherExpress Card, the overhead of doing two DMA operations is more expensive than copying the payload each time.

5.2   Measurement Series B

The second measurement series was carried out on the same machine as series A, but with a RealTek® 8139 fast Ethernet adapter. We used the "8139too" device driver, version 0.9.26.

For the two larger packet sizes of 500 and 1000 bytes, all three implementations achieve the same throughput of 88 and 94 Mb/s, respectively. For 50-byte packets, "user space" achieves 36 Mb/s, "linear" 35.5 Mb/s and "scatter-gather" 35 Mb/s. When sending 100-byte packets, "user space" manages to send 56 Mb/s, the other two achieve 60.5 Mb/s. Figure 5 shows the CPU load of the three implementations for different packet sizes and numbers of receivers.

Again, the load measurements reveal that the kernel implementations are more efficient than the user-space implementation. An exception is the case of 50-byte packets with three receivers, where the kernel-space implementations are slightly worse than the user-space implementation. Apart from that, the following other points are noteworthy.

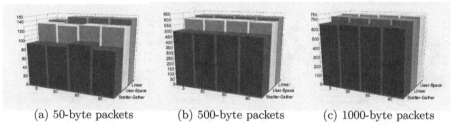

(a) 50-byte packets   (b) 500-byte packets   (c) 1000-byte packets

Fig. 6. Throughput in Mb/s using Intel E1000

- For smaller packet sizes, "linear" is the most efficient of all three implementations. This changes for larger packet sizes, where "scatter-gather" is more efficient. This indicates that copy operations in the kernel are less efficient for larger packets than two DMA transfers to the Realtek 8139 network device.
- For 100-byte packets, the kernel implementations are only slightly more efficient than the user-space implementation. At the same time, the kernel implementations also achieve 8% more throughput. This somewhat unexpected behavior seems to be a peculiarity of the RealTek device driver or the device itself, as the measurements done on the same machine with the Intel device do not show this effect.

5.3   Measurement Series C

The third measurement series was carried out on a machine equipped with a 2.66 GHz Intel⊙ Pentium⊙ 4 processor, PC2100 DDR memory subsystem and a Intel⊙ PRO/1000 MT gigabit Ethernet adapter.

The throughput achieved by the various implementations differs rather significantly for small packets, as shown in Figure 6. "Scatter-gather" shows the weakest performance. The conclusion is that for small packets, copying the packets is more efficient than executing two DMA transfers. For larger packet sizes, "scatter-gather" performs better, although it does not quite achieve the performance of the other two implementations.

The CPU load measurements show again that the kernel-space implementations, in general, are more efficient than the user-space implementation. Figure 7 shows the CPU load for the various parameter configurations. Figure 7(c) is rather surprising, as it shows that the user-space implementation is more efficient than "linear".

6   Discussion of the Results

The throughput achieved by the three implementations is in the same range. Assuming a client of a typical game produces a stream of 8 Kb/s using an average packet size of 100 bytes [1], then our software multicast reflectors are able to support 7'500 clients with fast Ethernet and between 20'000 and 30'000 for Gigabit Ethernet depending on which one is used. The throughput figures

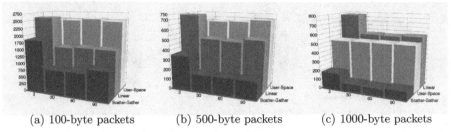

(a) 100-byte packets   (b) 500-byte packets   (c) 1000-byte packets

Fig. 7. CPU load using Intel E1000

are net numbers. For the gross throughput, the Ethernet, IP and UDP headers have to be taken into account. The resulting gross throughput for fast ethernet is about 85 Mb/s and for Gigabit Ethernet, it ranges from 230 Mb/s to 360 Mb/s. This shows that a software based solution is sufficient for fast Ethernet while hardware assists could increase the throughput for Gigabit Ethernet.

The measurement results for the CPU load revealed that the kernel-space implementations are up to six times more efficient. This gain in efficiency depends on the device and device driver used as well as on the number of receivers in the multicast group. The user-space implementation consumes most of the available CPU cycles for packet forwarding. If we take into account that the multicast reflector has to execute control code for registering and unregistering participants and other administrative tasks, we expect that the throughput of the user-space implementation will be lower for real-world implementations. The kernel-space implementations, on the other hand, consume considerable less CPU resources in packet forwarding thus leaving more resources available for control tasks.

7   Conclusions

By dividing large multi-players games into a federation of many peer-to-peer systems, we scale the resources with the number of participants. The actual data forwarding is performed by multicast reflectors. In this paper, we have described and measured the performance of three different implementations of multicast reflectors on Linux. Two implementations were done in the Linux kernel space; both require only modest modifications of the network layer, essentially adding an address list and a wait queue to the kernel. Compared with a user-space implementation, the CPU load is reduced by as much as a factor of six while the throughput is maintained over a wide range of packet- and multicast group sizes. The measurements also show that the network device and device driver have a significant effect on the resulting CPU load. The low load is achieved by eliminating the busy-wait loop that is necessary in the user-space implementation. The kernel-space implementations make sure that datagrams are not lost because of overflowing queues, a task that otherwise has to be done in the application. At the same time applications are simplified as they can use a single send operation for sending datagrams to an entire multicast group.

References

1. A. Abdelkhalek, A. Bilas, and A. Moshovos. Behavior and performance of interactive multi-player game servers. In *Proceedings of the International IEEE Symposium on the Performance Analysis of Systems and Software (ISPASS-2001)*, Nov. 2001.

2. D. Bauer, I. Iliadis, S. Rooney, and P. Scotton. Communication Architectures for Massive Multi-Player Games. Technical Report RZ3500, IBM Research, June 2003. http://www.research.ibm.com/resources/paper_search.shtml

3. A. Bharambe, S. Rio, and S. Seshan. Mercury: A Scalable Publish-Subscribe System for Internet Games. In *NetGames 2002 – First Workshop on Network and System Support for Games*, Braunschweig, Germany, Apr. 2002.

4. M. Clendenin. Dual-channel DDR chips aim for 5.3 Gbyte/s bandwith. http://www.eetimes.com/story/OEG20020809S0036, Aug. 2002. EETimes.

5. A. Cox. Network buffers and memory management. *Linux Journal*, Sept. 1996.

6. K. Morse. Interest management in large-scale distributed simulations. Tech report 96-27, Dept. of Information and Computer Science, University of California, Irvine, 1996.

7. OpenSkies. OpenSkies Network Architecture. http://www.openskies.net/papers/papers.html.

8. OpenSkies. Openskies performance test: Demonstration of scalability. http://www.openskies.net/papers/papers.html.

9. M. Pettersson. Linux x86 Performance-Monitoring Counters Driver. http://user.it.uu.se/~mikpe/linux/perfctr, Mar. 2003.

10. J. Postel. User datagram protocol. Request for Comments 768, Internet Engineering Task Force, Aug. 1980.

Performance Evaluation of Multicast for Small Conferences

Stefan Egger and Torsten Braun

Institute of Computer Science and Applied Mathematics
University of Bern
Neubrueckstrasse 10, CH-3012 Bern, Switzerland

Abstract. Many new Internet applications require data transmission from a sender to multiple receivers. Unfortunately, the IP Multicast technology used today suffers from scalability problems, especially when used for small and sparse groups. Multicast for Small Conferences aims at providing more efficient support for example to audio conferences. In this work, we present a performance study of the concept, based on simulations of real-world scenarios with the ns-2 network simulation software. The results indicate that Multicast for Small Conferences has the potential of replacing IP Multicast for many delay sensitive small group applications, even with very limited support from the network infrastructure.

1   Explicit Multicast

IP Multicast does not scale well for (many) small groups such as in audio conferences or multi-player games. Multicast routing entries cannot be aggregated such as unicast routing entries since multicast address selection is arbitrary. Moreover, multicast routing entries do not only consist of destination addresss but may include source addresses. With many small group applications routing table sizes are increasing massively, which deteriorates the performance of (backbone) routers. Explicit Multicast [3] (Xcast, the successor of Small Group Multicast [4]) is a multicast scheme designed for supporting a very large number of multicast sessions as present in audio/video conferencing, network games or collaborative working. It differs from native multicast in that the sending node keeps track of all session members and explicitly encodes the list of destinations in a special packet header. This newly defined header introduces a new protocol between the network (IP) and the transport (UDP/TCP) layer. Xcast capable routers that receive such a packet parse the Xcast header and use the ordinary unicast routing table to determine how to route the packet to each destination, generating a packet copy for every affected outgoing interface. Each address list contains only the addresses that can be reached via that interface. If there is only one destination address for a particular next hop, the packet may be sent as a standard unicast packet.

With the Xcast scheme, routers do not have to maintain per session state. This makes Xcast very scalable in terms of the number of sessions that can be

B. Stiller et al. (Eds.): NGC/ICQT 2003, LNCS 2816, pp. 226–233, 2003.

supported. Also, no multicast addresses are used, which eliminates all problems related to multicast address allocation. Another advantage is the fact that no multicast routing protocols are required, neither intra nor inter domain. Xcast packets always take the correct path as determined by the unicast routing protocols.

2 Multicast for Small Conferences

Like XCase, the Multicast for Small Conferences (MSC) [5] concept aims at solving the scalability problem of native multicast by explicitly carrying all destination addresses in the data packets while at the same time avoiding the problems of Xcast.

In contrast to Xcast, MSC defines mechanisms to integrate native multicast and Xcast concepts [5]. These are beyond the scope of this paper. The basic MSC packet forwarding mechanism is identical to Xcast. However, instead of introducing a new protocol, MSC relies solely on the existing IPv6 protocol, in particular on the IPv6 routing header. A sender will create a unicast address list of all group members and put the nearest one in the IPv6 destination address. All other member addresses are stored in the MSC routing header, preferably ordered by the distance from the sender (in hops). The group's multicast address should ideally be stored in the routing header as well. If members have to be reached via different outgoing interfaces, a packet for each affected interface is generated with the list of members that can be reached via this interface. This means that the sender divides the address list into N parts and sends N copies of the packet to the N generated lists.

A receiving end system which finds its address in the header creates a packet for the higher protocols encapsulated in the IPv6 packet by copying the multicast address into the IPv6 destination address and removing the routing header. An MSC gateway forwards the packet to local multicast receivers using the appropriate scope. If the routing header contains further unicast addresses, a new packet is generated with the address of the nearest node in the IPv6 destination address. As before, a routing header carries the remaining unicast addresses.

A router that does not understand the MSC header forwards the packet towards the address specified in the IPv6 destination field. This also means that no tunneling between MSC gateways is necessary, which simplifies a gradual deployment. MSC capable routers read the addresses from the destination field and the routing header and determine the outgoing interface for each destination. They then duplicate the packet for each involved link. Again, each packet contains only the unicast addresses that can be reached via that interface plus the multicast address identifying the group. In this document, this router behavior is denoted *standard MSC*.

A possible improvement of the basic MSC concept involves the use of topology information, which can for example be obtained from a link state routing protocol such as OSPF. The first MSC router that handles an MSC packet after it enters a certain network domain (e.g. a backbone network) determines the egress router

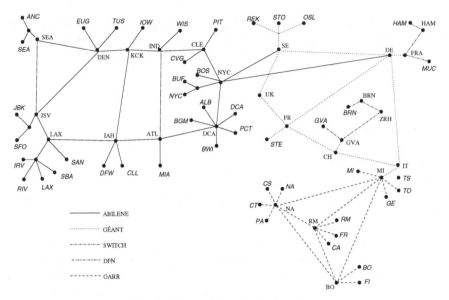

Fig. 1. The ns-2 simulation topology.

(i.e. the router where the packet leaves the domain) for the destination address and all addresses listed in the routing header. A packet is then created for each involved egress router. Thus, packet forwarding between destinations connected to the same network can be eliminated, which potentially reduces the delays. On the downside, multiple packets may be sent over the same link, if two or more egress routers are reached via the same outgoing interface. In this document, this advanced concept is denoted *enhanced MSC* (EMSC).

3   Simulation

In order to evaluate the performance of Multicast for Small Conferences, the protocol has been implemented in the ns-2 network simulator [6,7]. This software was subsequently used for a basic performance study of Multicast for Small Conferences. Due to the similarity of MSC and Xcast the results can be applied to Xcast as well.

   Since choosing an appropriate topology is critical for useful results, the simulations were based on real-world information. Since MSC has been proposed for use in backbones, the simulation scenarios were based on information from actual Internet backbone networks. Particularly, the structure of the simulation topology was formed on the basis of five research networks: The Pan-European Gigabit Research Network (Géant) [8], the Italian Academic and Reseach Network (Garr) [9], Abilene [10], the Swiss Academic and Research Network (Switch) [11] and the German Research Network (DFN/G-WiN) [12]. In order to obtain information about MSC's sensitivity to group size and clustering, fifteen different setups (sets of end systems) were defined. These include combinations of five different group sizes (4, 8, 12, 16 and 20 hosts) and three degrees of spatial locality (clustering). In this paper, we only present the results for a medium (or "weak") clustering. For example, in a group of eight end systems, there may be four pairs, each connecting to a node of the backbone network. In "strong" clustering scenarios, we would possibly have two clusters of four hosts each. Similarly, in a configuration with no clustering, each host might use a different node of a backbone network. Each setup was run in eight different configurations:

Native multicast. IP Multicast (PIM-SM)

Naive unicast. Unicast transmission from the sender to all recipients.

End system MSC. All end systems are MSC capable, but there are no MSC routers (which means that packets are forwarded between the receivers). The senders order the destination addresses by distance.

Full-scale MSC. Standard MSC functionality is deployed in all end systems and backbone routers.

(E)MSC at backbone interlinks. All end systems, and all nodes (routers) with a link to another network domain have MSC functionality. This scenario was simulated for both standard and enhanced MSC.

(E)MSC SIX. In this scenario, only six routers (LAX, KCK, NYC, DE, CH and MI) in the topology are considered MSC capable, but these are more evenly distributed over the topology than in the previous configuration. This scenario was also simulated for both standard and enhanced MSC.

All simulations involve each end system sending a single packet to the group. Packet size is calculated on the basis of an audio transmission with 80 bytes payload over RTP, UDP and IPv6. For the evaluation of the 120 simulation runs, four metrics were used. The average and maximum delays of all transmissions in a specific scenario can be used as indications of the performance of a given configuration. Usually, a delay of 150ms is the maximum that is acceptable for audio conferencing. Another important factor is *bandwidth consumption*. For this performance evaluation, the overall link usage in the scenarios has been measured. The *backbone usage* parameter uses the same data, but only data transferred on links in backbone networks is taken into account.

4   Results

4.1   Maximum Delays

There is a significant gap for maximum delays (Fig. 2) between native multicast, naive unicast, and full-scale MSC on one hand and end system MSC on the other. The other approaches deploying MSC partially are between both extremes. In particular (E)MSC at backbone interlinks suffer from higher maximum delays as group sizes increase (due to increased packet forwarding between end systems). There are a few cases where the measured maximum delay decreases as the group size increases, e.g. in the EMSC SIX configuration. The explanation of this effect is based on router distribution. When a new end system is introduced, the forwarding path of a packet from a given sender to the receivers may change, since

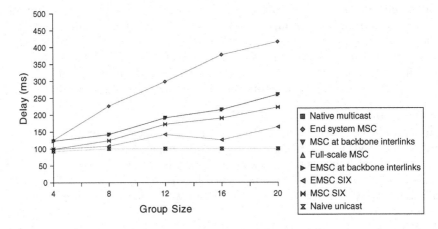

Fig. 2. Maximum Delays

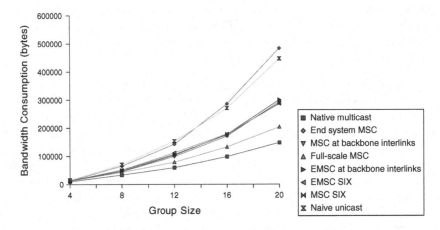

Fig. 3. Bandwidth Consumption

the senders order the recipient's addresses by distance. In some configurations, the new sequence (and the resulting forwarding path) is much more efficient, for example because an MSC capable router is encountered earlier in the forwarding process. This in turn can lead to completely dfferent, potentially significantly lower end-to-end delays. This effect and a similiar occurence in average delays highlight the impact that the selection of end systems (i.e. the composition of a multicast group) can have on the performance of multicast mechanisms.

4.2   Bandwidth Consumption

Bandwidth consumption (Fig. 3) is best for native multicast, but full-scale MSC is very close. Naive unicast and end system MSC perform worst, while the other MSC approaches are again between the extremes. As with the average and max-

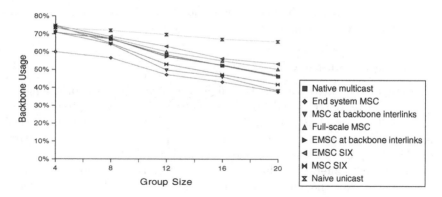

Fig. 4. Backbone Usage

imum delay parameters, the bandwidth consumption among the eight configurations increases when group sizes increase. While the link usage of native multicast increases almost linearly, it does so exponentially for some of the other approaches, particularly naive unicast and end system MSC. This is a good indication for the scalability problems of end system-based mechanisms.

4.3   Backbone Usage

The trend of increasing differences for larger group sizes is also noticeable in the diagrams showing the backbone usage (Fig. 4). End system MSC suffers from excessive packet forwarding between end systems, which most affects the links close to the hosts. For native multicast, the explanation is different: the backbone usage is relatively high for small groups, since each destination is served using an optimal forwarding path. This drives up the number of backbone links that have to carry the packet, while the number of used access network links is low. When new receivers are added, the core of the forwarding tree does not change very much. Thus, the load on the backbone links will not increase significantly. This is further emphasized by the fact that packet size is independent from group size (unlike in MSC scenarios). However, some new access network links are added to the forwarding tree, adding bytes to the non-backbone counter and thus reducing the backbone usage.

At the same time naive unicast shows almost constant values for all group sizes. The reason is that with the naive unicast approach, each packet travels all the way from the sender to the receiver, using backbone and access networks. In the other configurations, the senders produce less packet copies and instead rely on packet forwarding between end systems, which drives up the usage of access networks.

Another interesting aspect is the performance of the (E)MSC at backbone interlinks and (E)MSC SIX configurations. While the MSC and EMSC approaches show almost identical results in terms of bandwidth consumption, they have completely different values for backbone usage. The enhanced MSC approaches consistently show higher values than the standard MSC concepts. Also, the differences increase with group sizes.

4.4   Configuration-Specific Analysis

The results of the native multicast configuration form the basis of the performance evaluation. In terms of delay, native multicast is insensitive to group size, because packets are always forwarded along an optimal tree. The bandwidth consumption is low, since there is no unnecessary packet duplication. Compared to the MSC approaches, the backbone usage is relatively high.

Naive unicast suffers from high link stress, because many identical packet copies are sent over the same links. In combination with the excessive bandwidth consumption, this disqualifies the concept from being an alternative to IP Multicast.

The end system MSC approach suffers from very high delays due to the packet forwarding between receiving end systems. In terms of bandwidth consumption, end system MSC also shows poor performance. While bandwidth consumption increases linearly for native multicast, it grows exponentially in the case of end system MSC. The consistently low backbone usage percentage is an indication that this configuration heavily burdens the networks close to the end systems (access networks).

In full-scale MSC, packet forwarding between end systems is reduced to a minimum due to the optimal forwarding paths. This shows almost no delay penalty compared to native multicast and naive unicast. In terms of bandwidth consumption, full-scale MSC suffers from the routing header, which increases the packet size.

In terms of delays, the (E)MSC at backbone interlinks scenarios perform significantly better than end system MSC. Unfortunately, they also perform a lot worse that full-scale MSC or native multicast. Especially in scenarios with large groups, the uneven distribution of MSC functionality and the resulting packet forwarding between end systems severely deteriorates the performance. The major performance difference between standard and enhanced MSC in this scenario (and also in (E)MSC SIX) is the backbone usage. The packet duplication of enhanced MSC puts more strain on the backbone links, but exonerates the access networks because packet forwarding between receiving end system is minimized.

Compared to the previous configuration, the (E)MSC SIX concept yields an improvement in delays, as the number of delays in excess of 150ms is significantly lower. Also, a slightly lower bandwidth consumption has been measured. The results of these two configurations prove that MSC can deliver an acceptable performance with just a few MSC capable routers, at least for smaller groups, even with widely spread group members. Compared to full-scale MSC lower deployment costs (less routers) have been traded against higher delays and increased bandwidth consumption. The comparison of (E)MSC SIX against (E)MSC at backbone interlinks proves that router distribution is critical.

Overall, MSC can only achieve a performance similar to native multicast (in terms of delays) when full-scale MSC is used. With an optimized "intermediate" approach such as in the (E)MSC SIX scenarios, an average delay penalty of 30-40% (with a maximum of 90% for standard MSC and 60% of enhanced MSC) has to be accepted. However, depending on the group size, the difference may be significantly smaller. Due to the longer IP header, packet duplication and packet forwarding between end systems, MSC also has a higher link usage than native multicast.

5   Summary

In this paper we have presented a performance study of Multicast for Small Conferences (MSC). The results of the extensive simulations with ns-2 indicate that supporting delay-sensitive applications without dedicated routers is not feasible. However, we have shown that already a small number of MSC routers can significantly improve the performance of the concept. The simulation results of several configurations also highlight the importance of appropriate router distribution.

References

1. Explicit Multicast website. http://www.watersprings.org/links/xcast/.
2. Myung-Ki Shin, Ki-Il Kim, Dong-Kyun Kim, and Sang-Ha Kim. Multicast Delivery Using Explicit Multicast Over IPv6 Networks. *IEEE Communications Letters*, 7(2), February 2003.
3. R. Boivie et al. Explicit Multicast (Xcast) Basic Specification, Internet Draft, work in progress, January 2003.
4. R. Boivie, N. Feldman, and Ch. Metz. Small Group Multicast: A New Solution for Multicasting on the Internet. *Internet Computing*, 4(3), May/June 2000.
5. Torsten Braun. Multicast for Small Conferences. Technical Report IAM-00-008, Institute of Computer Science and Applied Mathematics, University of Berne, Switzerland, July 2000.
6. Ns-2 website. http://www.isi.edu/nsnam/.
7. Stefan Egger. Performance Simulation of Multicast for Small Conferences. Master's thesis, University of Berne, December 2002.
8. Géant website. http://www.dante.net/geant/.
9. Garr website. http://www.garr.it.
10. Abilene website. http://www.internet2.edu/abilene/.
11. Switch website. http://www.switch.ch.
12. DFN/G-WiN website. http://www.dfn.de.

Scalable Support for Source Specific Multicast in Differentiated Services Networks

Ning Wang, George Pavlou, and Konstantina Papantoni

Centre for Communication Systems Research
University of Surrey
Guildford, United Kingdom
{N.Wang,G.Pavlou}@eim.surrey.ac.uk
kpapa@hermes-technologies.com

Abstract. In this paper we propose a scalable framework for providing differentiated *QoS* multicast channels for end users with heterogeneous requirements based on the Source Specific Multicast (*SSM*) model, which we name *QoS* Source Specific Multicast (*QSSM*). By encoding each *QoS* service class into a multicast group address and by maintaining the corresponding mapping table at the edge of each DiffServ domain, the proposed *QSSM* architecture embraces per-group *QoS* statelessness at core routers, which is a vital requirement of the DiffServ paradigm. We construct independent trees for each class of service, i.e. *QoS*-specific trees, in order to reduce routing complexity and avoid *QoS* fairness issues among different classes.

1 Introduction

With the emergence of Quality of Service (*QoS*) support in the Internet through IP Differentiated Services (DiffServ [2]) and the requirement for group communications with heterogeneous *QoS* demands, research efforts have recently targeted DiffServ-enabled multicast solutions. The DiffServ architecture is seen as a promising technology for service differentiation in a large scale due to the fact that the core network is kept relatively simple, with most complexity confined at the network edge and the management plane (Bandwidth Broker). Admission control and traffic conditioning are performed at border routers, while core routers simply treat traffic aggregates on a Per Hop Behavior (*PHB*) basis according to the Differentiated Services Code Point (*DSCP*) in each packet. On the other hand, the basic mechanism of traditional *IP* multicast is to maintain group states where necessary *within* the network in order to route data to active receivers. It has been realised that the scalability of group state maintenance is one of the critical obstacles to the fast deployment of multicast services. When receivers demand the support for different *QoS* classes, existing schemes require core routers to record *QoS* service level information (e.g., *DSCP*) for downstream end users in addition to the original group state. This paradigm imposes even heavier memory overhead, which becomes a new issue concerning scalability.

In [1, 3, 9], for supporting receivers with heterogeneous *QoS* requirements, it is proposed that one single multicast tree containing multiple classes of services is constructed, with individual branches reflecting heterogeneous *QoS* requirements. The key idea of this type of tree is that branches with lower classes can be directly grafted from those with higher classes for the same group. We name this type of scheme

B. Stiller et al. (Eds.): NGC/ICQT 2003, LNCS 2816, pp. 234–241, 2003.

Hybrid *QoS* Multicast (*HQM*). Currently all the schemes belonging to *HQM* need to append an additional field to the underlying routing protocols (e.g., *PIM-SM* [5]) as well as core router's forwarding infrastructure, for the inclusion of *DSCP* values in order to support multicast with heterogeneous *QoS* requirements in DiffServ networks. When the *QoS*-aware join request is received from a particular interface, not only the group address but also the desired *DSCP* value are recorded at that interface for further traffic treatment. This is necessary for service differentiation with distinguished *DSCP* values when the packet reaches the branching point of the multicast tree where heterogeneous *QoS* classes meet each other. On receiving group data from its incoming interface (*iif*), the core router should first look up the outgoing interface (*oif*) list with the group state, and then forward the data with the right class by checking the *QoS* state (i.e., *DSCP* value) on those *oifs*.

In this paper we propose the integration of the emerging Source Specific Multicast (*SSM* [6, 7]) service model and DiffServ infrastructure. By using the dedicated *SSM* group address to express and convey *QoS* requirement during group subscription from receivers, the fundamental conflict between sender-based DiffServ and receiver-oriented multicast can be gracefully handled. Since the proposed solution requires no extensions to existing router architecture and to the underlying multicast protocols such as *IGMP* [4] and *PIM-SM*, we believe that this framework can be directly deployed in a large scale. On the other hand, we are not trying to propose an all-in-one architecture with full functionality, but just to introduce a simple solution from the viewpoint of scalability and backwards compatibility.

2   *QSSM* Framework

2.1 *QoS* Mapping Overview

The *QoS*-Source Specific Multicast (*QSSM*) scheme can be regarded as an integration of the Source Specific Multicast and Differentiated Services models, which both address scalability issue in multicast and service differentiation respectively. In *SSM* each group is identified by an address tuple (*S*, *G*) where *S* is the unique *IP* address of the information source and *G* is the destination channel address (in the 232/8 address range). Since channels exist on a per-source basis, issues such as class *D* address allocation and inter-domain source discovery which are problems in the *IP* multicast service model are successfully eliminated.

In the *QSSM* architecture, an *ISP* provides external content providers/receivers with finite classes of unified Olympic services, each of which is uniquely encoded into a class *D* address in the *SSM* address range 232/8. In such a situation, the interpretation of the *SSM* address tuple (*S*, *G*) becomes straightforward: *S* identifies the address of the information source and *G* identifies the *QoS* service level (we name it *QoS* channel) available from *S*. The distinct advantage of this scheme is that since the *QoS* class is embedded into the group address, no *QoS*-related states need to be maintained inside Diffserv core routers, and hence the group forwarding state extension for *DSCP* is not necessary. In order to support compatibility with the conventional *DSCP*-based forwarding in DiffServ environment, a logical mapping table is constructed with the responsibility of translating group address into a *DCSP* value that is associated with a specific *PHB* (Figure 1). In section 2.2 we indicate that this type of mapping only needs to be maintained at edge routers.

	SSM group address	DSCP
	G1	EF
Maximum length: 64	G2	AF11
	...	...
	Gn	BE

Fig. 1. *QSSM* mapping table

By effectively encoding *QoS* states into multicast addresses and maintaining these states within the network, no additional states need to be added to the existing multicast forwarding entries. On the other hand, the maximum number of *QoS* classes in DiffServ is restricted by 6 bits of the *DSCP* field, and the allocation of 64 dedicated class *D* addresses will not cause any problem in the usage of the *SSM* address range that contains 2^{24} addresses. However, there is one restriction regarding the implementation of this approach. Since the *QoS* channel is source specific, it is impossible for a single source with a unique *IP* address *S* to send multiple data streams with different content. In the classic *SSM* model, an information source can be simultaneously in multiple groups because (*S, G1*) and (*S, G2*) are completely independent. One short-term solution is to allow the content provider to use multiple unicast source addresses, each for a particular group/application.

2.2   *QSSM* Tree Management

Recent research works have shown that *HQM* might result in fairness problems for receivers with different service levels. For example, the "Good Neighbor Effect" takes place when a group member subscribing to lower class is physically located near another receiver with a higher *QoS* class [8]. Relevant simulation studies indicate that the two subscribers might receive group data with almost the same *QoS* performance, although they have subscribed/charged at different service/price levels.

In our proposed *QSSM* architecture, we build source specific trees on a per *QoS* class basis, i.e., different *QoS* channels for a specific source *S* are independently maintained even if some of them might have overlapping tree links within the DiffServ domain. The basic characteristic of *QSSM* is that one source specific tree only serves a particular *QoS* level and data packets delivered on this tree exhibit the same class of service. Moreover, the *QSSM* multicast session should be source specific, which satisfies the fundamental requirement of the conventional *SSM* service model.

The construction of *QSSM* trees is illustrated in Figure 2. Once an end user *R* decides to join the *QSSM* tree rooted at source *S* with a desired *QoS* class, it first negotiates with the Bandwidth Broker (*BB*) the bandwidth availability for that *QoS* channel. If successful, the user will send an *IGMPv3* [4] (*S, G*) group membership request to its Designated Router (*DR*) at the edge of the DiffServ domain, where *G* is the associated *QSSM* group address mapped to the negotiated *QoS* channel. On receiving the group membership request from *R*, the *DR* will send a *plain* (*S, G*) join request towards *S*, and this join request packet will either reach the source *S*, or it will be intercepted by an on-tree router with the same (*S, G*) state. It should be noted that when core routers receive the *QSSM* join request, they only create plain (*S, G*) state and they do not maintain any *QoS*-related information for the group, as it is required by the conventional *HQM* approaches. In effect core routers need not know about the mapping between *QoS* classes and group addresses. If the source *S* receives multiple (*S, G*) join requests with different group address *G*, it will initiate an independent *QoS* channel for each of them respectively. When the (*S, G*) group traffic flow back into the DiffServ domain along the reversed path created by the join request, the ingress router (*IR*) will mark the data packets with the matching *DSCP* value according to the address *G* being carried. This type of marking is fulfilled by means of looking up the locally maintained mapping table between group address and *DSCP* value at the ingress router. Thereafter, traffic from *S* will flow along the (*S, G*) tree back to the subscriber with the desired *DSCP*, based on which core routers will forward the packet in the proper DiffServ queue. If one (*S, G*) join request is intercepted at a core router already having this state, a new branch is grafted from the current (*S, G*) tree, in a similar fashion to the conventional *SSM* join procedure. Moreover, replicated packets in the new branch still contain the original *DSCP* value since core routers never re-mark them at the branching point. In this scenario, it is guaranteed that the resulting source specific tree is *QoS* specific as well. From the core routers' point of view, data carrying common *DSCP* values can still be treated in an aggregate fashion, and furthermore, treatment of group data is exclusively based on the *DSCP* value in the packet header, instead of *QoS* states maintained in core routers.

Maintaining *QSSM* trees has the following advantages. First, inter-class fairness problems are avoided thanks to the *QoS* specific tree approach, and this has been proved in [8] by simulation. Second, there is no need to perform traffic reconditioning at core routers, because this is done at the edge of the DiffServ domain. Finally, since *QSSM* group address is used as the carrier of *QoS* requirements from group members, neither protocols nor core routers need to be extended with *QoS* information.

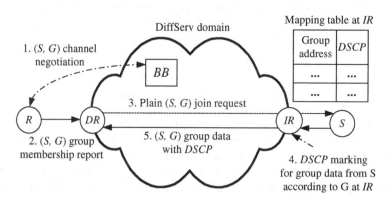

Fig. 2. *QSSM* group join procedure

3   Inter-domain *QSSM* Management

In this section we explain how *QSSM* trees are constructed and maintained across multiple Autonomous Systems (*ASes*). One of the challenges in handling inter-domain

QoS delivery lies in the fact that *ISPs* have heterogeneous DiffServ configuration policies. For example, each DiffServ domain might provide a different number of *QoS* classes, and for the purpose of flexibility, the *DSCP* identification for each class need not be necessarily consistent in all domains.

Similar to *DSCP* usage, *ISPs* should be allowed to map arbitrarily *QSSM* based group addresses to any class of service they provide within their own *ASes*. In this case, when two adjacent *ISPs* set up a domain-level peering Service Level Agreement (SLA) including bilateral *QoS* class mapping (i.e., multicast aggregates belonging to class *i* in domain A should be mapped to class *j* in domain *B* and vice versa), the *QSSM* group address might not be identical for class *i* and *j* in the two *ASes*. Considering this difference in *QoS* class identification between different *ASes*, we propose a mechanism for *QSSM* group address mapping at the edge of DiffServ domains. Figure 3 illustrates a scenario on inter-domain *QSSM* management between two adjacent *ISPs*. It is obvious from the figure that the peering SLA only involves *QSSM* group address conversion, with *DSCP*/PHB hidden from external peers.

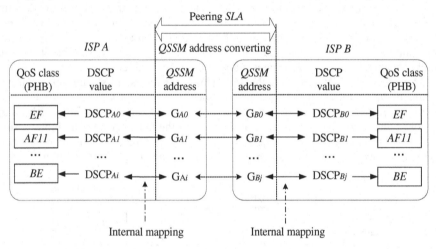

Fig. 3. Inter-domain group address conversion

If an end user wants to subscribe to a *QSSM* group whose source is located in a foreign domain, an inter-domain join request is issued, as in the conventional SSM group join. It should be noted that this user should choose one *QoS* channel available from its local domain. Suppose that the user selects *QoS* class i in its own domain A, then a (S, G_{Ai}) join request will be sent towards the remote source S. Once this join request is admitted into the adjacent domain, say domain B, the *QSSM* group address will be converted into G_{Bj} based on the peering SLA between domain A and B at the border node of domain B. Finally, what the source S or any grafting router already on the existing *QSSM* tree receives is the join request with a recognized group address in its own domain. When group traffic is transmitted back towards the new subscriber, the *QSSM* destination group address is also converted at the ingress router of the transit domains. When the data packet arrives at each DiffServ domain, the ingress router first changes its group address based on the peering SLA, and then by looking up the local mapping table, it remarks the *DSCP* value according to the new *QSSM* address. In such a scenario, all the following core routers will use the proper queue for scheduling by checking the local *DSCP* value contained in the group data packets.

4   Evaluation Through Simulation

We present below the evaluation of *QoS* specific trees in *QSSM* through simulation. We used the Network Simulator (*ns-2*) and extended it with DiffServ-aware source specific multicast (*SSM*) routing. To evaluate the performance of end-to-end group data delivery, we use the topology shown in Figure 4. This network comprises two ingress routers (*S1, S2*), three egress routers (*R1, R2, R3*) and two core routers (*C1, C2*). The bandwidth capacity of each link is 10Mbps. We assume that the *ISP* is providing 4 Assured Forwarding (*AF*) classes of service, i.e. *AF11, AF21, AF31* and *AF41*. The scheduling mechanism for individual *AF* queues is based on Weighted Round Robin (*WRR*), and the weight for each *AF* queue is set as follows: [*AF11 AF21 AF31 AF41*] = [4 3 2 1].

We use the adapted *PIM-SM* [5] for *SSM* (i.e. *PIM-SSM*) as the intra-domain multicast routing protocol. The metric of each link is set to 1 so that the join request always follows the path with the minimum number of hops back to the source.

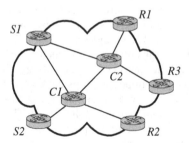

Fig. 4. DiffServ domain topology

In our first experiment, there are two active groups whose sources send data via the ingress routers *S1* and *S2* respectively. For simplicity we only consider two classes of service in this experiment, i.e. *AF11* and *AF21*. The source rate from *S1* is 2Mbps and that from *S2* is 1Mbps (both for *AF11* and *AF21*). We also set 3Mbps background traffic (both *AF11* and *AF21*) from each ingress router to all the egress routers. We consider the situation that each egress router joins both channels with *AF11* and *AF21* simultaneously, resulting in 4 distinct multicast trees: (*S1, AF11*), (*S1, AF21*), (*S2, AF11*) and (*S2, AF21*). We define the Transmission Ratio (*TR*) as the number of packets received by each group member over the total number of packets sent by the source. Figure 5 illustrates the *TR* performance of each source/receiver pair. We can see that in most cases the *TR* performance of *AF11* is significantly better than that of *AF21* (except *R2*). By examining the traffic load of each link, we find that all the links between *S1* and *R2* (i.e., *S1*→ *C1* and *C1*→*R2*) are under-loaded, resulting in 100% transmission ratio for both *AF11* and *AF21*. On the other hand, the performance of transmission ratio also depends on the location of the egress router through which group members are attached to the distribution tree. For example, both egress routers *R1* and *R3* have *AF21* group members for *S1*. Our simulation results show that the *TR* value for *R1* is 59.4% while that for *R2* is significantly higher (77.6%). This is caused by the more overloaded link $C2\rightarrow R1$.

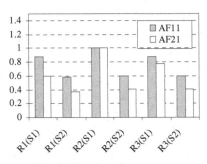

Fig. 5. *TR* value of two groups

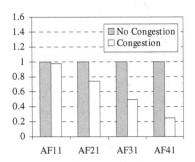

Fig. 6. Simultaneous *AF* joins

Next we investigate the performance of individual group members attached to the same egress router. The objective of this experiment is to examine the inter-class fairness in more detail without considering the receivers' physical location. The simulation scenario is as follows: The source rate of *S2* is fixed at 1Mbps and 4 receivers attached to egress router *R1* join the session by subscribing to 4 different channels, i.e. (*S2, AF11*), (*S2, AF21*), (*S2, AF31*) and (*S2, AF41*). The grey column of Figure 6 indicates that if none of the links on the tree branch $S2\rightarrow C1\rightarrow C2\rightarrow R1$ are congested, the transmission rate of all the four classes is 100%. In order to evaluate the performance in time of congestion, we impose 3Mbps background traffic for each of the four *PHBs*. From the figure we can observe the significant differentiation of the four *AF* classes when the network cannot handle all the traffic. The group member subscribing to the *AF11* channel achieves virtually no packet loss, whereas the one subscribing to *AF41* channel only receives 24.6% of the packets from *S2*. The "Good Neighbour Effect" [8] does not happen if we construct this type of *QoS* specific trees for each channel.

Finally we evaluate the relative inefficiency of *QSSM* compared with the *HQM* approaches. We define the bandwidth overhead O_t for class t as follows:

$$O_t = 1 - \frac{U_t^{HQM}}{U_t^{QSSM}}$$

where U_t^{HQM} is the bandwidth utilization of class t with *HQM* and U_t^{QSSM} is that with *QSSM*. In this simulation we create random graph networks with 100 core routers and 5 data sources using the GT-ITM topology generator. The simulation scenarios remain the same as before. Figure 7 presents the bandwidth overhead of 4 individual AF classes with a sequence of 450 join requests that randomly select group source S and *QoS* channel G. From the figure we can see that *HQM* is able to conserve bandwidth compared with *QSSM* on all classes of service except AF11, which is the highest *QoS* channel that obviously cannot be grafted from a higher *QoS* level. We also observe that the lower the *QoS* channel, the more bandwidth is conserved. The reason behind this is that in *HQM* join requests with lower *QoS* levels have a bigger chance to hit an on-tree node that can satisfy their requirement, and hence no further path to the source is required.

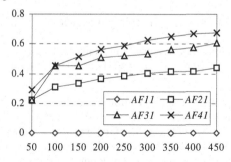

Fig. 7. Bandwidth overhead for 4 *AF* classes

5 Summary

In this paper we proposed the *QSSM* framework for supporting scalable multicasting in DiffServ networks. By encoding *QoS* state into SSM group address and maintaining a mapping table at edge routers, multicast with heterogeneous *QoS* requirements can be achieved in DiffServ networks without any extension of underlying multicast protocols or of the forwarding state entry of core routers. The advantage is that multicast service differentiation can be directly supported based on the current routing and forwarding infrastructure very soon. Moreover, routing complexity and inter-class fairness issues are avoided by constructing source specific trees on per *QoS* class basis. Our future work will address the *QSSM*-based Service Level Agreements and receiver-oriented admission control mechanisms.

References

1. G. Bianchi et al, "QUASIMODO: QUAlity of ServIce-aware Multicasting Over DiffServ and Overlay Networks", IEEE Network, special issue on multicasting, Jan/Feb. 2003, pp 38-45
2. S. Blake et al, "An Architecture for Differentiated Services", RFC 2475
3. R. Bless, K. Wehrle, "Group Communication in Differentiated Services Networks", Proc. IQ2001, pp. 618-625
4. B. Cain et al, "Internet Group Management Protocol, Version 3", RFC 3376
5. B. Fenner, "Protocol Independent Multicast - Sparse Mode (PIM-SM): Protocol Specification (Revised)", draft-ietf-pim-sm-v2-new-0*.txt, work in progress
6. H. W. Holbrook, D. R. Cheriton, "IP Multicast Channels: EXPRESS Support for Large-scale Single-source Applications", Proc. ACM SIGCOMM'99
7. D. Meyer et al, "Source-Specific Protocol Independent Multicast in 232/8", Internet Draft, draft-ietf-mboned-ssm232-0*.txt, Jan. 2003, work in progress
8. A. Striegel, G. Manimaran, "Dynamic *DSCPs* for Heterogeneous *QoS* in DiffServ Multicasting", Proc. IEEE GLOBECOM 2002
9. B. Yang, P. Mohapatra, "Multicasting in Differentiated Service Domains", Proc. IEEE GLOBECOM 2002

Programming Overlay Networks
with Overlay Sockets

Jörg Liebeherr, Jianping Wang, and Guimin Zhang

Department of Computer Science, University of Virginia, Charlottesville, USA
{jorg,jwang,gz8d}@cs.virginia.edu

Abstract. The emergence of application-layer overlay networks has inspired the development of new network services and applications. Research on overlay networks has focused on the design of protocols to
maintain and forward data in an overlay network, however, less attention
has been given to the software development process of building application programs in such an environment. Clearly, the complexity of overlay
network protocols calls for suitable application programming interfaces
(APIs) and abstractions that do not require detailed knowledge of the
overlay protocol, and, thereby, simplify the task of the application programmer. In this paper, we present the concept of an *overlay socket* as a
new programming abstraction that serves as the end point of communication in an overlay network. The overlay socket provides a socket-based
API that is independent of the chosen overlay topology, and can be configured to work for different overlay topologies. The overlay socket can
support application data transfer over TCP, UDP, or other transport
protocols. This paper describes the design of the overlay socket and discusses API and configuration options. The overlay socket has been used
to develop a variety of applications, from multicast-file transfer programs,
to multicast video streaming systems.

Keywords: Overlay Networks, Application-layer Multicast, Overlay
Network Programming.

1 Introduction

Application-layer overlay networks [5,10,14,18] provide flexible platforms for developing new network services [1,9,11,12,15,19,20,21,22] without requiring changes
to the network-layer infrastructure. Members of an overlay network, which can
be hosts, routers, servers, or applications, organize themselves to form a logical
network topology, and communicate only with their respective neighbors in the
overlay topology. A member of an overlay network sends and receives application
data, and also forwards data intended for other members.

This paper addresses application development in overlay networks. We use
the term *overlay network programming* to refer to the software development
process of building application programs that communicate with one another in
an application-layer overlay network. The diversity and complexity of building
and maintaining overlay networks make it impractical to assume that application
developers can be concerned with the complexity of managing the participation
of an application in a specific overlay network topology.

B. Stiller et al. (Eds.): NGC/ICQT 2003, LNCS 2816, pp. 242–253, 2003.
© Springer-Verlag Berlin Heidelberg 2003

We present a software module, called *overlay socket*, that intends to simplify the task of overlay network programming. The design of the overlay socket pursues the following set of objectives: First, the application programming interface (API) of the overlay socket does not require that an application programmer has knowledge of the overlay network topology. Second, the overlay socket is designed to accommodate different overlay network topologies. Switching to different overlay network topologies is done by modifying parameters in a configuration file. Third, the overlay socket, which operates at the application-layer, can accommodate different types of transport layer protocols. This is accomplished by using *network adapters* that interface to the underlying transport layer network and perform encapsulation and de-encapsulation of messages exchanged by the overlay socket. Currently available network adapters are TCP, UDP, and UDP multicast. Even though the overlay socket has been designed with the Internet protocols in mind, in principle, one can design network adapters for non-Internet protocols. Fourth, the overlay socket provides mechanisms for bootstrapping new overlay networks. We note that security-related issues are not emphasized in the design of the overlay socket. While mechanisms that ensure integrity and privacy of overlay network communication can be integrated in the overlay socket, they are not discussed here.

In this paper, we provide an overview of the overlay socket design and discuss overlay network programming with the overlay socket. The overlay socket has been implemented in Java as part of the HyperCast 2.0 software distribution [13]. The software has been used for various overlay applications, and has been tested in both local-area as well as wide-area settings. The HyperCast 2.0 software implements the overlay topologies described in [16] and [17]. This paper highlights important issues of the overlay socket, but it is not a comprehensive description. Additional information can be found in the design documentation available from [13].

Several studies before us have addressed overlay network programming issues. Even early overlay network proposals, such as Yoid [10], Scribe [4], and Scattercast [6], have presented APIs that aspire to achieve independence of the API from the overlay network topology used. Particularly, Yoid and Scattercast use a socket-like API, however, these APIs do not address issues that arise when the same API is used by different overlay network topologies. Several works on application-layer multicast overlays integrate the application program with the software responsible for maintaining the overlay network, without explicitly providing general-purpose APIs. These include Narada [5], Overcast [14], ALMI [18], and NICE [2]. A recent study [8] has proposed a common API for the class of so-called *structured overlays*, which includes Chord [21], CAN [19], and Bayeux [22], and other overlays that were originally motivated by distributed hash tables. Our work has a different emphasis than [8], since we assume a scenario where an application programmer must work with several, possibly fundamentally different, overlay network topologies and different transmission modes (UDP, TCP), and, therefore, needs mechanisms that make it easy to change the configuration of the underlying overlay network.

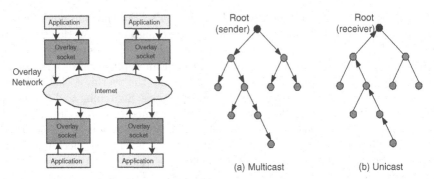

Fig. 1. The overlay network is a collection of overlay sockets.

Fig. 2. Data forwarding in overlay networks.

The rest of the paper is organized as following. In Section 2 we introduce concepts, abstractions, and terminology needed for the discussion of the overlay socket. In Section 3 we present the design of the overlay socket, and discuss its components. In Section 4 we show how to write programs using the overlay socket. We present brief conclusions in Section 5.

2 Basic Concepts

An *overlay socket* is an endpoint for communication in an overlay network, and an overlay network is seen as a collection of overlay sockets that self-organize using an overlay protocol (see Figure 1). An overlay socket offers to an application programmer a Berkeley socket-style API [3] for sending and receiving data over an overlay network. Each overlay socket executes an *overlay protocol* that is responsible for maintaining the membership of the socket in the overlay network topology.

Each overlay socket has a *logical address* and a *physical address* in the overlay network. The logical address is dependent on the type of overlay protocol used. In the overlay protocols currently implemented in HyperCast 2.0, the logical addresses are 32-bit integers or (x, y) coordinates, where x and y are positive 32-bit positive integers. The physical address is a transport layer address where overlay sockets receive messages from the overlay network. On the Internet, the physical address is an IP address and a TCP or UDP port number. Application programs that use overlay sockets only work with logical addresses, and do not see physical addresses of overlay nodes.

When an overlay socket is created, the socket is configured with a set of configuration parameters, called *attributes*. The application program can obtain the attributes from a configuration file or it downloads the attributes from a server. The configuration file specifies the type of overlay protocol and the type of transport protocol to be used, but also more detailed information such as the size of internal buffers, and the value of protocol-specific timers. The most important attribute is the *overlay identifier* (overlay ID) which is used as a global identifier for an overlay network and which can be used as a key to access the other attributes of the overlay network. Each new overlay ID corresponds to the creation of a new overlay network.

Overlay sockets exchange two types of messages, *protocol messages* and *application messages*. Protocol messages are the messages of the overlay protocol that maintain the overlay topology. Application messages contain application-data that is encapsulated in an overlay message header. An application message uses logical addresses in the header to identify source and, for unicast, the destination of the message. If an overlay socket receives an application message from one of its neighbors in the overlay network, it determines if the message must be forwarded to other overlay sockets, and if the message needs to be passed to the local application. The transmission modes currently supported by the overlay sockets are unicast, and multicast. In multicast, all members in the overlay network are receivers. In both unicast and multicast, the common abstraction for data forwarding is that of passing data in spanning trees that are embedded in the overlay topology. For example, a multicast message is transmitted downstream a spanning tree that has the sender of the multicast message as the root (see Figure 2(a)). When an overlay socket receives a multicast message, it forwards the message to all of its downstream neighbors (children) in the tree, and passes the message to the local application program. A unicast message is transmitted upstream a tree with the receiver of the message as the root (see Figure 2(b)). An overlay socket that receives a unicast message forwards the message to the upstream neighbor (parent) in the tree that has the destination as the root.

An overlay socket makes forwarding decisions locally using only the logical addresses of its neighbors and the logical address of the root of the tree. Hence, there is a requirement that each overlay socket can locally compute its parent and its children in a tree with respect to a root node. More specifically, given the logical address of some overlay socket R, an overlay socket with logical address A must be able to compute the logical address of A's parent and children in an embedded tree which has R as the root. This requirement is satisfied by many overlay network topologies, including [16,17,19,20,21,22].

3   The Components of an Overlay Socket

An overlay socket consists of a collection of components that are configured when the overlay socket is created, using the supplied set of attributes. These components include the overlay protocol, which helps to build and maintain the overlay network topology, a component that processes application data, and interfaces to a transport-layer network. The main components of an overlay socket, as illustrated in Figure 3, are as follows:

- The *overlay node* implements an overlay protocol that establishes and maintains the overlay network topology. The overlay node sends and receives overlay protocol messages, and maintains a set of timers. The overlay node is the only component of an overlay socket that is aware of the overlay topology.

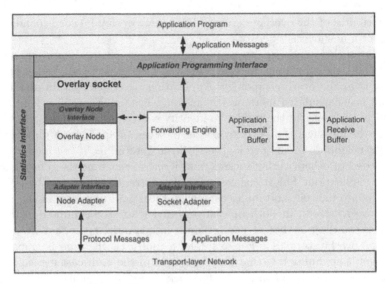

Fig. 3. Components of an overlay socket.

- The *forwarding engine* performs the functions of an application-layer router, that sends, receives, and forwards formatted application-layer messages in the overlay network. The forwarding engine communicates with the overlay node to query next hop routing information for application messages. The forwarding decision is made using logical addresses of the overlay nodes.
- Each overlay socket has two network adapters that each provides an interface to transport-layer protocols, such as TCP or UDP. The *node adapter* serves as the interface for sending and receiving overlay protocol messages, and the *socket adapter* serves as the interface for application messages. Each adapter has a transport level address, which, in the case of the Internet, consists of an IP address and a UDP or TCP port number. Currently, there are three different types of adapters, for TCP, UDP, and UDP multicast. Using two adapters completely separates the handling of messages for maintaining the overlay protocol and the messages that transport application data. Particularly, socket and node adapters in the same overlay socket need not use the same transport protocol. Having two adapters simplifies the support for multiple overlay network protocols, since changes to the overlay protocol and its message formats does not have an impact on the processing of application data.
- The *application receive buffer* and *application transmit buffer* can temporarily store messages that, respectively, have been received by the socket but not been delivered to the application, or that have been released by the application program, but not been transmitted by the socket. The application transmit buffer can play a role when messages cannot be transmitted due to rate control or congestion control constraints[1].

---

[1] The application transmit buffer is not implemented in the HyperCast 2.0 software.

– Each overlay socket has two external interfaces. The *application programming interface* (API) of the socket offers application programs the ability to join and leave existing overlays, to send data to other members of the overlay network, and receive data from the overlay network. The *statistics interface* of the overlay socket provides access to status information of components of the overlay socket, and is used for monitoring and management of an overlay socket. Note in Figure 3 that some components of the overlay socket also have interfaces, which are accessed by other components of the overlay socket. Specifically, the overlay node and the adapters have a uniform internal API when different overlay protocols and adapter types are used.

The following component is external to the overlay socket (and not shown in Figure 3), but it interacts closely with the overlay socket.

– The *overlay manager* is responsible for configuring an overlay socket when the socket is created. The overlay manager reads a configuration file that stores the attributes of an overlay socket, and, if it is specified in the configuration file, may access attributes from a server, and then initiates the instantiation of a new overlay socket.

Next we describe some of the components in more detail.

3.1 Overlay Node

Running an application program with a different overlay protocol simply requires a replacement of the type of overlay node in the overlay socket. Across different overlay protocols, all overlay nodes have a set of common features. First, each overlay node maintains a neighborhood table, which contains a list of its neighbors in the overlay network topology. Each entry of the neighborhood table contains the logical and the physical address of a neighbor. Each overlay node exchanges overlay protocol-specific messages with its neighbors, and maintains a set of protocol-specific timers. The overlay node is activated when timers expire and when protocol messages are received.

Even though not strictly required, overlay protocols should be soft-state protocols, where all remote state information is periodically refreshed. This can be done if each overlay socket maintains a timer, and periodically sends a protocol message to each of its neighbors. If an overlay node does not receive a message from a neighbor, the neighbor is eventually removed from the neighborhood table.

In the HyperCast 2.0 software, there are overlay nodes that build a logical hypercube [16] and a logical Delaunay triangulation [17].

3.2 Forwarding Engine

The forwarding engine forwards application messages to its children or to its parent in a tree that is embedded in the overlay network. The next-hop routing information for forwarding messages is obtained from the overlay node component. For example, when the forwarding engine wants to pass a message to the parent node with respect to the root with logical address *LARoot*, it issues a request '*getParent(LARoot)*' to the local overlay node. The overlay node returns the logical address and the physical address of the parent. Then, the forwarding engine sends the message to the given physical address via the socket adapter. When the overlay topology changes, it may happen that two consecutive next-hop requests, e.g., two requests '*getParent(LARoot)*', yield addresses of different overlay sockets. Here, the forwarding engine is left unaware that the overlay network topology has changed. The forwarding engine always assumes that the information provided by the overlay node is correct. This simplicity of the forwarding engine is intentional and contributes to the efficiency of the overlay socket when handling large volumes of data.

When a forwarding engine receives an application message, it passes the message to the application if the message is a multicast message, and then forwards the message to all children nodes with respect to the logical address of the sender. If the received message is a unicast message, it passes the message to the application if the local overlay socket is the destination, or, otherwise, forwards the message to the parent with respect to the logical address of the destination. If a message must be forwarded but cannot be transmitted due to flow control or congestion control constraints, then it is stored in the application transmit buffer.

There are two methods for passing an application message to the application program. If the application program has supplied a callback function for processing incoming messages, then the callback function is executed. If no callback function is available, the received message is written to the application receive buffer, from where the application program can retrieve the message with a receive operation.

3.3   Adapters

The adapter type determines how overlay sockets exchange overlay protocol and application messages. Each adapter can be configured to use TCP, UDP, or, at least in principle, other transport protocols. The type of the socket adapter determines the semantics of the data delivery service. Since UDP provides a best effort service, a socket with UDP provides an unassured message delivery between neighbors in the overlay. When the socket adapter is configured to use TCP, the data exchange between neighbors in the overlay is reliable. Note, however, that end-to-end reliability is not assured, since forwarding engines in intermediate overlay sockets may drop messages.

3.4   Message Format

Overlay sockets exchange two types of messages, overlay protocol messages and application messages. Overlay protocol messages are generated by the the overlay node and transmitted by the node adapter. Application messages are processed by the forwarding engine and transmitted via the socket adapter. Overlay protocol messages are defined by the overlay protocol and specific to a certain overlay

```
                    1                   2                   3
 1 2 3 4 5 6 7 8 9 0 1 2 3 4 5 6 7 8 9 0 1 2 3 4 5 6 7 8 9 0 1 2
+-------+-----------------+---+---+-----------------------------------+
|Version|LAS|Dmd| Traffic Class |  Flow Label   | Next Header        |
+-------+-----------------+---+---+-----------------------------------+
|  Overlay Message Length         |        Hop Limit                  |
+---------------------------------+-----------------------------------+
|                             Src LA                                  |
+--------------------------------------------------------------------+
|                             Dest LA                                 |
+--------------------------------------------------------------------+
```

Fig. 4. Common header of an application messages.

topology. Application messages, have a common format that is identical in all configurations of the overlay socket.

Each application message has a common header which is loosely modeled after the IPv6 message format. The fields of the application message header are shown in Figure 4. The version field is set to 0 in the current version. The *LAS* field determines the size of the logical address. Using the formula '(LAS+1)×4 bytes', the size of a logical address is between 4 and 16 bytes. The delivery mode indicates whether the packet is a multicast, flood, unicast, or anycast packet (Anycast is currently not implemented). The traffic class and flow label fields are intended to play a similar role as in IPv6, but are currently not used. The *Next Header* field allows a concatenation of different headers. There is a whole set of extension headers defined, for which we refer to [13]. The simplest form of a message is a 'raw messages' (*Next Header = 0x05*) where the overlay message has only a single payload field. The hop limit field plays the same role as in IPv6. Finally, the *SrcLA* field and the *DestLA* field are the logical addresses of the source and the destination. The length of the address fields is determined by the *LAS* field. Multicast messages (*Dmd=0*) do not have a *DestLA* field.

4   Overlay Network Programming

An application developer does not need to be familiar with the details of the components of an overlay socket as described in the previous section. The developer is exposed only to the API of the overlay socket and to a file with configuration parameters. The configuration file is a text file which stores all attributes needed to configure an overlay socket. The configuration file is modified whenever a change is needed to the transport protocol, the overlay protocol, or some other parameters of the overlay socket. In the following, we summarize only the main features of the API, and we refer to [13] for detailed information on the overlay socket API.

4.1   Overlay Socket API

Since the overlay topology and the forwarding of application-layer data is transparent to the application program, the API for overlay network programming can be made simple. Applications need to be able to create a new overlay network, they must be able to join and leave an existing overlay network, they must be able to send data to members in the overlay network, and they must be able to receive data sent by other members in the overlay.

The API of the overlay socket is message-based, and intentionally stays close to the familiar Berkeley socket API [3]. In fact, changing an application program that uses multicast datagram sockets to overlay sockets requires only few modifications. Even though the API presented here uses Java, the API is not bound to use Java. The effort to transcribe the API to other programming language is comparable to a corresponding effort for Berkeley sockets.

Since space considerations do not permit a description of the full API, we sketch the API with the help of a simplified example. Figure 5 shows the fragment of a Java program that uses an overlay socket. An application program configures and creates an overlay socket with the help of an overlay manager (*om*). The overlay manager reads configuration parameters for the overlay socket from a configuration file (*hypercast.prop*), which can look similarly as shown in Figure 6. The application program reads the overlay ID with command *om.getDefaultProperty ("OverlayID")* from the file, and creates a configuration object (*config*) for an overlay socket with the given overlay ID. The configuration object also loads all configuration information from the configuration file, and then creates the overlay socket (*config.createOverlaySocket*). Once the overlay socket is created, the socket joins the overlay network (*socket.joinGroup*). When a socket wants to multicast a message, it instantiates a new message (*socket.createMessage*) and transmits the message using the *sendToAll* method. Other transmission options are *sendToParent*, *sendToChildren*, *sendToNeighbors*, and *sendToNode*, which, respectively, send a message to the upstream neighbor with respect to a given root (see Figure 2), to the downstream neighbors, to all neighbors, or to a particular node with a given logical address.

4.2   Overlay Network Properties Management

As seen, the properties of an overlay socket are configured by setting attributes in a configuration file. The overlay manager in an application process uses the attributes to create a new overlay socket. By modifying the attributes in the configuration file, an application programmer can configure the overlay protocol or transport protocol that is used by the overlay socket. Changes to the file must be done before the socket is created. Figure 6 shows a (simplified) example of a configuration file. Each line of the configuration file assigns a value to an attribute. The complete list of attributes and the range of values is documented in [13]. Without explaining all entries in Figure 6, the file sets, among others, the overlay ID to '*1234*', selects version 2.0 of the DT protocol as overlay protocol (*'Node=DT2-0'*), and it sets the transport protocol of the socket adaptor to TCP (*'SocketAdapter=TCP'*).

Next we provide additional background on the management of attributes of an overlay socket. Each overlay network is associated with a set of attributes that characterize the properties of the overlay sockets that participate in the overlay

```
// Generate the configuration object
OverlayManager om = new
OverlayManager("hypercast.prop");
String MyOverlay =
   om.getDefaultProperty("OverlayID");
OverlaySocketConfig config =
      new om.getOverlaySocketConfig(MyOverlay);
   // create an overlay socket
OL_Socket socket =
   config.createOverlaySocket(callback);
   // Join an overlay
socket.joinGroup();
   // Create a message
OL_Message msg = socket.createMessage(byte[]
data, int length);
   // Send the message to all members in overlay network
socket.sendToAll(msg);
   // Receive a message from the socket
OL_Message msg = socket.receive();
```

```
# OVERLAY Server:
OverlayServer =
   # OVERLAY ID:
OverlayID = 1234
KeyAttributes= Socket,Node,SocketAdapter
   # SOCKET:
Socket = HCast2-0
HCAST2-0.TTL = 255
HCAST2-0.ReceiveBufferSize = 200
   # SOCKET ADAPTER:
SocketAdapter = TCP
SocketAdapter.TCP.MaximumPacketLength = 16384
   # NODE:
Node = DT2-0
DT2-0.SleepTime = 400
   # NODE ADAPTER:
NodeAdapter = NodeAdptUDPServer
NodeAdapter.UDP.MaximumPacketLength = 8192
NodeAdapter.UDPServer.UdpServer0 =
128.143.71.50:8081
```

Fig. 5. Program with overlay sockets.

Fig. 6. Configuration file (simplified).

network. As mentioned earlier, the most important attribute is the overlay ID, which is used to identify an overlay network, and which can be used as a key to access all other attributes of an overlay network. The overlay ID should be a globally unique identifier. The overlay ID is an arbitrary string and does not require a specific format or naming convention.

A new overlay network is created by generating a new overlay ID and associating a set of attributes that specify the properties of the overlay sockets in the overlay network. Hence, changing the overlay ID in Figure 6 to a new value effectively creates a new overlay network (which has initially no members). To join an overlay network, an overlay socket must know the overlay ID and the set of attributes for this overlay ID. This information can be obtained from a configuration file, as shown in Figure 6.

All attributes have a name and a value, both of which are strings. For example, the overlay protocol of an overlay socket can be determined by an attribute with name *NODE*. If the attribute is set to *NODE=DT2-0*, then the overlay node in the overlay socket runs the DT (version 2) overlay protocol. The overlay socket distinguishes between two types of attributes: *key attributes* and *configurable attributes*. Key attributes are specific to an overlay network with a given overlay ID. Key attributes are selected when the overlay ID is created for an overlay network, and cannot be modified afterwards. Overlay sockets that participate in an overlay network must have identical key attributes, but can have different configurable attributes. The creator of an overlay ID is responsible for deciding which attributes are key attributes and which are not. This is done with the attribute *KeyAttributes*. In Figure 6, the attribute *KeyAttributes= Socket,Node,SocketAdapter*, sets *Socket*, *Node*, and *SocketAdapter* as key attributes. In addition, the attributes *OverlayID* and *KeyAttributes* are key attributes by default in all overlay networks. Configurable attributes specify parameters of an overlay socket, which are not considered essential for establishing communication between overlay sockets in the same overlay network, and which are considered 'tunable'. However, having different values for the configurable attributes of overlay sockets may have a significant impact on the performance of the overlay network.

5   Conclusions

We discussed the design of an *overlay socket* which attempts to simplify the task of overlay network programming. The overlay socket serves as an end point of communication in the overlay network. The overlay socket can be used for various overlay topologies and support different transport protocols. The overlay socket supports a simple API for joining and leaving an overlay network, and for sending and receiving data to and from other sockets in the overlay network. The main advantage of the overlay socket is that it is relatively easy to change the configuration of the overlay network. This is done with the help of configuration parameters, called attributes, that configure the components of an overlay socket, when an overlay socket is created. This provides a substantially increased flexibility, as compared to existing APIs for overlay networks.

An implementation of the overlay socket is distributed with the HyperCast2.0 software. The software has been extensively tested. A variety of different applications, such as distributed whiteboard and a video streaming application, have been developed with the overlay sockets. Currently ongoing work consists of adding services that enhance the simple message-oriented API of the overlay socket and provide better support for security, data aggregation, synchronization, service differentiation, streaming.

Acknowledgements

In addition to the authors of this article the contributors include Bhupinder Sethi, Tyler Beam, Burton Filstrup, Mike Nahas, Dongwen Wang, Konrad Lorincz, Jean Ablutz, Haiyong Wang, Weisheng Si, Huafeng Lu, and Guangyu Dong.

References

1. D. G. Andersen, H. Balakrishnan, M. F. Kaashoek, and R. T., Morris. Resilient overlay networks. In *Proceedings of the 18th ACM Symposium on Operating Systems Principles*, pp. 131-145, Lake Luise, Canada, October 2001.
2. S. Banerjee, B. Bhattacharjee, and C. Kommareddy. Scalable Application Layer Multicast. In *Proceedings of ACM SIGCOMM*, pp. 205-220, Pittsburgh, PA, August 2002.
3. K. L. Calvert, M. J. Donhahoo. TCP/IP Sockets in Java: Practical Guide for Programmers. *Morgan Kaufman*, October 2001.
4. M. Castro, P. Druschel, A-M. Kermarrec and A. Rowstron. SCRIBE: A large-scale and decentralized application-level multicast infrastructure. *IEEE Journal on Selected Areas in Communications (JSAC)*, Vol. 20, No. 8, October 2002.

5. Y. Chu, S. G. Rao, and H. Zhang. A case for end system multicast. In *Proceedings of ACM SIGMETRICS*, pp. 1-12, Santa Clara, CA, June 2000.
6. Y. D. Chawathe. Scattercast: An Architecture for Internet Broadcast Distribution as an Infrastructure Service. *Ph.D. Thesis, University of California, Berkeley*, December 2000.
7. Y. Chu, S. G. Rao, S. Seshan and H. Zhang. Enabling Conferencing Applications on the Internet using an Overlay Multicast Architecture. In *Proceedings of ACM SIGCOMM*, pp. 55-67, San Diego, CA, August 2001.
8. F . Dabek, B. Zhao, P. Druschel, J. Kubiatowicz, and I. Stoica. Towards a Common API for Structured Peer-to-Peer Overlays. In *Proceedings of the 2nd International Workshop on Peer-to-Peer Systems (IPTPS '03)*, Berkeley, CA, February 2003.
9. H. Deshpande, M. Bawa, and H. Garcia-Molina. Streaming live media over a peer-to-peer network. *Technical Report 2001-30*, Stanford University (Computer Science Dept.), August 2001.
10. P. Francis. Yoid: Extending the Internet multicast architecture, Unpublished paper, April 2000. Available at http://www.aciri.org/yoid/docs/index.html.
11. *The FreeNet Project.* http://freenetproject.org.
12. *The Gnutella Project.* http://www.gnutella.com.
13. *The HyperCast project.* http://www.cs.virginia.edu/~hypercast.
14. J. Jannotti, D. K. Gifford, K. L. Johnson, M. F. Kaashoek, and J. OToole. Overcast: Reliable multicasting with an overlay network. In *Proceedings of the Fourth Symposium on Operating Systems Design and Implementation*, pp. 197-212, San Diego, CA, October 2000.
15. *The JXTA Project.* http://www.jxta.org.
16. J. Liebeherr and T. K. Beam. HyperCast: A protocol for maintaining multicast group members in a logical hypercube topology. In *Proceedings of First International Workshop on Networked Group Communication (NGC 99)*, In Lecture Notes in Computer Science, Vol. 1736, pp. 72-89, Pisa, Italy, November 1999.
17. J. Liebeherr, M. Nahas, and W. Si. Application-layer multicasting with Delaunay triangulation overlays. *IEEE Journal on Selected Areas in Communications*, Vol. 20, No. 8, October 2002.
18. D. Pendarakis, S. Shi, D. Verma, and M. Waldvogel. ALMI: An application level multicast infrastructure. In *Proceedings of 3rd Usenix Symposium on Internet Technologies and Systems*, pp. 49-60, San Francisco, CA, March 2001.
19. S. Ratnasamy, P. Francis, M. Handley, R. Karp, and S. Shenker. A Scalable Content-Addressable Network. In *Proceedings of ACM SIGCOMM*, pp. 161-172, San Diego, CA, August 2001.
20. A. Rowstron, and P. Druschel. Pastry: Scalable,distributed object location and routing for large-scale peer-to-peer system. In *Proceedings of IFIP/ACM International Conference on Distributed System Platforms (Middleware)*, pp. 329-350, Heidelberg, Germany, November 2001.
21. I. Stoica, R. Morris, D. Karger, F. Kaashoek, and H. Balakrishnan. Chord: A Scalable Peer-To-Peer Lookup Service for Internet Applications. In *Proceedings of ACM SIGCOMM*, pp. 149-160, San Diego, CA, August 2001.
22. S. Q. Zhuang, B. Y. Zhao, A. D. Joseph, R. H. Katz, and J. Kubiatowicz. Bayeux: An Architecture for Scalable and Fault-tolerant Wide-Area Data Dissemination. In *Proceedings of the Eleventh International Workshop on Network and Operating System Support for Digital Audio and Video, (NOSSDAV 2001)*, pp. 11-20, Port Jefferson, NY, January 2001.

Enhancing Peer-to-Peer Parallel Data Access with PeerFecT

Laurent Dairaine, Laurent Lancérica, and Jérôme Lacan

ENSICA / TéSA, 1, place Emile Blouin 31056 Toulouse cedex 5, France
{Laurent.Dairaine,Laurent.Lancerica,Jerome.Lacan}@ensica.fr
Tel : +(33)561618683 / Fax : +(33)561618688

Abstract. Data access performances over a Peer-to-Peer (P2P) network is a critical issue since downloading time remains the longest phase of P2P usage by end-user. In the present effort, we propose an innovative approach called PeerFecT (*Peer-to-peer with Fec dissemination Technique*) based on an erasure code, often called Forward Error Correction (FEC) code, to speed-up data access into P2P networks. The main idea is to use the erasure code to dilute the information over the peers. This dilution allows a greater and flexible choice among all the disseminated encoded data and then statistically enhances the overall throughput of the transfer. This paper focus on the performance gain this technique can provide. A performance evaluation based on an original model using the results of a measurement campaign of sequential and parallel downloads in a real P2P network over Internet is presented. The results show that for the same amount of information disseminated into the P2P network, our solution is more efficient compared to classical file replication approaches.

Keywords: P2P (Peer-to-peer), Erasure codes, parallel data access.

Introduction

The popularity of Peer-to-peer (P2P) file sharing applications offers new prospects to Internet end-users. The main benefits of P2P networks are to enhance the utilization of information, bandwidth, and computing resources. As a result, numerous research level issues are related to the conception of such a system. Scalability, fault tolerance, authentication, routing or data localization are examples of hot topics concerning this domain. Nevertheless, the performance of data access and downloading time over the P2P networks is the crucial aspect in such systems. The contribution of this paper concerns these last issues.

A classical approach to cope with data access performance consists in enhancing the localization of replicated copies [1]. The end user then simply downloads one of them from the closest peer. Typical enhancement of this scheme consists in getting various blocks from different peers in parallel. In the present effort, we propose a complementary approach based on the use of an erasure code, also called Forward Error Correction (FEC) codes, to speed-up the data access into the P2P network. We named PeerFecT (Peer-to-peer with FEC dissemination Technique) this approach. This paper focus on the gain in terms of downloading time provided from the use of

B. Stiller et al. (Eds.): NGC/ICQT 2003, LNCS 2816, pp. 254–261, 2003.

erasure codes in P2P networks. The FEC usage allows the information to be diluted over a set of different data blocks. Those blocks once disseminated over the P2P network, FEC properties induce that only a subset of the total set of blocks is necessary to reconstitute the original information. Due to the universal value of each encoded block, any client will be statistically situated closer to the minimal necessary amount of blocks among the multiple FEC blocks copies than in the case of classical approaches. Then, the overall downloading performance will be enhanced. This paper shows that for the same amount of information disseminated into the P2P network, this solution is statistically more efficient in terms of data access performance compared to classical file replication. This property is verified whatever the downloading technique used, i.e., sequential or parallel access to remote peers.

The paper is structured as follows. The first section describes the PeerFecT idea, explaining how the FEC are used into the P2P network to enhance data access time. The second section presents and analyses the technique used into parallel data access context, context largely implemented into today's P2P systems. The last section considers main issues for implementing PeerFecT. Finally, concluding remarks and future work are given.

Using Erasure Codes to Enhance Data Access Performance in P2P System

A P2P system uses a peering architecture that offers the support for various P2P services such as applicative multicast communications or file sharing between peers. Examples of implemented file sharing P2P systems are Napster or Gnutella. Using these systems, each node is able to determine its peers and to localize data over the peer network. Furthermore, the peering algorithms allow data dissemination and cost determination in terms of bandwidth, for peer to peer data transfers. Concerning the data localization among peers, several efficient techniques have already been proposed (see e.g.[2]). Recall that erasure codes are a mechanism classically used to protect information against errors or losses in transmissions (see e.g. [6]). The principle is to add redundancy to the transmitted information, permitting receivers to recover the whole original data, even after experiencing transmission errors.

The PeerFecT approach is based on the following method. When a file must be published into the network, it is firstly cut into k blocks which are encoded using an erasure code to obtain a set of n blocks. The last phase of publication is the dissemination stage of the various blocks over the P2P network (briefly discussed in Implementation Issues Section).

Considering the various encoded blocks disseminated into the network, and thanks to the erasure code properties, downloading a complete file is equivalent to downloading any k blocks among the total n ones. Hence, compared to classical approaches, there are greater choices for the sets of k blocks to get, to reconstitute the original data. Note that the availability and the robustness of the system are also increased (for a fault-tolerant point-of-view of similar systems, see e.g. [9]). When these blocks are disseminated over the P2P network, searching and throughput measurement services help to determine the closest ones by considering a certain cost function (e.g., the largest throughput). Then, the k closest blocks are downloaded in a classical way. The original data file can be finally obtained from the decoding of those k blocks.

An evaluation of the PeerFecT performance was proposed in [4] for sequential downloading, i.e. when the blocks are downloaded one after the other. Three dissemination strategies were studied: The first approach, *a) Entire File Replication*, consists in simply replicating the entire file into the network. The second approach, *b) no-FEC Block Dissemination*, splits the file into several blocks and distributes them. The last approach, *c) FEC Block Dissemination*, disseminates the blocks previously encoded with an erasure code. Note that the three approaches disseminate the same amount of data in the network. The first result shown in [4] is that no performance gain is obtained when using a simple *No-FEC Block dissemination* compare to *Entire File Replication*. This result is not amazing and the equivalence of the two approaches has been mathematically proved. The second important result was that PeerFecT approach was always more efficient than Entire File Replication and *No-FEC Block dissemination*.

Parallel Data Access Performance Evaluation

It should be noted that the context of sequential downloading is not realistic. Indeed, one major characteristic of recent P2P systems is to support a parallel access to several peers [1] (i.e., several blocks are downloaded at the same time). This parallel strategy drastically improves the downloading time. Those gains are evaluated in the context of mirror sites in [7].

Problem Modeling

We propose a simple model allowing computing the cost to get a file with the three previously considered approaches.

For the first strategy, *(a) Entire File Replication*, we consider that the r file replicas are downloaded independently with the bandwidths $Bw_1, Bw_2, ..., Bw_r$. By opening r parallel connections towards the r peers and assuming that each connection downloads different parts of the file, it could be obtained a total bandwidth up to $Bw_1 + Bw_2 + ... + Bw_r$. This maximum is reached if all the connections are bottleneck-disjoint i.e., without any side-effect between the various connections. In a P2P network, where the connections can be established among several thousands different peers, it is very difficult to evaluate the presence of bottlenecks due to parallel-downloads of different parts of the same file. Thanks to the over-provisioning of the network infrastructure, we consider that the bottleneck are necessary situated near the client, at access network, due to bandwidth limitation. This assumption is strongly confirmed by the campaign of measures presented in the next part of this section.

Let us denote this access bandwidth by Bw_0. By using this new parameter, we can state that the available bandwidth is now equal to $\min(\sum_{i=1}^{r} Bw_i, Bw_0)$. The cost to get the entire file is then $C_{(a)} = S_F / \min(\sum_{i=1}^{r} Bw_i, Bw_0)$. For the second strategy, (b) no-FEC Block Dissemination, the file is segmented into k blocks of size S_b, and each block is replicated r times in the network. Let us denote by $Bw_{i,j}$ the available bandwidth for the download of the ith replica of the jth block. This block can be downloaded for a cost equal to $S_b / Bw_{i,j_i}$ where $Bw_{i,j_i} = \max_{j=1..r}(Bw_{i,j})$. Note that parallel accesses to several replicas of the same block could be opened, but this would be equivalent to have a larger number of blocks and could also decrease performance due to the added load. So we only consider one connection per block. With this hypothesis, k parallel connections are opened. The minimal cost to get the entire file is then $\max_{i=1..r}(S_b / Bw_{i,j_i})$. As stated previously, this expression holds if there is no bottleneck due to the parallel downloads.

If $\sum_{i=1}^{k} Bw_{i,j_i} < Bw_0$, where Bw_0 denotes the access bandwidth limitation, then the minimal cost is given by the previous formula. On the other hand, if $\sum_{i=1}^{k} Bw_{i,j_i} \geq Bw_0$, due to the TCP fairness, the bandwidth Bw_0 is equally split into the k connections, i.e. a bandwidth of Bw_0 / k is supposed to be available for each connection. But if there is a bandwidth $Bw_{i,j_i} < Bw_0 / k$, the corresponding connection is not modified by the limitation resulting from this bandwidth limitation. The previously given cost value only depends on the minimum value of the Bw_{i,i_i}, then we can state that

$$C_{(b)} = \frac{S_b}{\min_{i=1..k}(Bw_{i,j_i})} \; if \; \min_{i=1..k}(Bw_{i,j_i}) < Bw_0 / k \; and \; \frac{S_b}{Bw_0 / k} else \, .$$

The case (c) FEC-block Dissemination can be analysed in the same way than case (b). The k original blocks constituting the file become now n blocks due to FEC redundancy. Getting the file consists now in downloading the k blocks of minimum cost over the n blocks. If the n blocks are replicated r' times over the network, we define $Bw_{i,j_i} = \max_{j=1..r'}(Bw_{i,j})$ for i=1,..n and the function $f : \{1,...,n\} \longrightarrow \{1,...,n\}$ such that $Bw_{f(1),j_{f(1)}} > Bw_{f(2),j_{f(2)}} > ... > Bw_{f(n),j_{f(n)}}$. Using similar considerations than in the previous case, the cost is expressed as follows $C_{(c)} = \frac{S_b}{Bw_{k,j_{f(k)}}}$ if $(Bw_{f(k),j_{f(k)}} < Bw_0 / k)$ and

$$C_{(c)} = \frac{S_b}{Bw_0 / k} else \cdot$$

Simulation Study

The simple model given in the previous section has been implemented for simulation. The main idea is to consider 3 arrays of size r for entire file dissemination and of size k.r and n.r' for respectively no-FEC block dissemination and FEC-block dissemination. These arrays contain the available bandwidth towards the peers containing the blocks or the files. To be fair between the three studied approaches in terms of data storage load over the P2P network, we assume the total number of blocks disseminated into the network to be constant, then $r' = k.r / n$. The arrays are randomly filled following a bandwidth distribution deduced from a campaign of real measurements on the Gnutella network. This campaign was realized between the 1st and the 29th of January 2003 on ENSICA local area network, connected to a Gigabit Metropolitan network, this network being connected to the French research backbone RENATER network with a 155 Mbits/s access bandwidth. In this campaign, 1000 files were downloaded from 1000 different peers in sequential then in parallel (10 simultaneous connections) accesses. The measurements results, given in Figure 1, strongly confirm the assumption that "no bottleneck will appear in the backbone due to the traffic generated by the parallel downloads" (the curve representing the bandwidth towards a peer in a parallel access is the same than for the sequential access).

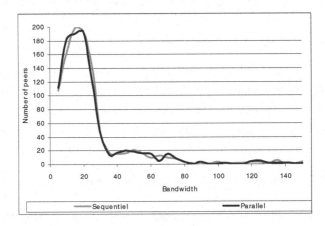

Fig. 1. Topology of the Gnutella network in terms of bandwidth (Kb/s).

The arrays were independently filled and analysed 1.000.000 times. The results of the simulations are presented in the next Section. Note that in all simulations except the last one, the access bandwidth at transport level is supposed to be 500Kb/s.

Results

In the following Figures, the results are presented in terms of gain percentages of the FEC and/or No FEC dissemination approaches compared to the entire file dissemination in a parallel downloading context.

Figure 2(a) evaluates the impact of the number of blocks k constituting the file for the case of No FEC and FEC disseminations. In the No FEC approach, the number of replicas is r=10. In the FEC approach, the redundancy factor n/k is equal to 5 and the number of replicas is r'=2. The main conclusions are that the FEC approach is always better than the No FEC approach and that the maximum gain (up to 60%) is obtained very soon. 10 blocks seems to be a good compromise between the performance gain and data storage load. Note that the negative gain for the No FEC approach is explained by non sufficient number of blocks compared to the entire file replication in the parallel approach.

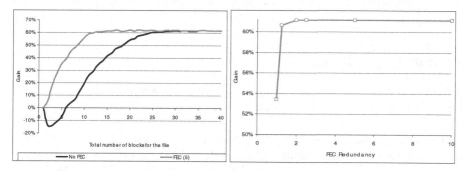

Fig. 2. (a) Impact on the number of blocks. (b) Impact on FEC redundancy factor

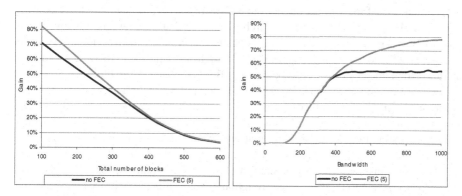

Fig. 3. (a) Impact of total number of blocks (b) Impact of access throughput (Kb/s)

The impact of the FEC redundancy factor (i.e. n/k) is shown on Figure 2(b). In this simulation, the number of file blocks is k=20 and the number of replicas is r=10 for the reference case (entire file dissemination). In order to be fair, the number of replicas r' is varying to satisfy the equality $r' = k.r/n$. The results show that a low redundancy factor n/k (2 or 3) is sufficient to obtain very important gain (up to 61% here).

Figure 3(a) presents the results of simulations which make the number of replicas r and r' vary. The value of k is fixed to 20 and the redundancy factor is equal to 5 (then, n=100). These results clearly show that PeerFecT is more powerful with a limited total number of blocks (up to 400). This observation can be explained by the fact that a large number of file or blocks replicas make them very accessible and then the FEC become less interesting.

The last simulation studies the impact of access bandwidth variation on performance. The file is split into k=20 blocks, each one being replicated r=10 times for the No FEC approach. The FEC approach uses a redundancy factor of n/k=5 and so a number of replicas r'=2. Figure 3.(b) presents the obtained results. This curve determines the domain of interest of PeerFecT. The left part shows that up to 350 Kb/s, there is no significant gain between No FEC and FEC approaches. This result illustrates that no performance gain is obtained when the bottleneck is situated on the access network. The right part of the curve illustrates the gain compared to the No FEC technique.

Implementation Issues

This section considers the implementation of PeerFecT over a typical P2P architecture by analysing the main modifications of the classical P2P services due to Peer-FecT.

The main classical P2P service used by PeerFecT is the *Searching* service. Indeed, the increasing of the global number of different blocks in the network may introduce a potential bandwidth overhead due to the signalisation messages generated by the searching phase. Nevertheless, depending on the underlying searching algorithm, an adapted naming of the various blocks can easily cope with this problem. For example, Gridella P2P system [1] provides a searching service that finds, with a low overhead, a set of files whose filename matches the same prefix. Then, using such a service in PeerFecT, all encoded blocks names are build from a prefix associated to the researched filename. The suffix can be an identifier associated to the block.

Another potential problem concerns the throughput estimation between peers. This estimation is crucial in PeerFecT because it is used to choose the location the blocks are to be downloaded from. Most of P2P systems provide mechanisms for such throughput estimation. Even these estimations are not accurate, recent research results indicate how to obtain an accurate estimation of the throughput [5][3]. Moreover, simple algorithms already implemented in classical P2P architectures allow classifying peers according to their relative throughput, even if it is not really accurate.

The implementation of the main functional blocks of the core of PeerFecT system can be described as follows. The main problem of the encoding/decoding phases is that they could be expensive in time for large files. However, the encoding/emission (resp. reception/decoding) can be organized in order to pipeline these operations. Since the encoding/decoding throughputs are in most cases greater than the transmission one [6], the latency due to this phase can be neglected.

The other important point of the PeerFecT scheme is the dissemination of the encoded blocks. A detailed description of the different possibilities is beyond the scope of this short paper, but two approaches are possible. First one is a user-driven scheme only using the downloading of blocks to ensure the block dissemination. This solution takes advantage of being costless in terms of downloading overhead (i.e., the downloading is achieved by users) and ensures the property of disseminating blocks depending on file popularity. The second approach is a pro-active scheme that spreads a given number of blocks onto the network before any user-download. This scheme enhances the performance for a given content as soon at it is published. The blocks distribution can be managed in such a way to control the total number of blocks disseminated over the P2P network.

Concluding Remarks

In this paper, we have presented a P2P file sharing system that uses an erasure code to disseminate information over the peers. Performance gains were estimated by comparing our system to classical approaches of various P2P systems.

Several lessons emerge from the obtained results. First, the use of FEC allows increasing the average availability of data and decreasing the access time. Secondly, although the obtained results depend on the distribution law of the bandwidth over the peer network, there is a set of values (number of blocks, FEC redundancy factor, and number of replicas) that optimize the peering architecture. Finally, the use of such FEC-based system enhances robustness and data availability, while keeping constant the storage capacity of every peer. All the simulations are based on a real measurement campaign providing an accurate estimation of the bandwidth distribution law of the peer. As a result, an accurate and realistic estimation of the PeerFecT performances are provided. In the sights of the obtained results, future work mainly concerns real implementation of PeerFecT and development of an adapted erasure code.

References

1. K. Aberer, M. Punceva, M. Hauswirth, R. Schmidt, "Improving Data Access in P2P Systems", IEEE Internet Computing 6, 1, pp. 58-67, Jan./Feb. 2002.
2. E. Cohen, S. Shenker "Replication Strategies in Unstructured Peer-to-peer Networks", ACM SIGCOMM 2002, August 2002.
3. T.S. Eugene Ng, Y. Chu, S. Rao, K. Sripanidkulchai, H. Zhang, "Measurement-Based Optimization Techniques for Bandwidth-Demanding Peer-to-Peer Systems", INFOCOM 2003.
4. J. Lacan, L. Lancérica, L. Dairaine, "When FEC Speed Up Data Access in P2P Networks", in Proc. of IDMS-PROMS, LNCS, Springer, 2002
5. K. Lai, M Baker, "Nettimer : a tool for measuring bottleneck link bandwidth", Proc. USENIX Symp. on Internet Technologies and Systems, 2001.
6. L. Rizzo, "Effective Erasure Codes for Reliable Computer Communication Protocols", In *Computer Communication Review*, April 1997.
7. P. Rodriguez, A. Kirpal, E. W. Biersack, "Parallel-Access for Mirror Sites in the Internet", In Proceedings of IEEE/Infocom'2000, Tel-Aviv, Israel, 2000.
8. S. Saroiu, P. Gummadi, S. Gribble, "A Measurement Study of Peer-to-Peer File Sharing Systems", T.R. UW-CSE-01-06-02, Seattle, July 2001
9. H.Weatherspoon, J. D. Kubiatowicz, "Erasure Coding vs. Replication: A Quantitative Comparison", inProc. of IPTPS '02, March 2002

An Approach to the Charging of
Secure IP Multicast Services

Sylvie Laniepce and Mohammed Achemlal

France Telecom R&D
mohammed.achemlal@rd.francetelecom.com

Abstract. The massive deployment of IP multicast-based services raises important issues, as far as the security is concerned. In particular, there is a growing
need for ISPs to be able to provide some guarantees with respect to the identification and authentication of sources and receivers, not to mention the preserva-
tion of the confidentiality of the traffic that will be forwarded along the dynamically computed distribution trees. In this paper, we propose a generic
scheme where service providers will play a key role for the provisioning of secure IP multicast services, based on the ongoing standardisation effort being
conducted within the msec working group of the IETF. A first part relates to
cryptographic services, e.g. data authentication and encryption, and highlights
the role a telecom operator could play in securing group communications. In
particular, various opportunities for providing GCKS (Group Controller and
Key Server) services and cryptographic treatment services, are discussed depending on the targeted market and the use made of the deployed IP multicast
network. A second part emphasizes the opportunities offered by multicast content security and the associated key management, to perform accounting. The
way a telecom operator could take advantage of such possibilities in order to offer value-added services is discussed. Various accounting and billing models,
made possible by the msec facilities, are demonstrated.

1 Introduction

Multicast content security aims at providing some guarantees to the receivers as far as
the authentication, the integrity and the confidentiality of the multicast data are concerned. We believe service providers have a key role to play to address the aforementioned issues appropriately, partly based on some work currently being specified by
the Internet community. This paper is organized as follows:

Section 1 highlights the difficulties raised when willing to secure *group* communication (as opposed to one-to-one communication). Then, Section 2 presents a brief
overview of MSEC[1], an on-going IETF standardization effort involved in the specification of protocols that will enable multicast content security. The core of the paper
addresses some issues about the application part of the subject, from a telecom operator's point of view: Section 4 relates to cryptographic services, *e.g.* data authentication
and privacy, and highlights the role a telecom operator could play within the security
treatment integrated value chain. Section 5 emphasizes the opportunities offered by
multicast content security and the associated key management, to perform accounting.
Again, the way a telecom operator could take advantage of such possibilities in order
to offer value-added services is discussed.

---

[1] MSEC: Multicast SECurity

B. Stiller et al. (Eds.): NGC/ICQT 2003, LNCS 2816, pp. 265–275, 2003.

2 What Is Specific to Group Communication Security

This section introduces the major motivations and goals for securing multicast data, as well as the encountered difficulties to address in order to perform *multicast* content security.

2.1 Secrecy

Within the context of IP multicast [RFC-1112], two main reasons can motivate secrecy, either to prevent unauthorized users from accessing the data – subscribers being charged to access the data (according to a pay-per-view scheme for a TV broadcasting service for example) – or to preserve the confidentiality of the information forwarded along the multicast distribution tree (corporate video-conferencing, for example).

Encryption of multicast data can provide the requested secrecy. Encryption by means of symmetric cryptography involves mechanisms based on symmetric keys, meaning that all members of the multicast group share a single common group key, which is used to cipher and decipher messages. Therefore, secrecy is subject to issues related to key management and distribution, moreover to dynamic re-key process, in the case of *forward/backward access control* requirement for example. Forward access control consists of preventing a member who leaves a multicast group from accessing the multicast data exchanged within the group *after* he left. The counterpart, called *backward access control*, aims to guarantee that a member who joins a given multicast group, *cannot* access the data exchanged within the group *before* he joins. Forward/backward access control is achieved by means of re-key process, each time the group membership changes (either a member leaves the group or a new member joins the group). Re-key consists of generating and distributing a *new* cryptographic encryption/decryption common key, in replacement of the one that was in use just before the group membership characteristics changed.

Other situations can motivate re-keying process, such as compromise recovery, if a group member loses its key or a group member's key is stolen, exclusion of a group member or key lifetime limitation.

2.2 Authentication and Integrity

Authentication and integrity provide some guarantees about the data originator (who sent the data) and some means to detect – hence prevent from - alteration and/or unauthorized changes in the data forwarded to the receivers. This is achieved by providing the receivers with an authentication value, computed by the sender, and specific to each message transmitted. Two input data come into the authentication value calculation: a secret (*i.e.* a key) owned by the sender, and the message itself. The receivers have the capabilities to check the received authentication value.

Within the context of IP multicast, the authentication of the data sender may refer either to *group* authentication or to *source* authentication. The *group* authentication only guarantees that it is for sure[2] a '*group* member', whoever this member may be (provided he is entitled to participate to the group communication), that sent the data

---

[2] Within the limits of the cryptographic algorithm robustness.

on the group. In this case, the receivers have no means to identify which member among those that are members of the group actually sent the data. The *source* authentication provides receivers with a means to check that the originator of the received data is for sure[2] a given sender, i.e. a specific legitimate and identifiable sender, hereafter called the *source*. Requirements for one of these two authentication modes are basically dependent on the application and on the trust 'group members' place in each other (a group member may trust a given source, but not all group members).

This *source* authentication capability raises some issues and requires new mechanisms when one chooses to use "regular" symmetric cryptography mechanisms, as shown in Figure 1. The principle of symmetric cryptography is that all the members would share a single common group key, used to perform the calculation of the authentication value. All members would therefore be able to calculate the authentication value of a given message. This authentication value would therefore become unusable to discriminate one sender from another.

Moreover, such a (unsatisfying) method would be unable to provide any means to detect a malicious alteration (performed by any member of the group) of a message sent by an authorized source. Indeed, a member would have the possibility to intercept a message sent by the source, to modify it, and to insert the appropriate authentication value – he would be able to do so because he knows the key that is necessary to perform a correct authentication value calculation – before re-sending it to the group. This yields a situation where the receivers would believe that "nothing is wrong", although this is actually wrong: the received data are not identical to those sent by the initial originator whereas the authentication value check has passed!

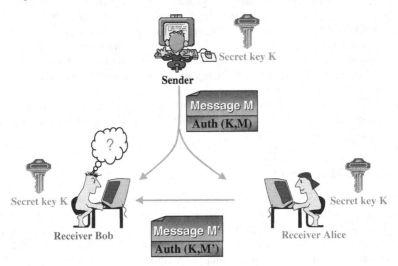

Fig. 1. Source authentication issue

Moreover, such a (unsatisfying) method would be unable to provide any means to detect a malicious alteration (performed by any member of the group) of a message sent by an authorized source. Indeed, a member would have the possibility to intercept a message sent by the source, to modify it, and to insert the appropriate authentication value – he would be able to do so because he knows the key that is necessary to perform a correct authentication value calculation – before re-sending it to the group. This yields a situation where the receivers would believe that "nothing is wrong", although this is actually wrong: the received data are not identical to those sent by the initial originator whereas the authentication value check has passed!

This is why some *new* authentication schemes become necessary when dealing with *source* authentication, within the context of group communication.

3 The MSEC Working Group of the IETF

Our reflections on opportunities for providing multicast content security-related services, whose results are presented in the next two sections, have been inspired by ongoing IETF standardization efforts, namely the specifications that are currently chartered by the MSEC working group which is involved in multicast content security.

This section is an extremely brief (and non-exhaustive) overview of *msec*, which tends to provide the *msec*-unaware reader with (hopefully) enough information to understand the rest of this paper.

To a certain extent, IPSEC (Internet Protocol SECurity, [RFC-2401]), a protocol suite providing content security for *unicast* IP communication between peers, represents a reference framework for the *msec* working group.

The way *msec* security protection is provided by the IP layer or the application layer, consists of adding an *msec* header, in order to transport security information related to the payload contents of the PDU (Protocol Data Unit) and to its associated header, basically:

- The result of the authentication value computation,
- Some means allowing the receiver to validate, interpret and process the received security information; this includes a means to retrieve the cryptographic material (key, algorithm, *etc.*) necessary to check the received authentication value,
- Additional security mechanisms to preserve the security of the transmitted security-related information, such as an anti-replay mechanism.

In addition, when secrecy is required, the *msec* engine ciphers the PDU. As for the authentication process, the means allowing the receiver to validate, interpret and process the enciphering are retrieved from the additional *msec* header.

This security transformation of the PDU is performed by *data treatment protocols*. Already existing data treatment protocols, such as the Encapsulating Security Payload (ESP, [RFC-2406]) that has been designed by the *ipsec* working group, could be applicable to multicast content security to some extent, although there are severe limitations in its current form (no source authentication, manual configuration of the cryptographic material). A couple of variants of ESP, namely Multicast Encapsulating Security Payload (MESP) and its equivalent at the application layer (AMESP), have been proposed by the SMUG (Secure Multicast Group) IRTF (Internet Research Task Force) Research Group and should be specified in the near future by the MSEC WG. These new protocols address the group communication-specific issues by adding new specific fields to the aforementioned protocols, in order to support source authentication for example.

The cryptographic material, such as the keys and the cryptographic algorithms, to be used by these data protocols to perform the security transformation of the data, is treated under the concept of *Group Security Association* (GSA, [DRAFT-GSA-00]), *i.e.* an aggregate of Security Associations (SAs).

The definition, creation, maintenance and deletion of the SAs are performed under the control of an entity called the 'Group Controller and Key Server' (GCKS).

The security policies that regulate the behaviour of the operations and the entities within the multicast group, are determined by the group owner (or a moderator who can be assimilated to a group owner). The group owner usually designates a GCKS and a sender who are responsible for both distribution and enforcement of policy.

In order to insure the distribution of the security rules and the associated crypto-graphic material (GSA), the GCKS implements particular 'group key' management protocols, such as Group Domain Of Interpretation (GDOI, [DRAFT-GDOI-02]) or Group Security Association and Key Management Protocol (GSAKMP, [DRAFT-GSAKMP-01]).

These latter 'group key' management protocols are designed to support re-key algorithms, such as Logical Key Hierarchy Protocol (LKH, [RFC-2627], a secure and scalable mechanism which handles group re-key, in an efficient manner, thanks to a logical tree architecture including intermediate virtual nodes).

The following 0[DRAFT-MFRAME-00], illustrates a global framework for multicast content security.

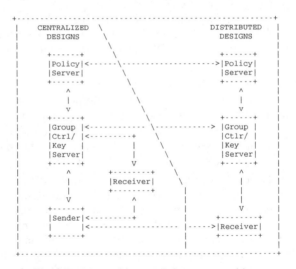

Fig. 2. Reference framework for secure multicast

4   The Inevitable Security Offer:
Authentication, Integrity and Confidentiality

The needs, if any, for security treatment of multicast data can vary from one application to another and the two following examples illustrate some of them:

Stock exchange quotation diffusion may require authentication of the source in order to avoid bogus data transmission by a malicious impersonator. However, the information being publicly available, there may be no need for confidentiality, thus neither for encryption.

To the opposite, broadcasting pay-per-view programs may require encryption to avoid non-subscribers from accessing the data. Also, in this case, source authentication may allow the receiver to check the legitimacy of the sender before starting some expensive decryption processes in order to, to a certain extent, protect himself from Denial of Service (DOS) attacks, in case malicious and/or unexpected data flows were sent supposedly encrypted, on the multicast distribution tree.

4.1 GCKS Services

It seems quite natural that content providers are likely to outsource, presumably to a service provider, the services provided by the Group Controller and Key Server entity, *i.e.* the members authentication facility and the key management services required for encryption/decryption, though this may depend on the targeted market as further discussed within the following proposals we suggest.

Regarding the residential market of multicast-based content distribution, pay-per-view TV for example, content providers are likely to ally with telecom operators for *msec* key management services (if required), in addition to data transport, source hosting and end-users portal purposes. Outsourced and centralized GCKS could lead to worthwhile mutualisation for complementary content packages and for efficient end-users management (*msec* initialisation or accounting, for example).

Regarding the corporate market, intranet multicast issues appear more numerous and complex, and they may differ as follows:

If both the source and receivers belong to a unique common intranet, it is likely worthwhile to manage an internal GCKS located in the intranet (if any needs for *msec* protection). Such an internal GCKS maintains the security material management within the protected network.

A different case refers to an internal source located inside an intranet, likely to multicast data to external group-members located outside the intranet, or even to external *and* internal group-members (within the context of extranet applications, for example). In this case, GCKS, as well as the source, are likely to be located in a demilitarised zone (DMZ), *i.e.* a protected area of a network having an interface with the internal corporate network and another interface with the external Internet, usually between firewalls.

Another case corresponds to internal receivers located inside the intranet, willing to receive *msec* protected multicast data from external sources situated outside the intranet and not under the control of the intranet. If one aims at enforcing end-to-end security – *i.e.* encryption between the every source and the group-members – delegation of the GCKS operations to a subordinate GCKS or a GCKS proxy located in the intranet DMZ should be considered. Direct entering key management data from an external GCKS to internal group members is another solution, though unlikely to be used for obvious security reasons.

These proposals are based on usual security architectural concepts recommending to keep the intranet as protected as possible, by splitting functionalities dedicated to internal purpose from the ones provided for external purposes, and by limiting the number of hosts that can communicate directly over Internet.

Therefore, hosting and/or managing GCKSs, on behalf of content providers and group receivers, seems to be a business enabler from the perspective of a service provider.

4.2 Cryptographic Services

Regarding the actual data cryptographic treatments, *i.e.* encryption/decryption and authentication of the data, the service opportunities may be not as large, from the perspective of a telecom operator.

An end-to-end security model, *i.e.* encrypted data from the content source to the very end-users (the group-members), would confine the potential data security services that may be provided by telecom operators, to data encryption on behalf of the sources hosted by the operator.

However, we believe that network-to-network security or host-to-network security, should not be excluded from investigations, especially for the corporate market. For example, an *msec* gateway makes sense if operating as a boundary between an unsecured network – where *msec* protection would be required - and a safe network - an intranet for example, with fewer security protection requirements. In this case, decryption of the received multicast data would occur at the *msec* gateway and not at the group member end. In particular, this scenario fits well into the corporate market environment, where multicast data would be distributed from one site to numerous remote sites located across the Internet.

This security model is restrictive in a sense that the access control to the data by means of encryption, is no longer performed at the user level, since in this case key management exchanges no more occur between the GCKS and the end-users, but between the GCKS and the *msec* gateway. In particular, this disallows opportunities for backward/forward access control. Still, it's worth keeping in mind the reality of the current IPSec practice market, which is nowadays not as end-to-end security oriented as apparently expected at the very beginning of IPSec design. This could avoid mis-consideration of possible future market needs for network-to-network security or host-to-network security dedicated to confidential information protection over public networks for example. If such an application should be confirmed, a telecom operator service could consist in hosting and/or more likely (remotely) managing *msec* gateways.

5 Multicast Content Security as a Business Enabler within the Domain of Accounting

Let us remember the meaning of provisioning group members with decryption keys for data deciphering. It is stating the obvious to say that, the *solely* group members holding the necessary key to decrypt the multicast data will be able to access the data in clear; the others – those who do not hold the required key – will be unable to access the data in clear. Charging group members for accessing the data is then equivalent to charging them for getting the key required to decrypt the data, which have been encrypted for restricted access purposes.

Key management is performed by the Group Controller and Key Server entity. Initial distribution of the key occurs during a registration phase initiated by a group member. Refresh of the key may be performed, thanks to a re-key phase and at the initiative of the GCKS. Key management exchanges between the GCKS and the group members include identification of the parties for security reasons, thus the ability of the GCKS to make accounting and billing, on behalf of the content provider.

In a way, the GCKS entity could act as a virtual kiosk, where users could get rights (the key) to receive a particular multicast stream in clear against money, as one can buy concert or movie or whatever tickets to attend events where admission fee is payable.

We believe this proposal is compliant with various billing models whose relevance is strongly dependent on the application:

- Set price: the user pays a fixed price against the key information (and the associated security policies) needed for the session, at the time of registration or selection of a session (like a pay-per-view payment scheme, for example). In this case, the encryption key may remain unchanged during the whole session.

- Pay-per-duration: the user pays as long as (and as much as) he is able to access the multicast data in clear. This model requires implementation of backward/forward access control, that is, the key used for encryption/decryption and shared by the whole group varies each time the group composition varies. The key hold by a member who just left the group, becomes invalid. Per duration billing means charging as long as a user holds a valid key, *i.e.* an up-to-date key being able to decrypt the transmitted data. Possibilities to charge as a function of quantity of received data should be investigated (by combining duration information and source rate). This scenario may be applicable to e-learning applications, for example.

- Contract price: this proposal would be based on a 'source-to-network' multicast content security model. An *msec* gateway would act as a point of decryption of encrypted multicast data received from a source, on behalf of several end-receivers who would receive multicast data in clear. In this case, the GCKS would exchange with one entity only – the *msec* gateway – and would then be unable to count the actual number of group members. For this scenario, one can imagine a contract price, possibly varying as a function of the size (to be defined) of the intranet.

Obviously, this chapter is an attempt to demonstrate the business opportunities of providing accounting services to multicast content providers, thanks to GCKSs hosting, running and managing on behalf of content providers. There is room for telecom operators to take advantage of this business potential.

6   Additional issue

Another major issue to address is piracy, *i.e.* the threat related to group members who are willing to reveal illegitimately either the cryptographic keys or unencrypted group messages to non-members. A telecom operator is not likely to propose multicast content encryption services, supposedly vouching for no data access to non subscribers, to content providers (broadcasting pay-per-view TV programs providers, for example), if no means provides some guarantees to limit the ability to illegally forward keys. There is a need for investigating some appropriate key-control facilities, a telecom operator – the one who would vouch the restricted access to the multicast data – acting as a third party on behalf of content providers, could control.

7 What about Implementation Status?

Msec implementations still remain at a very early stage. However industrials seem ready to actively look at business opportunities in which theirs products could support IP multicast security.

At the time this paper is written, efforts seem to focus on implementing 'group key' management protocols. Once this is achieved, a first significant step will consist in demonstrating "basic" *msec* services, thanks to the use of already existing data security treatment protocol, namely Encapsulating Security Payload. What is here called "basic" *msec* services refers to multicast content confidentiality and *group* authentication, for single source multicast sessions. A next worthwhile step would consist in implementing a re-key protocol, in order to allow backward/forward access control. Finally, *msec* dedicated data treatment protocols such as Multicast Encapsulating Security Payload will complete the *msec* offer by adding new functionalities such as *source* authentication, thanks to compliance with TESLA (Timed Efficient Stream Loss-tolerant Authentication, [2]) for example.

8 Conclusion

A multicast content security protocol suite, such as *msec*, is a source of future prospects that a telecom operator may take advantage of, in order to provide new security-related services for both residential market and corporate markets.

A major interest comes from 'group key' exchange protocols, which allow on line 'group key' management. By this means, a telecom operator could act, on behalf of content providers, such as pay-per-view TV providers for example, to multicast and encrypt the data, in order to restrict their access to members being charged to obtain the 'group key' that is necessary to access the data in clear. This "open" application on Internet would require a high degree of interoperability, hence standardisation, for GCKS modules to be able to exchange with as much users on Internet as possible. For corporate market, network-to-network security protection of multicast data, between the various sites of a company may also be a business enabler to evaluate.

To conclude this paper on multicast content security applications, one has to recall that multicast is an efficient transmission scheme for group communication, and content security should not compromise the scalability achieved thanks to the multicast model. Hence the need to evaluate how the security protocols scale for various applications. Do the security protocols handle well memberships in bursts? How does convergence of very large groups fit with unpredictable and highly dynamics of members' leaving and joining operations? How acceptable are the delays to process joins and leaves? There is still a rather long way to go before stating on multicast content security applications opportunities.

Acknowledgment

A France Telecom corporate mutlicast-related R&D program, sponsored by Pierre Rolin, has funded this work. The authors would like to acknowledge the MSEC IETF WG members for the technical specifications they currently promote, which contributes to some large extent to this application-oriented reflection, including Lakshminath Dondeti for his helpful discussions. Numerous valuable comments came from Christian Jacquenet.

References

[1] Deployment issues for the IP multicast service and architecture, Diot, Levine, Lyles, Kassan, Balsiefien. IEEE Network, Special issue on multicasting, January/February 2000

[2] Efficient authentication and signing of multicast streams over lossy channels, Perrig, Canetti, Tygar, Song. In Proceedings of IEEE Symposium on Security and Privacy, pages 56-73, Oakland, CA, May 2000

[3] Multicast security: A taxonomy and efficient constructions, Canetti, Garay, Itkis, Micciancio, Naor, Pinkas. In Proceedings of IEEE INFOCOM, New York, March 1999

[DRAFT-GDOI-03] The Group Domain of Interpretation, Baugher, Hardjono, Harney, Weis, draft-ietf-msec-gdoi-08.txt, work in progress, May 2003

[DRAFT-GSA-00] GKM Building Block: Group Security Association (GSA) Definition, draft-irtf-smug-gkmbb-gsadef-01.txt, Harney, Baugher, Hardjono, Expired, September 2000

[DRAFT-GSAKMP-03]   Group Secure Association Key Management Protocol, Harney, Colegrove, Harder, Meth, Fleischer, draft-ietf-msec-gsakmp-sec-01.txt, work in progress, February 2003.

[DRAFT-MFRAME-00]   Secure IP Multicast: Problem areas, Framework, and Building Blocks, Hardjono, Canetti, Baugher, Dinsmore, draft-irtf-smug-framework-01.txt, Expired, September 2001

[RFC-1112] Host Extensions for IP Multicasting, Deering, August 1989

[RFC-2401] Security Architecture for the Internet Protocol, Kent, Atkinson, November 1998

[RFC-2406] IP Encapsulating Security Payload (ESP), Kent, Atkinson, November 1998

[RFC-2627] Key Management for Multicast: Issues and Architectures, Wallner, Harder, Agee, June 1999

Glossary

AMESP	*Application Multicast ESP*. A variant of ESP, adapted to multicast needs and operating in the application layer.
ESP	*Encapsulating Security Payload*. An IPSec security header providing the same protection as AH plus confidentiality and traffic analysis protection (in certain conditions).
GCKS	*Group Controller and Key Server*. An entity providing the functions of both the membership management (group controller) and group key management (key server)
GDOI	*Group Domain Of Interpretation*. The Domain Of Interpretation (DOI) of Internet Security Association and Key Management Protocol (ISAKMP) for *group* key management.
IPSEC	*Internet Protocol SECurity* is an IETF standard suite of content security mechanisms, developed for unicast communication protection

ISAKMP   *Internet Security Association and Key Management Protocol.* A framework which defines a generic and versatile abstract set of exchanges for key management.

LKH   *Logical Key Hierarchy.* A key management technique for multicast communication sessions. In particular, LKH allows re-key of the multicast group, in an efficient manner, in terms of number of transmissions and storage requirements.

MESP   *Multicast ESP.* A variant of ESP, adapted to multicast needs and operating in the network layer.

MSEC   *Multicast SECurity,* an on-going IETF working group which aims at standardizing building blocks and protocols for secure group communications and multicast (www.securemulticast.org/msec-index.htm). MSEC is also the name of the technology.

SA   *Security Association.* Define the nature of the security to be applied to the communications: which cryptographic algorithms, the secret keys, the security headers, and so forth.

TESLA   *Timed Efficient Stream Loss-tolerant Authentication.* A secure source authentication mechanism for multicast or broadcast data streams.

Accounting Mechanism for Membership Size-Dependent Pricing of Multicast Traffic

David Breitgand[1], Danny Dolev[1], and Danny Raz[2]

[1] School of Engineering and Computer Science, The Hebrew University, Givat-Ram
91904 Jerusalem, Israel
{davb,dolev}@cs.huji.ac.il
[2] Department of Computer Science, The Technion
32000 Haifa, Israel
danny@cs.technion.ac.il

Abstract. A number of schemes for membership size-dependent pricing of multicast traffic have been proposed recently. The enabling accounting technology, however, is lagging behind. Retaining an exact count of the active receivers is very difficult. To target an accounting mechanism, we suggest novel monitoring algorithms that combine a hierarchical control structure with event-driven monitoring. The efficiency and tradeoffs of the proposed solutions are thoroughly studied through simulations using both synthetic, and real MBone workloads. As we show, depending on the workload and the required accuracy, we can reduce the monitoring traffic by factor of 2 to 10 compared to other known alternatives.

1 Introduction

IP multicast is an important technology that allows distributing large volumes of data to millions of receivers in an economic fashion. Usually, IP multicast tree construction is guided by receivers. The network provider bears the control overhead of joining the group's tree when the first receiver appears in the domain. The provider also absorbs the overhead of maintaining this new tree branch for as long as there exists at least one receiver in the domain.

In general, network providers are interested in encouraging both receivers and senders to use the most cost-efficient network service type (*i.e.*, unicast or multicast). The senders, however, need to assess the utility of transmitting into a specific multicast group, *i.e.*, the size of the audience that they can reach.

Recently, a number of proposals [1,2,3] addressed these issues via group size-dependent pricing of transmissions. However, it is very difficult to find out the exact number of host receivers in a multicast group at any given moment [4].

We argue that for applications like pricing and billing it may suffice to know at any given moment that the group size is between some two predefined threshold values. These bounds determine the group's *rank*. Traffic being sent into the group is priced depending on the rank of the group, and the price does not change until the group changes its rank.

B. Stiller et al. (Eds.): NGC/ICQT 2003, LNCS 2816, pp. 276–286, 2003.

The group size estimation is disseminated to the multicast ISPs worldwide using a peer-to-peer application level network being set up among the ISPs as is explained later. The ISPs then *locally* compute the price of transmitting a unit of bandwidth to the group, and present this price to senders in their domain. Senders are also presented with the group rank information, so that they can assess the utility of reaching a particular audience size by transmitting to a specific group while paying the price charged by their local ISP.

We assume that the charging scheme will be applied locally both to receivers and senders by their respective ISPs as in [2,17]. However, we do not require that ISPs will be involved in additional cost apportionment process among themselves based on the local population of receivers. If they do, the question of trust should be solved, since ISPs may have incentive to exaggerate the number of their local receivers to make extra profit when reassigning the costs with other ISPs, as is the case in the spilt-edge pricing proposal in [16], or EXPRESS [3], for instance.

Additional factors such as spatial distribution of users, time of day, *etc.* may be taken into account by the pricing scheme. However, in this paper we focus specifically on the group size estimation. We propose the following generic approach to monitoring the size of a multicast group for the sake of pricing. A specific pricing scheme requires knowing the group size up to some predefined constant factor $1 \leq \gamma < \infty$. Suppose that initially the group size is known to be S_0. As long as the group size S remains such that $\frac{S_0}{\gamma} < S < \gamma \cdot S_0$, there is no need in any additional accounting activity because it brings no benefit. We say that γ defines the *low* and *high* thresholds values. Multicast ISPs need to be notified about the new group size *if and only if* either the low, or high threshold value is violated. This way each ISP knows the group size up to factor γ at all times. Given this estimation each ISP locally computes the price of transmitting a unit of bandwidth to the given group, and presents it to the local senders. Our accounting mechanism ignores membership fluctuations that are insufficient to change the rank of the group.

There is a trade-off between the accuracy of the group size approximation, and the communication cost paid for it. Thus different pricing schemes may choose different QoS levels of accounting for controlling their overhead, while still maintaining a precision that suits them.

When we consider the typical lifespan of a multicast group, we identify three successive periods: membership build-up, saturation, and membership termination. Membership build-up and membership termination phases are characterized by rapid membership changes. However, these two periods are short relatively to the saturation phase. Therefore, it is natural to consider an event-driven (*reactive*) monitoring scheme that generates more traffic in the first and last phases of the multicast transmission, and conserves bandwidth in the second stage. Thus, the total communication overhead of reactive group size accounting will be lower compared to a monitoring scheme based on periodic polling.

When we consider multicast, it is very natural to assume that we have a (bounded out-degree) tree structure where the leaves are the end routers that have a local count regarding the number of participants in the group. Since we want to know the total size of the group, our aim is to calculate the sum of the values of the leaves. This can be done in a hierarchical way in the internal nodes of the tree. Every polling step consists of calculating the sum of the values up the tree and disseminating the value from the root to all the leaves if needed.

This hierarchical polling process is a natural way to overcome the feedback implosion problem, and it also saves a factor of $\log N$ messages in each polling interval, where N being the number of ISPs. The next step is to combine it with the reactive monitoring process. This leads us to constructing a hierarchical and reactive monitoring algorithm that allows to maintain the multicast membership size estimation with very low communication overhead.

Unfortunately, deployment of this mechanism would require changes to most of the existing standard multicast routing protocols. We are not proposing any changes to the existing routing protocols, but rather suggest that the accounting function to be implemented as a separate service over a peer-to-peer network of ISPs, be orthogonal to the routing functionality. In this respect, our proposal constitutes a protocol independent multicast accounting mechanism, in an analogy to PIM [15] that promotes protocol independence with respect to routing, and protocol independent multicast pricing proposal [2].

2   Related Work

The cost-effectiveness of multicast was first expressed in [1] as a simple power-law function of the active membership size. Namely, $N^{k-1} = \frac{L_m}{L_u N}$, where L_m is the total number of links in a multicast tree, L_u is the average length of the unicast route, and N is the number of leaf routers. The exponent k is called *Economy of Scale* (EoS) factor, $0 \le k \le 1$.

This power law suggests a straightforward multicast pricing scheme: $P_m = N \cdot (P_u)^k$ where P_u being the price of unicast, and P_m being the price of multicast. It should be noted that in order for the sender to decide which service to use, it should know the number of individual hosts, N_h, and not only N. The sender will prefer the multicast service over the unicast one as long as $P_m < P_u \cdot N_h$.

It is assumed in [1] that N, the number of leaf multicast routers, can be discovered using distributed monitoring. However, no specific accounting mechanism has been suggested, and the problem of finding N_h was left open. In this work, we provide a solution that can be used to discover both the number of leaf routers, and that of the individual hosts.

The reactive monitoring algorithms presented in [5] constitute the starting point for this research. However, these algorithms cannot be used as is for multicast group size estimation, since they ignore the network distances, the feedback implosion problem, and the statistical nature of the monitored data is different.

In [3] a new IP multicast routing protocol called EXPRESS was proposed. Part of the proposal is ECMP, the management protocol that accounts for the group size at the granularity of individual hosts. The event-driven version of ECMP is close in spirit to our hierarchical reactive monitoring algorithm of

Section 5. However, our algorithms can be used with any multicast protocol, and as we show later, is superior to ECMP in terms of bandwidth.

In [12], a fast and cost-effective algorithm for estimating the number of leaf multicast routers was presented. This algorithm leverages on the empirical properties of the realistic multicast topologies that exhibit a linear ratio between the number of high degree nodes, and the number of leaves. The algorithm as is does not help finding the number of individual hosts. However, it provides a better initial estimation for the probabilistic methods for faster convergence.

The need to know the number of active receivers in a multicast session often arises at the transport and application levels [8]. To this end, a number of probabilistic estimation methods have been proposed [?,9,10,11]. A comprehensive comparative study of all probabilistic estimation algorithms is beyond the scope of this paper. In Section 6, we define a generic probabilistic monitoring algorithm that embodies the functionality common to all probabilistic group size estimation methods. We use this generic algorithm as a baseline.

3   Model and Problem Definition

Let $G(V, E)$ be partially synchronous network. Let $V' \subseteq V$ be a set of nodes representing the ISPs participating in a multicast group spanning tree. We assume that there exists a reliable unicast channel between each pair of nodes in V' in addition to the spanning tree of the multicast group. Each $v \in V'$, maintains a variable $x_i \in I^+ \bigcup \{0\}$, $x_i < \infty$. By $x_i(t)$ we denote the value of x_i at time $t \in I^+ \bigcup \{0\}$. The physical meaning of this variable is the number of active receivers in the domain represented by node v.

The system proceeds in rounds where all messages sent at the beginning of a round are received by their destinations by the end of the round. Each round is completed within one time unit. In practice, the actual value of the time unit may be important. This is the maximal round trip time between any two neighbors in the network. In addition, each node in V' can send or receive no more than a fixed number of messages in a round. All messages that exceed this threshold get lost. All messages are assumed to be of a fixed limited length.

Definition 1. *Let $\omega(n)$ be some function assuming non-negative integer values, and bounded from above. $f(t) = f(x_1(t), x_2(t), ..., x_N(t))$ is ω-constant function if and only if it is being constant on the semi-open intervals of length ω: $[0, \omega), [\omega, 2\omega)$, etc.*

Every node knows only its local variable x_i. The estimation of the total membership size is computed in a fully distributed manner that involves network communication among some nodes. The communication delay being inherent to any distributed algorithm, precludes knowing the exact membership count at any given moment. We compute the $O(\log^2 N)$-constant approximation of our target function $f(t) = \sum_{i=1}^{N=|V'|} x_i(t)$. In other words, we do not account for the fluctuations in the target function value if these changes last for less than $O(\log^2 N)$ time units.

> Given synchronous reliable network $G(V, E)$, a collection of variables $x_1(t), x_2(t), ..., x_N(t) \in I^+ \bigcup\{0\}$, each being maintained by some $v \in V' \subseteq V$, a target function $f(t) = \sum_{i=1}^{n=|V'|} x_i(t)$, being ω-constant function, a set of threshold values $X_1, X_2, ..., X_m$, find an algorithm that guarantees that if and only if at time t_a a global threshold violation event occurs, all nodes in V' are notified about this event by time $t_a + \omega$.

Fig. 1. Problem Definition

Definition 2. *If at time t, $f(t) \leq H$, and at time t_a, $t_a > t$ and $f(t_a) > H$, t_a being minimal such time, we say that a* global upper threshold event *(or simply* cross-over*) has occurred at t_a.*

Cross-down is defined similarly. Figure 1 provides the rigorous definition of the problem. Let $C(A, \delta)$ denote the total number of messages sent by algorithm A over time δ. In this work, we compare the algorithms using this metric. *It is important to stress that we count traversing of each hop between any two neighbors in the network as a separate message.*

4   Estimation Methodology

The estimation accuracy requirements come from a specific pricing scheme. The following general methodologies are conceivable.

- **Relative to Total (R2T):** the purpose is to show what percentage of the total maximum population is active. The total space is partitioned into percentiles that implicitly define the sensitivity parameter, γ. R2T is applicable when the maximal size is known in advance.
- **Relative to Last (R2L):** the purpose is to capture the change of the group size relatively to its last known size. Precision of the estimation, γ, should be specified explicitly. At every given moment the estimation provides the group size up to a multiplicative factor γ. R2L is more flexible and scalable.

5   Hierarchical Reactive Monitoring Algorithm

This section briefs Hierarchical Reactive Monitoring Algorithm (HRMA) that overcomes the problems of feedback implosion and bandwidth inefficiency that are common to all flat algorithms[1]. The common structure of all flat algorithms is as follows. The monitored targets can directly communicate with a distinguished *monitor* over a reliable unicast channel. The relay can communicate with the targets using either multicast, or unicast channels. When a target detects a local threshold event, it reports to the monitor. The latter either initiates a global

---

[1] A detailed presentation of the algorithm along with the thorough discussion on flat event-driven monitoring can be found in [4]

poll of all targets, or discards the reported event. This structure is inherently unsuitable for our context because as the group size grows, the monitor becomes overwhelmed by the reports (the feedback implosion problem), many of which do not have global implications (bandwidth inefficiency).

The basic idea of HRMA is as follows. Instead of using the direct unicast communication channels for reporting local values of ISP variables, and the multicast communication channel for propagating the polling requests, we organize the nodes into a logical hierarchy in which the same node may act at different levels. The inter-nodal links are realized as reliable unicast FIFO channels.

The optimal hierarchy formation and maintenance need a special study since one can look for several optimization functions. For the sake of simplicity, we assume that the logical hierarchy is a full binary tree.

The leaf nodes (ISPs) report their traps up the hierarchy, and the intermediate nodes act as local relays deciding whether to propagate the trap further toward the root depending on the total values reported by their children.

Each node has values l and h that hold the current low and high thresholds for the subtree rooted at this node. The root also has an array of threshold values, $thresh$, as determined by the ranking service.

Initially, a converge-cast is performed to compute the total number of active receivers at time 0, S_0. The root calculates the leaf thresholds as $l = \frac{S_0}{N \cdot \gamma}$, $h = \frac{S_0 \cdot \gamma}{N}$, and multicasts them on the tree. Initially, the intermediate nodes do not have l and h. They compute them upon receiving traps from their children.

When a node sends a trap to its father in the tree, we say that it starts verifying the threshold condition. This process ends either at some intermediate node, or at the root of the whole tree. A node stops the propagation if it discovers that neither high, nor low threshold of the subtree being rooted at it is violated. In this case, the node does not send more messages. The leaf nodes in its subtree will discover that no global event has occurred after a timeout. If the root discovers that a global threshold event has happened, it sends an *update* message down the hierarchy informing the ISPs about the new group size estimation. It is not difficult to verify that if the root informs about the global event, then there was at least one local threshold violation. In the worst case, any local event is verified after $O(\log^2 N)$ time units. Thus, *HRMA* correctly solves the membership size monitoring problem defined in Figure 1.

6 HRMA Performance

First, we establish a baseline algorithm against which the cost gain factor of *HRMA* will be computed. To this end, we define a *Hierarchical Straightforward Monitoring Algorithm*, denoted OB_h that uses the hierarchical structure as explained in Figure 2. We argue that evaluating against OB_h, also is indicative for other known alternatives. Obviously, $C(OB_h, \delta) = 2(N-1)(\frac{\delta}{2\log^2 N} + e_\delta)$, where e_δ being the number of TVEs detected by the root. It is easy to observe that $C(HRMA, \delta)$ may be higher than $C(OB_h, \delta)$.

> The leaf nodes initiate a converge-cast of their local values towards the root of the logical hierarchy every $2\log^2 N$ time units. The root checks whether a global TVE occurs, and if so, multicasts the new group size using the same hierarchy.

Fig. 2. Hierarchical Straightforward Monitoring Algorithm (OB_h)

An alternative baseline is offered by popular probabilistic polling techniques. A generic probabilistic estimation procedure communicates directly with the receivers, and not with their ISPs. The algorithm proceeds in rounds. In each round, an increasing probability of response is multicast by the dedicated node, usually the source. The receivers respond with the advertised probability. Each such response constitutes a single Bernoulli trial. Based on the number of the responses (that are not aggregated), an estimation of the total number of receivers is performed. Although there are many more details involved, this *Generic Probabilistic (GeP)* algorithm captures the essence of the methodology. *GeP* avoids the problem of feedback implosion. However, it is easy to see that the communication cost of *GeP* approximately equals that of OB_h. Indeed, in our model, the cost of multicasting the response probability in *GeP* equals the cost of converge-cast in OB_h, and the cost of informing the members about the TVE is the same in both techniques. Thus, comparing *HRMA* to OB_h is indicative of *GeP*.

Yet another alternative is ECMP of EXPRESS. It is again easy to observe that the communication cost incurred by ECMP is *at least* that of OB_h when the maximal silence period of ECMP is set to $O(2\log^2 N)$. Thus, comparing *HRMA* to OB_h is sufficient is indicative of the relative ECMP performance.

In this work, we focus on the short-lived multicast sessions. The reason for this is that shorter sessions are less stable, and, therefore are more challenging. Following [6,13] we model the inter-arrival and stay times of the multicast receivers as exponentially distributed variates with means μ_{arr}, μ_{stay}. Throughout the simulations we assume that users are uniformly distributed over ISP domains. We assume a fixed ratio of the users over domains, thus having a knowledge of the total population size. The thresholds are computed using R2T estimation methodology with the group ranks being 15-percentiles.

Figure 3(a) shows a sample synthetic trace of the group membership for 512 multicast domains, 15360 potential receivers acting according to the exponential model above, and being uniformly distributed among the domains with the average user/domain ratio being 30. There are 10 different multicast sessions per trace. All sessions are of equal length. This is the maximal load scenario. In reality the membership not necessarily drops to 0 at the end of each session, and there exist larger periods of stability during, and between the sessions. The basic scenario can be changed by adding stability periods to the trace that freeze the membership activity for the certain percentage of the total trace duration.

Figure 3(b) shows the average performance of *HRMA* versus OB_h under the maximal load condition, and for 90% inactivity time trace. The same figure also shows the performance of *HRMA* versus ImpVal (the most efficient flat event driven algorithm of [5]) under the maximal load. Under a very high probability

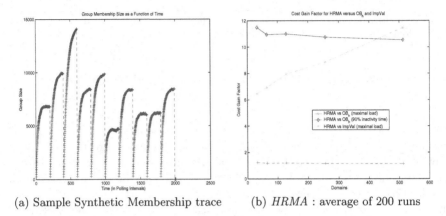

(a) Sample Synthetic Membership trace   (b) $HRMA$: average of 200 runs

Fig. 3. Performance of HRMA

of violating a local threshold, $HRMA$ produces a message cost-gain factor of 14%-20%. Notice that this cost-gain remains constant with the number of domains.

The relative cost-gain of $HRMA$ versus ImpVal grows with the number of domains. $HRMA$ does not save communication on multicasting the notifications about the global TVEs. It saves communication by suppressing the non-significant local threshold violation events though. In our traces, $HRMA$ pays $\approx 1.5 * N$ messages per round. This is due to the fact that some edges are traversed twice: one message to solicit the value, and another one to report the value itself. In the same circumstances, ImpVal pays $\approx 2 * N \log N$ messages per round. Thus, the expected improvement is around $1.33 * \log N$ and is indeed expected to grow with the number of domains, N. These are very important observations suggesting that $HRMA$ is scalable.

7   Adaptive HRMA

Basic $HRMA$ is not adaptive. Namely, if there exist local threshold events, but there is no global TVE, then the verification process stops at some level in the hierarchy, However, $HRMA$ learns no lesson from this, and if the situation remains similar also for the next step, the unnecessary verification will be repeated.

There is an apparent trade-off between leaving the local thresholds in the subtree intact in case of a false alarm in this subtree, and changing them. The latter requires multicasting in the scope of this subtree, and therefore increases the communication cost of the algorithm in this round. However, if it succeeds in tuning the thresholds in such a way that no false alarms would follow, the total communication cost of the algorithm will be reduced over time. To this end, we define two simple modifications to the basic $HRMA$.

– **Oblivious Adaptive HRMA:** When a false alarm is detected at time t by the root of some subtree (an intermediate node i), this node computes $\alpha_1 = f_i(t)/l$, and $\alpha_2 = h/f_i(t)$ where $f_i(t)$ being the sum of the leaf variables

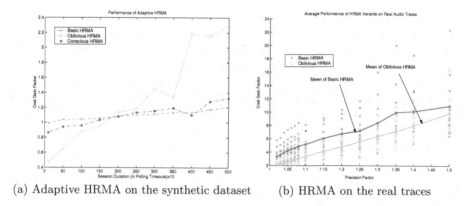

(a) Adaptive HRMA on the synthetic dataset   (b) HRMA on the real traces

Fig. 4. Adaptive Heuristics; Validation on real traces

of the subtree rooted at i, and l, h being the lower and higher local thresholds of this node respectively. Then, i multicasts the ▯▯▯▯▯▯ message containing α_1, α_2, and indicating that there was no global threshold event. The nodes in the subtree recalculate their local thresholds using these values as they would upon reception of this message from the global root. However they do not change their current estimation of the group size.

- **Conscious Adaptive HRMA:** The main difference from Oblivious is that the root of the subtree computes the chance of suppressing local TVEs of no global significance. It compares the distance of the current value of the sum for its subtree with the median of the interval defined by its l, and h threshold values. The chances of suppressing false alarms are highest when the current value of the subtree is close to the median, and decrease as it gets close to either l, or h. Accordingly, Conscious Adaptive $HRMA$ sends ▯▯▯▯▯▯ message with the higher probability in the former case, and lowers the probability of sending an ▯▯▯▯▯▯ message in the latter case.

Figure 4(a) demonstrates the adaptivity trade-off. For a fixed number of domains, we vary the trace duration. As one would expect, for shorter sessions the adaptivity heuristics are inferior to the basic form of $HRMA$. However, as sessions become longer, they become advantageous over the basic $HRMA$. Oblivious Adaptive $HRMA$ is always inferior to the the Conscious and and Basic variants when sessions are short. This is natural since Oblivious Adaptive $HRMA$ needs more time to compensate for the extra costs of updating the thresholds.

8   Validation with Real Traces

In this section we evaluate $HRMA$ vs. Ob_h using the real membership traces collected using *mlisten* tool [6]. The purpose of this study is to inspect the behavior of $HRMA$ when statistical assumptions on the user behavior used so far are not necessarily preserved.

Most multicast groups that were present in the traces were quite small ranging from a few users to a few tens of users at any given moment, and have not exhibited particularly high activity[2]. However, this makes the data even more interesting. So far our algorithms have been evaluated on the synthetic data that simulated very large groups (thousands of highly dynamic users) spanning hundreds of domains. This may be way too far from the current state of the Internet. The question that we asked was whether the hierarchical reactive monitoring will be useful also for estimating the size of very small groups in such a way that it would be useful for pricing applications.

To this end, we used R2L estimation methodology that defines only a single pair of thresholds $H \overset{\text{def}}{=} \gamma * f(0)$, $L \overset{\text{def}}{=} f(0)/\gamma$, where $f(0)$ is the total size of the group as measured at time 0. The local thresholds l, h are computed as before. If at some time instance t a global TVE is detected, $HRMA$ re-calculates L, H using $f(t)$. This way we always know the size of the group with precision γ as being set by the pricing application.

Out of ≈ 200 different traces we found only 11 traces with considerable activity. All these traces were comprised out of ≈ 256 ISPs. We analyzed only the first $300,000$ seconds (≈ 80 hours) of these traces. Figure 4(b) illustrates performance of $HRMA$ variants for various values of γ. One thing to notice is that on the average Conscious Adaptive $HRMA$ obtained exactly the same results as the Basic $HRMA$. This means that the distribution of values in the tree was always such that the values of the subtrees were far from the median of the intervals defined by their local thresholds. We do not have an explanation for this. Also, it would be difficult to come to a decisive conclusion without inspecting more traces. However, the traces we used represent a certain type of real life traffic, and $HRMA$ performance on these traces is very satisfactory. The cost-gain factor of $HRMA$ versus other known techniques represented by OB_h ranges from 5 to 10 on the average. As one would expect, the variance is high because the sample is too small. The variance is lower when threshold values are lower which generates more threshold events irrespective of the nature of the trace. It gets higher when thresholds grow. The variance diminishes as the thresholds grow even more since large thresholds preclude any local violation events.

9   Conclusions

We proposed a protocol-independent group size accounting mechanism. It allows explicitly to control the trade-offs between the accuracy of accounting and expected benefit from it, and between the cost-effectiveness of the multicast and unicast. As simulations show, the communication costs it incurs are low. On the average, it reduces management bandwidth by factor of 2 to 10 compared to other existing techniques while yielding acceptable precision.

---

[2] See [7] for discussion on the reasons.

Acknowledgments

We thank K. Almeroth, and R. Chalmers for sharing MBone traces with us.

References

1. J. Chuang and M. Sirbu, "Pricing Multicast Communication: a Cost Based Approach," in *INET'98*, Geneva, Switzerland, July 1998.
2. T. Henderson and S.N. Bhatti, "Protocol independent multicast pricing," in *10th International Workshop on Network and Operating Systems Support for Digital Audio and Video (NOSSDAV'00)*, The Univ of N. Carolina, USA, June 2000.
3. H. Holbrook and D. Cheriton, "Multicast channels: Express support for large-scale single-source applications," in *ACM SIGCOMM'99*, USA, Sept. 1999.
4. D. Breitgand, , D. Dolev, and D. Raz, "Hierarchical reactive monitoring of multicast membership size," Tech. Rep. TR2002-45, School of Engineering and Computer Science, Hebrew Univ. of Jerusalem, July 2002.
5. Mark Dilman and Danny Raz, "Efficient reactive monitoring," *IEEE Journal on Selected Areas in Communications (JSAC), special issue on recent advances in network management*, Apr. 2001.
6. K. Almeroth and M. Ammar, "Multicast group behavior in the internet's multicast backbone (mbone)," *IEEE Communications*, June 1997.
7. K. Sarac and K. Almeroth, "A Long-Term Analysis of Growth and Usage Patterns in the Multicast Backbone (MBone)," in *INFOCOM'00*, Israel, Mar. 2000.
8. Dan Rubenstein, Jim Kurose, and Don Towsley, "A study of proactive hybrid fec/arq and scalable feedback techniques for reliable rea-time multicast," *Computer Communications Journal*, vol. 24, no. 5–6, pp. 563–574, Mar. 2001.
9. C. Liu and J. Nonnenmacher, "Broadcast audience estimation," in *IEEE INFOCOM'00*, Tel-Aviv, Israel, Mar. 2000, vol. 2, pp. 952–960.
10. T. Friedman and D. Towsley, "Multicast session membership size estimation," in *IEEE INFOCOM'99*, New York City, NY, USA, Mar. 1999, vol. 2, pp. 965–972.
11. Sara Alouf, Eitan Altman, and Philippe Nain, "Optimal on-line estimation of the size of a dynamic multicast group," in *INFOCOM'02*, NY, USA, June 2002.
12. D. Dolev, O. Mokryn, and Y. Shavitt, "On Multicast Trees: Structure and Size Estimation," in *INFOCOM'03*, San-Francisco, USA, Apr. 2003.
13. Robert C. Chalmers and Kevin C. Almeroth, "Modelling the Branching Characteristcs and Efficiency Gains in Global Multicast Trees," in *INFOCOM 2001*, Anchorage, Alaska, USA, Apr. 2001.
14. Robert C. Chalmers and Kevin C. Almeroth, "Developing a Multicast Metric," in *GLOBECOM 2000*, San-Francisco, CA, USA, Dec. 2000.
15. D. Estrin, D. Farinacci, A. Helmy, D. Thaler, S. Deering, M. Handley, V. Jacobson, C. Liu, P. Sharma, and L. Wei, "Protocol independent multicast sparse mode (PIM-SM): Protocol specification," June 1997, RFC2117.
16. S. Herzog, S. Shenker, and D. Estrin, "Sharing the cost of multicast trees: An axiomatic analysis," in *SIGCOMM'95*, Cambridge, USA, Aug. 1995, pp. 315–327.
17. B. Briscoe, "The direction of value flow in connection-less networks," in *NGC'99*, Pisa, Italy, Nov. 1999.

A Low-Cost Packet Originator Verification for Metering at Access-Routers

Bernd Lamparter and Dirk Westhoff

NEC Europe Ltd., D-69115 Heidelberg, Germany
{bernd.lamparter,dirk.westhoff}@ccrle.nec.de

Abstract. To provide a mobile device wireless last hop access to packet switched networks, authentication is a necessary pre-requisite for most charging and billing solutions. A lot of work has already been done to establish an initial user and device authentication both within a single administrative domain and across several administrative domains. Unfortunately, initially authenticating the mobile device and even ensuring mutual authentication with the involved access-router does not prevent all types of fraud. Similar to the well-known IMSI-Catcher attack in GSM networks, a malicious mobile node in IP-based networks may spy on the IP-address of a node with access to the wired part of the network. Such an attack is of considerable advantage for a malicious node since it can send traffic free of charge, masquerading as the mobile node by spoofing its IP-address. In this paper, we evaluate different existing protocols to prevent such fraud and finally propose, by presuming an initial device authentication, a new low-cost packet originator verification for access-routers. Such an approach suits realtime-responsive traffic and is even extendable to support the metering of traffic per device over different access technologies.

Keywords: Packet originator verification, wireless last hop, charging support, unpredictable bits.

1 Introduction

With the goal to prepare for flexible and solely packet switched network architectures suitable for a variety of different access technologies, we have to face the security problems of such architectures. In particular the necessity to prevent fraud and to support charging and billing issues should be taken for granted. Additionally, such security approaches should be transparent and independent from the wireless communication systems.

Related to an initial device authentication, in addition to IETF's RADIUS [1] or Diameter [2], some other architectural solutions [3], [4] have been proposed. Protocols focus on the features untraceability [5] or mutual authentication of mobile device and access-router [6]. Contrary to [5] the focus in [7] explicitly is on enhanced location based authentication services. But none of these approaches additionally focuses on the authentication of resource usage, more precisely volume-based resource usage. Although, with respect to a) fraud and

B. Stiller et al. (Eds.): NGC/ICQT 2003, LNCS 2816, pp. 287–297, 2003.

b) metering issues for charging and billing this becomes even more important for packet switched networks with shared wireless last hop. Actually, because of its large performance overhead, traffic authentication at an access-router is not sufficiently supported in any of the solutions from related works. This paper intends to be a first step into this direction. It evaluates different existing protocols to doubtlessly map in a volume-based manner all IP-traffic originated from a mobile device to this device. Here, we take into account the resulting computational overhead as well as the additional traffic over the scarce wireless link. Current security protocols either for this reason, for transparency reason or/and because of their general security lacks are less suited.

The rest of this paper is structured as follows. Section 2 explains our motivation for an additional originator verification of traffic at the access-router. In section 3, we evaluate the suitability of existing security protocols at different layers against IP-catching. Section 4 describes an architecture that we feel will be self-financing available in future. By using this architecture we describe and analyze our approach in sections 5 and 6.

2   Motivation

When sending IP-traffic over a wireless link that frequently is not sufficiently protected at the link layer[1], a malicious mobile node (*MN*), that is currently resident in the same cell as an honest *MN*, may act like following:

IP-Catcher: It can read the IP-address of the honest *MN* on the wireless shared medium and wait until the initial device authentication of the honest *MN* is finished. From this point of time the malicious *MN* can send traffic to any destination for free. It just has to apply the honest *MN*'s IP-address in the source address fields of its own IP-packets. In such case the honest user has to pay the fees of the malicious user. Note, that the described attack has strong impact on usage- as well as on flat-fee based charging: whereas for the first the honest user is the sufferer in case of flat-fees the provider is the one to suffer.

Credential-Catcher: Obviously, the malicious *MN* that currently resides in the same cell as the honest *MN*, is also enabled to catch the authentication credential during the honest *MN*'s initial device authentication. It may later use it for its own bogus access. Fortunately, by encryption and additionally integrating a random value within the credential the attack is to be prevented. We do not deal further with this attack.

Possible candidates to protect an honest *MN* from IP-catching are described in the next sections. All candidates do not solve the man-in-the-middle problem where a malicious *MN* acts under the masquerade of *AR*. Such an attack is to be prevented by also authenticating *AR*.

---

[1] This statement is substantiated in section 3.

3   Related Work

3.1   Link Layer Security

We start evaluating exemplary hop-by-hop protection schemes at the link layer. Can we assume from the moment *MN* configures an IP-address (stateless, stateful, link-local, Care-of-Address, etc.) that each potential underlying access technology has established a secure hop-by-hop channel? ETSI's HIPERLAN/2 [8] provides only an optional confidential channel. Even in case of using the proposed block cipher *Data Encryption Standard with Output Feedback (DES-OFB)* mode and an un-keyed *cyclic redundancy check (CRC)* there is obviously still the problem of integrity deficiency. Further, this standard does not specify how authentication keys are distributed.

IEEE 802.11 a/b WLAN includes a *Wired Equivalent Privacy (WEP)* standard [9] which does again not provide a standardized key distribution. Even assuming succeeded distribution the challenge-response based shared-key authentication may reveal the key. An eavesdropper can watch both, the plaintext challenge and the ciphered response of this plaintext. Borisov et al. [10] describe how to infer from given initial vector, plaintext, and cipher to the key by making use of the stream cipher RC4's and the exclusive-or operator's characteristics.

The lack of key distribution schemes in HIPERLAN/2 and IEEE 802.11 a/b WLAN gets even more risky when nodes from different administrative domains have to establish such one. For 802.11 the concept of default keys becomes necessary. Such keys are widely distributed to many stations and may be more likely to be revealed. As a consequence, even the relatively weak WEP is often not used, leaving many of today's WLANs without any protection.

Just trusting such optional and weak security protocols at the link-layer may encourage fraud. Particularly, if subscribers pay for IP-based services, fraud gets advantageously and thus some additional protection schemes have to be introduced. Even if hop-by-hop protection over the wireless link would be mandatory for all existing access technologies, with respect to real-time traffic and envisioning that in any case there has to be established a secure end-to-end channel between *MN* and a corresponding node (*CN*) additional delays at *MN* and *AR* for en-/decryption would not be acceptable.

3.2   Network Layer Security

Next, we evaluate the suitability of existent end-to-end security approaches at the network layer to detect IP-catching. To guarantee beside an obligatory end-to-end authentication also the originator verification of packets at *AR*, IPsec (v6) [11] has to run in tunnel mode (Fig 1). Again, we assume the non-trivial case that *MN* and *AR* have established session keys in advance. By applying the authentication key, *AR* verifies the packet's originator on base of IPsec's (outer) *authentication header* AH1[2]. In case of IP-catching, although a malicious *MN* is

---

[2] IETF's proposed authentication mechanisms for IPsec's AH (as well as ESP) are HMAC-MD5-96 [12], HMAC-SHA1-96 [13] or HMAC-Ripmed-160-96 [14].

enabled to spoof the honest *MN*'s IP-address, it does not know the authentication key and thus the verification at *AR* fails. The fraud has been prevented and *AR* drops the packet. The *encapsulating security payload* (ESP) header and another (inner) authentication header AH2 ensure an encrypted payload flow from the source address ($SA : MN$) to the final destination address ($DA : CN$) and *CN*'s data originator verification[3].

Generally, an authentication header AH is calculated on all data that do not change in transit or are predictable. AH is solely checked by that node which IP-address is equal to the destination address of the received IP-packet's header. Thus, for an additional intermediate check, the tunnel mode serves introducing two different destination addresses (DA), namely those of *AR* and *CN*. Authentication headers AH1 and AH2 are separately checked at *AR* and *CN*. Obviously, this approach presumes the establishment of two session keys for *MN* with different parties. After a succeeded authentication at *AR*, the remaining inner IP-packet is forwarded to *CN*.

$MN \rightarrow AR$ *(wireless):*

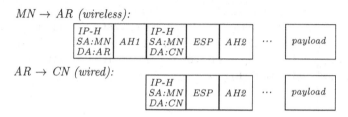

$AR \rightarrow CN$ *(wired):*

Fig. 1. End-to-End plus intermediate IP-packet authentication with IPsec in tunnel mode ($MN \rightarrow CN$).

Unfortunately, the additional traffic over the wireless link may increase to more than 60 bytes per IP-packet. Each IPv6-header's static length is 40 bytes, whereas AH's length is about 24 bytes, depending on the chosen hash function. Elkeelany et al. in [15] argue in the same direction although their performance analysis is on IPsec v4.

Assuming a maximum length of 1500 bytes or more per IP-packet such additional signaling data are neglectable. But with respect to real-time, e.g. audio responsive traffic the additional signaling data for this approach may increase from 12% to 59% per IP-packet. We refer to Degermark et al. [16] which consider maximum packet lengths for different audio applications in the range of at most 108-512 bytes. Such a distension of signaling data to be sent over the scarce wireless link is not acceptable for these applications. On the contrary, a lot of work is even done in the area of header compression to reduce traffic over the wireless link.

---

[3] ESP's mandatory encryption alogrithms is DES-CBC (resp. 3DES-CBC). ESP does also provide authentication (see footnote 4). Since ESP unlike AH does solely authenticate all its successor data and in particular it does not authenticate IP-addresses we prefer also applying AH2.

3.3   Transport Layer Security

Protection schemes on top of the transport layer, e.g. *Secure Shell* (*SSH*), *Secure Socket Layer* (*SSL*) [17], *Transport Layer Security* (*TLS*) [18] are not suited to prevent the described fraud. First, these protocols just work over TCP, and do not support UDP. Second, they transmit their own header information and the header information of the underlying protocols, e.g. the IP-header, in plaintext. Finally, authentication is solely based on all successor data of the TCP-header and thus preceding data like the source IP-address are not authenticated at all.

4   Architecture

Our approach that will be presented in the sections 5-8 presumes the initial authentication of *MN*. An authentication, authorization and accounting (AAA) architecture may be realized by IETF's *Remote Authentication Dial in User Service (RADIUS)* [1] or Diameter [2]. We envision, that such an architecture will be an essential building block of the future Internet that is self-financing available for our approch. It supports beside the transport of metering data also an initial device authentication (Fig 2).

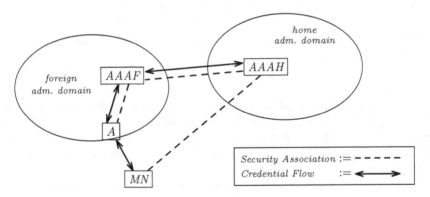

Fig. 2. Initial authentication plus security associations.

Depending on the underlying security infrastructure such authentication may be based on challenge-response protocols, digital signatures or even zero-knowledge protocols [19]. If *MN* accesses a foreign administrative domain, the initial authentication requires a control flow of *MN*'s credentials to a foreign domain's service interface (*A*) (deposited at *AR*), to the foreign AAAServer (*AAAF*) and from there to its home AAAServer (*AAAH*). The presence of such an architecture implicitly provides security associations between *A* and *AAAF*, *AAAF* and *AAAH* as well as between *AAAH* and *MN*. They are applicable also for our approach.

5 Packet Originator Verification

For the subsequent authentication of incoming traffic at AR caused by MN, we propose an approach that works at the network layer. After the device authentication our approach additionally maps IP-packets to each authenticated MN by not just mapping to the source address. The approach is reasonable as it

- causes much less overhead than the IPsec tunnel mode,
- is extendable to a volume-based metering at AR that supports charging over different access technologies, .
- supports metering even in case of a cell-dependent change of an IP-address (and a ciphered static home address when using e.g. Mobile IP plus IPsec's ESP).

5.1 Approach

In parallel to a successful initial authentication $AAAH$ offers a secret r_{AAAH} to MN and A via confidential channels established by the security associations of the described AAA architecture. Note, that our approach presumes a direct physical radio link with MN and verifier, i.e. there is no relay between them. We thus propose co-locating A, AR and the functionality of the access-point. In particular, the approach is not suited for a wireless multi-hop scenario.

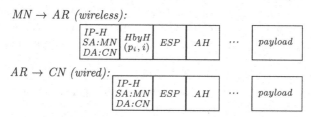

Fig. 3. End-to-end and intermediate IP-packet authentication with unpredictable bits and IPsec ($MN \rightarrow CN$).

The secret r_{AAAH} is a pseudorandom bit-stream $b_1, \ldots, b_n$ [20] generated each time anew in $AAAH$ (e.g. by ANSI X9.17) when $AAAH$ is involved in the device authentication.

If MN sends IP-packets it creates for each packet an IPv6 hop-by-hop options header (HbyH) (Fig 3) that contains a proof p_i based on r_{AAAH} as well as a cyclic sequence number i. Including the sequence number i into the options header is necessary to discriminate packet loss from an attack as well as to handle the sequence of incoming IP-packets. For the i-th IP-packet where $|p|$ notes the number of each proof's bits is $p_i := b_{(i-1)|p|+1}, \ldots, b_{i|p|}$.

Note, that with such a marking of IP-packets originated from MN, p_i and i must not be encrypted and thus there are no additional computation costs for decryption at AR. When receiving IP-packets, in general for verification only a simple and low-cost comparison of the received p_i with the bits $b_{(i-1)|p|+1}, \ldots, b_{i|p|}$

from AR's stored r_{AAAH} is necessary. In the general case it is even not necessary for AR to read and compare i. After each successful verification AR directly shifts r_{AAAH}'s pointer $|p|$ positions ahead.

6   Analysis

The proposed scheme is stateless in a sense that the previous bits and in particular p_1 to p_{i-1} ideally have no impact on p_i. This characteristic suits on the one hand to handle the risk of packet loss over the wireless link as described below. On the other hand it is a necessary condition that a malicious MN by reading the current proof cannot infer to the proof for the next packet to be sent. Because of the shared medium's characteristic the originally transmitted data are readable for every connected entity and especially for AR.

6.1   Fraud Detection

A malicious modification of data at a dishonest MN and its forwarding results at AR in additional comparisons on base of the current proof p_i. After two negative verifications of this proof AR stops the transmission and fraud has been prevented. A second verification is neccessary to ensure transmission robustness in the presence of our approach. Fraud detection is possible since in particular the dishonest MN cannot drop original data. Due to gradually shifting r_{AAAH}'s pointer ahead, in case of an attack this means that AR checks the manipulated data on behalf of the following $|p|$ bits from r_{AAAH}. Obviously, such verification is negative.

The attacker may try to flood the link by sending $2^{|p|}$ packets with equivalent sequence number and payload, each with another permutation of p. Replay attacks and in particular this attack does not work because AR again keeps the current sequence number not more than for two comparisons. After each positive check it implicitly increases i by shifting r_{AAAH}'s pointer $|p|$ positions ahead. In case of a single negative check, by explicitly reading i from the received packet, AR shifts r_{AAAH}'s pointer to position i and exactly once more checks on base of the currently received proof. If the second check is negative as well, AR stops the transmission. The fraud has been prevented and re-authentication starts anew.

Summing it up: Whereas in the presence of our protection scheme the forwarding of a single manipulated IP-packet is possible, forwarding of more than one packet from a dishonest MN will most probably be prevented. In subsection 6.3 we analyse the correctness of the approach in more detail.

6.2   Robustness

Packet loss varies depending on some parameters like the assumed wireless link's bit error frequency, that may typically lie in the range of 10^{-3} to 10^{-5}, the medium access layer's error correction functionality, the maximum packet length of 108 bytes to 1500 bytes, etc. Naturally, the mobility scenario also has a strong impact. Zorzi [21] stated an average packet loss in the range of $3 \cdot 10^{-1}$ to 10^{-5} for different types of wireless links.

Whereas generally AR can select $b_{(i-1)|p|+1}, \ldots, b_{i|p|}$ from r_{AAAH} in advance before receiving the i-th packet from MN and thus this causes no additional delay, in case of a negative comparison some additional computation becomes necessary. Reasons for a negative comparison may be

- fraud,
- packet loss, and
- a changing packet sequence.

Assuming no congestion at AR, the last can be excluded in almost all cases for a single hop over a wireless link. A changing packet sequence as well as packet loss, in comparison to the previous much more probable over a wireless link, are to be handled at AR by explicitly reading in case of a single negative compare the sequence number i of the received packet and afterwards selecting bits $b_{(i-1)|p|+1}, \ldots, b_{i|p|}$ from r_{AAAH}. If this second comparison is positive, AR can infer with high probability that the previous negative check was not caused by fraud, but by a packet loss.

6.3   Correctness

Generally, in case of a positive check at AR, the probability to assure that IP-packets stem from the authenticated honest mobile device, strongly relates to $|p|$. An attacker's chance to guess the correct proof p_i of the actual packet can be denoted as the event E_i 'p_i guessed' and the probability for this is $Pr[E_i] = 2^{-|p|}$. Assuming half a byte for $|p|$, means the probability of $1/16$ to guess the current proof.

Since our proposed scheme is stateless, the E_i's are independent. Therefore, when MN sends a couple of packets, it holds for m $(m \geq 1)$ proofs $p_i, \ldots, p_{i+m-1}$ that an attacker's chance to guess all of them is

$$Pr[E_i \wedge E_{i+1} \wedge \ldots \wedge E_{i+m-1}] = \frac{1}{2^{|p|m}}. \tag{1}$$

Thus, an attacker can send m packets with probability $1/2^{|p| \cdot m}$, meaning that the probability for sending 10 sequential IP-packets for free is less than 10^{-11}.

Although in any case an attacker is able to send one IP-packet for free, we feel that the reached security level is relative to the required security of this application.

6.4   Costs

As well as our approach minimizes additional computation costs at MN and AR, traffic should not be increased unnecessarily. We propose for $|i|$ and $|p|$ all together one byte, resulting in 8 bytes IPv6 hop-by-hop options header. Whereas the reasonable lower limitation of $|p|$ should be $|p| > 3$ with a lower probability bound of 10^{-3} to 10^{-4} to be the victim of IP-packet fraud of more than one packet, the lower limit of $|i|$ strongly depends on the average and peak packet loss rate. Further, it depends on AR's verification strategy. The cyclic sequence number's maximum value i_{max} should be large enough to make it very seldom that a sequence of lost packets is larger and thus AR'a i points to the wrong proof.

Assuming an average packet loss of 10^{-1} with a normal distribution means that, if we want to support the sending of 1000 IP-packets without multiple selection and comparison of different bit-streams $b_{(i-1)|p|+1}, \ldots, b_{i|p|}$, we have to choose $|i| \gg 3$. Such a value results from the probability $1/10^{peak\_loss}$ at which a bundle of *peak_loss* packets is expected. For an average packet loss rate of 10^{-1}, every 1000 packets a peak loss of three packets occurs.

Table 1. Bits for sequence number and proof.

loss rate	peak loss 2	3	4	5	6	i_{max}	$|i|$	$|p|$
$3 \cdot 10^{-1}$	0.09	0.027	0.0081	0.000243	0.000729	> 6	4	4
$2 \cdot 10^{-1}$	0.04	0.008	0.0016	0.00032	-	> 5	4	4
10^{-1}	10^{-2}	10^{-3}	-	-	-	> 3	3	5
10^{-2}	10^{-4}	-	-	-	-	> 2	3	5
10^{-5}	10^{-10}	-	-	-	-	2	2	6

Table 1 proposes values for $|i|$ and $|p|$, assuming different rates of packets loss for different wireless LAN characteristics. Note, that for each of the different average packet loss rates only one additional byte is reasonable enough. Having also in mind the traffic caused by sending r_{AAAH}, the hop-by-hop options header's next header field, the extension length field, etc., this means an overhead of 9 bytes per packet over the wireless link (Fig 4).

Next Header	Length $= 0$	Opt. Type $= x$	Opt. Len. $= 0$	Opt. Data $= (i, p_i)$	PadN. $= 1$	Length $= 1$	Value $= 0$

Fig. 4. Format and value of the IPv6 hop-by-hop extension header with hop-by-hop options header (two bytes), our option (three bytes), and a three byte padding.

In comparison to the IPsec tunnel mode approach this means 7 times less additional signaling overhead over the scarce wireless link for packet originator verification at AR. Again assuming maximum packet lengths of at most 108-512 bytes, for real-time, e.g. audio traffic, the additional amount of signaling data related to the maximum packet length could be decreased for at most 50.7

Table 2. Data efficiency gain of unpredictable bits compared to IPsec tunnel mode approach.

	packet length [byte]			
	108	160	200	512
Sig. data IP tunnel mode [%]	59	40	32	12
Sig. data unpredictable bits [%]	8.3	5.6	4.5	1.7
data efficiency gain [point]	50.7	34.4	27.5	10.3

points. Table 2 lists the data gain for different packet lengths that were proposed in [22] and [16] for various audio applications[4].

7   Conclusions and Open Issues

A low-cost packet originator verification at the access-router extendable for volume-based metering was introduced. It supports metering data at the network layer over different access technologies. All data originated from and destined to a mobile device can be mapped with reasonable high probability to this device. Our scheme prevents fraud and reduces for real-time, e.g. audio responsive traffic and varying maximum packet lengths additional signaling data over the scarce wireless link in the range of 10.3 points to 50.7 points compared to the IPsec tunnel mode approach.

The method was implemented in a diploma thesis as a proof of concept [23]. We applied the Netfilter architecture and IPtables for IPv4 under Linux kernel 2.4.4. For the integration of our approach we queued IP-packets from kernel space into user space and performed IP-packet modification as well as verification.

To reduce traffic for transit of the pseudorandom bit-streams r_{AAAF} we integrate key-stream generators at the mobile device and the access-router. Thus, the AAA architecture only has to send initial keys. The handling of DoS attacks that enforce an honest mobile device's re-authentication needs to be investigated more detailed.

To avoid re-authentication in case of an intra-domain handover, a context-transfer including $(r_{AAAF}, |p|, |i|, p)$ from the current access-router to the following access-router becomes necessary.

References

1. C. Rigney, S.W. Livingston, A.R. Merit, W.S. Daydreamer, 'Remote Authentication Dial In User Service (RADIUS)', IETF RFC 2865, 2000.
2. P.R. Calhoun, J. Arkko, E. Guttman, G. Zorn, J. Loughney, 'Diameter Base Protocol', Internet Draft, IETF, Jun. 2002, Work in progress.

---

[4] JMF values for CBR audio codecs are 108 bytes for G.723 (6.5kbps, 8000Hz, 8bit), 160 bytes for GSM (13kbps, 8000Hz, 8bit) 200 bytes for G.711 (μLaw) (64kbps, 8000Hz, 8bit).

3. S. Glass, T. Hiller, C. Perkins, 'Mobile IP AAA Requirements', IETF RFC 2977, 2000.
4. T. Braun, L. Ru, G. Stattenberger, 'An AAA Architecture Extension for Providing Differentiated Services to Mobile IP Users', 6th IEEE Symposium on Computers and Communications (ISCC 2001), Hammamet, Tunesia, 2001.
5. D. Samfat, R. Molva, N. Asokan, 'Untracebility in Mobile Networks', Procedings of MOBICOM'95', Berkeley, CA, 1995.
6. Y. Zheng, 'An Authentication and Security Protocol for Mobile Computing', IFIP World Conference on Mobile Communications, 1996.
7. M. Looi, 'Enhanced Authentication Services for Internet Systems using Mobile Networks', IEEE GLOBECOM 2001, San Antonio, Texas, 2001.
8. ETSI TS 101 761-1: 'Broadband Radio Access Networks (BRAN); HIPERLAN Type 2; Data Link Control (DLC) Layer; Part 1: Basic Transport Functions'.
9. B. O'Hara, A. Petrick, 'IEEE 802.11 Handbook A Designer's Companion', Standards Information Press IEEE Press, 1999.
10. N. Borisov, I. Goldberg, D. Wagner, 'Intercepting Mobile Communications: The Insecurity of 802.11', ACM MOBICOM 2001, 2001.
11. S. Kent, R. Atkinson, 'Security architecture for the Internet Protocol', IETF RFC 2401, 1998.
12. C. Madson, R. Glenn, 'The Use of HMAC-MD5-96 within ESP and AH', IETF RFC 2403, Nov. 1998.
13. C. Madson, R. Glenn, 'The Use of HMAC-SHA-1-96 within ESP and AH', IETF RFC 2404, Nov. 1998.
14. A. Keromytis, N. Provos, 'The Use of HMAC-RIPEMD-160-96 within ESP and AH', IETF RFC 2857, Jun. 2000.
15. O. Elkeelany, M.M. Matalgah, K.P. Sheikh, M. Thaker, G. Chaudhry, D. Medhi, J. Qaddour, 'Performance Analysis of IPSec Protocol: Encryption and Authentication', IEEE International Conference on Communications, IEEE ICC'02, NY, USA, April 2002.
16. M. Degermark, M. Engan, B. Nordgren, S. Pink, 'Low-loss TCP/IP Header Compression for Wireless Networks', 1996.
17. A. Frier, P. Karlton, P. Kocher, 'The SSL 3.0 Protocol', Netscape Communication Corporation, Nov. 1996.
18. C. Allen, T. Dierks, 'The TLS Protocol Version 1.0', Internet Draft, IETF, Nov, 1997, Work in progress.
19. A.J. Menezes, P.C. v. Oorshot, S.A. Vanstone, 'Handbook of Applied Cryptography', CRC Press, 1996.
20. O. Goldreich, 'Modern Cryptography, Probabilistic Proofs and Pseudorandomness, Algorithms and Combinatorics', Springer-Verlag Volume 17, 1998.
21. M. Zorzi, 'Packet dropping statistics of a data-link protocol for wireless local communication', ICUPC'97, San Diego, 1997.
22. SUN Micro Systems, 'The Java Media Framework Version 2.0 API', http://java.sun.com/products/java-media/jmf, 1999.
23. A. Aijaz, 'Framework for device and traffic authentication of mobile subscriber nodes', Master Thesis, University of Stuttgart, Germany, 2002.

Problem Statement: Metering and Accounting in the Full-IP 4G Environment

Jürgen Jähnert

Communication Systems & Belwue Development, National Supercomputing Center, University of Stuttgart
jaehnert@rus.uni-stuttgart.de

Abstract. The current migration from traditional circuit-switched networks towards a packet-based wireless-IP network infrastructure is adding significant pressure for the provision of commercialized IP-based services. However, due of the lack of suitable mechanisms to provide scalable and efficient support for IP-based charging and billing, the commercialization of the Internet has only been progressing slowly. Such IP-based charging and billing support is crucial to the overall success of a commercialized wireless IP-based network as aspired in 4G. Within the IETF, both an IP-based metering framework and an AAA architecture dealing with authentication, authorization and accounting have been developed which targets the missing functions and mechanisms. Although the basic mechanisms are available and widely understood, their efficient and scalable integration into a mobile environment is still an open point.

1 Introduction

Virtually all papers with the title 'Beyond 3G Mobile Networks' are considering IP as the final means for integrating access networks from any technology - wireless or wired - and the, equally IP-based, core network. This migration from traditional circuit-switched networks towards a packet-based wireless-IP network infrastructure adds considerably to the pressure to provide commercialised services in this network.

In the wired-network infrastructure, circuit-switched voice communication still dominates the telecommunications market. Packet-switched voice and data communications are currently the key drivers for the development of new communication systems and technologies. The paradigms of the circuit-switched and packet-based networks are well known and, looking deeper at the current migration process, the circuit-switched network already provides full mobility support and has a well-established business model describing in detail the relationship between the customer and the network operator. Here, the users widely accept the pricing model offered by the operator and this relationship between customer and operator has led to an overly successful commercialised network. However, looking at the Internet, there is still no overall mobility support available and there is not yet a well-established business model in place, which is widely accepted by the users and able to generate significant revenue.

Currently, concepts on how to describe, define and detect IP service usage at a finer grain and finally how to charge for this kind of service usage in an efficient

B. Stiller et al. (Eds.): NGC/ICQT 2003, LNCS 2816, pp. 298–307, 2003.

manner is still an open issue in both the wired Internet and in the wireless packetbased mobile Internet. Pursuing this goal, but often focussing on different aspects, several working groups in the IETF and other consortia such as 3GPP/2 or MWIF etc. have started to identify both the key concepts and the missing components and have proposed complementary and sometimes competitive concepts or approaches. Along with the IETF a metering architecture has been developed which provides a promising base for the missing functions and mechanisms. Although basic mechanisms are available and widely understood, their efficient and scalable integration is not yet solved. This integration has to consider not only technology-driven aspects, but also the basic principles of a commercialised network. The rest of the paper is organized as follows: In chapter 2 relevant metering- and accounting-related issues coming from marketing and economy are discussed. In chapter 3 existing mechanisms from the IETF and IRTF are briefly presented. Chapter 4 summarizes requirements for costefficient metering and accounting in commercialised 4G networks. Chapter 5 highlights open issues not yet considered sufficiently in the current approaches and chapter 6 closes the paper with a summary.

2 Cost Model and Pricing Mechanism

The cost structure of a network-service provider consists of high fixed costs and relatively low variable costs which is typical for the whole Telco/IT sector [10]. So, in order to operate a network economically efficient, the overall operating costs, being part of the variable costs, must be lowered. Major parts of the fixed costs are network equipment, personnel and licensing costs. Variable costs are directly linked to the operator's incremental costs for an additional customer. One major item of these variable costs are those for user management. This includes the costs for metering, accounting, charging and billing.

Figure 1 shows a generic overview of a cost model for a network provider. The left side shows the more facilities-related branch comprising metering accounting and charging issues. The rest shows the customer-related management part. During a customer care and sales process, costs relating to the customer's contract and the storage of the customer specific data in a customer-care system are generated.

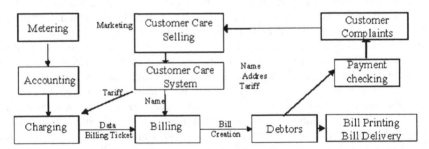

Fig. 1. Generic Cost Model of a Network Provider

The service-specific data per user has to be combined with the usage-data to calculate the final charge. This process is one of the most expensive and contributes significantly to a network operator's variables cost. It depends on the total amount of data to be handled. Input to this process is coming from the customer-care system in terms of the differences in the contracts offered to the customers mainly described by the variou s pricing models. The details of this pricing model in turn influence greatly the total amount of data to be captured per individual customer in order to charge and bill accordingly. Assuming that a network offers most of its customers a flat-rate contract, it makes no sense at all to capture the flat-rate customer's usage-data. Further, input to the costly usage-data management process is the total amount of accounting data, which should be very low. If customers can individually select, for example, the QoS/session as supported by most of the actual QoS provisioning strategies, and even have the possibility to change them during a session, then the usage-data must be captured at a correspondingly finer grain. A network operator might offer its customer such a fine-grained service only if he can be assured of a good profit margin. Thus, the additional revenue must overcompensate the additional cost for user management including the metering/accounting/charging/ billing process in order to evaluate the overall concept from a commercial point of view.

In order to be able to create a cost-effective metering and accounting framework, a pricing model must be considered, since this determines which parameters of the usage-data are relevant for metering and accounting at all. Pricing models are part of market research. However, some simple requirements derived from the basic concepts of pricing models can be determined at this early stage. Any pricing model deployed in a competitive environment has to provide a level of dynamic flexibility so as to be able to react to any changes in a competitor's pricing strategy. The use of service-bundling concepts is, for example, one widely used mechanism in pricing models. Service bundling describes a method for binding different services together in one package and to offer this to the user at a price cheaper than pricing each individual item of the bundle separately. In [10] it has been shown that, through a prudent composition of the bundles, overall revenue can be increased significantly. Furthermore, for reasons of user acceptance, service bundles are a necessity as customers prefer to have a clearly indicated but limited business relationships. Another mechanism to be considered within this context is price differentiation [10]. This concepts' basic assumption is that each customer is willing to pay differently for each individual service. In order to maximize revenue, services should be sold to each user by exactly this maximum willingness-to-pay. The challenge is to discover this maximum willingness-to-pay for each customer. For this reason, classes of customers are defined as, for example, airlines creating three categories: students, tourist traveller and business traveller. Students are identified by their age, tourist travellers stay the weekend and business travellers make up the rest.

3 AAA and IP Metering in the IETF

Since the future Internet will offer a wide range of commercialised services, commercial systems and services need metering, authentication, authorization, accounting, auditing and charging to ensure a return on the operator's investment for providing these services. These economic and market-driven aspects are even more important to the future mobility enabled multi-service provider networks because here the existing and, from a business model point-of-view, well-established circuit switched networks will merge towards a packet-based network architecture where IP acts as a convergence layer managing heterogeneous access to this multi-service network platform.

In recent years, within both the IETF and IRTF, working groups have been established to overcome the lack of an efficient user management framework which is able to manage, from a technical point of view, the interface of the Internet where business meets technology. Under the acronym AAA, a common platform is currently under development for authentication, authorization and accounting to meet these business driven requirements. Further, under the acronym RTFM, the Real-Time Flow Measurement group has been defined a reference architecture for IP metering.

3.1 AAA Terminology

Accounting is the collection and aggregation of information relating to customers' service usage. Accounting should be expressed in units relevant to its final purpose. For charging, the accounting units must be derived from the parameters derived from the deployed pricing model.

Authorization is the verification of whether an entity is allowed to perform an action, which is generally bound to resource usage.

Auditing is the verification of correctness of a process with respect to service delivery and is done by examination of logged data in order to verify the correctness of operational procedures.

Authentication mechanisms are mostly credential-based and describe the verification of a user's (entities) identity.

*AAA mechanism*s can be distinguished between those, which determine methods to perform authentication, authorization and accounting.

AAA protocols specify an appropriate interaction between the typically distributed entities as well as performing the above-mentioned tasks.

AAA *architecture* addresses the interworking between components [7].

3.2 IETF AAA Work

The IETF's AAA working group is focusing on the requirements for supporting authentication, authorization, and accounting access to and services provided by network resource managers (e.g.: bandwidth brokers), [7]. The additional requirements for mobility-enabled networks are summarized in greater detail in [2].

For authentication, there are currently two different protocols: Radius, Remote dial in User Service Protocol [3] and its successor Diameter [1], which was developed due to shortcomings in Radius especially if deployed in the mobile environment. Diameter is the major output of the IETF's AAA working group and was designed for being used by different access technologies, distributed security models and, with some limitation, for multi-domain roaming scenarios. Diameter consists of a sessionoriented base protocol operated ideally over a reliable transport protocol. Diameter exchanges information by means of so-called attribute-value pairs (AVPs). Here, a standardized set of AVPs is defined, but the protocol has the flexibility for further proprietary extensions. To support specific scenarios, so-called Diameter applications [7] must be added to the Diameter base protocol. Here some effort was made in [8] to support IP mobility scenarios adequately.

3.3 IRTF AAA Architecture

Within the Internet Research Task Force (IRTF), a group is working on the definition of an AAA architecture [4] to be deployed on a heterogeneous network-provider environment. The main focus of this group is on authorization and accounting. The basic concept of this architecture is that in each administrative domain there is at least one AAA server offering authorization, authentication and accounting services. Multiprovider scenarios are supported by appropriate communication between these servers via the Diameter protocol [1]. Here, an agent in the foreign domain (AAA Attendant) receiving the client's request is likely to require that the client provide some credentials, which can be authenticated before resources in the foreign domain can be consumed. The attendant consults an authority attached to its administrative domain (AAA.f), which checks the credentials of the requesting client. This authority forwards this request to the authority of the home domain (AAA.h), and once this local authority has obtained authorization, the attendant is informed about resources, which can be committed to the requesting client.

Based on this elementary scenario, several functional requirements relating to security, authorization, user identification and accounting have been identified. Further, the architecture should be extensible across a wide variety of Internet services spanning many stakeholders, provide application-independent sessionmanagement mechanisms and of course should be scalable to the size of the global Internet which includes operations across administrative boundaries.

3.4 IETF Policy-Based Accounting Approach

In [13] a policy-based accounting framework is introduced which provides a generic description of the accounting policies describing the configuration of an accounting architecture in a standardized way. The policies are supposed to be used to instrument the accounting architecture and can be exchanged between AAA entities in order to share configuration information. The described building blocks and message sequences for policy-based accounting in the generic AAA architecture are underlined with examples for the usage of accounting policies in different scenarios and its potential integration into the AAA authorization framework. The proposed approach refers to the IETF Metering approach, which will be introduced in the next chapter and generically describes how an AAA server will configure a meter remotely. The approach presents an inter-domain accounting scenario, which means that at least two administratively separated networks are involved in the accounting process. These can be two domains involved in a roaming scenario or a chain of providers if service provisioning involves data transfer and/or services from different domains. In these scenarios, the exchange of accounting policies between providers is necessary if accounting tasks are delegated to one provider or shared among multiple providers. The AAA servers exchange accounting policies. User specific service parameters are given to the visited AAA server and are forwarded to the service equipment where the user configuration is done. The user-specific service parameters could additionally include the desired policies for the configuration of the accounting infrastructure of the visited ISP.

3.5 IP Metering in the IETF

Measuring network traffic has a long history within the IETF. A working group within IETF, the so-called Real Time Traffic Flow Measurement (RTFM) Working Group, was founded in 1995 and has been developing an architecture for traffic measurement [6]. Central to this architecture is the notion of traffic flows. An IETF RTFM flow is a bi-directional stream of packets between two endpoints, each defined by a set of attribute values, which can be determined flexibly. Via these flows, the notion of a virtual "connection" is introduced to the IP layer. The most important flow attributes describe endpoint addressees as, for example, the 128-bit IPv6 address of a flow's source. Further attributes are, for example, transport protocol port and the Differentiated Services Code Point. Historically, this architecture was designed for accounting purposes and as a base for further charging and billing processes in order to detect and economically handle the resource/service usage more accurately. Currently, the architecture has been extended for traffic analysis purposes.

Figure 2 depicts the overall architecture. Heart of the traffic flow measurement architecture is the Meter. Meters are placed at measurement points determined by the network operator. Each meter selectively records network activity as directed by its configuration settings. It can also aggregate, transform and further process the recorded activity before the data is stored. The processed and stored results are called the usage-data. This data has to be collected and aggregated for further processing which the Meter Reader does before being passed to the accounting layer.

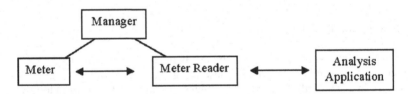

Fig. 2. The IETF Real Time Traffic Flow Measurement Architecture

Metering policies define how this collection and aggregation is done. The application, which configures Meter entities and controls Meter Reader entities, is called the Meter Manager. The Meter Manager controls the proper interworking between Meter and Meter Manager. Via requirements analysis, it further determines the appropriate configurations for each Meter and the proper operation of each Meter Reader. Finally, the Analysis Application processes and aggregates the usage-data in order to provide information and reports, according to the operator's specific purposes. This process is done offline.

4 Requirements

Before going into the limitations of the currently available solutions to be deployed in a 4G-infrastructure, figure 3 shows an overview of a 4G-mobility scenario as defined in [9]. An end-system is able to roam within and between administrative domains by changing dynamically the IP-network address across different network cells. To efficiently meter the usage-data, hierarchical distributed metering is required, which should be configured flexibly and remotely. At the lowest hierarchy, each access point providing access to either the wired or wireless-access network needs to have a metering instance. Since a data session launched by the user of an end-system can take place across this heterogeneous-network infrastructure, an overall session concept allowing very early usage-data consolidation and assignment of usage-data to a user is desirable. To minimize the total amount of gathered usagedata, this metering concept must be linked to the pricing concept of each individual user since the pricing concept finally decides which usage-data are relevant to the billing process. Looking at the two fundamental pricing mechanisms, price differentiation and service bundling described in chapter 2, both mechanisms can be characterized as user-centric. Deploying these mechanisms on the Internet, different customers have to pay different prices for the same service and the services must be somehow bundled before being offered to the customer.

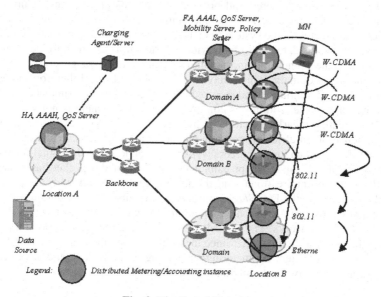

Fig. 3. Distributed Metering

So, the first requirement to be extracted from this correlation is an efficient user-centric approach for capturing usage-data, where different services can be assigned and bundled dynamically to individual customers, since service-centric metering, accounting and charging is not sufficient in commercialised 4G-networks. Overlaying this requirement with the dynamic 4G network, a distributed metering architecture is required. In principal, in the home domain service-centric usage data can be assigned to the different users, but this method will increase complexity which can be easily avoided by gathering usage data user-centric right from the beginning. To clarify this statement lets assume that user A has a flat rate contract and user B has to pay for certain service on a fine granularity. Deploying service-centric metering and accounting would result in gathering all the usage data on the finest granularity offered to any customer and to assign in the home domain the serviced to the different users since the IP addresses used do not provide any information about the user itself. The total amount of data to be transmitted is quite huge and partially useless. Dependant of the variety of services offered to the customer and assuming that some of the customers have a prepaid contract, several terabytes of usage data might be transferred through the network and even more, must be handled in a complex post process in order to transfer service-centric data into user-centric data. Assuming an user-centric metering/accounting process, basically there are three major factors influencing the overall amount of data to be gathered. They are: the manifoldness of the pricing scheme offered to the customers, the QoS support offered to the users and the ability to detect as early as possible the data relevant for the charging process.

If the pricing scheme is manifold, all the separate details from a large variety of services have to be captured during the metering process. For this case, there is simply not enough time to consolidate the data during the accounting process.

If the QoS support is manifold i.e. a user can decide individually or even dynamically which resources he wants to consume, then again all fine-grain details of the usage-data have to be gathered and provided to the charging process. Current QoS concepts intend to offer exactly such fine-grained QoS often allowing customers to dynamically interact with the system to increase the QoS – also during a session.

If the usage-data is detected to be service-centric and is assigned to individual customers back in the home domain, quantities of data are being generated and transferred to the home domain, which may be of no use and could therefore be deleted, assuming price differentiation and service bundling concepts to be in place.

A further open issue, within this context, is the fact that there is not yet a concept available indicating clearly which party pays for which service, which in turn has a major influence on an efficient metering and accounting process. While in the POTS world the billing and charging process was directly attached to the signaling and connection setup phase, this concept cannot be adopted in the packet-based network. Here IP flows are unidirectional and do not provide the meter with the parameters currently deployed in the POTS/2G environment like distance and duration. Does the caller of a voice-over-IP session have to pay for the whole call, as currently deployed in most of the 2G networks? Is it the callee or do we share the costs among them, as is currently the case for the Internet? Since these are still open issues and depend also on the services to be charged, the metering/accounting framework should have the flexibility to support all flavors of combinations efficiently.

5   Limitations and Weaknesses of Existing Solutions

Key limitations to of the presented IP based mechanisms are the lack of integration of fundamental mechanisms to provide commercial services such as auditing, charging and metering. Additionally, the existing AAA mechanisms were originally designed for a fixed-wired network infrastructure. The need for interdomain mobility support has been identified but solutions fulfilling all requirements are not yet available. Here especially, the optimisation of the accounting framework to lower the overall management costs does not yet adequately consider 4G-mobility scenarios. Furthermore, the inclusion of QoS-related services across administrative domain boundaries has not been considered.

Both, the IETF RTFM architecture and the current AAA architecture have significant limitations with respect to efficient metering and accounting support for charging and billing purposes scenarios as described in [5] and [15].

The limitations of the IETF RTFM framework are due to the lack of remotely assigned attributes extracted from the pricing scheme to the Meter configuration dynamically and user-centric. Here, integration into the AAA framework is lacking as well as the possibility to remotely assign metering rules to the meter dynamically.

The limitations of the IETF AAA framework are the missing overall session concept, which supports the very early accounting data consolidation already in the foreign domain, corresponding to a middle hierarchical level of the data consolidation process. Here, a more active behaviour of the AAA server playing the role of an AAA.f server is required and some functions currently covered by the AAA server in the home domain should be delegated as close as possible to the end-system to be charged. This includes the temporary storage of usage-data. Because of the lack of a generic definition of this mechanism, this process is further complicated. So, the integration of generic pricing schemes via dynamic user-centric profiling has not yet been sufficiently considered in the AAA activities and has not been considered at all in the currently inactive RTFM working group. Recently under the acronym IPFIX, a new working group was founded [11], taking up some of the open issues, however the recently published requirement document [12] does not consider the aforementioned needs specific to a commercialised 4G network sufficiently.

The limitations of the policy-based accounting [13] are the missing compression of gathered usage-data in order to minimize the overall amount of data to be captured and processed. Here no concept about when to forward data in a scalable and efficient manner in an IP based mobility environment is provided. Further, the lack of an overall accounting session management concept considering these provider driven scalability aspects is open and can be regarded as key factor to slow down the process of commercialising the wireless Internet.

Despite of mentioning that significant work has been done so fare and for most of the problems solutions which can be partly regarded as a first step are available, an integration into Mobility Management, an overall QoS provisioning strategy, security, a policing concept and an AAA infrastructure suitable to support multi-provider scenarios are not yet in place. Initial effort to come up with an integrated solution has been undertaken [14], however there is still some open issues left.

6 Conclusion and Further Steps

There is an increasing need for AAA services and services related to AAA. These are not yet included sufficiently in the existing AAA and RTFM architecture to allow the commercial deployment of services in a real all-IP 4G-network infrastructure. Amongst others, the lack of an efficient metering framework in the AAA architecture such that mobile scenarios can be supported in a cost-lowering manner, might become one reason for slowing the commercialization process of the 4G-network infrastructure. Due to the significant pressure of the existing 2G value chains, plus the enormous 3G licensing costs in Europe and the need to open the network platform in order to offer services provided by third party service providers as pushed by deregulation, fundamental enhancements of the existing interworking between AAA, metering, accounting and the pricing scheme are required.

Acknowledgement

The work presented in this paper was partially funded by the EU project IST-2000-25394 "Moby Dick" (Mobility and Differentiated Services in a Future IP network).

References

1. P. Calhoun, J. Loughney, E. Guttman, G. Zorn, J. Arkko, *Diameter Base Protocol*, draft-ietf-aaa-diameter-16.txt, IETF work in progress, December 2002.
2. S. Glass, T. Hiller, S. Jacobs, C. Perkins, *Mobile IP Authentication, Authorization, and Accounting Requirements*, IETF RFC 2977, October 2000.
3. Rigney, C., *RADIUS Accounting*, IETF RFC 2139, April 1997.
4. C. de Laat, *Generic AAA Archit*ecture, IETF RFC 2903, August 2000.
5. J. Arkko, P. Calhoun, G. Zorn, *Diameter Accounting Extensions*, IETF draft-ietfaaa- diameter-accounting-01.txt, work in progress, March 2001.
6. N. Brownlee, C. Mills, G. Ruth, *Traffic Flow Measurement: Architecture,* IETF RFC 2722, October 1999.
7. C. Rensig, Hasan, M. Karsten, B. Stiller, *AAA: A survey and a Policy-Based Architecture and Framework*, IEEE Network Nov./Dec. 2002.
8. S. M. Faccin, F. Le, B. Patil, C. Perkins, *Diameter Mobile IPv6 Application,* IETF draft-le-aaa-diameter-mobileipv6-02.txt, September 2002.
9. Moby Dick: Mobility and Differentiated Services in a Future IP Network, http://www.ist-mobydick.org, Jan. 2003.
10. Shapiro, C., Varian, H. R., *Information Rules: A Strategic Guide to the Network Economy*, ISBN 0-87584-863-X, Harvard Business School Press, 1999.
11. http://www.ietf.org/html.charters/ipfix-charter.html
12. Quittek, T. Zseby, B. Claise, S. Zander, G. Carle, K.C. Norseth, *Requirements for IP Flow Information Export*, draft-ietf-ipfix-reqs-07.txt, September 2002.
13. T. Zseby, S. Zander, G. Carle, *Policy-based Accounting*, IETF RFC 3334, October 2002.
14. Sarma, et.al.: *Solutions for Ipv6-based mobility in the EU project Moby Dick*, World Telecom Congress, Paris, September 2002.
15. Juergen Jähnert: *Cost-efficient Metering and Accounting in 4G Networks,* International Teletraffic Congress (ITC), Berlin, September 2003.

Incentive Based Inter-domain Routeing

Richard Mortier[1] and Ian Pratt[2]

[1] Microsoft Research Ltd., 7, JJ Thomson Avenue, Cambridge CB3 0FB, UK*
`mort@ieee.org`, Tel.: +44 1223 479830, Fax.: +44 1223 479999
[2] University of Cambridge Computer Lab, 15, JJ Thomson Avenue, Cambridge CB3 0FD, UK
`ian.pratt@cl.cam.ac.uk`, Tel.: +44 1223 334639

Abstract. The Internet's inter-domain routeing system has evolved to keep pace with the Internet's rapid growth, from a few co-operatively managed administrative domains to a large number of competetive domains. This growth has brought to light one of the Internet's shortcomings: lack of support for efficient control and management of traffic, particularly between domains. This paper presents an extension to BGP, the inter-domain routeing protocol, that enables congestion to drive route selection and thus allows economic incentives to play their part in traffic distribution. Implementation in a deployed BGP stack is discussed and a simple simulation presented, showing better traffic distribution.

1 Introduction

The Internet has evolved from a small number of co-operatively managed interconnected networks. It now consists of approximately 16 000 networks, or Autonomous Systems (ASs), with a similar number of competitive administrative domains. Rather than rely on co-operation, interconnecting networks enter into Service Level Agreements (SLAs) that contractually specify the parameters of the services to be provided. The process of managing the allocation of network resources to meet such obligations is known as *traffic engineering* [1].

Unfortunately, control and management protocols in the Internet have struggled to evolve to manage this increased complexity. The only mechanism available to operators to manage the distribution of traffic throughout the Internet is the inter-domain routeing protocol, Border Gateway Protocol v4 (BGP) [2,3]. This is used to advertise connectivity to particular Internet Protocol (IP) prefixes, since either the network advertising the prefix owns that prefix, or the network is providing transit for traffic belonging to a prefix owned by another network.

By controlling the distribution of adverts for these prefixes, based on the adverts' properties such as the originating AS, BGP provides for separation between topology and policy. However, the mechanisms it currently provides are generally not easily automated, requiring substantial manual intervention on the part of operators. Received wisdom has long held that BGP configuration is highly prone to errors, and there is increasing evidence that such errors both occur *and* significantly impact the operation

---

* The work presented in this paper was carried out while the author was a Ph.D. student at the University of Cambridge Computer Lab, UK.

B. Stiller et al. (Eds.): NGC/ICQT 2003, LNCS 2816, pp. 308–317, 2003.
© Springer-Verlag Berlin Heidelberg 2003

of the Internet [4]. Furthermore BGP does not provide any facility for changing routes based on more dynamic metrics such as the current performance of different routes. This makes it difficult to correctly implement policies such as multi-homing, where a customer connects via multiple providers for performance and reliability reasons.

This paper presents an incremental modification to BGP allowing ASs to advertise a load-based price for carrying traffic from their peer ASs. This provides two significant benefits: it provides a globally valid metric that should improve the stability properties of BGP; and it allows route selection to be made incentive-compatible and more dynamic. This has a number of benefits: it allows more flexible traffic engineering policies to be implemented; it increases the potential for automation of Internet network management; and it increases the likely performance of the network.

Section 2 describes Internet routeing and related work using BGP and its mechanisms for Internet traffic engineering. Section 3 discusses issues surrounding the design of the pricing extension to BGP and its implementation. Sections 4 and 5 present a simulator built around a deployed BGP implementation, and a simple simulation demonstrating that stability of routes and a more even distribution of load can be achieved. Finally, Section 6 concludes with a pointer to some discussion of issues surrounding deployment.

2   Internet Routeing and Related Work

Traffic in the Internet is routed by each router matching the destination address of a packet against the longest (and so most specific) address prefix known to that router. The corresponding routeing table entry tells the router on which interface the packet should be transmitted in the hope that it will progress towards its destination. Information about which networks and routers 'own' prefixes is disseminated via routeing protocols.

In a given network there are effectively two classes of prefix, and so two classes of routeing protocol. The Interior Gateway Protocol (IGP) disseminates information about those prefixes that belong to the network in question. Common examples of such protocols include the Intermediate System-Intermediate System protocol (IS-IS) [5,6] and the Open Shortest Path First protocol (OSPF) [7]. The Exterior Gateway Protocol (EGP) disseminates information about those prefixes that are external to the AS in question; the only currently deployed example is the Border Gateway Protocol v4 (BGP) [2,3].

BGP is a *path-vector* routeing protocol, an extension of a distance-vector routeing protocol. Each node distributes to its neighbours, or peers, its current preferred routes to the destination prefixes of which it is aware along with *path attributes* that apply to those prefixes. BGP is used in two ways: as internal-BGP (iBGP), to readvertise externally learnt prefixes within the enclosing AS; and as external-BGP (eBGP), to advertise prefixes (both internal and external) to neighbouring ASs. A session is iBGP if both ends use the same AS number, and the effect is that all the path attributes are trusted.

When a node receives adverts for the same destination prefix from multiple neighbours, it executes some preference function to decide which it will use and continue to advertise. In this way nodes build up information about their current best *next hop* choices for the destination prefixes available in the network. Key path attributes include:

the mandatory AS‑PATH attribute which lists the ASs on the path that this advert has taken to reach the current router, enabling loop detection and also application of policy; the first applied path attribute, the LOCAL‑PREF, a simple locally valid preference; and the ultimate tie-breaker, selecting the peering router with numerically lowest IP address.

Existing work has addressed the problems of resource allocation and effective route choice in IGPs [8,9]. The key point about such work is that the problems are all contained within a single network and thus a single administrative domain. Consequently, more co-operation can be expected from network elements, and it is more reasonable to assume that implementation of a single consistent policy is desired. However, as BGP is used to distribute prefixes between ASs and thus administrative domains, there will be multiple policies to be implemented in a given AS based on those to which it connects, and little co-operation between competitors may be assumed.

To deal with these problems, BGP provides two basic mechanisms to enable operators to express policy. The first is *filtering*, controlling the routes that individual routers will accept and advertise based on properties of the peer or advert in question. The second is based on use of *path attributes*, associated by routers with each set of advertised prefixes, and used to influence the preference function at the receiving router. There are approximately fifteen different types of path attribute that may be used, and their treatment is standardised by the IETF [2].

The sheer number of available path attributes itself causes problems. For example, it makes understanding their interaction difficult, increasing the chances of misconfiguration, and can lead to problems with persistent oscillation [10,11]. Since correctly managing so many attributes is difficult, operators tend to use just a small well-understood subset. Two of the most commonly used are the AS‑PATH and COMMUNITY attributes.

COMMUNITY attributes are opaque 32-bit tags associated with adverts that have semantics defined on a pairwise ad hoc basis between operators. They are commonly used to control the application of filters to adverts, or the modification or assignment of other path attributes to the advert. For example, the number of terms in the AS‑PATH is used as part of the route preference function (shorter AS‑PATHs being preferred), so by inserting multiple copies of their own AS number, operators gain some control over the routes their peers will prefer. The number of copies to insert is commonly controlled using different COMMUNITY attribute values as agreed between the operators.

In conclusion, BGP currently provides no mechanism allowing simple and consistent inter-domain traffic management. The mechanisms it does provide are ad hoc and difficult to make consistent between operators. Although extensions have been proposed to make particular functions consistent [12], they are limited in scope, and do not provide a generic mechanism for consistent inter-domain traffic engineering. The remainder of this paper presents a new path attribute that should enable consistent network-wide traffic engineering policies to be implemented, and also simplify the management process for the operator. Furthermore, it can be used to increase the control the operator has over traffic entering and leaving their network, allowing more flexible service differentiation.

3   Inter-AS Pricing

The principal aim of inter-AS pricing is to give greater control over traffic distribution to operators offering and receiving transit services. The current measured network load is transformed first into a per-AS *price*, and this is then transformed into a per-customer *charge* and advertised to customers. Note that in this context, an operator's *customers* refers to other network operators, both its clients and peers.

In fact, current peering policies are already influenced by network load: before operators decide to peer they attempt to calculate their traffic matrices and decide appropriate ratios for ingress to egress traffic on their respective networks. However, such decisions and measurements are taken over very long timescales, typically on the order of months. The mechanism presented in this paper should allow these timescales to be shortened to hours or perhaps even minutes.

Furthermore, those who desire higher quality service should have some mechanism to express this, for both transmitted *and* received traffic. Conversely, those operators providing transit services should have some mechanism allowing them to encourage or discourage customers (i.e. other operators) from routeing traffic toward them. Prices should be based on network load since that is the major cause of service variation in an operational network. Retaining the separation between price and charge allows arbitrary policy to be imposed by operators, while basing the network's route selection process on its load.

The natural mechanism to implement inter-AS pricing is as a new path attribute for BGP. Such a path attribute should be *optional* and *non-transitive* (i.e. not all BGP implementations need support it, and it need not always be communicated to peers). This preserves compatibility with prior versions of BGP whilst enabling incremental deployment. Inter-AS pricing can be split into three parts: *measuring congestion*, performed by the routers in the AS, based on metrics such as round-trip time estimates, packet drop rates, or packet mark rates; *calculating prices*, based on aggregated congestion measurements from the network; and *charging customers*, allowing policies to be applied by the provider based on customer, time-of-day, etc.

Dividing inter-AS pricing in this way achieves a number of goals. The principal from a technical point of view is that operators are given a rational mechanism to select between available routes. More nebulous effects include the easing of network management since usage based charging in this way gives a basis for automated settlement of bilateral peering arrangements; potential structural changes to the network, both technical and economic; and the possibility for operators to influence the route taken by traffic destined for them. This allows operators to begin to offer differentiated service in the Internet which can include some form of statement about the treatment of traffic in networks other than their own: a movement toward true end-to-end differentiated services.

3.1   Calculation of Prices

There are a number of design decisions implicit in the above description which will now be discussed in turn: the measure of congestion on which the price is based; the association of the price with a node and not a link; and the constraints on the calculated prices.

Using marking information provided by routers seems a good basis for calculating a useful AS-wide measure of congestion as it takes into account both the remaining capacity and queueing delay on links. The price will thus be based on, and usually related to, the congestion that the router is experiencing. Effective schemes for smoothing and utilising the information available from packet marking are not discussed in this paper but are the subject of ongoing work.

Three constraints on the calculated price are identified here. The first two are fairly straightforward: the price should be positive[1] and should increase as the measure of congestion increases. The third is that the price should become less sensitive to changes in the load as the load increases.

As the network becomes excessively congested, route stability becomes more important as changing routes has a progressively more disruptive effect. In particular, route stability is likely to be a more important constraint than maximising the revenue generated by these price-based mechanisms: operators have other means to generate revenue, and there is not much that the routeing protocol can do to deal with a network which is simply overloaded. When the network does become overloaded, measures such as admission control and the end-to-end congestion control mechanisms of the transport protocols must play their part to reduce congestion. Such measures might be implemented through pricing visible to end users, but it is not within the remit of the routeing protocol to calculate or advertise these prices.

3.2 Expression of Policies

Before advertising the calculated price it is transformed according to local policy into a *charge*, then used by peers to calculate a LOCAL - PREF value as input to their own route selection process. This serves two purposes: (*i*) allowing the AS advertising the route to influence the route selection process of those receiving the advert; and (*ii*) allowing the AS receiving the advert to express more complex route selection policies. Such policies may be separated into two categories: static and dynamic.

Static policies include current BGP configurations such as 'always choose AS_i over AS_j' for a given prefix. For such policies the price path attribute acts purely as an accounting mechanism, simplifying the construction, parameterization and settlement of SLAs; it plays no direct part in the distribution of traffic through the network, and hence should not affect routeing stability.

Dynamic policies are more interesting and enable more expressive semantics but are harder to understand and predict in detail. Perhaps the most obvious such policy would be 'pick the cheapest route.' More complex policies could be implemented if the operator could measure the load neighbouring ASs were experiencing.

When calculating the price, a node has knowledge of the load its links are experiencing and the charges advertised to it from its peers. The price, p_i, at a node, N_i, may

---

[1] This is perhaps debatable if this mechanism were to be used to give discounts to peers, but such use is not considered further here.

thus be viewed as a function, $p_i = p(l_i^j, c_j^i)$ $\forall j \neq i$ where l_i^j is the load between nodes N_i and N_j, and c_j^i is the charge node N_j advertises to node N_i.

Using such load measurements, the operator could implement policies such as 'pick the highest quality route,' 'pick the cheapest route j such that $c_j^i l_i^j < C$' or 'pick the highest quality route j such that $c_j^i l_i^j < C$,' for some total cost C, perhaps itself time varying. The implementation of such remote monitoring facilities is not covered here; route server *looking glasses* already allow queries of the routes available to particular destinations, and these might be extended if the facility was considered desirable. In fact, companies offering such Internet performance measurement services now exist [13,14].

3.3   Settlement of Bills

Schemes for *settlement*, the process of converting into bills the charges associated with traffic, may be arbitrarily complex. The simplest and most obvious is to use traffic volume. This has a number of advantages: it is straightforward to understand and to measure; it is generally slowly varying between ASs, allowing operators to make relatively accurate predictions about future bills; and many operators already have to collect such information in order to police the SLAs into which they have entered.

Of course, scope exists for more complex settlement schemes. For example, if suitable feedback could be arranged, settlement might be performed based on the number of packets marked. Although this links the final bill more closely to congestion (since charges will not be levied unless congestion is occurring and hence packets being marked), such a scheme is more complex to understand and predict, and requires more infrastructure to support.

4   Simulation

Existing network simulators typically simulate at a per-packet level, making them inappropriate for BGP (and routeing in general) simulation: in such cases it is the macroscopic properties of the protocol that are of interest. Furthermore, they tend to use models of protocol behaviour rather than actual protocol implementations; since routeing protocols are notoriously difficult to implement correctly, such modelled versions must be viewed with some scepticism.

To avoid these problems, a simulator was developed based on a deployed implementation of routeing code: the GNU Zebra protocol suite [15]. This provides a number of dæmons which operate individual routeing protocols, and multiplex forwarding table updates to the kernel via a further *Zebra* dæmon. This suite was modified in three ways: (*i*) the Zebra dæmon was restricted to provide only logging and not to modify kernel forwarding tables; (*ii*) the BGP dæmon was modified to enable multiple copies to run on the local machine[2]; (*iii*) a simple harness was written that scheduled among the many BGP instances and provided simulation of load.

---

[2] Essentially by binding the BGP connection's local socket to a virtual IP interface on the local machine.

Realistic load simulation is complex and so for the initial simulator it was assumed that (*i*) the network is homogeneous in capacity, and (*ii*) each node sources equal amounts of traffic to all known prefixes. Although both are untrue in practice, they allowed some basic protocol properties to be investigated; furthermore, the Internet core currently uses technologies with commensurate, if not identical performance characteristics.

Under these two assumptions, load at a node is then calculated as the sum of two terms: (*i*) one unit per prefix advertised in the network, representing the load sourced by the node itself; and (*ii*) one unit per prefix per source for which the node's neighbours are using the node as next hop. For example, in a network of n nodes each advertising a single prefix, stub nodes should carry $2n - 1$ units: n units representing the load that the stub node is itself generating, and $n - 1$ units representing the load generated for it by every other node in the network.

Finally, code was added to implement the price path attribute, mimicking the usual way that path attributes are implemented. The result is a BGP simulator where the basic BGP code is essentially unmodified from a genuine deployed BGP implementation, and the extension under test is implemented in the same way that it would be implemented in reality. Although the simulation of load makes simplifying assumptions about the behaviour of traffic in the network, the state machine and routeing protocol behaviour are not simplified in any way.

5   Results and Discussion

The results in Figure 1 are intended as a simple illustration of this approach; more complete evaluation has yet to be carried out. Each AS contains a single router which introduces a single prefix to the system; the price is equal to the load incident to an AS; and the simplest non-trivial charging policy is uniformly applied: prefer the cheapest route. The nodes are numbered in the numeric order of their IP addresses with T_x nodes being transit nodes and S_x nodes being stub nodes.

In all simulations the stub nodes carry 11 units of load as expected. With unmodified BGP, the deterministic default tie-breaker[3] makes node T_1 preferred for transit to node T_2, which is then preferred to node T_3. The result is that nodes (T_1, T_2, T_3) carry (17, 15, 13) units of load respectively. With the BGP price attribute in place, a much more even distribution of load is achieved: all transit nodes carry 15 units of load each. The cost of this better balancing of load is an approximate doubling in the convergence time.

It should be noted that Zebra version 0.91a on which the simulator was based separately modifies the standard BGP route selection process. This version of Zebra changes the default tie-breaker to prefer the first-received route, in an attempt to reduce route-flap. The result using otherwise unmodified BGP is that the load distribution is then based on the precise ordering of message arrivals at nodes. This allows situations with evenly balanced load to arise at the price of the system becoming non-deterministic. Such a modification is actually required when using the price path attribute to prevent permanent oscillation: after the system equalizes load through the transit ASs, stub ASs

---

[3] All other things being equal, select the next hop with the numerically lowest IP address.

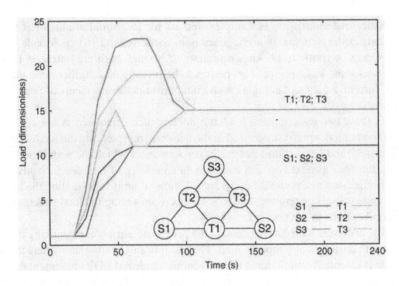

Fig. 1. Multi-homing with a small core. The embedded figure displays the simulated topology. The graph of results with unmodified BGP is omitted for space.

see equal prices; however, by default they would tie-break on lowest IP address, causing one transit AS to become overloaded and the pricing mechanism once again to take effect.

Two other mechanisms were also introduced to avoid route change synchronization leading to permanently oscillating routes. First, the number of routes that may have their LOCAL-PREF altered on the basis of a change in price is limited to one. This implements the most conservative load shedding policy; changes in price are still re-advertised as soon as they are processed. Second, the LOCAL-PREF may only be modified after a delay proportional to the maximum AS-PATH length in the network.

These changes attempt to ensure that changes in price have a chance to propagate throughout the network so that routes are not changed on the basis of out-of-date prices. An alternative, less pessimistic, scheme would be to choose the delay randomly from $[0, n]$ where n is proportional to the diameter of the network; this should decrease convergence times while still preventing synchronisation.

We remark here that several issues did become clear even with such a simple simulation. First, the number of BGP messages appears to increase when pricing is applied, as changes in load cause changes in prices which must be readvertised, potentially causing further changes in load. The magnitude of the increase in number of messages seems dependent on the topology and initial condition. With more realistic sizes of network and routeing tables this might become a problem and so deserves further investigation.

Second, correct choice of which routes to move to the cheaper AS can be difficult. If an AS advertises a reduction in its charge, the natural reaction is to cause as many routes as possible to use that AS as transit. However, doing so can increase the load on that AS to the extent that the price reduction is destroyed, and replaced by a price increase. This can cause the AS receiving the advert to now choose to move its routes back, resulting in needless route flap.

There are two straightforward responses to this problem of increased route flap. First, the assumption that each AS sources traffic from only one prefix means that BGP has no flexibility over how much traffic to shift: it must move all or nothing. In a real deployment, a single AS is unlikely to both source sufficient traffic and do so toward a single prefix to cause this effect – where such a situation occurs, dynamic SLAs can be considered inappropriate without application of other techniques such as prefix disaggregation. Second, route flap damping [16] can be used to rate limit adverts in such situations.

However, it is clear that further work must include more detailed investigation of stability properties, particularly using more complex topologies and realistic load distributions coupled with different load redistribution policies. Mechanisms for providing useful measures of network load that can deal with Internet phenomena such as flash-crowds also need investigation, as do ways to turn such measures into prices. In particular, appropriate ways to aggregate mark information from routers to calculate AS-wide prices has not been addressed. Finally, given the freedom such a system potentially gives to operators to measure load and calculate prices, the interactions between different such mechanisms is yet another area requiring investigation.

6   Conclusion

This paper presented an incentive-based approach to routeing using the Internet's inter-domain routeing protocol, BGP. It presented the design of a new path attribute for BGP that enables choice between routes to be made on a more rational and incentive-compatible basis than currently possible. It continued with discussion of a BGP simulator written to test the behaviour of the new path attribute and presented a result from this implementation. Although detailed evaluation is beyond the scope of this paper, the simulation served to illustrate the ideas outlined here, and the simulator may prove useful in the future. Even such a simple simulation provided some directions where further work is needed to make pricing for BGP in this way viable.

The other area for further investigation not touched upon in this paper concerns more operational details of BGP: the behaviour of iBGP with pricing, and algorithms for combining iBGP advertised prices to achieve a price for the AS should be studied. Implementing more complex dynamic policies involving 'quality' estimates of neighbouring ASs, interaction between ASs applying different policies, and interactions between static and dynamic policies should also all be studied further. More details may be found in [17].

References

1. Xipeng Xiao, A. Hannan, B. Bailey, and L.M. Ni, "Traffic engineering with MPLS in the Internet," *IEEE Network Magazine*, vol. 14, no. 2, pp. 28–33, March/April 2000.
2. Y. Rekhter and T. Li, "A Border Gateway Protocol 4 (BGP-4)," RFC 1771, IETF, Mar. 1995.

3. J.W. Stewart III, *BGP4 Inter-Domain Routing in the Internet,* Addison Wesley Longman, 1999.

4. R. Mahajan, D. Wetherall, and T. Anderson, "Understanding BGP misconfiguration," in *Proceedings of ACM SIGCOMM 2002,* Aug. 2002.

5. "OSI IS-IS Intra-domain Routing Protocol," RFC 1142, IETF, Feb. 1990.

6. R.W. Callon, "Use of OSI IS-IS for routing in TCP/IP and dual environments," RFC 1195, IETF, Dec. 1990.

7. J. Moy, "OSPF Version 2," RFC 2328, IETF, Apr. 1998.

8. B. Fortz and M. Thorup, "Internet traffic engineering by optimizing OSPF weights," in *Proceedings of IEEE Infocom 2000,* Tel Aviv, Israel, Mar. 2000.

9. C. Villamizar, "OSPF optimized multipath (OSPF-OMP)," in *Proceedings of the Forty-Fourth Internet Engineering Task Force.* IETF, Mar. 1999, available as Internet Draft `draft-ietf-ospf-omp-02`.

10. T. Griffin and G.T. Wilfong, "An analysis of BGP convergence properties," *Computer Communication Review (CCR),* vol. 29, no. 4, pp. 277–288, Oct. 1999, Proceedings of ACM SIGCOMM 1999.

11. C. Labovitz, A. Ahuja, A. Bose, and F. Jahanian, "Delayed internet routing convergence," *Computer Communication Review (CCR),* vol. 30, no. 4, pp. 175–187, Oct. 2000, Proceedings of ACM SIGCOMM 2000.

12. L. Gao, T. Griffin, and J. Rexford, "Inherently safe backup routing with BGP," in *Proceedings of IEEE Infocom 2001,* Anchorage, Alaska, Apr. 2001, pp. 547–556.

13. Keynote.com, "Keynote.com," `http://www.keynote.com/`, 2001.

14. Matrix.net, "Matrix.net," `http://www.matrix.net/`, 2001.

15. DML Networks, Inc., "The GNU Zebra Routeing Protocol Suite," `http://www.zebra.org/`, 2002.

16. C. Villamizar, R. Chandra, and R. Govindan, "BGP Route Flap Damping," RFC 2439, IETF, Nov. 1998.

17. Richard Mortier, "Internet traffic engineering," Tech. Rep. UCAM-CL-TR-532, University of Cambridge, Computer Laboratory, JJ Thomson Avenue, Cambridge CB3 0FD, United Kingdom, phone +44 1223 763500, Apr. 2002.

The Economics of Smart Routing and Quality of Service*

Rui Dai[1], Dale O. Stahl[2], and Andrew B. Whinston[3]

[1] Dupree College of Management, Georgia Institute of Technology,
Atlanta, GA 30332, USA
rui.dai@mgt.gatech.edu
[2] Department of Economics, The University of Texas at Austin,
Austin, TX 78712, USA
stahl@eco.utexas.edu
[3] Department of MSIS, The University of Texas at Austin,
Austin, TX 78712, USA
abw@uts.cc.utexas.edu

Abstract. This paper studies an emerging technology in network service market: smart routing technology. We focus on the economics issues related to the adoption of this new technology, such as contracting, bandwidth allocation and cost-benefit analysis. This study shows the advantage of deploying smart routers assuming efficient contract and usage, and quantifies the extra benefit they can generate. Interestingly, we find smart routing technology can also potentially help ISPs in todays sluggish service market: smart router users tend to contract more capacities and ISPs can raise their service prices without losing customers.

1 Introduction

Internet quality of service (QoS) has always been a major concern of business network service subscribers who use the Internet to communicate with internal branch offices, customers and suppliers. According to a 2001 survey of Fortune 1000 companies conducted by Morgan Stanley, 71% picked QoS as the No.1 criterion when they choose network service provider. However, theoretically network reliability and performance is impossible to be guaranteed by service provider given the current technology and structure of the Internet.

A possible way to solve QoS problem is to change Internet service framework on service providers' side. Two architectures have been proposed by computer scientists and engineers: Integrated Service (Intserv) [1] [3] and Differentiated Service (Diffserv) [2][4][5]. Theoretically, if all network service providers implement one of these frameworks, service quality can be guaranteed to a certain extend. But in a competitive market where different players have different budget constraints, serve different customer groups and face different costs, it is hard for service providers to coordinate on this move.

Compared with solutions on the providers' side, it is much easier to implement multi-homing solutions on the service subscribers' side to improve QoS. In order to avoid the problems that can occur within a particular ISP, network users are

---

* This research is supported by Intel Corp.

B. Stiller et al. (Eds.): NGC/ICQT 2003, LNCS 2816, pp. 318–331, 2003.

increasingly subscribing services from multiple service providers. The most widely used protocol to direct traffic at gateways between Intranets and ISPs is called Border Gateway Protocol (BGP) [6]. BGP can tell which ISPs' networks are reachable at a certain time and find the path with the least hops between the endpoints for each specific connection.

Nevertheless, the path found by BGP is not necessarily the fastest path for a session, since it cannot tell the congestion condition in networks and less hops may take longer to get through. To circumvent the limitation of BGP and help network users fully exploit the benefit from this multi-homing approach, smart routing technology has been proposed and increasingly deployed, especially by large companies who deliver content through the Internet, such as Microsoft, Sony and SAP, etc. Many suppliers are providing smart routing devices or services in today's market, including Internap, RouteScience, NetVmg, Equinix, etc[7]. Although the implementation details might be different among different suppliers, the basic idea of smart routing is the same: monitoring the performances of different ISPs in real time and determining the optimal path based on these probes. Figure 1 illustrates how smart routing works.

The most significant advantage of smart routing technology is its simple implementation. However, quite a few economics and management questions need to be answered to ensure efficient adoption of this technology. First of all, a service subscriber needs to decide how much capacity she should contract with different service providers given her demand. Then she has to decide the policy to allocate available bandwidth efficiently. For example, which traffic can use the faster network given limited capacity? Based on the optimal solutions of these two decision problems, the service subscriber can estimate the benefit of adopting smart routing technology

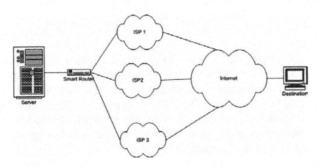

Fig. 1.

and decide whether to go or not to go. This paper uses a generic economic model to study previously addressed questions. We find deploying smart routing technology will always generate more benefits for service subscribers. The magnitude of the benefit depends on total demand and characteristics of the user's traffic (for example, whether it is delay sensitive). Our model also predicts that the adoption of smart routers will increase service providers' profits.

This research is closely related to the Internet pricing literature[8][9][10], which tries to employ different pricing mechanisms to allocate network resources efficiently. Most of the papers in this literature assume a network service provider has full control of the whole network (or a company has full control of its internal network) and network traffic will only pass through a single domain. In this paper, we stress the multi-domain feature of the Internet, and use shadow price to control traffic going through a gateway between company's internal network and the Internet.

2 Model Setup

For expositional convenience, we consider the case where there are two ISPs providing Internet service in a local service market. Each ISP's network has two states: H and D. The H state represents the normal state of an ISP's network and the D state is the down state. When the network is in state D, no traffic can be transmitted. We model network delay in an ISP's network as a random variable when the network is in state H. Let t_i denote network delay in ISP i's network domain and $f_i(t)$ denote the probability density function of t_i. We assume t_i (i=1,2) are independent[2] random variables with an upper limit of t_0. The BGP protocol can tell if an ISP's network is in state D or not. When one ISP's network is down, all the traffic will be routed to other networks. But it can not compare t_1 and t_2 when both networks are in state H. Instead, BGP protocol will choose the route with the shortest path. However, smart routers make routing decisions based on network delays.[3] When a network user has access to multiple ISPs' networks, the smart router at the gateway can help to decide which network will be used for each specific application. For example, the user might want to use a faster network to handle online transactions, and use a slower network to send emails. The smart router can use the collected information to make the right choices for the user. Let P_{iH} and P_{iD} denote the probabilities that an ISP i's network is in state H and D at any certain time, $P_{iH}+P_{iD}=1$. Usually, the network system uptime is much larger than the downtime, $P_{iH} >> P_{iD}$. The average network delay in ISP i's network domain is

$$\bar{t}_i = \int_0^{t_0} t f_i(t) dt,$$

when the network is in state H. In this paper, we focus on the symmetric case where

$$P_{1H}=P_{2H}=P_H, \ P_{1D}=P_{2D}=P_D, \ \bar{t}_1 = \bar{t}_2 = \bar{t} \ .$$

This assumption reflects the current status of the Internet service market to some extent: there is no way to guarantee QoS with best effort service framework and Internet traffic passes through different ISPs networks so that all ISPs are basically offering the same level of service.

Each ISP charges a price to service subscriber according to the capacity specified in the service contract[4]. The duration of the contract is fixed. In this paper we use linear pricing scheme for service contract. There is no further charge for

---

[2] Network delays might be correlated in real world. In order to enjoy the advantage of smart router, network subscribers should try to pick ISPs with distinct path and uncorrelated network delays.

[3] For simplicity, we assume the smart router can retrieve instant delay information from the networks.

[4] There are four major billing schemes are used in network service market: Tiered, Full pipe, 95percentile, and Burstable with minimum commitment. Our model is an approximation of the first two billing schemes.

network service, such as an installation fee or usage based prices. In the next section, we present the benchmark case where network users can only subscribe one ISP's service and show optimal contracting strategy of those end users. Then we study how network users should change their strategies when using BGP and smart routers at their gateway respectively in section 2.2 and 2.3. We also analyze the social impacts of these technologies.

Before the appearance of smart routers, since ISPs are providing homogenous services, they engage in Bertrand competition and set marginal price equal to marginal operating cost. However, when smart routing technology is available, network services from different ISPs are no longer perfect substitutes. Instead, they are complementary with each other to some extent. This will change the pricing strategy of ISPs. We also discuss how smart routing technology may change ISPs' pricing strategies in this paper.

2.1 Single ISP Model

We assume smart router and BGP are not available to network subscribers, so that they can only use one ISP's network service. The expected net benefit of submitting a data packet into the network for user i is

$$U_i(V, \delta | \, t_j \leq t_0) = V - \delta \bar{t} \,,$$

when the network is in state H. Here V is the user's total value of the packet, δ is the user's delay cost and $\bar{t}$ is the expected network delay. We assume that all packets generate the same load on network.[5] Following our previous assumption, when the network is in state D, network users will not receive any benefit from submitting a packet since for any positive V and δ, we have V- $\delta *$ ∞<0. Therefore, the user's utility is 0 when network is in state D.

Each network subscriber sends traffic from different applications through the Internet, such as telnet, ftp, online video or the World Wide Web, etc. Different applications may have different quality requirements. Moreover, these streams have different values and delay costs. For example, online stock transactions usually have higher values and delay costs, while online chatting, on the other hand, usually have lower values and delay costs. In order to capture this diversity in traffic from a single user, let $g_i(V, \delta)$ denote the probability density function for user i's V and δ. Here $g_i(V, \delta)$ represents density of traffic (packets) from user i with specific V and δ. It is on the packet level and the packets may come from different applications or different instances of the same application.

Since all the ISPs are offering identical service and price, network user can just randomly pick a service provider. The decision problem faced by a network user is two-fold.: First, how much capacity should be contracted with the ISP? Second, given the contracted capacity, how should the network resources be allocated among different applications?

In order to characterize network users' submission decisions, let $\pi_i(V, \delta)$ denote the probability that user i will submit a packet given certain V and δ, where $0 \leq \pi_i(V, \delta) \leq 1$. Then user i's decision problem can be described as

---

[5] It might be hard to tell the benefit and delay cost of a single packet. However, we can first estimate these values at application level and then map them to packet level by assuming that all the packets from one instance of the application have the same V and δ.

$$Max \quad EU_i(\pi_i(V,\delta)) = TP_{II}X_{i0}\iint(V-\delta\bar{t})\pi_i(V,\delta)g_i(V,\delta)dVd\delta - TcX_{i1}$$

$$s.t. \quad X_{i0}\iint\pi_i(V,\delta)g_i(V,\delta)dVd\delta \leq X_{i1}, \qquad (1)$$

where X_{i0} is the rate of total exogenous traffic from user i, X_{i1} is the contracted rate at which user i can send packets into ISP's network, T is the contract length, and cT is ISP's marginal operational cost of the network.[6] User i cannot send traffic into the network at a rate larger then the contracted rate. The user receives positive benefit from service when the network is in state H, and 0 benefit in state D.

Let L denote the Largrangian function of (1). For any V' and δ',

$$\frac{\partial L}{\partial \pi_i(V',\delta')} = TX_{i0}(P_H(V'-\delta'\bar{t}) - \lambda/T)g_i(V',\delta'), \qquad (2)$$

where λ is the Lagrangian multiplier. From the Kuhn-Tucker theorem, we know $\pi_i^*(V',\delta')$ solves (2), where

$$\pi_i^*(V',\delta') = \begin{cases} 1 & V'-\delta'\bar{t} > \lambda/TP_H \\ any\ value\ in\ [0,1] & V'-\delta'\bar{t} = \lambda/TP_H \\ 0 & V'-\delta'\bar{t} < \lambda/TP_H. \end{cases} \qquad (3)$$

Here, λ/TP_H is the threshold for submission decision. When the surplus of submitting a packet excesses the threshold, the packet should be submitted; if the surplus equals to the threshold, it doesn't matter whether it is submitted or not; otherwise, the user should choose not to submit the packet. We can then illustrate the optimal solution to the decision problem with figure 2.

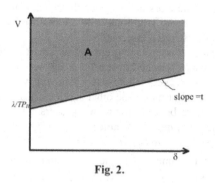

Fig. 2.

The shaded area A indicates where it is optimal to submit packets with probability one, while the blank area indicates the packets that should not be submitted.

---

[6] Here we assume ISPs only impose constraints on average packets arrival rate, and do not impose any constrains on the variance in arrival rates.

Also from the Kuhn-Tucker Theorem, we have

$$\frac{\partial L}{\partial X_{i1}} = \lambda - Tc = 0. \tag{4}$$

The shadow price for optimal capacity should be set equal to the marginal cost, which implies

$$X^{*}_{i1} = X_{i0} \int_{0}^{\infty} \int_{c/P_{H}+\delta}^{\infty} g_{i}(V,\delta) dV d\delta , \tag{5}$$

where X^{*}_{i1} is the optimal capacity. From (4), we can see that marginal unit cost c and network uptime P_{H} are crucial to users' contract decision. For any given c, if ISPs can lower the probability of network failure, users will subscribe more capacities. Lowering c can lead to the same result if we fix P_{H}.

2.2 Two ISPs with Smart Routers

When smart routing technology is available, network subscribers can sign multiple contracts with several ISPs and use the smart routers at the gateway to choose the optimal path for each network connection at any certain time. Originally, smart routers were designed and developed to find the fastest network route for those jobs that are critical to network users. How to define "critical" and how to decide the cutoffs are fundamental questions to be answered by network managers. Moreover, the slower networks should not be left unused. How to effectively utilize this capacity is also a challenging question. In this paper, we focus on using smart router as a device to differentiate traffic from a company's LAN, which in essence provides multiple service quality levels to the end users. The motivation is to extract more benefits from the information gathered by smart routers and to provide managerial insights for network managers on how to allocate the available network resources efficiently.

Since smart routing technology is quite new and not widely adopted, in this model, we keep the ISPs' network access price the same as in the previous model. We still focus on the user side and study how the adoption of smart routers will change contracting decisions of network subscribers.

Two new service classes can be created by smart routers when both networks are in state H. One of the service classes, e, is the service commonly delivered by smart routers in today's market, where users can always use the ISP with shorter network delay (at any certain time). The other service class, l, uses the slower network, which could generate extra benefits for network users. The network delays of these two new service classes are random variables:

$$t_{e} = \min(t_{1}, t_{2}), \quad t_{l} = \max(t_{1}, t_{2}).$$

The cumulative distribution functions of these two random variables are

$$F_{e}(x) = F_{1}(x) + F_{2}(x) - F_{1}(x)F_{2}(x), \; F_{l}(x) = F_{1}(x)F_{2}(x).$$

With simple calculations, we have

$$\bar{t} - \bar{t}_e = \int_0^{t_0} (F_e(t) - F_1(t)) dt = \int_0^{t_0} F_2(t)(1 - F_1(t)) dt > 0 \text{ and } \bar{t}_l - \bar{t} = \int_0^{t_0} F_2(t)(1 - F_1(t)) dt > 0.$$

$$(6)$$

The quality differences between ISPs' original service and these two new service classes are equal. If only one network is in state H, while the other network is in state D, then the smart router cannot provide service classes e or l.[7]

Next, we study service subscribers' optimal contracting problem. Assume the smart router distinguishes between two kinds of incoming traffic: high and low priority. When both ISP's are up, high priority traffic is always routed to the faster ISP, while low priority traffic is routed to the slower ISP. When only one ISP is up, traffic is routed to that ISP based on $\bar{t}$.

There are eight control variables for the user's submission decision: $\pi_{ik}^{j(H)}(V, \delta)$, the probability of submitting to ISP k when both are up and ISP $j(H)$ is the faster ISP; and $\pi_{ik}(V, \delta)$, the probability of submitting to ISP k when only k is up. Note that the ex ante probability that $j(H) = k$ is ½ for all k. Then, the user i's decision problem can be expressed as:

$$EU_i(\pi_i) = \{T(1 - P_D)^2 X_{i0} \iint (V - \delta \bar{t}_e)[\pi_{i1}^1(V, \delta) + \pi_{i2}^2(V, \delta)]g_i(V, \delta)dVd\delta +$$

$$T(1 - P_D)^2 X_{i0} \iint (V - \delta \bar{t}_l)[\pi_{i1}^2(V, \delta) + \pi_{i2}^1(V, \delta)]g_i(V, \delta)dVd\delta +$$

$$T(1 - P_D)P_D X_{i0} \iint (V - \delta \bar{t})[\pi_{i2}(V, \delta) + \pi_{i1}(V, \delta)]g_i(V, \delta)dVd\delta\}/2 \quad (7)$$

$$s.t. \quad X_{i0} \iint \pi_{ik}^{j(H)}(V, \delta)g_i(V, \delta)dVd\delta \le X_{ik} \text{ for all } k \text{ and } j(H),$$

$$X_{i0} \iint \pi_{ik}(V, \delta)g_i(V, \delta)dVd\delta \le X_{ik}, \quad \text{for all } k.$$

As with only one ISP, the submission decision can be represented by graphs like Figure 2 with vertical intercept λ / TP_H. The optimal control when only one ISP is up can be expressed in terms of this intercept.

$$\pi_{ik}(V, \delta) = 1 \text{ if and only if } (V - \delta \bar{t}) \ge \lambda / TP_H \text{ and only ISP } k \text{ is up.}$$

The Lagrangian λ is determined so the quantity constraint is satisfied. It is evident from Figure 2 that the flow of admissions will decrease as λ increases; therefore, λ is a decreasing function of capacity X_{ik}.

When both ISPs are up, the user can send some of her packets to each ISP, depending on how delay sensitive (δ) the packets are. In particular, low delay sensitive packets will be sent to the ISP in state L, while packets with high delay sensitivity will

---

[7] It is not difficult to tell $\bar{t}_l$ and $\bar{t}_e$ have smaller variances than $\bar{t}$, which implies smart router can provide more consistent performance to end user.

be sent to the ISP in state H. This allocation is determined by two costate variables μ_{iL} < μ_{iH} as illustrated in Figure 3.

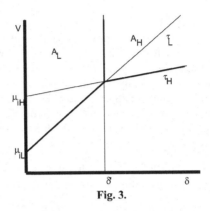

Fig. 3.

The cutoff value of delay sensitivity, δ', is equal to $(\mu_{iH} - \mu_{iL})/(t_L - t_H)$. Packets with less delay sensitivity are never sent to the ISP that is faster [denoted $j(H)$], and packets with greater delay sensitivity are never sent to the ISP that is slower [denoted $j(L)$]. The area A_L indicates values of (V, δ) for which it is optimal to submit packets to ISP $j(L)$, and area A_H indicates values of (V, δ) for which it is optimal to submit packets to ISP $j(H)$, while the blank area indicates values for which it is optimal not to submit the packets at all. Integrating the density $g_i(V, \delta)$ over A_L (A_H) and multiplying by X_{i0} gives the total flow of submissions which must not exceed the contract capacity $X_{ij(L)}$ ($X_{ij(H)}$). Let $\mu_{iH}(X_{ij(L)}, X_{ij(H)})$ and $\mu_{iL}(X_{ij(L)}, X_{ij(H)})$ denote the vertical intercepts in Figure 3 such that the total flow to the ISP $j(H)$ is exactly equal to $X_{ij(H)}$ and total flow to the ISP $j(L)$ does not exceed to $X_{ij(H)}$. These functions are jointly decreasing in the capacities. Unless $X_{ij(L)} = X_{ij(H)}$, the (μ_{iL}, μ_{iH}) intercepts will depend on which ISP is in which state. Let $(\mu_{iL}^{LH}, \mu_{iH}^{LH})$ denote the values for state LH, and let $(\mu_{iL}^{HL}, \mu_{iH}^{HL})$ denote the values for state HL.

Lemma 1. If $X_{i1} > X_{i2}$, then $(\mu_{iH}^{HL} - \mu_{iL}^{HL}) < (\mu_{iH}^{LH} - \mu_{iL}^{LH})$.

Proof:

$$X_{i1} = X_{i0} \int_0^{\delta'} \int_{\mu_{iL}^{LH} + \delta \, \bar{t}_l}^{\infty} g_i(V, \delta) dV d\delta = X_{i0} \int_{\delta''}^{\infty} \int_{\mu_{iH}^{HL} + \delta \, \bar{t}_e}^{\infty} g_i(V, \delta) dV d\delta \qquad \text{and}$$

$$X_{i2} = X_{i0} \int_0^{\delta''} \int_{\mu_{iL}^{HL} + \delta \, \bar{t}_l}^{\infty} g_i(V, \delta) dV d\delta = X_{i0} \int_{\delta'}^{\infty} \int_{\mu_{iH}^{LH} + \delta \, \bar{t}_e}^{\infty} g_i(V, \delta) dV d\delta$$

where $\delta' = (\mu_{iH}^{LH} - \mu_{iL}^{LH})/(t_L - t_H)$ and $\delta'' = (\mu_{iH}^{HL} - \mu_{iL}^{HL})/(t_L - t_H)$. Suppose that $X_{i1} > X_{i2}$ and that $(\mu_{iH}^{HL} - \mu_{iL}^{HL}) \geq (\mu_{iH}^{LH} - \mu_{iL}^{LH})$ which implies that $\delta'' \geq \delta'$. Comparing the first terms in each row above, we must have $(\mu_{iL}^{HL} > \mu_{iL}^{LH})$. Then using the supposition, we must have $(\mu_{iH}^{HL} > \mu_{iH}^{LH})$. But then comparing the second terms in each row, we would have $X_{i1} < X_{i2}$, a contradiction.   Q.E.D.

Proposition 1. In an optimal contract, a network user will subscribe the same capacityfrom each ISP, i.e. $X_{i1}^{SR*} = X_{i2}^{SR*}$.

Proof: The Kuhn-Tucker conditions for an interior optimum require that

$(1-P_D)^2[\mu_{iH}^{HL} + \mu_{iL}^{LH}] + (1-P_D)P_D[v_{iA}(X_{i1})] = 2c = (1-P_D)^2[\mu_{iH}^{LH} + \mu_{iL}^{HL})] + (1-P_D)P_D[v_{iA}(X_{i2})]$.

Where $v_{iA}(X_{ij}) = min\{ v \geq 0 \mid X_{i0} \int_0^\infty \int_{v+\delta i}^\infty g_i(V,\delta)dVd\delta \leq X_{i1}\}$. Subtracting,

$(1-P_D)^2[(\mu_{iH}^{HL} - \mu_{iL}^{HL}) - (\mu_{iH}^{LH} - \mu_{iL}^{LH})] + (1-P_D)P_D\{v_{iA}(X_{i1}) - v_{iA}(X_{i2})\} = 0$.

Suppose that $X_{i1} > X_{i2}$, implying that the term in $\{\}$ is negative, since the $v_{iA}()$ and $v_{iA}()$ functions are strictly decreasing. This implies that the first term in $[]$ is positive, contradicting Lemma 1. A similar contradiction arises supposing that $X_{i1} < X_{i2}$. Q.E.D.

We can now rewrite (7) by applying Proposition 1,

$$EU_i(\pi_{i1}(V,\delta),\pi_{i2}(V,\delta),\pi_{i3}(V,\delta),X_i^{SR}) =$$

$$TP_H^2 X_{i0} \iint (V-\delta \tilde{t}_e)\pi_{i1}(V,\delta)g_i(V,\delta)dVd\delta +$$

$$TP_H^2 X_{i0} \iint (V-\delta \tilde{t}_l)\pi_{i2}(V,\delta)g_i(V,\delta)dVd\delta +$$

$$2TP_H P_D X_{i0} \iint (V-\delta \tilde{t})\pi_{i3}(V,\delta)g_i(V,\delta)dVd - 2TcX_i^{SR}$$

$$s.t. \quad X_{i0} \iint \pi_{i1}(V,\delta)g_i(V,\delta)dVd\delta \leq X_i^{SR} \qquad (i)$$

$$X_{i0} \iint \pi_{i2}(V,\delta)g_i(V,\delta)dVd\delta \leq X_i^{SR} \qquad (ii)$$

$$X_{i0} \iint \pi_{i3}(V,\delta)g_i(V,\delta)dVd\delta \leq X_i^{SR} \qquad (iii)$$

$$\pi_{i1}(V,\delta) + \pi_{i2}(V,\delta) \leq 1 \qquad (iv)$$

(8)

Again, $\pi_{i1}(V,\delta)$ denotes the probability that user i will submit a packet of (V, δ) to the faster network and $\pi_{i2}(V,\delta)$ denotes the probability that user i will submit a packet of (V, δ) to the slower network when both networks are in state H. $\pi_{i3}(V,\delta)$ denotes the probability that user i will submit a packet of (V, δ) to the only network in state H. Let L denote the Lagrangian function of (8). The Kuhn-Tucker conditions are

$$\frac{\partial L}{\partial X_1^{SR}} = \lambda_1 + \lambda_2 + \lambda_3 - 2Tc = 0, \qquad (9)$$

where λ_i is the multiplier for constraint i in (8). Now we want to proof the network user i would increase her total network subscription comparing with the single ISP case.

At first, suppose $\dfrac{\lambda_3}{2TP_HP_D} \le \dfrac{c}{P_H}$, then

$$X_{i0}\int_0^\infty \int_{\frac{\lambda_3}{2TP_HP_D}+\delta i}^\infty g_i(V,\delta)dVd\delta \ge X_{i0}\int_0^\infty \int_{c/P_H+\delta i}^\infty g_i(V,\delta)dVd\delta .$$

Let $X_i^{SR}*$ denote the optimal contract in (8),

$$X_i^{SR}*= X_{i0}\int_0^\infty \int_{\frac{\lambda_3}{2TP_HP_D}+\delta i}^\infty g_i(V,\delta)dVd\delta . \tag{10}$$

From (5) and (10), we have

$$2X_i^{SR}*>X_i^{SR}*\ge X_{i1}*. \tag{11}$$

Otherwise, let's assume $\dfrac{\lambda_3}{2TP_HP_D} > \dfrac{c}{P_H}$. Since $P_H + P_D =1$,

$$\frac{2Tc-\lambda_3}{2TP_H^2} < \frac{c}{P_H} . \tag{12}$$

From (9), we know

$$\lambda_1 -(2Tc-\lambda_3)/2 = (2Tc-\lambda_3)/2-\lambda_2 = (\lambda_1 - \lambda_2)/2. \tag{13}$$

Using (6) and (13),

$$\delta_{12} = \frac{\lambda_1-\lambda_2}{TP_H^2(\bar t_l -\bar t_e)} = \frac{\lambda_1-(2Tc-\lambda_3)/2}{TP_H^2(\bar t-\bar t_e)} = \frac{(2Tc-\lambda_3)/2-\lambda_2}{TP_H^2(\bar t_l -\bar t)} . \tag{14}$$

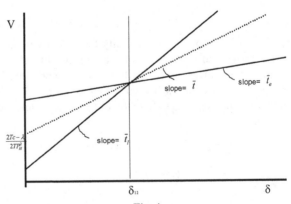

Fig. 4.

To explain (14), we show the partition of the jobs when both ISPs are in state H in figure 4. If we draw a line with slope of $\bar{t}$ and vertical intercept of $\dfrac{2Tc - \lambda_3}{2TP_H^2}$, it intersects with the two lines partitioning the jobs right at the intersection of those two lines. From (12), It is obvious

$$2X_i^{SR}* \geq X_{i0} \int_{0}^{\infty} \int_{\frac{2Tc-\lambda_3}{2TP_H^2}+\delta\bar{t}}^{\infty} g_i(V,\delta)dVd\delta \geq X_{i0} \int_{0}^{\infty} \int_{c/P_H+\delta\bar{t}}^{\infty} g_i(V,\delta)dVd\delta = X_{i1}* \qquad (15)$$

Combining (11) and (15) together, we can conclude $2X_i^{SR}* \geq X_{i1}*$. This gives us the following proposition:

Proposition 2. Suppose $(X_i^{SR}*, X_i^{SR}*)$ are the optimal contracts for user i, then $2X_i^{SR}* > X_{i1}*$.

Proposition 2 tells us that the employment of a smart router will increase the demand for network capacity. Since a lot of ISPs network capacities are left unused nowadays, the introduction of smart routing technology will be able to boost the utilization level of the network capacity.

Given Lemma 1 and Proposition 2, it is not difficult to deduce that using smart routers will improve overall social welfare of network service:

$$\sum_i (EU_i(X_i^{SR}*) + cX_i^{SR}*) - \sum_i (EU_i(X_{i1}*) + cX_{i1}*)$$

$$\geq \sum_i TP_H^2 X_{i0}(\iint (V-\delta\bar{t}_e)\pi_{i1}*(V,\delta)g_i(V,\delta)dVd\delta +$$

$$\iint (V-\delta\bar{t}_l)\pi_{i2}*(V,\delta)g_i(V,\delta)dVd\delta - \int_{0}^{\infty}\int_{c/P_H+\delta\bar{t}}^{\infty}(V-\delta\bar{t})g_i(V,\delta)dVd\delta) +$$

$$\sum_i TP_H P_D X_{i0}(2\iint (V-\delta\bar{t})\pi_{i3}*(V,\delta)g_i(V,\delta)dVd\delta - \int_{0}^{\infty}\int_{c/P_H+\delta\bar{t}}^{\infty}(V-\delta\bar{t})g_i(V,\delta)dVd\delta))$$

$$> 0.$$

Proposition 3. The adoption of smart routers will increase total welfare generated by network services.

Since we are assuming the price is equal to the marginal cost, network users extract all the extra surplus. This is unrealistic if smart routing technology prevails. We will show that the ISPs will try to improve their profits by changing their pricing strategy.

2.3 Multiple ISPs with BGP

Traditionally, network users who care about availability of Internet service can subscribe services from several ISPs and use BGP at their gateways to direct traffic. BGP can find a path with the fewest hops between two connection points. Therefore, when one ISP's network is down, BGP will not choose to submit traffic into that network. However, this protocol cannot tell traffic conditions in networks and a shorter path doesn't mean a faster one.

Again, we have to ISPs in the market. Let X_{ij}^{BGP} denote user i's contracted capacity with each ISP. Then user i's expected utility can be expressed as:

$$EU_i(X_{i1}^{BGP}, X_{i2}^{BGP}) = TP_H^2 X_{i0} \iint (V - \delta t\,)\pi_{i1}(V,\delta)g_i(V,\delta)dVd\delta$$

$$+ TP_H P_D X_{i0} \iint (V - \delta t)\pi_{i2}(V,\delta)g_i(V,\delta)dVd\delta$$

$$+ TP_H P_D X_{i0} \iint (V - \delta t)\pi_{i3}(V,\delta)g_i(V,\delta)dVd\delta$$

$$- Tc(X_{i1}^{BGP} + X_{i2}^{BGP}) \tag{16}$$

$$s.t. \qquad X_{i0} \iint \pi_{i1}(V,\delta)g_i(V,\delta)dVd\delta \le X_{i1}^{BGP} + X_{i2}^{BGP}$$

$$X_{i0} \iint \pi_{i2}(V,\delta)g_i(V,\delta)dVd\delta \le X_{i1}^{BGP}$$

$$X_{i0} \iint \pi_{i3}(V,\delta)g_i(V,\delta)dVd\delta \le X_{i2}^{BGP}$$

Here $\pi_{i1}(V,\delta)$ denotes the probability that user i will submit a packet of (V, δ) when both networks are in state H. $\pi_{i2}(V,\delta)$ and $\pi_{i3}(V,\delta)$ denote the probability that user i will submit a packet of (V, δ) to the network in state H when the other network is in state D.

Let L denote the Lagrangian function of (16). The Kuhn-Tucker conditions are:

$$\frac{\partial L}{\partial X_{i1}^{BGP}} = \lambda_1 + \lambda_2 - Tc = 0 \quad \text{and} \quad \frac{\partial L}{\partial X_{i2}^{BGP}} = \lambda_1 + \lambda_3 - Tc = 0.$$

We have $\lambda_2 = \lambda_3$, which implies the network user will subscribe the same amount of capacity from each ISP. This is similar to the result we get in the smart router case. Moreover, since $\lambda_1 < TcP_H$, the total capacity signed in two contracts will exceed the case when only single ISP is used. The following proposition states this result.

Proposition 4. Suppose $(X_{i1}^{BGP}*, X_{i2}^{BGP}*)$ are the optimal contracts for user i, then

$$X_{i1}^{BGP}* + X_{i2}^{BGP}* > X_{i1}*.$$

At this point, a network manager might ask whether she should switch from BGP to smart router: Will smart routing technology return more benefit to the organization than BGP? We can get the answer by comparing objective functions (8) and (16). Suppose the network user has the same network capacity for these two cases, she can derive the same amount of benefits when only one network is in state H. For the case when both networks are in state H, from previous discussion, it is always preferred to differentiate traffic. Since all extra surpluses are captured by network users, we can conclude with the following proposition.

Proposition 5. Assuming optimal contract and submission decision,

$$NW^{SR} > NW^{BGP} > NW^{S},$$

where NW^{SR}, NW^{BGP} and NW^{S} are the net surplus for smart router, BGP and single ISP respectively.

2.4 ISPs' Pricing Strategy

Without smart routers, ISPs engage in Bertrand competition and drive the profits to zero. However, smarter routing technology provides complementarities among services from different ISPs, which helps ISPs escape from the Bertrand paradox: An ISP will not lose all of her customer by charging a price higher than marginal cost. We can demonstrate this result with the following proposition:

Proposition 6. When smart routing technology is available to network users, pricing at marginal cost is no longer an equilibrium.

Proof: Let ISP 1 still charge price at marginal cost c, while ISP 2 charge price at $c+\varepsilon$, where $\varepsilon>0$. We assume network user i's optimal choice is to contract with ISP 1 only, the capacity will be X^*_{i1}. Let's consider another contract $(X^*_{i1}-\Delta, \Delta)$, where $X^*_{i1}-\Delta$ are Δ contracted capacity with ISP 1 and ISP 2 respectively. Since when both ISPs are in state H, we can use smart router to differentiate traffic and generate extra benefit, $b_i(X^*_{i1}-\Delta, \Delta) > 0$. When only ISP 1 is in state H, the total network service

value is $X_{i0}\int_{0}^{\infty}\int_{v_{iA}(X^*_{i1}-\Delta)+\delta\,\bar{t}}^{\infty}(V-\delta\,\bar{t})g_i(V,\delta)dVd\delta$. Similarly, when only ISP 2 is in state

H, the total network service value is $X_{i0}\int_{0}^{\infty}\int_{v_{iA}(\Delta)+\delta\,\bar{t}}^{\infty}(V-\delta\,\bar{t})g_i(V,\delta)dVd\delta$. Since $v_{iA}()$ is

decreasing, the total benefit of this contract is larger than contract $(X^*_{i1},0)$:

$$P_H P_D(X_{i0}\int_{0}^{\infty}\int_{v_{iA}(X^*_{i1}-\Delta)+\delta\,\bar{t}}^{\infty}(V-\delta\,\bar{t})g_i(V,\delta)dVd\delta + X_{i0}\int_{0}^{\infty}\int_{v_{iA}(\Delta)+\delta\,\bar{t}}^{\infty}(V-\delta\,\bar{t})g_i(V,\delta)dVd\delta X_{i0}$$

$$-X_{i0}\int_{0}^{\infty}\int_{v_{iA}(X^*_{i1})+\delta\,\bar{t}}^{\infty}(V-\delta\,\bar{t})g_i(V,\delta)dVd\delta) + P_H^2 b_i(X^*_{i1}-\Delta,\Delta) > 0$$

Notice the extra cost for this contract is $\varepsilon^* \Delta$. We can let $\varepsilon \to 0$ and lead to the contradiction. Therefore, ISP 2 can be better off by charging a slightly higher price than marginal cost.   Q.E.D.

3 Conclusion

The introduction of smart routing technology provides network subscribers a possible means to improve their Internet QoS. But it also complicates their contract decision problem and network resource allocation problem. The foregoing analysis characterizes the optimal service contract and the best network management practice for smarter router users. We have shown that smart routing technology can improve network user surplus comparing with the single ISP case and the BGP case. Furthermore, network users tend to subscribe more capacity, since the traffic condition information provided by smart routers can increase the marginal benefit of network service. This will improve network utilization level, which might have positive impacts on network service market where a lot of bandwidths are left unused nowadays. These results assume that the deployment of smart router just begin and network and ISPs still charge prices at marginal cost. In the last part of our analysis, we show with the diffusion of smart routing technology, ISPs can potentially charge higher prices since their services are no longer pure substitutes. However its impact on social welfare still needs further study.

References

[1] Braden, R., D. Clark and S. Shenker, "Integrated Services in the Internet Architecture: an overview," Internet Engineering Task Force, Request for Comments 1633, Jun. 1994

[2] Nichols, K, V. Jacobson, and L. Zhang, " A Two-bit Differentiated Services Architecture for the Internet," Internet Draft, Nov. 1997.

[3] Zhang, Lixia, Steve Deering, Deborah Estrin, Scott Shenker and Daniel Zappala,"RSVP: a new resource reservation protocol," in Proceedings of the International Networking Conference (INET), (San Francisco, California), pp. BCB-1, Aug. 1993.

[4] Heinanen, J., et al.,"Assured Forwarding PHB Group," Internet Draft, June 1999.

[5] Jacobson,V., et al., "An Expedited Forwarding PHB," Internet Draft, June 1999.

[6] Meyer, D. et al, "BGP-4 Protocol Analysis," Internet Draft, March 2003.

[7] http://www.internap.com/;
http://www.routescience.com/ ;
http://www.netvmg.com/ ;
http://www.equinix.com/.

[8] Mendelson, Haim and S.J. Whang, "Optimal Incentive-Compatible Priority Pricing for the M/M/1 Queue," Operations Research, Vol. 38 (1990), pp. 870-883.

[9] Masuda,Y. and S.J. Whang, " Dynamic Pricing for Network Service: Equilibrium and Stability, " Management Science, Vol. 45, 1999, 867-869.

[10] Gupta, A., Stahl, D. and Whinston, A., "A Stochastic Equilibrium Model of Internet Pricing," Journal of Economic Dynamics and Control, 21, 1997, pp. 697-722.

A Progressive Second Price Mechanism with a Sanction Bid from Excluded Players[*]

Patrick Maillé[1] and Bruno Tuffin[2]

[1] ENST Bretagne, 2 rue de la Châtaigneraie
CS 17607, 35512 Cesson Sévigné Cedex, France
pmaille@rennes.enst-bretagne.fr
[2] IRISA-INRIA, Campus universitaire de Beaulieu
35042 Rennes Cedex, France
btuffin@irisa.fr
http://www.irisa.fr/armor/lesmembres/Tuffin/Tuffin_en.htm

Abstract. In the large number of papers published on pricing schemes for telecommunication networks in the past few years, auctionning for bandwidth has been proved to be one of the main streams. We deal here with a method called *Progressive Second Price (PSP) Auction*, that we point out to have two drawbacks: first, the initial bidder has no interest in giving his true valuation of the bandwidth, and second, switching the order of bid between players can provide different Nash equilibria resulting in different seller revenues. We then design an adaptation of PSP allowing to solve these problems by asking to the players excluded from the game to submit a specific bid, which acts as a sanction on the other players.

1 Introduction

Designing charging schemes for telecommunication networks has become a challenging task in the networking community. Indeed, even if the capacity keeps increasing, it is commonly admitted that demand will still be ahead. Also, since different applications with different quality of service requirements are concerned, differentiating the services is becoming mandatory. For these reasons, switching from the usual flat-rate pricing, like in the current Internet, to a usage-based scheme seems relevant. Many different ways to charge for telecommunication services have been devised (see for instance [1] and the references therein). We focus here on the schemes where users compete for bandwidth by means of auctions, and more specifically on the Progressive Second Price (PSP) Auction [2,5,6,7] where the players (i.e., the users) sequentially bid for bandwidth until an equilibrium is reached.

In this paper, we show that the PSP presents two major drawbacks. First, we show that the first bidding player has an incentive to overestimate his bandwidth

---

[*] This work has been partially supported by the INRIA project PRIXNET (see http://www.irisa.fr/armor/Armor-Ext/RA/prixnet/ARC.htm)

B. Stiller et al. (Eds.): NGC/ICQT 2003, LNCS 2816, pp. 332–341, 2003.
© Springer-Verlag Berlin Heidelberg 2003

unit price, so that the following players will be detered from entering the game, giving him the maximum bandwidth at a minimum price. Second, we show that switching the order of the bids among players leads to different Nash equilibria, and then different revenues for the seller, which is an unpleasant (since unpredictable) behavior of the scheme. We have then designed an extension of the PSP mechanism that solves these problems. Basically, the players excluded from the game are asked to submit, at no cost, a specific bid that depends on their valuation of the bandwidth. We prove that both of the above problems are then solved. It requires a slight modification of the best-reply strategy that will be described.

The layout of the paper is the following. In Section 2 we present the PSP mechanism and its properties. Section 3 highlights some drawbacks of the scheme, that are solved in Section 4 by requiring that the players excluded from the game bid as we suggest. Finally, we conclude in Section 5.

2   The PSP Mechanism

The PSP mechanism has been first designed to allocate bandwidth among users for a single communication link [2], and was afterwards extended to a general network [6]. Because of lack of space, and for the sake of understanding, we limit ourselves here to the case of a single resource. Assume that its capacity is Q and that there are I players competing for it in an auction process, where players bid sequentially. Player i's bid is $s_i = (q_i, p_i)$ where q_i is the capacity player i is asking and p_i is the unit price he is proposing. The bid profile is $s = (s_1, \cdots, s_I)$. Let $s_{-i} = (s_1, \cdots, s_{i-1}, s_{i+1}, \cdots, s_I)$ be the profile where player i's bid is excluded from the game. We write s as $s = (s_i; s_{-i})$ in order to emphasize player i's bid. For $y \geq 0$ define

$$\underline{Q}_i(y; s_{-i}) = \left[Q - \sum_{k \neq i \ : p_k \geq y} q_k \right]^+.$$

The progressive second price allocation rule [2,5] gives to player i a bandwidth

$$a_i(s) = q_i \wedge \underline{Q}_i(p_i; s_{-i}), \tag{1}$$

(where $\wedge$ is for the minimum), and sets the total cost to

$$c_i(s) = \sum_{j \neq i} p_j [a_j(0; s_{-i}) - a_j(s_i; s_{-i})]. \tag{2}$$

Thus the highest bids are allocated the desired quantity and the cost is given by the declared willingness to pay (bids) of the users who are excluded by player i's presence. The allocation and pricing rules are illustrated in Figure 1. In [7], the allocation rule given by Equation (1) has been modified to make sure that the bandwidth is optimally allocated, as rule (1) punishes bids with the same price.

If we define

$$Q_i(y, s_{-i}) = \left[Q - \sum_{k \neq i \; :p_k > y} q_k \right]^+ \tag{3}$$

as the remaining bandwidth at a given unit price, we allocate

$$a_i(s) = q_i \wedge \frac{q_i}{\sum_{k \; :p_k=p_i} q_k} Q_i(p_i, s_{-i}) \tag{4}$$

to player i, with the total cost still computed by Equation (2).

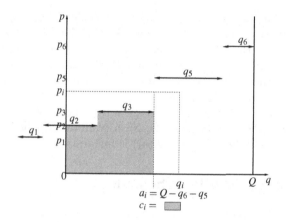

Fig. 1. Allocation and price to pay for player i

Assume that player i attemps to maximize his utility $u_i(s) = \theta_i(a_i(s)) - c_i(s)$ where θ_i is his valuation function, i.e. $\theta_i(q)$ is the total price that player i is willing to pay to obtain quantity q. Notice that Lazar and Semret also suggest that a budget constraint can be taken into account, but we omit it in this paper for sake of simplicity. We note $\mathcal{I}$ the set of players, and we use the following smoothness and concavity assumptions for functions $\theta_i, i \in \mathcal{I}$:

- $\theta_i(0) = 0$,
- θ_i is differentiable with $\theta_i'(0) < +\infty$,
- $\theta_i' \geq 0$, is non-increasing and continuous,
- $\exists \gamma_i > 0, \forall z \geq 0, \theta_i'(z) > 0 \Rightarrow \forall \eta < z, \theta_i'(z) < \theta_i'(\eta) - \gamma_i(z - \eta)$.
- $\exists \kappa > 0, \forall i \in \mathcal{I}, \forall z, z', z > z' \geq 0, \theta_i'(z) - \theta_i'(z') > -\kappa(z - z')$.

As a consequence, we have that

$$0 \leq a < b \text{ and } \theta_i'(b) > 0 \quad \Rightarrow \quad \gamma_i(b - a) \leq \theta_i'(a) - \theta_i'(b) < \kappa(b - a), \tag{5}$$

which will be used later on in the paper.

Also, a bid $s_0 = (Q, p_0)$ is introduced, meaning that the resource owner will not sell the bandwidth under a minimum unit price p_0, which is called the reserve price. The seller can thus be seen as a player (not in $\mathcal{I}$) with a valuation function $\theta_i(q) = p_0 q$.

The following results are then shown (see [2,5]):

- **(Incentive Compatibility).** Let

$$G_i(s_{-i}) = \{z : z \leq Q_i(\theta_i'(z), s_{-i})\} \qquad \text{and} \qquad x_i = \sup G_i(s_{-i}). \qquad (6)$$

Under the above assumptions on θ_i and $\forall 1 \leq i \leq I$, for all s_{-i} such that $Q_i(0, s_{-i}) = 0, \forall \varepsilon > 0$, there exists a truthful ε-best reply

$$t_i(s_{-i}) = (v_i = [x_i - \varepsilon/\theta_i'(0)]^+, \omega_i = \theta_i'(v_i)) \qquad (7)$$

where a truthful bid is a bid $s_i = (q_i, p_i)$ such that $p_i = \theta_i'(q_i)$.

- **(Convergence).** If all the players bid like described by Equation (7) while they can improve their utility by more than ε (it is assumed that there is a bid fee $\varepsilon > 0$ each time a player submits a bid), the game converges to a 2ε-Nash equilibrium, where an ε-Nash equilibrium is a bid profile s such that $\forall i \in \mathcal{I}, s_i \in \mathcal{S}_i^\varepsilon(s_{-i}) = \{s_i \in \mathcal{S}_i : u_i(s_i; s_{-i}) \geq u_i(s_i'; s_{-i}) - \varepsilon, \forall s_i' \in \mathcal{S}_i\}$ (with $\mathcal{S}_i = [0, Q] \times [0, +\infty))$, meaning that s is a fixed-point of $\mathcal{S}^\varepsilon = \prod_{i \in \mathcal{I}} \mathcal{S}_i^\varepsilon(s_{-i})$.

- **(Optimality).** For the previous 2ε-Nash equilibrium, the resulting overall utility (social welfare) $\sum_{i \in \mathcal{I} \cup \{0\}} \theta_i(a_i)$ is maximized.

3   Drawbacks of the PSP Scheme

Notice that the PSP mechanism is based on sequential bids (see [5], p36) and that it is assumed that there are never two players bidding at the same time, since each player must know the bid profile s_{-i} when submitting a new bid.

As previously said in the introduction, the first player has no incentive to bid his truthful best-reply. Indeed, denote by player 1 this initial player, and assume that he knows the maximal valuation $p_{max} = \max_{i \in \mathcal{I}} \theta_i'(0)$ and that $\theta_1'(Q) > p_0$. Then, if player 1 submits the bid $s_1 = (Q, p_{max})$, he will be allocated the total amout of bandwidth at unit price p_0. Consequently, the next players will be detered from entering the game (i.e., they will ask for 0 units of bandwidth) since whatever they would ask, their utility would be negative, i.e., $\forall i \geq 2$,

$$u_i = \theta_i(a_i) - a_i p_{max} \leq (\theta_i'(0) - p_{max}) a_i \leq 0.$$

We then actually obtain a Nash equilibrium that is undesirable, since the social welfare is not maximized: player 1 gets all the resource, and the resulting overall utility is $\theta_i(Q)$.

As a second undesirable effect, even when using the truthful best-reply as the initial bid, switching the order of bids among players may lead to different Nash equilibria, with different final seller revenues. Consider the following example to illustrate the problem, with $I = 2$ players, $\theta_1(x) = A \ln(1 + x)$ and $\theta_2(x) = \frac{A}{2} \ln(1 + x)$ for $A > 0$, and $Q = 1$. Table 1 displays the different outcomes depending on the bid order when $p_0 < A/4$, and where in the resulting 2ε-Nash equilibrium, the bid fee ε tends to 0 to simplify the formulas.

Table 1. Different outcomes depending on the bid order

	Player 1 bids first	Player 2 bids first
bid s_1	$(1, A/2)$	$(1, A/2)$
bid s_2	$(0, 0)$	$(1, A/4)$
Allocation a_1	1	1
Allocation a_2	0	0
Cost c_1	p_0	$A/4$
Cost c_2	0	0
Seller revenue	p_0	$A/4$

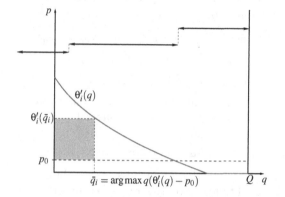

Fig. 2. Sanction bid made by an excluded player. Player i is excluded because his marginal valuation is below the lowest price that i should bid to obtain some resource. The area in grey corresponds to the cost (sanction) that player i can impose on others by bidding $(\bar{q}_i, \theta_i'(\bar{q}_i))$

4   A Sanction Bid from Excluded Players

We present here a way to tackle the problems highlighted in the previous section. The players that cannot get any bandwidth by submitting a truthful bid are required to submit a specific bid, at no cost, which will punish players who cheatingly take all the resource. As described in Figure 2, the idea is to find the quantity $\bar{q}_i$ that maximizes the quantity $q_i(\theta_i'(q_i) - p_0)$, and submit bid $(\bar{q}_i, \theta_i'(\bar{q}_i))$.

Remark 1. Since there is no bid fee for excluded players, they are indifferent about the bid they submit here. However, the fact that the bid we suggest prevents other players from cheating can incitate excluded players to effectively give that bid. Moreover, we can consider that excluded players want to be truthful in their sanction bid, because they can be allocated some resource if there are other players who leave the game.

4.1   Solving the Initial Bid Problem

Using this policy, the first player bid drawback is circumvented. Indeed, assuming that the first player has bet (Q, p_{max}), the second player is then excluded from the game, but submits $(\bar{q}_2, \theta'_2(\bar{q}_2))$, so that player 1 will pay $p_0 Q + \bar{q}_2(\theta'_2(\bar{q}_2) - p_0)$, and his utility becomes $\bar{u}_1 = \theta_1(Q) - [p_0 Q + \bar{q}_2(\theta'_2(\bar{q}_2) - p_0)]$, which is not always positive.

Even in terms of equilibrium, the cheating strategy can lead to a utility loss: consider a 2-player game where $\theta'_1(Q) < \theta'_2(0)$ and $\theta'_2(Q) < \theta'_1(0)$. It is proved in [3] that truthful strategies will lead to a 2ε-Nash equilibrium $s^* = (s_1^*, s_2^*)$ where, as $\varepsilon \to 0$, we have $q_1^* + q_2^* = Q$ and $\theta'_1(q_1^*) = \theta'_1(q_2^*)$. We use that result to compare the outcomes for both strategies from player 1's point of view:

$$
\begin{aligned}
u_1^* - \bar{u}_1 &= \theta_1(q_1^*) - p_0 q_1^* - \theta_1(Q) + p_0 Q + \bar{q}_2(\theta'_2(\bar{q}_2) - p_0) \\
&\geq -(\theta'_1(q_1^*) - p_0)(Q - q_1^*) + \bar{q}_2(\theta'_2(\bar{q}_2) - p_0) \quad \text{(concavity of } \theta_1) \\
&= \bar{q}_2(\theta'_2(\bar{q}_2) - p_0) - q_2^*(\theta'_2(q_2^*) - p_0) \geq 0. \quad \text{(definition of } \bar{q}_i)
\end{aligned}
$$

This proves that making a high bid is not a dominant strategy anymore, as in that case the truthful strategy is better for player 1.

4.2   Uniqueness of the Nash Equilibrium

In this subsection, we prove the uniqueness of the obtained Nash equilibrium, provided that the truthfull best-reply strategy is slightly modified as follows.

Proposition 1. *Under the smoothness and concavity assumptions over θ_i $\forall i \in \mathcal{I}, \forall s_{-i} \in S_{-i}$ such that $Q_i(0, s_{-i}) = 0$, $\forall \varepsilon > 0$, there exists a truthful ε-best reply $\tilde{t}_i(s_{-i})$ providing a larger utility than the one described in the Incentive Compatibility property of Section 2. If we note*

$$
\tilde{v}_i = \max \left\{ [x_i - \varepsilon / \theta'_i(0)]^+, \underline{Q}_i(\theta'_i(x_i), s_{-i}) \right\} \tag{8}
$$

where x_i is defined in Equation (6), then $\tilde{t}_i = (\tilde{v}_i, \theta'_i(\tilde{v}_i)) \in S_i^{\varepsilon}(s_{-i})$, and $\tilde{t}_i$ gives a larger utility than if submitting $t_i = (v_i, \theta'_i(v_i))$ like in the Incentive Compatibility property of Section 2.

Proof. A proof of Proposition 1 is given in the Appendix A.1. The possible situations are depicted in Figure 3, and the gray areas correspond to the difference $u_i(\tilde{v}_i, s_{-i}) - u_i(v_i, s_{-i})$.

Using the strategy defined above, we now focus on the uniqueness of the resulting Nash equilibrium. We first introduce the *demand function* of a user $i \in \mathcal{I}$ (see [3]):

Definition 1. *For every unit price $p > 0$, define*

$$
d_i(p) = \arg \max_q \{\theta_i(q) - pq\}. \tag{9}
$$

The application d_i is called the demand function of player i. $d_i(p)$ corresponds to the resource quantity that player i would want to buy in order to maximize his utility, if the unit price of the resource were fixed to p.

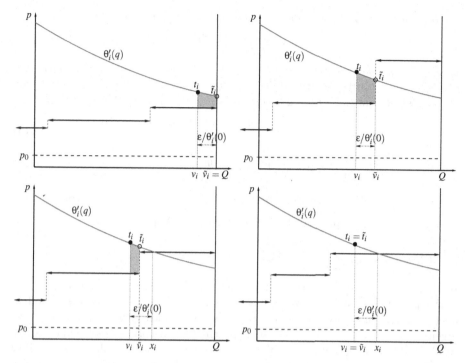

Fig. 3. The strategy $t_i = \left(v_i = [x_i - \varepsilon/\theta_i'(0)]^+ , \theta_i'(v_i) \right)$ *versus* the modified strategy $\tilde{t}_i = \left(\tilde{v}_i = \max [x_i - \varepsilon/\theta_i'(0)]^+ , \underline{Q}_i(\theta_i'(x_i), s_{-i}), \theta_i'(\tilde{v}_i) \right)$

We now define the *market clearing price* as the unique price such that

$$\sum_{i \in \mathcal{I}} d_i(u) = Q. \tag{10}$$

Define also $\mathcal{I}^+ = \{i \in \mathcal{I} | d_i(u) > 0\}$, as the subset of players requiring some bandwidth at this market clearing price. It can then be proved [3] that, for every truthful ε-Nash equilibrium, and for a sufficiently small ε,

$$\max_{i \in \mathcal{I}^+} |u - p_i| \leq C\sqrt{\varepsilon}, \qquad \text{with} \qquad C = 2\sqrt{2}\kappa \max_{i \in \mathcal{I}^+} \left\{ \frac{1}{\sqrt{\gamma_i}} \right\}. \tag{11}$$

We can state the result concerning the uniqueness of the equilibrium reached in the auction game:

Proposition 2. *Suppose that the smoothness and concavity assumptions over θ_i hold $\forall i \in \mathcal{I}$, and that:*

- *the players who can obtain some bandwidth follow the modified best-reply strategy (defined in Proposition 1) while it increases their utility by more than ε,*

- *the players i excluded from the game bid $s_i = (\bar{q}_i, \theta'_i(\bar{q}_i))$ with*

$$\bar{q}_i = \arg \max_{q \in [0,Q]} \left\{ q(\theta'_i(q) - p_0) \right\}, \tag{12}$$

then if the market clearing price u exists, is larger than p_0, and is such that $u > \sup_{i \in \mathcal{I} \setminus \mathcal{I}^+} \theta'_i(0)$, the bid-profile converges to a unique Nash 2ε-equilibrium s^* for ε small enough, where uniqueness is provided upto ε. More precisely:

$$\forall i \in \mathcal{I}^+ , \begin{cases} |u - p_i^*| \leq C\sqrt{2\varepsilon} \\ q_i^* = d_i(p_i^*) \end{cases} \tag{13}$$

$$\forall i \in \mathcal{I} \setminus \mathcal{I}^+ , \begin{cases} q_i^* = \bar{q}_i \\ p_i = \theta'_i(q_i^*) \end{cases} \tag{14}$$

where C is the constant in Equation (11), and $\bar{q}_i$ is defined by Equation (12).

Proof. We provide a proof of Proposition 2 in the Appendix A.2.

5   Conclusions

In this paper, we have illustrated two drawbacks of the PSP mechanism: the initial player has an incentive to cheat about his bandwidth valuation and to declare a high unit-price in order to get all the bandwidth at a minimal cost given by the reserve price. Also, changing the bidding order among players can result in different outcomes in terms of seller revenue, even if the overall utility is still maximized. By requiring that the excluded players submit a specific bid which acts as a sanction against liers, those two problems are proved to be solved.

As a direction for future research, we plan to look at the behavior of this mechanism in a stochastic environment where players enter or leave the game like we have done for the initial PSP mechanism in [4].

References

1. M. Falkner, M. Devetsikiotis, and I. Lambadaris. An Overview of Pricing Concepts for Broadband IP Networks. *IEEE Communications Surveys & Tutorials*, 3(2), 2000.
2. A. A. Lazar and N. Semret. Design and analysis of the progressive second price auction for network bandwidth sharing. *Telecommunications Systems - Special issue on Network Economics*, 1999.
3. P. Maillé. Market clearing price and equilibria of the progressive second price mechanism. Technical Report 1522, IRISA, Mar 2003.
4. P. Maillé and B. Tuffin. The progressive second price mechanism in a stochastic environment. to appear in *Netnomics*, 2003.
5. N. Semret. *Market Mechanisms for Network Resource Sharing*. PhD thesis, Columbia University, 1999.
6. N. Semret, R.R.-F. Liao, A.T. Campbell, and A.A. Lazar. Pricing, provisioning and peering: Dynamic markets for differentiated internet services and implications for network interconnections. *IEEE Journal on Selected Areas in Communications*, 18(12):2499–2513, 2000.
7. B. Tuffin. Revisited Progressive Second Price Auctions for Charging Telecomunication Networks. *Telecommunication Systems*, 20(3):255–263, 2002.

Appendix

A.1   Proof of Proposition 1

We first prove that $\tilde{v}_i \leq x_i$: if this were not the case, we would have $\tilde{v}_i = \underline{Q}_i(\theta_i'(x_i), s_{-i}) > x_i$. But the continuity of θ_i' and the left-continuity of $\underline{Q}_i(., s_{-i})$ would ensure the existence of a $z > x_i$ such that $z \leq \underline{Q}_i(\theta_i'(z), s_{-i}) \leq \overline{Q}_i(\theta_i'(x_i), s_{-i})$, which is in contradiction with the definition of x_i (Equation (6)). Thus

$$v_i \leq \tilde{v}_i \leq x_i \tag{15}$$

(the first inequality is a direct consequence of Equations (7) and (8)).
  Moreover, we have

$$\tilde{v}_i \leq \underline{Q}_i(\theta_i'(\tilde{v}_i), s_{-i}); \tag{16}$$

this can be seen as follows:

- if $[x_i - \varepsilon/\theta_i'(0)]^+ > \underline{Q}_i(\theta_i'(x_i), s_{-i})$, then necessarily $0 < \tilde{v}_i = [x_i - \varepsilon/\theta_i'(0)]^+ = x_i - \varepsilon/\theta_i'(0) < x_i = \sup G_i(s_{-i})$, and thus there exists a $r > 0$ such that $\tilde{v}_i + r \in G_i(s_{-i})$. We therefore have

$$\tilde{v}_i \leq \tilde{v}_i + r \leq Q_i(\theta_i'(\tilde{v}_i + r), s_{-i}) \leq \underline{Q}_i(\theta_i'(\tilde{v}_i), s_{-i}).$$

  The second inequality stems from the assumption that $\tilde{v}_i + r \in G_i(s_{-i})$, and the last one from the relation $Q_i(y, s_{-i}) = \lim_{z \searrow y} \underline{Q}_i(z, s_{-i})$, from the fact that θ_i' is strictly decreasing on $[\tilde{v}_i, \tilde{v}_i + r]$ (following the assumptions on the valuation functions), and from the property that $\underline{Q}_i(., s_{-i})$ is non-decreasing. Equation (16) is thus verified.
- if $[x_i - \varepsilon/\theta_i'(0)]^+ \leq \underline{Q}_i(\theta_i'(x_i), s_{-i})$, then $\tilde{v}_i = \underline{Q}_i(\theta_i'(x_i), s_{-i})$, and Equation (15) and the non-increasingness of $\underline{Q}_i(\theta_i'(.), s_{-i})$ imply Equation (16).

Now define as in [5]

$$P_i(z, s_{-i}) := \inf \{y \geq 0 : z \leq Q_i(y, s_{-i})\},$$

which implies that $c_i(s) = \int_0^{a_i(s)} P_i(z, s_{-i}) dz$ for all bid profile s, and that $\forall y, z$, $z \leq \underline{Q}_i(y, s_{-i}) \Rightarrow P_i(z, s_{-i}) \leq y$.
  Thus Equation (16) implies that $P_i(\tilde{v}_i) \leq \theta_i'(\tilde{v}_i)$, and also that $a_i(\tilde{t}_i, s_{-i}) = \tilde{v}_i$ (following the allocation rule (1)). Moreover $a_i(t_i, s_{-i}) = v_i$ since

$$v_i \leq \tilde{v}_i \leq \underline{Q}_i(\theta_i'(\tilde{v}_i), s_{-i}) \leq \underline{Q}_i(\theta_i'(v_i), s_{-i}).$$

Thus,

$$u_i(\tilde{t}_i, s_{-i}) - u_i(t_i, s_{-i}) = \theta_i(a_i(\tilde{t}_i, s_{-i})) - \theta_i(a_i(t_i, s_{-i})) - \int_{a_i(t_i, s_{-i})}^{a_i(\tilde{t}_i, s_{-i})} P_i(z, s_{-i}) dz$$

$$= \theta_i(\tilde{v}_i) - \theta_i(v_i) - \int_{v_i}^{\tilde{v}_i} P_i(z, s_{-i}) dz$$

$$\geq \theta_i'(\tilde{v}_i)(\tilde{v}_i - v_i) - \int_{v_i}^{\tilde{v}_i} \theta_i'(\tilde{v}_i) dz \geq 0$$

from which the proposition is obtained (we have used the concavity of function θ_i, and the property that function $P_i(., s_{-i})$ is non-decreasing): bidding $\tilde{t}_i = (\tilde{v}_i, \theta_i'(\tilde{v}_i))$ gives player i a larger utility than bidding t_i. As $t_i \in \mathcal{S}_i^\varepsilon(s_{-i})$, we also have $\tilde{t}_i \in \mathcal{S}_i^\varepsilon(s_{-i})$.

A.2   Proof of Proposition 2

We first show a lemma about the modified strategy:

Lemma 1. *Assume that the smoothness and concavity assumptions over θ_i hold $\forall i \in \mathcal{I}$, and that $p_0 > 0$. If a player $i \in \mathcal{I}$ follows the modified best-reply strategy, and bids $(\tilde{v}_i, \theta_i'(\tilde{v}_i))$ (following Proposition 1), we have thereafter*

$$Q - \sum_{p_k \geq \theta_i'(\tilde{v}_i) - \varepsilon\kappa/\theta_i'(0)} q_k \leq 0.$$

This implies that a player j entering the game (or who had bidden (p_j, q_j) before with $p_j < \theta_i'(\tilde{v}_i) - \varepsilon\kappa/\theta_i'(0)$) can not obtain some resource if he bids at a too low price (below $\theta_i'(\tilde{v}_i) - \varepsilon\kappa/\theta_i'(0)$), since

$$\underline{Q}_j(\theta_i'(\tilde{v}_i) - \varepsilon\kappa/\theta_i'(0), s_{-j}) = 0, \tag{17}$$

Proof. Equation (8)) implies that $\tilde{v}_i \geq [x_i - \varepsilon/\theta_i'(0)]^+$, which gives $0 \leq x_i - \tilde{v}_i \leq \varepsilon/\theta_i'(0)$, as we saw that $\tilde{v}_i \leq x_i$ (Equation (15)). Relation (5) then leads to

$$\theta_i'(x_i) \geq \theta_i'(\tilde{v}_i) - \kappa\varepsilon/\theta_i'(0). \tag{18}$$

Equation (8) also implies

$$\tilde{v}_i \geq \underline{Q}(\theta_i'(x_i), s_{-i}). \tag{19}$$

Since $\underline{Q}_i(., s_{-i})$ is non-decreasing, Equations (18) and (19) prove that

$$\tilde{v}_i \geq \underline{Q}(\theta_i'(\tilde{v}_i) - \kappa\varepsilon/\theta_i'(0), s_{-i}) \geq Q - \sum_{k \neq i: p_k \geq \theta_i'(\tilde{v}_i) - \varepsilon\kappa/\theta_i'(0)} q_k,$$

which gives the result (as $q_i = \tilde{v}_i$).

Proof of Proposition 2: First, it can be shown that the algorithm converges (in $O(\sum_{i \in \mathcal{I}} \theta_i(Q)/\varepsilon)$): the proof strictly follows the one given in Proposition 4 of [5] for the initial best-reply strategy. The obtained convergence point is then a 2ε-Nash equilibrium. We can thus apply Relation (11), leading to Equation (13).

We choose ε small enough to make sure that there exists r such that $u - C\sqrt{2\varepsilon} > r > \sup_{i \in \mathcal{I} \setminus \mathcal{I}^+} \theta_i'(0) + \varepsilon\kappa \sup_{i \in \mathcal{I}^+}\{1/\theta_i'(0)\}$. This means that each player of $\mathcal{I}^+$ has bet a unit price strictly greater than r. Lemma 1 shows that for each player j in $\mathcal{I} \setminus \mathcal{I}^+$, we have $\underline{Q}_j(\theta_j'(0), s_{-j}) = 0$, which is equivalent to saying that the players of $\mathcal{I} \setminus \mathcal{I}^+$ are excluded from the game at equilibrium. Equation (14) is then verified.

Capacitated Network Revenue Management through Shadow Pricing

Mustapha Bouhtou[1], Madiagne Diallo[2], and Laura Wynter[3]

[1] France Télécom R&D, DAC/OAT,39-40, rue du Général Leclerc, 92131,
Issy-Les-Moulineaux, France, Mustapha.Bouhtou@rd.francetelecom.com
[2] Laboratoire PRiSM, Université de Versailles, 45 Av. des Etats-Unis, 78035
Versailles-Cedex, France, Madiagne.Diallo@prism.uvsq.fr
[3] IBM Watson Research Center P.O. Box 704, Yorktown Heights, NY 10598, USA,
lwynter@us.ibm.com

Abstract. In this paper, we analyze a method that links Lagrange multipliers from a resource allocation problem to the problem of revenue or profit maximization. This technique, first proposed in the transportation science literature by [7] has important implications for telecommunication network pricing. Indeed, the framework provides a generalization of telecommunication resource allocation/shadow price-based schemes such as those of [6] and [9], in that it permits the optimization of the shadow prices themselves, through a computationally simple procedure. We analyze the extent to which revenue can be maximized on a network that uses shadow-price-based prices, and how to deal with cases of unbounded multipliers.

Keywords: Internet Pricing, Network Equilibrium, Revenue Maximization, Proportional Fairness, Bilevel Program, congestion control.

1 Introduction

Traditionally, models of telecom pricing set prices independently of consumer behavior [3], [4]. A number of recent methods, however, take into account the user by considering his or her willingness to pay, or some QoS requirements, through either a non-linear utility function [6], a system of price-equations [2], [5] or a pre-defined maximum budget [10].

Models that take into account user behavior, in particular, [6], and [9], through the incorporation of user utility functions, often define link prices as Lagrange multipliers. While the existence of the prices is thus guaranteed under the hypotheses of the models, *the uniqueness is not guaranteed*, and in fact, is usually not satisfied, as we shall see in this paper. Furthermore, defining link prices in terms of Lagrange multipliers has one very important consequence. Namely, the price on a link is zero until that link is congested. This property may seem at odds with a provider's goal of revenue maximization; indeed, it was derived rather from the concept of fairness, especially proportional fairness

B. Stiller et al. (Eds.): NGC/ICQT 2003, LNCS 2816, pp. 342–351, 2003.
© Springer-Verlag Berlin Heidelberg 2003

allocation [6]. We shall show in this paper that the two notions, that of a fair allocation and of revenue maximization, are not necessarily incompatible.

In the next section, we recall the frameworks of Proportional Fairness [6] Resource Allocation and Pricing, and Toll Optimization [7]. In Section 3, we provide the numerical study and analysis. Section 4 concludes the paper.

2   Fair Resource Allocation and Revenue Optimization Models

In some cases, we would like for the prices not to be tied to Lagrange multipliers, but rather to be freely optimized so as to obtain the highest possible revenue. This implies the resolution of two models, which are linked by their common variables: on the one hand, the network operator problem includes prices and total resources allocation, and on the other hand, the users' model determines the level of usage taking into account the different links prices with respect to resources availability.

Mathematically, this combination of two linked models is formalized as a bi-level, or hierarchical, program. It allows the operator to set network prices and service levels which take into account their effect on the user response. The resulting problem is a highly complex non-convex optimization problem, for which real-time solutions cannot be expected, despite recent advances on computational methods.

In other cases, however, it is desirable for link prices to be defined by Lagrangian multipliers. Proportional Fairness Resource Allocation and Pricing [6], advocates this point of view. In particular, a proportionally fair resource allocation h^* is one that satisfies for all users, $r \in R$, with a willingness to pay w_r, the inequality

$$\sum_{r \in R} w_r \frac{(h_r{}^* - h_r)}{h_r{}^*} \geq 0 \tag{1}$$

for all feasible allocations h_r. This inequality amounts to the optimality condition of the following optimization program:

$$\max \sum_{r \in R} w_r \log h_r \tag{2}$$

such that h_r is feasible with respect to user demand, the capacity constraints on the network links are satisfied, and flows are non-negative. Kelly and colleagues then interpreted the Lagrangian multipliers on the link capacity constraints as the added costs that would drive the allocation to proportional fairness, without imposing them explicitly.

Our approach generalizes the method of pricing suggested by the Proportional Fairness model. The model combines two problems. When the framework of Larsson and Patriksson [7] is applied to our setting, one must first solve optimally a non-linear resource allocation problem (such as the Proportional Fairness allocation model). Then, one uses the optimal solution and the Lagrange multipliers of this first problem to maximize the operator's revenue function over a restricted set of prices.

Let $G(N, A)$ denote a strongly connected network, where N is the set of nodes and A the set of links. Each link a has associated with it a capacity $u_a \in R_+ \cup \{\infty\}$, $a \in A$. For certain ordered pairs of nodes, $s = (o, q) \in S \subset N \times N$, there is a demand for communication from o to q, known as d_s. The flow associated with the set of all such demands over the network can be expressed as a flow on each link a, or on each origin-to-destination route. We shall assume here that several routes serve the same origin-to-destination pair. The set of all routes on the network will be referred to as R. This may represent the case of several physical routes that a request may take, or the presence of more than one network operator serving that pair.

Indicator matrices can be used to convert from the flow on links to flow on routes. Let Δ be the link-route indicator matrix, where $\Delta_{ar} = 1$ if link a is present along on route $r \in R$, and 0 otherwise. Let Γ be the od-route indicator matrix, where $\Gamma_{rs} = 1$ if route r serves the od-pair $s \in S$, and 0 otherwise.

Here, we shall suppose in the remainder of this paper that the users on each od pair are homogeneous in their quality of service (QoS) requirements. Adding user differentiation and/or multiple QoS classes within each od-pair is straightforward, but complicates the notation.

The method of [7] works as follows. Consider a canonical network optimization problem with capacity constraints:

$$\min f(x) \tag{3}$$

subject to

$$\Gamma y = d \tag{4}$$
$$\Delta y \leq u \tag{5}$$
$$d, y \geq 0, \tag{6}$$

where the flow on a link, a, is $x_a = \sum_{r \in R} y_r \Delta_{ar}$. Then, the system based on the Karush-Kuhn-Tucker (KKT) optimality conditions for the problem (3)–(6) as expressed in [7] is given below:

$$T(\lambda, \pi) = \begin{cases} \Delta^T [\nabla f(x^*) + \lambda] - \Gamma \pi \geq 0, \\ [\nabla f(x^*) + \lambda]^T x^* - d^T \pi = 0, \\ \lambda^T (x^* - u) = 0, \\ \lambda \geq 0 \end{cases} \tag{7}$$

where π is the Lagrange multiplier vector for constraints (4). Line 2 of Equation set (7) can be obtained by writing the following linear programming formulation of (3)–(6), solving for x^*:

$$\min_x \nabla f(x^*)^T x \tag{8}$$

subject to constraints (4)–(6). The function $\nabla f(x^*)$ is the value of the gradient of the function f *evaluated at the optimal solution value*, x^*. While this model is clearly not solvable in practice, since the function value $f(x^*)$ at x^* is not known, it permits writing a linear programming dual to the original nonlinear problem (3)–(6). Taking the Lagrangian relaxation of the capacity constraints (5) and adding that into the linear programming objective function (8), we obtain

$$
\begin{aligned}
\min_x \; & \nabla f(x^*)^T x + \lambda^T(x - u) = \\
\min_x \; & \nabla f(x^*)^T x + \lambda^T x.
\end{aligned}
\tag{9}
$$

Then, the linear programming dual of (9) with constraints (4) and (6) is:

$$
\max_\pi \; d^T \pi
\tag{10}
$$

subject to

$$
\Gamma^T \pi \le \Delta^T [\nabla f(x^*) + \lambda].
\tag{11}
$$

Strong (linear programming) duality gives the term analogous to that of Line 2 of Equation set (7), that is:

$$
[\nabla f(x^*) + \lambda]^T x^* - d^T \pi = 0.
\tag{12}
$$

For a fixed, optimal, value of x^*, the System (7) describes a polyhedron in λ and π. Furthermore, it can be observed that the multiplier vector λ will not necessarily be unique in network flow problems.

Indeed, the requirement of linear independence of binding constraint gradients is not always satisfied in networks, as the constraint gradients take the form of indicator matrices for the graph, which are not constructed so as to have linear independent rows. When these multipliers are not unique, then, the authors in [7] proposed optimizing a secondary objective over the set of those multiplier values. That is, given the System (7), they posed the following secondary optimization problem:

$$
\max_{\lambda \in T \cap P} \; \phi(\lambda),
\tag{13}
$$

where in our setting T is the set of link prices, λ, given by the System (7), P the set of the manager's possible price decisions and $\phi : \Re^{|A|} \mapsto \Re$ is coercive, and preferably convex. Since the feasible set is polyhedral, when P is bounded, this secondary, or network manager's optimization problem is easy to solve using standard linear or nonlinear programming algorithms (depending on whether ϕ is a linear or nonlinear function of λ).

The network manager's objective can take various forms. Larsson and Patriksson [7], in the context of transport planning, discussed at length the network objective of trying to achieve a particular flow of (transport users) by adding prices judiciously; this includes trying to adjust link flows from their user-equilibrium values to a system optimum (using marginal cost pricing) or to some other flow (which then changes the prices that are produced by the model), or even prices to be positive or negative, in which case, travel subsidies are considered (negative prices).

The interest in the model stems from the possibility to optimize network revenue through prices, and to do so using a restricted, and therefore simpler, model than the general bi-level program. Furthermore, the model has the advantage of possessing a unique solution, under very mild and natural conditions.

In [7], it was claimed that the maximization of operator revenue in the model they propose, will very often be unbounded, leading to infinitely large prices; in other words, they claim that the revenue maximization problem is usually ill-defined for this model. *This outcome is not, however, valid when the network is constructed so as to always contain a non-priced path, for each user, that is, linking every origin-to-destination pair. In the case of Internet networks, this assumption will always be verified, as explained further below. When the network is constructed as such, link prices cannot be made arbitrarily large as long as the free path has sufficient capacity.* A non-trivial solution (that is, non-zero revenue) arises when the free paths offer lower quality of service than the paths priced by the network operator.

However, in order to be of use in practice, it is necessary to explore the extent to which one can optimize revenue over the polyhedral set of prices, in System (7).

3   Numerical Experience

The purpose of the tests presented in this section was to evaluate the extent to which link prices that are tied to Lagrange multipliers can be optimized toward revenue maximization. We were therefore interested in evaluating whether the non-uniqueness of the prices that is theoretically possible in the context of the network flow problem arises in practice, and whether it can be optimized sufficiently to allow for revenue maximization. More such instances, for different networks and price structures, can be found in the longer paper [1].

To that end, by solving the fair network resource allocation problem via an augmented Lagrangian algorithm, relaxing the link capacity constraints, an optimal "fair" link flow, x^* is obtained, along with an initial multiplier, or price, vector λ. With this optimal flow x^* to the (for example, proportional) fairness problem in hand along with λ, it is possible to explore the polyhedron of feasible $\lambda(x^*)$, and, in principle, optimize over that set. We are thus interested in to what extent, *in practice* this secondary, revenue maximizing optimization is feasible.

The results that follow were all obtained using the Network Equilibrium Toolbox, *CiudadSim* found at

http://www-rocq.inria.fr/scilab/CiudadSim

in Scilab [8] to solve the fair resource allocation problems and the linear programming solver of Scilab to solve the linear revenue maximization problems in λ.

The networks were constructed to represent several possible choices for the user. For each user, characterized by an origin-to-destination pair, there is always a "best effort" choice, that is, a path with generally higher delay (low QoS) but very high capacity relative to demand levels and consequently not subject to pricing by the network operator. The term "best effort" comes from the current allocation strategy of the Internet: usage is free but no quality guarantees are provided; this service is known as "best effort" service since capacity is allocated to a user "as best as possible".

In addition, to the best effort path available to each user, there is at least one path, offering service with higher QoS, meaning here lower delay; consequently capacity on those links is lower. The delay functions we chose were quadratic. In our setting we are interested in a particular form of (13). In particular the revenue maximization problem

$$\max_{\lambda \in T \cap P} \phi(\lambda) = (x^*)^T \lambda. \tag{14}$$

Note that, through the set P, this may represent a joint maximization of all providers revenues, or the maximization over a subset of link prices, corresponding to one of several possible providers on the network.

3.1   Network Instances with Non-unique, but Finite Link Prices

The present example makes use of the network of Figure 1, and delay data from Table 1. Here, there are two users represented on this network. The first requires 2.5 units from node 1 to 5; the second requires 3 units from node 2 to 6. As before at least one path with high QoS exists for each user as well as a "best effort" choice for each.

Table 1. Network Data for Figure 1

Link #	1	2	3	4	5	6	7	8	9
Link Definition	(1,2)	(1,4)	(2,4)	(2,3)	(2,5)	(3,4)	(3,6)	(4,6)	(6,5)
Link Capacity	100	1.5	100	1.8	1	0.3	1.5	100	100
Link Delay	$5+4x_1$	$9x_2$	$7+9x_3$	$9x_4$	$4x_5$	$1x_6$	$6x_7$	$4+5x_8$	$6+2x_9$
Fair Link Flow x^*	1	1.5	1.2	1.8	1	0.3	1.5	3	1.5
Initial Link Price λ	0	0	0	1.3	28.5	0	10.3	0	0

Using the augmented Lagrangian method, we obtained the fair resource allocation illustrated on the network of Figure 1 and in Table 1. As in Section ??, this method provides along with the solution a feasible vector of prices, denoted Initial Prices, λ. The initial revenue with respect to the fair link flow and the Initial prices, λ is

$$\textbf{Initial Revenue} = (\mathbf{x}^*)^T \lambda = \textbf{46.3}.$$

With the fair link flow x^* of Table 1 at hand, we write explicitly the set of fair link prices, $T(\lambda, \pi)$, for the present example as follows:

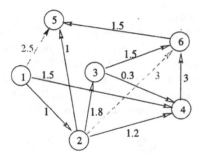

Fig. 1. Network with Fair Flows

$$T(\lambda, \pi) =$$

$$
\left\{
\begin{array}{l}
\lambda_1 \qquad\qquad +\lambda_5 \qquad\qquad\qquad\qquad\qquad -\pi_{15} \qquad\quad \geq\ -13 \\
\lambda_1 \qquad +\lambda_4 \qquad\quad +\lambda_7 \qquad +\lambda_9\ -\pi_{15} \qquad\quad \geq\ -43.2 \\
\lambda_1 \quad +\lambda_3 \qquad\qquad\qquad\qquad +\lambda_8\ +\lambda_9\ -\pi_{15} \qquad\quad \geq\ -54.8 \\
\lambda_1 \qquad +\lambda_4 \qquad +\lambda_6 \qquad +\lambda_8\ +\lambda_9\ -\pi_{15} \qquad\quad \geq\ -53.5 \\
\quad +\lambda_2 \qquad\qquad\qquad\qquad\qquad +\lambda_8\ +\lambda_9\ -\pi_{15} \qquad\quad \geq\ -41.5 \\
\quad +\lambda_3 \qquad\qquad\qquad\qquad +\lambda_8 \qquad\qquad -\pi_{26} \ \geq\ -36.8 \\
\qquad +\lambda_4 \qquad\qquad\qquad\qquad\qquad\qquad\qquad -\pi_{26} \ \geq\ -25.2 \\
\qquad +\lambda_4 \qquad +\lambda_6 \ +\lambda_7\ +\lambda_8 \qquad\qquad -\pi_{26} \ \geq\ -35.5 \\
\lambda_1\ +1.5\lambda_2\ +1.2\lambda_3\ +1.8\lambda_4\ +1\lambda_5\ +0.3\lambda_6\ +1.5\lambda_7\ +3\lambda_8\ +1.5\lambda_9\ -2.5\pi_{15}\ -3\pi_{26}\ =\ -167.86 \\
-99\lambda_1 \qquad\quad -98.5\lambda_3 \qquad\qquad\qquad\qquad\qquad -97\lambda_8\ -98.5\lambda_9 \qquad\qquad =\ 0 \\
\lambda_1,\qquad \lambda_2,\qquad \lambda_3,\qquad \lambda_4,\qquad \lambda_5,\qquad \lambda_6,\qquad \lambda_7,\qquad \lambda_8,\qquad \lambda_9, \qquad\qquad\quad \geq\ 0
\end{array}
\right.
$$

When the multipliers are not unique, the polyhedron of prices T need not be a singleton, and we may be able to maximize the network manager's revenue further than that which was obtained from the initial Lagrange multipliers λ.

Again, we examine the KKT necessary conditions, denoting by I the set of the active and the equality constraints gradients. It is easy to verify that the capacity constraints relative to arcs 2, 4, 5, 6, and 7 are active since those arcs are saturated. Using the arc-route and od-route matrices, respectively Δ and Γ, we construct the set I. We use:

$$
\Delta = \begin{vmatrix}
1 1 1 1 0 0 0 0 \\
0 0 0 0 1 0 0 0 \\
0 0 1 0 0 1 0 0 \\
0 1 0 1 0 0 1 1 \\
1 0 0 0 0 0 0 0 \\
0 0 0 1 0 0 0 1 \\
0 1 0 0 0 0 1 0 \\
0 0 1 1 1 1 0 1 \\
0 1 1 1 1 0 0 0
\end{vmatrix}
\qquad
\Gamma = \begin{vmatrix}
1 1 1 1 1 0 0 0 \\
0 0 0 0 0 1 1 1
\end{vmatrix}
\qquad
I = \begin{vmatrix}
0 0 0 0 1 0 0 0 \\
0 1 0 1 0 0 1 1 \\
1 0 0 0 0 0 0 0 \\
0 0 0 1 0 0 0 1 \\
0 1 0 0 0 0 1 0 \\
1 1 1 1 1 0 0 0 \\
0 0 0 0 0 1 1 1
\end{vmatrix}
$$

We compute the rank of I, which is $6 < 7$; indeed, summing rows 4 and 5 in I gives row 2. Thus, the Lagrange multipliers need not be unique and an optimization over the set of prices could be effectively performed.

In this case, we are interested in *the extent to which revenue can be maximized by performing the secondary optimization (14) over the set of prices, T*. In order to do so, we evaluate the size of the polyhedron of feasible prices, T, solving the following pair of optimization problems

$$\max_{\lambda \in T} <e^i, \lambda>, \qquad \min_{\lambda \in T} <e^i, \lambda>, \tag{15}$$

We denote e^i the ith coordinate vector, i.e, $i = 1, \ldots, 11$, where the 11 variables are the 9 price multipliers, 1 for each arc, and the two demand constraints multipliers, π_{15} and π_{26}. All of the solutions to the above problems were finite; the set T is therefore bounded in all coordinate directions.

The next step is then to solve the revenue maximization problem over the polyhedral (and, in this case, bounded) set of multipliers, T. That is, given the fair allocation x^*, the revenue maximization problem is:

$$\max_{\lambda \in T} \; \phi(\lambda) = (x^*)^T \lambda$$

which gives rise to the optimal prices summarized in Table 2.

Thus, we obtain the maximal revenue

Max Revenue = $(\mathbf{x}^*)^T \lambda^* = 79.54$.

This value is substantially higher than the initial revenue of 46.3. Recall that the initial link prices were obtained by solving the fair resource allocation problem and taking prices to be the Lagrange multiplier values output by the augmented Lagrangian algorithm. The optimal link prices were obtained by maximizing revenue over the set of Lagrange multipliers. The financial advantage of solving the secondary linear program is significant in this example.

Table 2. Optimal Link Prices for Network of Figure 1

Link #	1	2	3	4	5	6	7	8	9
Optimal Link Prices λ^*	0	13.3	0	1.3	41.8	0	10.3	0	0

3.2 Unbounded Prices Set and Alternative Optimizations

In this last example, we illustrate the possibility of T to be unbounded in the direction of the profit maximization objective. We consider the network of Figure 2 with 7 nodes and 13 links with three user demands. Demands are from nodes 2 to 6, 4 to 2 and 3 to 4 with respective quantities 40, 5, and 5. The network data, the resulting fair link flows and the initial link prices obtained with the augmented Lagrangian routine are summarized in Table 3. Although the polyhedral set is unbounded, it is possible to maximize revenue over subsets of arcs or routes.

In this instance, the initial revenue, as obtained through the initial Lagrange multipliers, is

Initial Revenue = 164.

Applying the KKT conditions shows that the multipliers are not unique, and, furthermore, solving the pair of optimization problems (15) shows that T is unbounded in the direction of the objective $(x^*)^T \lambda$. However, here, we may choose a restricted set of arcs, such as $S_1 = \{2, 4, 7, 9\}$, and optimize the revenue over this

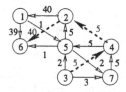

Fig. 2. Network with Fair Flows

Table 3. Network Data for Figure 2

Link #	1	2	3	4	5	6	7	8	9	11	12	13
Link Definition	(1,6)	(1,5)	(2,1)	(3,2)	(3,5)	(3,7)	(4,5)	(5,6)	(5,7)	(5,2)	(6,3)	(7,4)
Link Capacity	100	1	100	8	2	100	100	1	2	100	4	100
Link Delay Data	(4,4)	(6,0)	(7,5)	(3,0)	(6,0)	(9,5)	(8,6)	(6,0)	(6,0)	(8,5)	(7,0)	(6,7)
Fair Link Flow x^*	39	1	40	0	2	3	5	1	2	5	0	5
Initial Link Price λ	0	74	0	0	4	0	0	74	4	0	0	0

set. From Table 3, we compute the initial revenue: **Initial Revenue over S_1 = 82**. Solving the following revenue maximization problem over S_1, we then obtain:

$$\max_{\lambda \in T} \phi(\lambda) = \sum_{i \in S_1} x_i^* \lambda_i$$

which gives **Max Revenue = 904**, which is much better than before where $\lambda_{i \in S_1}^* = (148, 8, 148, 8)$.

4   Perspectives and Related Results from the Literature

This paper presented the application of a special case of the bilevel programming problem for the solution of a set of fair prices on a telecommunication network, where a network manager optimizes a revenue maximization objective over a particular set. The set is determined by the optimality conditions for a multi-commodity flow problem over the network, subject to capacity constraints. A restriction on the prices states formally that the link prices must be Lagrange multipliers for the capacity constraints, and will therefore be strictly positive only when capacity is reached. This approach generalizes some popular approaches to pricing through fairness, and other Lagrangian schemes for solving telecommunications network flow problems. It draws a parallel between a large body of telecommunications network modeling and the more general bi-level mathematical programming model. A natural next stage of this work would involve developing a characterization of the telecommunication networks that exhibit sufficiently large Lagrange multiplier sets so as to permit considerable revenue maximization. This work also leads naturally into a study of the more general bi-level programming model, by freeing the prices of the complementarity constraints that define them to be Lagrange multipliers.

The numerical exercises have shown that at least, on the quadratic cost fair resource allocation problem, the method of optimizing a secondary objective over the set of Lagrange multipliers, or shadow prices, is worthwhile. Indeed, we have seen that in most instances, revenue maximization is possible for some subnetwork, if not for the entire network, and for some network data. Furthermore, the complexity of the secondary optimization is lower than that of the fair resource allocation problem as it is a linear program, rather than a nonlinear program. An interesting topic for future research would be to test whether the solution to this two-step procedure may come quite close to the true bi-level optimization solution. In other words, the solution to the system described here could be used as a good approximation to the true optimal pricing problem in which prices are not restricted to be Lagrange multipliers.

References

1. M. Bouhtou, M. Diallo, and L. Wynter. Fair network ressource allocation and link pricing: A numerical study. Technical Report RR-4680, INRIA-Rocquencourt, December 2002.
2. R. Cocchi et al. Pricing in computer networks: Motivation, formulation, and example. *ACM/IEEE Trans. Net.*, 1:614–627, 1993. available from ftp://ftp.parc.xerox.com/pub/net-research/pricing1.ps.Z.
3. M. Falkner, M. Devetsikiotis, and I. Lambadaris. An overwiew of pricing concepts for broadband ip networks. *IEEE Communications Surveys and Tutorials*, 3(2), Second Quarter 2000. available from URL: http://www.comsoc.org/pubs/surveys/.
4. P. C. Fishburn and A. M. Odlyzko. Dynamic behavior of differential pricing and quality of service options for the internet. In *Proc. First Intern. Conf. on Information and Computation Economies (ICE-98)*, pages 128–139, ACM Press, 1998. Extended version in Decision Support Systems, 28 (2000), 123-136, available from URL http://www.research.att.com/~amo.
5. A. Gupta et al. Priority pricing of integrated services networks. In L. W. McKnight and J. P. Bailey, editors, *Internet Economics*, pages 323–352, Cambridge, Massachusetts, 1997. MIT Press.
6. F. P. Kelly. Charging and rate control for elastic traffic. *European Trans. Telecommunications*, 8:33–37, 1997. available from URL http://www.statslab.cam.ac.uk/~frank/elastic.html.
7. T. Larsson and M. Patriksson. Side constrained traffic equilibrium models—traffic management through link tolls. In P. Marcotte and S. Nguyen, editors, *Chapter 7 in Equilibrium and Advanced Transportation Modelling*, pages 125–151, Boston, MA, 1998. Kluwer Academic Publishers. available from the URL http://www.math.chalmers.se/~mipat/traffic.html.
8. Scilab Scientific Computing Library. www-rocq.inria.fr/scilab/.
9. S. H. Low and D. E. Lapsley. Optimization flow control, 1: Basic algorithm and convergence. *IEEE/ACM Transactions on Networking*, 7(6):861–875, December 1999.
10. J. K. Mackie-Mason and H. R. Varian. Pricing congestible network resources. *IEEE JSAC*, 13(7):1141–1149, September 1995.

Author Index